Sabina Spielrein

Sabina Spielrein

Forgotten Pioneer of Psychoanalysis

Edited by
Coline Covington and
Barbara Wharton

Brunner-Routledge
Taylor & Francis Group

HOVE AND NEW YORK

First published 2003 by Brunner-Routledge
27 Church Road, Hove, East Sussex BN3 2FA

Simultaneously published in the USA and Canada
by Brunner-Routledge
29 West 35th Street, New York, NY 10001

Brunner-Routledge is an imprint of the Taylor & Francis Group

Typeset in Times by RefineCatch Limited, Bungay, Suffolk
Printed and bound in Great Britain by
MPG Books Ltd, Bodmin, Cornwall
Cover design by Sandra Heath

British Library Cataloguing in Publishing Data
A catalogue record for this book is available from the British Library

Library of Congress Cataloging-in-Publication Data
Sabina Spielrein: forgotten pioneer of psychoanalysis/editors, Coline
Covington, Barbara Wharton.
       p. cm.
Includes bibliographical references and index.
   ISBN 1-58391-903-1
   1. Spielrein, Sabina. 2. Women psychoanalysts–Europe–Biography.
3. Mentally ill women–Europe–Biography. 4. Jung, C. G. (Carl Gustav),
1875–1961–Relations with women. 5. Psychoanalysts–Europe–
Correspondence. 6. Psychoanalysis–History. I. Covington, Coline,
1953–   II. Wharton, Barbara.

RC440.82.S66S23 2003
616.89'17'092–dc21   2003002575

ISBN 1-58391-903-1

Contents

Contributors

Coline Covington, PhD, is Chair of the British Confederation of Psycho-therapists and consultant editor of the *Journal of Analytical Psychology*. She is a training analyst of the Society of Analytical Psychology and a training therapist of the British Association of Psychotherapists (Jungian Section). She is co-editor with Paul Williams, Jean Arundale and Jean Knox of *Terrorism and War: Unconscious Dynamics of Political Violence*, published in 2002 by Karnac Books.

Johannes Cremerius (1918–2002) was co-editor of the former *Psyche* journal and the series *Conditio Humana*. He was highly regarded at the psycho-therapeutic and psychosomatic hospital in Freiburg, which he also founded and directed. He taught for several years in the psychoanalytic departments of Bern and Milan Universities. He always emphasized the function of enlightenment in psychoanalysis and fought for this under-standing against the orthodoxy of the science with great enthusiasm, fearless of controversy. His publications include: *Neurose und Genialität: Psychoanalytische Biographien* (ed.), 1971; *Psychoanalytische Textinterpreta-tionen* (ed.), 1974; *Zur Theorie und Praxis der psychosomatischen Medizin*, 1978; *Vom Handwerk des Psychoanalytikers: Das Werkzeug der psychoana-lytischen Technik*, 2 vols, 1984; *Arbeitsberichte aus der psychoanalytischen Praxis*, 1998; *Die Zukunft der Psychoanalyse* (ed.), 1995.

Angela Graf-Nold, PhD, is a psychotherapist in practice in Zürich. She worked as a research fellow at Zürich University on the role of women in the early history of psychotherapy and at the Burghölzli Psychiatric Hos-pital on epidemiology. She has published several works on the early history of child analysis, Hermine von Hug-Hellmuth, the history of Swiss psychiatry and current issues in Swiss psychiatry, and Jungian theory and practice.

Nicolle Kress-Rosen, MA, is a psychoanalyst. She lectured in linguistics and psychoanalysis at the Universities of Strasbourg, Brest and Paris VIII until 1982. She was a member of the Ecole Freudienne de Paris, and until

2000 was the director of Arcanes, a publishing company specialising in psychoanalysis. She is the author of *Trois Figures de la Passion, Freud, Jung, Sabina Spielrein* (1993) and *Du Côté de l'Hystérie* (1999). Her most recent work is a collection of short stories entitled *Chez les Thomas, on est très famille* was published in 2002 by Editions J.-C. Lattès. She has been practising as a psychoanalyst since 1977, currently in Paris.

Zvi Lothane, MD, is Clinical Associate Professor of Psychiatry at Mount Sinai-New York University School of Medicine, New York, senior member and training analyst, the National Psychological Association for Psychoanalysis, New York, Fellow of the American Psychiatric Association and Member of the International Psychoanalytical Association and the American Psychoanalytic Association. Zvi Lothane is author of *In Defense of Schreber/Soul Murder and Psychiatry*, now being prepared for publication by Psychosozial Verlag, Giessen; and of papers on the methodology of psychoanalysis and psychotherapy.

Bernard Minder, Dr Med., works as a psychiatrist and psychotherapist in private practice in Lenzburg, Switzerland, and is interested in the history of medicine, especially the pioneering years of clinical psychoanalysis. His work includes various publications on Sabina Spielrein, C.G. Jung and Eugen Bleuler.

Sabine Richebächer, PhD, is a psychoanalyst, sociologist and writer in Zürich. Her first book on the Socialist Women's Movement in Germany (1890–1914) was published in 1982 by Fischer Verlag, Frankfurt. For many years she wrote a column on new psychoanalytic literature in the *Neue Zürcher Zeitung*. Her writings and research are now focused on the history of psychoanalysis, especially on forgotten pioneers like Wilhelm Reich, Otto Fenichel and Sabina Spielrein.

Fernando Vidal is a research scholar at the Max Planck Institute for the History of Science in Berlin. He works on the history of the human sciences, and has published on Jean Piaget, psychoanalysis and psychiatry, the progressive education movement, and psychology from the 16th to the 20th century.

Barbara Wharton, MA, is a training analyst of the Society of Analytical Psychology, London. She is a consultant editor for *The Journal of Analytical Psychology* and author of numerous papers on analytical psychology. She is in private practice.

Preface

This compilation of papers has been drawn together as a tribute to the life and work of Sabina Spielrein. The papers include the records of Sabina Spielrein's treatment by C.G. Jung at the Burghölzli Hospital in Zürich and reflect over five years of research and detective work. In 1995, I, along with my co-editors of the *Journal of Analytical Psychology*, learned about the publication a year earlier in the Swiss journal *Luzifer-Amor* of a paper by Dr Bernard Minder on Jung's treatment of Spielrein that incorporated the hospital records. We wrote to Dr Minder requesting information on obtaining permission to publish the records in English translation. This was the start of several years of research and waiting while questions about copyright and ownership of the records could be sorted out. We were assisted initially by Sophie Slaata, who was acting at the time as the legal representative for the Spielrein estate, and who informed us about other unpublished material written by Sabina Spielrein. Prior to her return to Moscow, Spielrein left a cache of letters and papers in the safekeeping of a psychologist colleague in Geneva, Edouard Claparède. Claparède's papers, containing Spielrein's letters and manuscripts, were subsequently inherited by his nephew, the Genevan neurologist Georges de Morsier. This material has remained in the de Morsier family archives and is now in the process of being catalogued by the Archives Institut Rousseau in Geneva.

The search to gain permission to publish the hospital records in English took me to Rostov-on-Don, Sabina Spielrein's birthplace, where I participated in the Second Sabina Spielrein Memorial Conference in May 1997 and met Spielrein's niece, Meniche Shpilrain. Although Meniche Shpilrain was in favour of the publication of the records, we had to wait for two years while other questions relating to the Sabina Spielrein estate were being addressed. Sadly, Meniche Shpilrain suffered a severe stroke during this time and the business of the estate was passed on to her younger cousin, Evald Shpilrain. I met with Evald Shpilrain twice during this time, once in London and once in Moscow. The Journal editorial board and members of the Society of Analytical Psychology in London made a contribution towards helping with Meniche Shpilrain's care until her death in April 2000. It was not until 1999, when the Sabina Spielrein estate reverted to the control of the Shpilrain family, that we were able to obtain permission from the Jung Estate to publish the hospital records in English.

This collection of papers follows on from the special issue of the *Journal of Analytical Psychology*, published in January 2001, on Sabina Spielrein. There is some overlap amongst these papers but we have also selected a number of new papers, not published before, to complement and expand on the material already available. The selection of papers is intended to shed light on different aspects of Spielrein's life and work. The historical context in which Sabina Spielrein's hospital treatment took place is described (see Minder, Chapters 6 & 7, and Graf-Nold, Chapter 8) along with commentaries on her therapeutic relationship with Jung (see Covington, Chapter 9) and her relationship with Jung following her discharge from hospital in 1905 (see Lothane, Chapter 10, and Cremerius, Chapter 4). Spielrein's subsequent professional development as a psychoanalyst in her own right is also discussed (see Kress-Rosen, Chapter 12, Richebächer, Chapter 11, and Vidal, Chapter 14). In addition to these papers, we include extracts from Spielrein's diary, never before published in English (Chapter 2), along with some short theoretical pieces written by Spielrein (Chapter 13) and her paper 'The origin of the child's words Papa and Mama' (Chapter 15, part II). We also include the letters of C.G. Jung to Sabina Spielrein (Chapter 3) that were discovered in the de Morsier archives and published in the German edition of Carotenuto's *A Secret Symmetry* (1986). For readers who would like to delve further into the work and life of Sabina Spielrein, we would recommend Spielrein's seminal paper 'Destruction as the cause of coming into being', originally published in *Jahrbuch* in 1912 and in English in the *Journal of Analytical Psychology* of April 1994. This paper is now widely regarded as the forerunner to Freud's concept of the death instinct. We would also recommend two articles by Victor Ovcharenko, the Russian historian, that appeared in the July 1999 issue of the *Journal of Analytical Psychology*. These articles, 'The history of Russian psychoanalysis and the problem of its periodization' and 'Love, psychoanalysis and destruction', give a fascinating account of the development of psychoanalysis in Russia and Spielrein's involvement in this, as well as more detailed biographical information about her life.

We have made no attempt to synthesize the material we have collected for this publication and there remain inevitably many gaps and questions. This collection of papers is our attempt to bring together these historical documents so that they are accessible to the English-speaking world, with the hope that this may in turn encourage and facilitate further historical research as well as the development of the many ideas we have inherited from Sabina Spielrein's treatment, from her writing, and from her relationships. Finally, we hope the publication of this material will also contribute to the ongoing dialogue between analytical psychologists and psychoanalysts about theory and practice – a dialogue that Sabina Spielrein was the first to try to preserve.

Acknowledgements

We would like to give thanks to the following people who have helped in this publication and in the earlier publication of the special issue of the *Journal of Analytical Psychology*: Pramila Bennett, the Burghölzli Clinic, Angela Connolly, Hélène de Morsier, the C.G. Jung Estate, Angela Graf-Nold, Leo La Rosa, Bernard Minder, Victor and Ira Ovcharenko, Sabine Richebächer, the Rostov Psychoanalytical Association, Sonu Shamdasani, Sophie Slaata, Dorothee Steffens, Sergei Ulyanitsky and Fernando Vidal. Finally, we are indebted to Meniche and Evald Shpilrain for their support, generosity, and faith in this work.

Text acknowledgements

Chapter 2

The extracts first appeared in French, translated from the German by Jeanne Moll, entitled 'Extraits inédits d'un journal' in *Le Bloc-Notes de la Psychanalyse*, 1983, No. 3, pp. 147–171, ed. Mario Cifali, Geneva. Reprinted in English by kind permission of *Le Bloc-Notes de la Psychoanalyse*.

Also reproduced with the kind permission of the Spielrein Estate.

Chapter 3

'The Letters of C.G. Jung to Sabina Spielrein', translated by B. Wharton, *Journal of Analytical Psychology, January 2001, 46*, 1:173–199. First published in the Journal of Analytical Psychology, reprinted with permission.

Also reproduced with the permission of the Heirs of the Estate of C.G. Jung.

Chapter 4

'Foreword to Carotenuto's *Tagebuch einer heimlichen Symmetrie*' by Johannes Cremerius. Reproduced with the permission of Psychosozial-Verlag. Copyright © Kore Verlag.

Also reproduced with kind permission of the author.

Chapter 5

'Burghölzli Hospital Records of Sabina Spielrein', translated by Barbara Wharton, *Journal of Analytical Psychology, January 2001, 46*, 1:15–42. First published in the Journal of Analytical Psychology, reprinted with permission.

Also reproduced with the kind permission of the Spielrein Estate.
Also reproduced with the permission of the Heirs of the Estate of C.G. Jung.

Chapter 6

'Sabina Spielrein: Jung's Patient at the Burghölzli' by Bernard Minder, *Journal of Analytical Psychology, January 2001, 46*, 1:43–66. First published in the Journal of Analytical Psychology, reprinted with permission.

Reproduced with the permission of the Heirs of the Estate of C.G. Jung.
Also reproduced with kind permission of the author.

Chapter 7
'A Document. Jung to Freud 1905: A Report on Sabina Spielrein' by Bernard Minder, *Journal of Analytical Psychology, January 2001, 46*, 1:67–72. First published in the Journal of Analytical Psychology, reprinted with permission.

Reproduced with the permission of the Heirs of the Estate of C.G. Jung.

Chapter 8
'The Zurich School of Psychiatry in Theory and Practice. Sabina Spielrein's Treatment at the Burghölzli Clinic in Zurich' by A. Graf Nold, *Journal of Analytical Psychology, January 2001, 46*, 1:73–104. First published in the Journal of Analytical Psychology, reprinted with permission.

Also reproduced with kind permission of the author.

Chapter 9
'Comments on the Burghölzli hospital records of Sabina Spielrein' by Coline Covington, *Journal of Analytical Psychology, January 2001, 46*, 1:105–116. First published in the Journal of Analytical Psychology, reprinted with permission.

Also reproduced with kind permission of the author.

Chapter 10
'Tender Love and Transference: Unpublished Letters of C.G. Jung and Sabina Spielrein' by Zvi Lothane, *International Journal of Psycho-Analysis, 80*, 6:1189–1204.

Also reproduced with the kind permission of the author.

Chapter 11
'In league with the devil, and yet you fear fire? Sabina Spielrein and C.G. Jung: A suppressed scandal from the early days of psychoanalysis' by Sabine Richebächer. Reproduced with the permission of Staatsarchiv des Kantons Zürich. Copyright © Staatsarchiv des Kantons Zürich.

Also reproduced with kind permission of the author.

Chapter 12
'Kindred Spirits' by Nicolle Kress-Rosen. Reproduced with kind permission of the author.

Chapter 13

'Sabina Spielrein: Three Psychoanalytic Studies', translated by C.J. Wharton, *Journal of Analytical Psychology, January 2001, 46,* 1:201–208. First published in the Journal of Analytical Psychology, reprinted with permission.

Also reproduced with the kind permission of the Spielrein Estate.

Chapter 14

'Sabina Spielrein, Jean Piaget – going their own ways', by Fernando Vidal.

Reproduced by kind permission of the author.

Chapter 15

Part I Comment on Spielrein's paper 'The origins of the child's words Papa and Mama', by Barbara Wharton. Reproduced with the permission of Psychosozial-Verlag. Copyright © Kore Verlag.

Part II The origin of the child's words Papa and Mama. Some observations on the different stages of language development.

Both parts have been reproduced with kind permission of the author.

Chapter 1

Introduction

Coline Covington

> No ashes, no coal can burn with such glow
> as a secretive love
> of which no one must know.
> > From the diary of Sabina Spielrein, 22 February 1912
> > (Carotenuto 1982: 43)

Sabina Spielrein is perhaps best known for her love affair with Carl Jung. While it is debatable whether their relationship was actually consummated, it bore fruit for them both in giving rise to psychological insights and discoveries that were to become the basis for fundamental theoretical concepts in psychoanalysis and analytical psychology – concepts such as the anima, countertransference, and the death instinct. We can see the seeds of Spielrein's erotic transference to Jung in his account of her treatment at the Burghölzli Clinic in Zürich where she was admitted to his care in 1904. At the time Spielrein was 19 years old; she had been sent for treatment by her parents from her home in Rostov-on-Don near the Black Sea in Russia. She was highly intelligent and lively and also diagnosed as suffering from hysteria on her admission to hospital. Jung was ten years older, he had recently taken up an appointment to work under Prof. Bleuler, head of the Burghölzli Clinic, and he had also recently married. He was laying the foundations for both his professional and his domestic life. Jung had read Freud's *Interpretation of Dreams*, published in 1900, and was impressed with Freud's new technique of psychoanalysis – so much so that he adopted it in his treatment of Spielrein, along with developing his word association test as a means of exploring and explaining the links between memory, image, and repression in what was to become his theory of the complexes. Two years later, Jung began his correspondence with Freud and in a letter dated 23 October 1906 he first referred to his 'difficult case', a 'Russian girl student', asking Freud for his opinion.

By June 1905 Spielrein had been discharged from the Burghölzli and had enrolled as a medical student at the University of Zürich. She was still under Jung's care and from this point on it becomes evident from her diaries and correspondence with Jung that Jung's own erotic transference towards

Spielrein was beginning to emerge. The intensity of their relationship reached its peak during the years 1908 to 1911, during which time they were both in correspondence with Freud, seeking his help. Jung, frightened of jeopardizing his career and family, broke off relations with Spielrein in March 1909 and wrote to Freud about the 'scandal' that was being spread about him by a female student and his troubles with Spielrein. Several months later, Spielrein contacted Freud, requesting a consultation that Freud declined. Sympathetic to Jung's position, Freud wrote to Jung in June 1909 (McGuire 1974: 230):

> ...after receiving your wire I wrote Fräulein Sp. a letter in which I affected ignorance, pretending to think her suggestion was that of an over-zealous enthusiast. I said that since the matter on which she wished to see me was of interest chiefly to myself, I could not take the responsibility of encouraging her to take such a trip and failed to see why she should put herself out in this way. It therefore seemed preferable that she should first acquaint me with the nature of her business. I have not yet received an answer.
>
> Such experiences, though painful, are necessary and hard to avoid. Without them we cannot really know life and what we are dealing with. I myself have never been taken in quite so badly, but I have come very close to it a number of times and had a *narrow escape*. I believe that only grim necessities weighing on my work, and the fact that I was ten years older than yourself when I came to A, have saved me from similar experiences. But no lasting harm is done. They help us to develop the thick skin we need to dominate 'countertransference', which is after all a permanent problem for us; they teach us to displace our own affects to best advantage. They are a '*blessing in disguise*' ...

Spielrein was never to be granted a consultation with Freud and renewed her contact with Jung over a year later when she received Jung's comments on her dissertation. While Spielrein and Jung continued to meet and correspond, the necessity to sublimate their erotic desire for each other in favour of an intellectual union became the central focus of their relationship. The theme of sacrifice, appealing to Spielrein's religious nature, emerged powerfully in her writing at this time, and was to colour her thinking and to shape the events of her life in significant ways from this time onwards. On the eve of her final medical examination in December 1910 and prior to her departure for Vienna, Spielrein described her parting with Jung:

> ... My friend and I had the tenderest 'poetry' last Wednesday. What will come of that? Make something good of it, Fate, and let me love him nobly. A long, ecstatic kiss in parting, my beloved little son! Now – may luck be with me! What a difference between his diary entry and mine ... in spite of the colossal similarity between us. How remarkable the

difference in the way he, the man, and I, the woman, contemplated the tasks ahead of us! With him the sacredness of his profession occupied the foreground, with me the sacredness of love . . .

8 December 1910 (Carotenuto 1982: 37)

It was in October 1911 that Spielrein first met Freud in Vienna. The following month Spielrein read her first theoretical paper, 'Destruction as the cause of coming into being', at one of Freud's meetings in the presence of Freud, Federn, Rank, Sachs, Stekel and Tausk amongst others. Here she introduced the concept of the death instinct, later to be incorporated and developed by Freud in *Beyond the Pleasure Principle* (1920) in which he refers in a footnote to Spielrein's idea of the 'destructive' component of the sexual instinct. Commenting on her paper some months later, Freud wrote to Jung: 'She is very bright; there is meaning in everything she says; her destructive drive is not much to my liking, because I believe it is personally conditioned. She seems abnormally ambivalent' (McGuire 1974: 494).

While Jung, in a note to his revised edition of *Transformation and Symbols of the Libido* (1952), acknowledged Spielrein as the originator of the idea of the death instinct (*Symbols of Transformation, CW* 5: 328, n.38), he also concurred with Freud's opinion, responding that her paper was 'over-weighted with her own complexes'. Jung went on to write, 'My criticism should be administered to the little authoress in *refracta dosi* only, please, if at all. I shall be writing to her myself before long' (McGuire 1974: 498).

It is interesting to note here that Spielrein in her diary entry of 26 November 1910 expressed her fear that Jung would 'simply borrow the whole development of the idea' (of the death instinct). She questioned herself:

Is this another case of unfounded distrust on my part? I wish so fervently that might be so, for my second study will be dedicated to my most esteemed teacher, etc. How could I esteem a person who lied, who stole my ideas, who was not my friend but a petty, scheming rival? And love him? I do love him, after all. My work ought to be permeated with love! I love him and hate him, because he is not mine. It would be unbearable for me to appear a silly goose in his eyes. No, noble, proud, respected by all! I must be worthy of him, and the idea I gave birth to should also appear under my name.

(Carotenuto 1982: 35)

Two years later, in a letter dated 25 March 1912, Jung tried to reassure Spielrein with regard to her fears and the matter of the 'uncanny' similarities in their views. He wrote:

. . . Your study is extraordinarily intelligent and contains splendid ideas whose priority I am happy to acknowledge as yours. The death tendency or death wish was clear to you before it was to me, understandably! . . . I express myself so differently from you in my work that no one could imagine that you had borrowed in any way from me. There is no question of it at all . . . Perhaps I borrowed from you too; certainly I have unwittingly absorbed a part of your soul, as you doubtless have of mine. What matters is what each of us has made of it. And you have made something good. I am glad that you are representing me in Vienna. The new work will certainly be misunderstood. I hope you will be able to represent my ideas.

(Jung 1912; this volume, Chapter 3: 46)

Jung's letter reads like a sleight of hand – he reverses the suggestion that he might be borrowing her ideas by reassuring her that no one would accuse her of borrowing from him; he goes on to say it does not matter what he has borrowed from her because she is part of his soul and they will inevitably express themselves differently in any case. What seems of paramount importance to Jung is that Spielrein is able to represent his ideas in Vienna.

Spielrein continued to work in Vienna and to become closer to Freud. She became accepted as a member of the Psychoanalytic Society, writing in her diary that it was 'on the strength of [her] dissertation'. She commented:

Prof. Freud, of whom I have become very fond, thinks highly of me and tells everyone about my 'magnificent article,' and he is also very sweet to me personally. Everything I wished for up to now has come true, with the exception of one thing: where is the man I could love, whom I could make happy as a wife and the mother of our children? Still completely alone.

Vienna, 7 January 1912 (Carotenuto 1982: 41)

By now Spielrein and Jung are 'friends'. However, her relations with Jung soon began to sour and there is some indication that, at least for a time, her erotic transference may have shifted onto Freud. In February 1912, hurt upon the receipt of a terse and businesslike letter from Jung, Spielrein wrote in her diary, analysing a dream:

. . . I am sliding down a mountain, arrive at a railroad station – whose name I have forgotten (I think it had an 'ine' ending). It was like Switzerland. I meet Frl. Aptekmann, a patient of Dr. Jung's, who is going to take her exam soon and is looking very pale. She took her exam shortly after me, and left Zürich. I feel malicious pleasure at the effect of Dr. Jung's treatment on her. I ask her about Dr. J. She says he has already become director. To this I remark with anxiety, indignation, and scorn: no, Prof. Bleuler is the director. 'He, Prof. B., is only allowed to go down to the coal cellar now.' Prof. Bleuler in my dreams also means Prof. Freud, because I am always confusing the two names. 'Coal cellar' seems on the one hand to suggest that poor Prof. B. has been relegated to a miserable and painful little role, but it also has an erotic significance: 'No ashes, no coal can burn with such glow/ as a secretive love/ of which no one must know.' Cellar = subterranean grotto = womb, a symbolism I encounter in my patient. Further analysis superfluous. Now Prof. Freud is the one who causes me to glow; if Dr. J. were also the director, his love would leave one cold (Frl. A.).

22 February 1912 (Carotenuto 1982: 43)

A further erotic reference to Freud appears in a subsequent diary entry dated 11 July 1912 in which Spielrein noted her marriage on 14 June to Dr Paul Scheftel and recounted a dream that in her associations led to the birth of a little girl. The diary entry ends, 'At night – "Freud"', suggesting that her erotised father transference continued to be powerfully present and active (ibid: 44).

Spielrein continued to be in correspondence with Jung until at least 1919 and with Freud until 1923. In this correspondence we can see the continuation of her interest in the sexual instinct and its relation to early development, to the development of language and symbolization, and as a component of the self. The theme of sacrifice also continues to predominate in her writings in different forms. In a letter to Jung dated 19 January 1918, Spielrein posed the question, 'Does the subconscious give any indication of the arena in which one should live out the "heroic attitude" represented by the symbol?' She went on to write:

According to Freud, the Siegfried fantasy is *merely* wish fulfilment. I have always objected to this *merely*. I told myself I was slated for something great, I had to perform a heroic deed: if analysis now reveals that my love for X was not perfectly platonic, as I was convinced it was and wanted it to be – why should I resist and not view it as my heroic deed to sacrifice myself after all for this sacred love and create a hero?

(Carotenuto 1982: 80).

Siegfried was the name of the son Spielrein originally wished to conceive by Jung. It was her wish to give birth to 'a great Aryan-Semitic hero' who would unite these different and warring races forever. The sacrifices Spielrein was prepared to make to achieve this would also, in her mind, secure Jung's love for her. When it became apparent to her that she could not win his love in this way, Spielrein 'sublimated' her desire into what might be described as a 'heroic attitude' towards her work. While this proved to be fruitful in Spielrein's case, she continued to suffer from what she described as the 'Monday morning blues' (letter to Jung, 6 January 1918, Carotenuto 1982: 68) and her arguments with Jung over the meaning of Siegfried also continued. In a letter to Spielrein dated 21 January 1918, Jung argued:

> You are always trying to drag the Siegfried symbol back into reality, whereas in fact it is the bridge to your individual development. Human beings do not stand in one world only but between two worlds and must distinguish themselves from their functions in both worlds. That is individuation. You are rejecting dreams and seeking action. Then the dreams come and thwart your actions. The dreams are a world, and the real is a world. You have to stand between them and regulate the traffic in both worlds, just as Siegfried stands between the gods and men.
>
> (Chapter 3: 54)

In a later letter, Spielrein indicates that she is still grappling with Jung over the meaning of Siegfried. She wrote to Jung of her vision of Siegfried:

> What happened was too profound and shattering; I cannot yet speak of it. For a long time after the realization I remained as if paralysed; the realization was that one cannot eliminate a psychic element by killing it. Perhaps I shall tell you someday what I experienced, since it is really amazing, but as yet I cannot do that. I can say no more than that, after long amazement, which completely paralysed me, I awakened as from a dream with the words 'So he is alive after all, her Siegfried!' What is this, and what does it want of me?
>
> 28 January [1918?] (Carotenuto 1982: 88)

It is impossible not to speculate here that Freud was correct in his interpretation of the Siegfried fantasy as wish fulfilment and to regard Spielrein's tenacity in trying to understand this image as her veiled insistence on Jung's seductiveness towards her in reality, not in the dream world to which Jung would relegate it. Spielrein's unconscious rage towards Jung, as is perhaps revealed in her reference to wanting to 'eliminate a psychic element by killing it', seems to have remained largely unacknowledged and unworked through. Perhaps this is what Freud perceived in Spielrein when he described her as 'abnormally ambivalent'.

It is very likely that we have Spielrein to thank today for the Jungian concept of the anima, which she most certainly represented for Jung, and for deepening Jung's awareness of the countertransference. Her work on early development, symbolization and language is not widely known and is represented in this volume to illustrate her pioneering research and insights into these subjects. Her most significant contribution to psychoanalysis has undoubtedly been her concept of the 'destructive drive', later to be formulated by Freud as the 'death instinct'. Ironically, it can be argued that it was Spielrein's erotic transference to Jung (and his to her) that led her to conceptualise a destructive aspect in the drive to love. Against the back-ground of the love affair between Spielrein and Jung that I have outlined briefly, it is possible to view Spielrein's idea of the 'destructive drive' in a somewhat different light and to consider its historical ramifications as it has influenced our conception of the death instinct.

When Spielrein delivered her paper on the 'destructive drive', she made the extraordinary link with the sexual instinct by locating the destructive drive as a component *within* the reproductive drive. Spielrein started her paper by noting the 'frequency with which sexual wishes are associated with images of death' and continued, quoting Jung from *Symbols of Transformation*:

> Passionate longing, i.e., the libido, has two aspects: it is power that beautifies everything and, in certain cases, destroys everything . . . to be fruitful provokes one's downfall; at the rise of the next generation, the previous one has exceeded its peak. Our descendants become our most dangerous enemies for whom we are unprepared. They will survive and take power from our enfeebled hands. Anxiety in the presence of erotic Fate is completely comprehensible, for there is something immeasurable within it. Fate usually contains hidden dangers. The wish not to wrestle in the dangerous struggle of life explains the continual hesitation of neurotics to take risks. Whoever relinquishes experiencing a risky under-taking must stifle an erotic wish, committing a form of self-murder. This explains the death fantasies that often accompany the renunciation of the erotic wish.
>
> (Spielrein 1912 in *JAP*, 39, 2: 155–6)

Jung describes the inextricable interweaving of love and death and implicitly links this with the idea of sacrifice in the sense that nothing new can come into being without the destruction of the old order. In psychological terms, one way we can understand this idea today is in the formulation of the depressive position in which the ego must relinquish its narcissistic illusion of omnipotence in order to accept reality and to overcome the Oedipal conflict. Spielrein's contribution was to take this passage of Jung's a step further in her attempt to demonstrate that the destructive drive, derived as it was from the libido, was an integral element in the development of sexuality. Freud, as he noted in *Beyond the Pleasure Principle* (1920), found Spielrein's descrip-tion of the sadistic components of the sexual instinct as 'destructive' unclear. Furthermore, as Freud wrote to Jung: 'Fräulein Spielrein read a chapter from her paper yesterday . . . What troubles me most is that Fräulein Spielrein wants to subordinate the psychological material to biological considerations; this dependency is no more acceptable than a dependency on philosophy, physiology, or brain anatomy . . .' (286F).

While Spielrein's essay, 'Destruction as the cause of coming into being', is at times dense and difficult to decipher, her conclusion is nevertheless clear.

She explains: 'I believe that my examples sufficiently show that, corresponding to the biological facts, the reproductive drive also consists psychologically of two antagonistic components, a destructive drive as well as a drive for coming into being' (Spielrein 1912 in *JAP*, 39, 2: 184).

Spielrein was not, as Freud was to hypothesize later, arguing that the destructive drive was a separate and opposing force to the life instinct or libido. Freud, Jung and Spielrein were trying to explain similar phenomena in the juxtaposition of sexual impulses and destructive ones in hysteria and masochism, yet Freud on the one hand and Jung and Spielrein on the other developed very different theories, perhaps as a direct result of their different experiences. Following Freud's idea 'that the germ of sexual pleasure in the adult resides in the infantile sources of pleasure', Spielrein comments that:

> ... We could just as readily derive everything from the nurturing instinct [as] from sexuality. Here I might mention the views of a French author who derives all psychic impulses from the instinct of self-preservation. Essentially, he proposes that the mother loves the child because sucking relieves the mammary glands; one loves a man or a woman because coitus releases the organism's bothersome excretions innocuously. Pleasurable sensation thus is transferred to the object that brings relief ...
>
> (Spielrein 1912 in *JAP*, 39, 2: 159)

Spielrein seems to predict here what might be considered an object relations approach to instinct, in that the 'nurturing instinct' necessarily entails and is reliant upon the primary relationship between mother and infant. In this formulation, Spielrein locates the destructive drive not simply within the reproductive drive but more fundamentally within the 'nurturing instinct' as the first experience of pleasure. In this sense, the destructive drive is traced to its pre-Oedipal roots. The regressive pull towards loss of self within the other, as can be experienced within the sexual act, is therefore present in its precursor in the image of the suckling of the infant at the breast, i.e. of the experience of being at one with the world.

Spielrein clarifies that the destructive component within the reproductive drive can exert itself in a benign or a malignant manner depending on circumstances. She writes:

> The instinct for preservation of the species, a reproductive drive, expresses itself psychologically in the tendency to dissolve and assimilate (transformation of the I to the We), differentiating a new form of the 'primal substance.' 'Where love reigns, the ego, the ominous despot, dies.' When one is in love, the blending of the ego in the beloved is the strongest affirmation of self, a new ego existence in the person of the beloved. If love fails, the image becomes one of destruction or death, a psychic or

physical alteration in the individual image under the influence of an exceptional power such as the sexual act.

(Spielrein 1912 in *JAP*, 39, 2: 174)

In this passage Spielrein reveals her conception of love as a merging or loss of ego, 'the ominous despot'. She contrasts this expression of the destructive drive with what happens if love should fail and give rise to the image of death. We can imagine Spielrein is writing very much from her own experience here. In her first example of being in love, she does not seem to be describing the relinquishment of omnipotence that is necessary in order to love another, or the depressive position, nor is she referring to the surrender of the ego to the Self. Spielrein's conception of the loss of ego seems much more bound up with her conception of sacrifice as a pathological reaction to her own experience of failed love. The regressive pull to be merged with the other is at the expense of the ego in an effort to find the nurturing satisfactions that were lacking in infancy. We could postulate that Spielrein had to defend herself against the 'image of death', resulting from her experience of failed love through her attempts to lose her ego within an idealized love, i.e. as a way of denying her reality. Seen in this light, Spielrein's emphasis on the importance of the 'nurturing instinct' can be linked to her own search for a father figure to provide the maternal understanding she lacked. Sexuality replaces orality, just as the father is used to stand in for the mother, with the result that sexuality is then confused with love. In writing about Shakespeare's ill-fated lovers who can only find peace ultimately in complete annihilation, Spielrein identifies the incestuous dynamic at work:

The strong fixation of libido on the parents makes [attachment] to the external world impossible; no object completely resembles the parents. Unsatisfied libido may re-attach itself to parents, resulting either in incest fantasies in the outer world or in more sublimated symptomatic fantasies such as nature worship or religious symptoms. At the same time, the unsatisfied destructive urge contained in the reproductive drive gains tension, producing either more concrete or more sublimated death fantasies. The death image connected with the incest wish, however, does not express: 'I am dying because I [am forbidden to] commit this sin'; 'I am dead' means 'I have attained the desired regression to the parent and I am disappearing there.' In slightly differentiated incestuous love, a distinctly intense destructive wish develops from a vigorous wish for coming into being.

(Spielrein 1912 in *JAP*, 39, 2: 173)

In this account of the child's fixation of libido onto the parents, Spielrein fails to explain how such a strong fixation occurs within certain individuals and whether it is possible to consider this type of fixation as resulting from a failure in the love relation with a parent. According to Britton, 'the fixation is to the infantile imago of an idealised parent who is more likely to be represented as God than as a human being' (Britton 2002: 3). In such cases, regression, whether it is in the context of a love relationship or within the transference of an analytic relationship, may be malignant rather than benign. As Spielrein points out, the purposive aspect of regression to find a new object relation within which the immature ego can emerge and 'come into being' can be perverted in cases of incestuous love into 'a distinctly intense destructive wish'. Here I am assuming Spielrein means that the destructive wish is turned against the self. The desire to 'disappear' within the parent could then be seen as a regression in the service of denial rather than as a movement towards growth and individuation. Idealisation of the parental imago serves to protect the ego and the love object from hateful and destructive impulses with the consequence that frustration and self-deprivation are also glorified.

In locating the 'destructive drive' within the 'reproductive drive', Spielrein makes a further differentiation between the drive for self-preservation and that of preservation of the species. The underlying theme of sacrifice resurfaces in the following passage:

> The instinct for self-preservation is a simple drive that originates exclusively from a positive component; the instinct for preservation of the species, which must dissolve the old to create the new, arises from both positive and negative components. In its nature, preservation of the species is ambivalent. Therefore, the impulse of the positive component simultaneously summons forth the impulse of the negative component and opposes it. Self-preservation is a 'static' drive because it must protect the existing individual from foreign influences; preservation of the species is a 'dynamic' drive that strives for change, the 'resurrection' of the individual in a new form. No change can take place without destruction of the former condition.
>
> (Spielrein 1912 in *JAP*, 39, 2: 174)

Spielrein equates sacrifice, which she associates with the preservation of the species, with destructiveness, and herein lies the basic confusion in her argument. Britton argues that the location of the death drive within the 'reproductive drive' 'is characteristic of a particular pathological organisation (Steiner 1979), rather than it being a normal constituent of the sexual drive. In this system death is believed to produce eternal union rather than loss whereas continued life is felt to cause separation'(Britton 2002: 2). Britton goes on to note, 'In her paper Spielrein brings Nietzsche to bear on the topic, "Loving and dying have gone together from eternity. The Will to Love: that is to be willing to die" . . . (Spielrein 1912 in *JAP*, 39, 2: 168)' (ibid: 2). This confusion is strikingly apparent in a letter Spielrein wrote to Jung in 1912 in which she begins by writing:

Deepest depression, hopelessly lost, and what have you. Probably my unconscious had a premonition of what was to come when, after sending off my dissertation, I was filled with one intense sensation: I do not produce anything worthwhile and have no reason to exist in this world.

(Carotenuto 1982: 49)

Spielrein then refers to Stekel's interpretation of dreams and the image of dying as a harbinger of the life urge. Turning to Swoboda's law of the preservation of life, Spielrein goes on to write: 'There is a balance between life and death, he says, as a result of which the release of sexual cells – for not every sexual act leads to the creation of new life – causes a temporary diminution of life, death in some form and to some extent. He rightly refers to Celsus: "*Seminis emissio est partis animae junctura.*" Thus one can see why coitus so often appears in dreams as dying' (ibid: 49).

Following her own creative act (completing her dissertation), Spielrein complained of falling into a deep depression. This does not seem to be the experience of the 'little death' usually associated with the sexual act, but rather a more masochistic, self-destructive response. As Britton points out, Spielrein conflates the 'little death' with the 'big death', i.e. actual death.

In his paper on Anna O, entitled, 'Getting in on the act: the hysterical solution', Britton reiterates that

in hysteria sex and death are characteristically conjoined in what I would see as a "pathological organisation" (Steiner 1987); one that expresses the sexual and destructive drives in the form of a phantasy in which the subject becomes one of the primal couple by projective identification. Such a dramatised scene can represent sexual union in the form of an erotised phantasy of mutual death. I suggest that such enacted phantasies defend the individual from the pain of perceiving the reality of the Oedipal situation and the guilt of annihilating it.

(Britton 1999: 12)

In the case of Sabina Spielrein, her 'erotised phantasy of mutual death' is evident in her transference to Jung, most notably in the comparison Spielrein makes between herself and Jung and Wagner's Brunhilde and Siegfried in *The Ring of the Nibelung*. However, while Britton points to such phantasies as a defence against the perception of the reality of the Oedipal situation, in the case of Spielrein I think we can see how these phantasies may stem from and operate at a pre-Oedipal level. Spielrein's intense erotic transference to Jung, along with her recognition of and her implicit identification with Jung's search for a mother, seem to point instead to her need to defend herself against the perception of the reality of the pre-Oedipal situation – against knowing about the mother who was missing. In this case, in order to obtain love, the infant must in its mind relinquish the self and its needs, and in effect annihilate reality. Death becomes the ultimate transcendence of the self, a sacrifice of the self that ensures the continuing life of the loved object and, by this means, the perpetuation of the self in the eyes of the beloved.

Spielrein's conception of the death instinct can be traced to its roots in her own pathology, and specifically to her confusion or failure to differentiate between being loved narcissistically (i.e. being used) and being loved for herself. Seen from this perspective, Spielrein needed to develop the idea of the 'destructive drive' to explain – and to normalise – the destructive impulses and phantasies that arose as a result of the intolerable frustration she seems to have continued to experience in her love relations. For different reasons of their own, both Jung and Freud turned a blind eye to the causes underlying Spielrein's own continuing self-destructiveness and masochism. Their failure to understand Spielrein's re-enactment of her past within her analytic relationship with Jung undoubtedly influenced the way in which the idea of the death instinct was conceptualised and developed subsequently. While Freud came to view the death instinct as an innate force opposing the life instinct and emphasized its regressive nature in reducing the excitations and tensions created by the life instinct, Jung tended to view the death instinct as a regressive pull in which the ego would be dissolved for the purposes of renewal and reconstitution. Rather than being in opposition to the life instinct, the death instinct for Jung served the life instinct. What is missing in both perspectives is any acknowledgement of the role of the individual's history and its impact on psychological development and the strength of the repetition compulsion. Perhaps in the case of Freud, this was the result of his despair in working with difficult or intransigent patients who stolidly refused to get better. In Jung's case it may have been due to his own dismissal (and fear) of the importance of Freud's historical, reductive approach and his insistence on the autonomy of the psyche.

What is so remarkable when we begin to look at Spielrein's writings, many of which remain unpublished in English, is the extent to which she foresaw what we now regard as fundamental psychoanalytical concepts. The question, echoed throughout the papers in this book, is why has Spielrein's work been so relatively neglected? It is not sufficient simply to attribute this to the impenetrability and defensiveness of the 'old boy network', despite evidence of Spielrein's work being minimized and marginalized; in their correspondence Jung and Freud refer to her as a 'little authoress' and a 'little girl' respectively. Apart from her troubled childhood history, her passionate engagement with Jung, and her encounters with Freud and his circle in Vienna, we know very little about Spielrein's relationships. Piaget describes his experience of his 'didactic analysis' with Spielrein when she was working at the Jean-Jacques Rousseau Institute in Geneva in 1921. Spielrein ended the analysis after eight months, according to Piaget, when she 'discovered that he was "impervious to the theory" and that she would never convince him'(Vidal

2001 in *JAP*, 46, 1: 141). Although it is important to remember that these were early days for analysis, we must also wonder about the extent to which Spielrein was able to be emotionally and intellectually flexible in her relationships given her persistent depressions and self-destructive phantasies. There is also some indication that upon her return to Russia in 1923, Spielrein was not popular amongst her colleagues at the State Psychoanalytical Institute in Moscow where she worked. Whether this was due to professional jealousy, as 'no one in the Institute could match her professional psychoanalytic qualifications' (Ovcharenko 1999 in *JAP*, 44, 3: 366), or whether it was due more to her way of relating to her colleagues is difficult to determine. Certainly the secret transference love that Spielrein continued to harbour for Jung must have taken its toll.

Spielrein returned to Rostov-on-Don in 1924. She was for a time reunited with her husband who had returned some years before and had been living with another woman with whom he had had a child. Spielrein's remaining years in Rostov-on-Don are, as far as we know, undocumented. It is still possible to see the house in which she lived and worked. Her consulting room was located in the middle of the house, with a door and no windows so that it was entirely enclosed. This arrangement brings to mind Jung's criticisms that Spielrein was too concrete in her thinking, as it suggests her wish to provide a womb-like environment within which her patients could regress to experience the loss of ego that she sought herself. During this period of her life Spielrein was described by relatives as a solitary figure, intense, serious, working long hours and puritanical in her dress, wearing old clothes, some of them torn, so as not to spend money on herself. Her idealisation of self-sacrifice seems to have resulted in self-deprivation. The last report of her was in the summer of 1942 when she was seen with her two daughters in a column of Jews being herded by the Nazis towards the Zmeyevsky gully, approaching her final sacrifice (Ovcharenko 1999: 368).

References

Britton, R. (1999) 'Getting in on the act: the hysterical solution'. *International Journal of Psychoanalysis*, 80, 1: 1–14.

Britton, R. (2002) 'The eleventh of September massacre'. In *Terrorism and War: Unconscious Dynamics of Political Violence*, eds. Covington, C., Williams, P., Arundale, J., and Knox, J. London: Karnac.

Carotenuto, A. (1982) *A Secret Symmetry*. New York: Pantheon Books.

Jung, C.G. (1912–1919) 'The letters of C.G. Jung to Sabina Spielrein'. *Journal of Analytical Psychology*, 46, 1.

—— (1952) *Symbols of Transformation. CW* 5.

Ovcharenko, V. (1999). 'Love, psychoanalysis and destruction'. *Journal of Analytical Psychology*, 44, 3.

Spielrein, S. (1912) 'Destruction as the cause of coming into being'. *Journal of Analytical Psychology*, 39, 2.

Steiner, J. (1987) 'The interplay between pathological organisations and the paranoid-schizoid and depressive positions'. *International Journal of Psychoanalysis*, *68*, 1: 69–80.

Vidal, F. (2001) 'Sabina Spielrein, Jean Piaget – going their own ways'. *Journal of Analytical Psychology*, *46*, 1, and this volume, Chapter 14.

Chapter 2

Unedited extracts from a diary

With a prologue by Jeanne Moll

Sabina Spielrein

Translated into French by Jeanne Moll,[1] and into English by
Pramila Bennett in collaboration with Barbara Wharton

Prologue

It is a strange feeling to hold in my hands and read through these twenty-one
double pages measuring 18 × 11.5 cm, a little yellowed by time and covered in
small black writing; they have recently been unearthed from an attic where
they have lain for nearly seventy-five years. In them a young Russian woman
of twenty-two or twenty-three addresses herself in a picturesque and at the
same time vigorous German to a correspondent whose identity is soon
guessed.

I devoured these undated pages of Sabina Spielrein's diary at first in one
sitting, astounded by the proliferation of questions, the acuity of the
thoughts, the subtlety of the remarks, and at the same time moved by a
strange sympathy for this passionate young girl who, first through her theoretical reflections, and then in an unequivocal way, asserts her right to think
and love openly, in the face of resistance from the man who humiliates her in
order to defend himself. One does not tire of reading these fluent pages, of
enjoying their timeless sensuality, of getting involved in the game of passion
and intellect that Sabina stages in this slightly puzzling prologue; a game
which is both subtle and confused, where passion and spirit – *die Leidenschaft
und der Geist* –, the female confronting the male, wrestle to find a word to
express an authentic note, straightforward and without any indeterminate
coldness.

In this prelude for two voices in which Sabina ends up by awarding the
prize to the speaker who resists the impetuosity of his feelings and almost
ridicules them, I seem to perceive a tribute to the still unnamed man who
overcomes his passion to allow thought to triumph, and, at the same time, a
secret claim to the love which dares speak its name.

It is a disingenuous game and at the same time a *terrible* one – the prologue's last word; a game of hide-and-seek in which *she* starts her quest for
recognition while *he* continues to try to extricate himself.

As I sorted out these pages that have emerged from their silence, the
abbreviations became clear (n. = *nicht*, d. = *durch* . . .), and as I searched in

minute detail for indications that would determine the dates of the entries (allusions to a physics lesson, to a work by Binswanger on associations,[2] to an expected visit to Locarno, constitute rather poor clues, but cross-checking with other unedited pages of August 1906 suggests that they were written in either 1906 or 1907), my belief grew that this diary, teeming with new ideas, testifies to what Sabina Spielrein would be writing to Freud on 13 June 1909:[3] namely, that what 'bound [Jung and herself] so closely together', was 'not just a doctor/patient relationship'.

Here a young woman asserts herself with an authority of thought which is surprising, taking into account her older discussant; one wonders consequently if it is not she who has more than once engendered his thoughts.

Then in the last pages her passion overcomes her, revealing the prolonged, loving lamentation of a lonely woman.

And the space created by the introductory prologue of two passionate voices does not close up but in fact surrenders to the cruel game of destiny, echoing the 'derisive, playful and yet terrible' spirit of the opening lines.

JEANNE MOLL

Love, death and transformation

Two speakers

Of the two speakers, one reaches the summit of his art only when he gives himself up to passion: it is passion that warms his brain into life, irrigates it and forces his spirit to show its strength. The other, to be sure, sometimes tries to present his case passionately, indeed violently and thunderously, but his success is generally poor. He is soon expressing himself in an obscure and confused way; his exaggerations and omissions make one doubt the sincerity of his cause: he himself begins to sense the lack of confidence that he engenders, and this explains sudden diversions into the coldest and most rejecting tones, which make the listener doubt the genuineness of his passion. For this speaker, passion swamps spirit every time; perhaps it is even stronger than that of the first speaker. But he is at the peak of his power when he resists the impetuosity of his emotions and, as it were, makes fun of them: it is only then that his spirit comes right out of its hiding place, a logical spirit, derisive, playful but nonetheless terrible.

I The theory of transformation and its corollaries

Let us take as our point of departure the case of a young girl who has had an unhappy love affair and whom marriage to another man has not spared from *dementia praecox*. In her illness the complex manifests itself in a 'sublimated' form. Even this case raises a number of questions, the first one being: from the point of view of the preservation of the species, it is impossible to understand why one cannot love just any human being as long as he is in good health, why marriage has not been enough to eliminate the complex; it is impossible to understand why these endless tortures should be brought about by a person who perhaps provokes only an ironic smile from the people around him, who is perhaps mentally and physically deficient. You may say: 'it is a perverse instinct'.

All that is true, judged from the context of the conservation of the species. But from another point of view, the instinct is normal.

Let us leave aside the fundamental reasons as well as the aims, and let us continue to analyse: what really is this abominable thing called love? The more developed the human being, the more importance this word assumes for him. For a dog, there would hardly be a difference between love and sexual attraction; but a human being can only experience true and profound love a limited number of times; in most cases it will be only a passing fancy. Two years ago you yourself asked me a question that you considered essential for determining my love for you: you asked me, 'Do you have many points in common with me?' My answer was an angry 'no'. So, one has numerous points in common with the person one loves. Creatures who are very much like each other, like animals, are less discriminating in their choice; they also hardly ever suffer the sorrows of love (mark this); an untutored girl will find a lover very easily and if you need examples to prove this, remember Wilhelm Meister: you will find there a girl who remains single for a long time because she lives above her set. Goethe says the same thing. The more differentiated a person is, the more fatal the story becomes (let's not confuse the two: I refer to the degree of love that a person is capable of, not a passing attraction).

We must not forget the fundamental difference between man and woman, which is also, provisionally, the rule. Man wants to embrace, woman prefers to be embraced. The reverse can only take place provisionally because men are on average more differentiated. And what are the consequences of this?

Woman is more discriminating in her choice because it is more difficult to find a personality that fits the ideal; it is for these reasons that the woman is generally monogamous, when she truly loves; for opposite reasons, the man is less discriminating and is more or less polygamous. As a remedy for infidelity, Forel proposes that a woman should be more able to share a man's interests, be more of a friend, make herself more indispensable. Forel is the man who dedicates his book 'as a proof of his love and in homage' to his wife – he bears her the noblest of love. You will find the same idea in Ibsen, in *Nora* for example. A young man of the 'people' says to me: man is polygamous until he can find a woman he can truly love; then he becomes monogamous (short, transitory attractions excluded, of course). Do you need examples from history? 'Ivan the Terrible' (1533–1584): his rule was gentle and beneficial during the years when his love for his wife and her influence guided all his actions; then he was monogamous. He became 'the terrible' when his wife died, when his unsatisfied love wanted to be satiated – we may return to him later as an example. This is the way men feel – can you contradict me?

We always see that a beautiful woman is the determining factor in a man's choice – let us not get angry! What does that mean: a beautiful woman? It is well known that there is no absolute beauty; the ideal of beauty was simply developed from female forms most frequently encountered, that is, from characteristics that proved most pleasing. Beauty does not have to be linked to value, from the point of view of the preservation of the species – you know that only too well. This is generally the case with degenerate people. And is it not in fact degenerates whose ideas continue to survive, even if they present them in different garb? If a generation of women, conforming to the utmost subtlety in their emotions and the way of life resulting from these emotions, eventually has a finer subtlety of forms, a purely mechanical sexuality is immediately applied to those forms. Innovators are rare, especially where an instinct is concerned, and it is still always the rule that a certain shape engenders sexual excitement, a shape which perhaps only simulates a resemblance or in which is to be found only a slight resemblance, but which is more than a similarity between two persons. After all human beings and animals have similarities which are deemed sufficient by some to engage in sexual relationships; these people are even less discriminating in their choice because an animal can only correspond to a fraction of their personality; from this minimal affinity it would have to be concluded that one can be understood by a cow and confide one's sublime feelings to her. When she was still a child (an age when human beings and animals are close), a colleague of mine was tenderly attached to a dog: she always told him everything that was in her heart. This usually took place in the forest and she often shed bitter tears; she was sure that the dog understood her. And this was true up to a point! If all else fails, you can even confide in a tree and you would certainly feel that the tree understands you, and through the soft movement of its leaves expresses its sympathy for you.

'And I went on hearing the rustling of the leaves, as if they were telling me: "come nearer, my friend, by my side you will find peace, etc., *ad infinitum*".' Thus one can love nature as a living being, and confide one's inner thoughts to it; for example find similarities between the storm in nature and the storm in one's own heart, and this similarity is real because our world is a part of the universal world or, if you prefer, a reflection of it. That is why everyone loves nature, especially those who live very intensely; that is what forms the most important and powerful part of the personality. To quote Nietzsche again: 'We must sometimes take a rest from ourselves by looking at ourselves from a distance and in depth, and with the same detachment as the artist, and by laughing at ourselves or weeping over ourselves; we have to discover not only the hero in us but also the madman, hidden in our [reservoir] of knowledge, we must rejoice now and then in our madness so as to be able also to rejoice in our wisdom.'

The paper that I have written for the clinic about the value of reaction (Spielrein 1909),[4] makes me think that we see our own pain in the soul of the other, that is objectively – hence the relief.

Every complex tries to transcend the limits of personality; every complex looks for its twin, its reflection and, when it is shown itself in the mirror, it laughs, even though for ego consciousness there is nothing to laugh at. Freud's interpretation that laughter is born of the comparison of two different amounts of energy, the over-abundance of energy being eliminated by laughter, seems to me *to be very plausible*.[5] 'Why?' – that would take us too far, but it is a fact that work done as a team (not to be confused with work which is said to be done together but is not in fact so) is much easier; it is a fact that a shared sorrow is easier to bear. That means that if the same complex is found in both one's own soul and the mirror, that is to say transformed (everybody thinks – outrageous though it is – 'look! I am master now!'), the two act as one, and it is 'from the accumulation of energy that must have met some previous resistance' (Freud) that laughter is born.

Art is only a complex which has found its independence or which 'having turned wild, wants to express itself fully' (your words) or 'wants to be transformed' (my words). When the artist creates, it is not the manifestation of the need to communicate something to the world. It is rather that the complex itself simply wants to emerge! The artist can spend a long time admiring his work, keeping it to himself, until he finally feels the need to have it understood by others. (Is not laughter born here because there is no resistance to what is beautiful?) In science too a thought – whatever it is – which has been formulated after much anguish needs necessarily to be understood by others. It seems to me that researchers for whom celebrity is essential are rare. To love glory is to want to have everyone's attention focused on oneself: this can only be a dominant characteristic among 'normal' people who do not feel the force of their own personality. To those whose thoughts have been born of prolonged suffering, their thoughts are much more important than glory; at the most glory would be but a means of being better understood and of remaining alive eternally. Or perhaps – I must correct myself – celebrity is important for those artisans of science who look upon it as a means of attracting general attention to themselves. Those for whom thoughts have been born of long suffering and form an integral part of their personality, might at the most desire glory as a way for them to be better understood and to live eternally. Only someone who, for example, has the same feelings as Galileo can understand me: Galileo, whose words 'And yet, it turns', are believed to express the individual's life – *but more about that later. I come back to the apparent contradictions in sexual life;*[6] and this is because associations to death are sexual associations. But I shall come back to this. Looking at popular poetry – which must be taken into consideration as it always contains truths – we find that sexual power is considered to be demonic power, a destructive force; the sexual act is a sin! Where does that come from? How is it that everyone always puts up so much resistance to sexual feelings? Why are they hidden, why are they felt to be unbearable, why can they be expressed only in a sublimated or symbolic form? Why does every young girl[7] (and perhaps also young man) have to live through a period of extreme apprehension of everything sexual (even if she has no idea of the pains it may engender)? There is an indication here of a contrast between sexuality and the rest of the personality, a contrast which reaches a climax when sexual feelings begin to manifest themselves – as borne out by the numerous psychic problems at the time of puberty – until the 'demonic' instinct subdues in part the inner personality and is partly subdued by it. Why is it that this contrast is felt to be primary? (Primary emotions are always the most powerful for they act as logarithms of excitement.) Why it is that we do not accept this? What is this strangeness? You must not forget for an instant that present sexual feelings are not genuine but tamed. One day I asked a passionate and healthy young woman: 'How can one find out if one is in love? It is also possible to want to take your mother in your arms and kiss her, isn't it?' She explained: 'When you kiss your lover, you want him to die of your kisses and you want to disappear into him (she used another very characteristic word) etc.' – there is an infinity of expressions. The most elevated instincts always present themselves as murderous instincts. To begin with there is the little brother who calls the kitten: 'Puss! Puss! My little darling! I love you! I am going to torture you and make you die!'; besides there is the well-known fact that lovers love to tease and torment each other, and moreover there is martyrdom and crimes of passion. Everywhere you see the pleasure involved in destroying and dying. Young people have a strange need to sacrifice their lives for a great cause, a 'nobler' cause. The psyche surrenders in the face of this demand which is made in a very clever way. But that can also happen with any wish, however mild, the wish for example for an eight-hour working day; if a very large number of people wish for something and demand it simultaneously, then this feeling becomes so powerful that it takes over the personality; after that the feeling cannot find satisfaction unless it is the only one, unless the other minimal part of the personality is crushed. And that is how young people, completely transformed by their desires, strike magnificent poses, torches in hand, pathetic speeches on their lips, and leap to their death. Let their desire live eternally in this new fascinating form – let everything else perish!

Basically, all complexes feel the need to mould the whole of the personality to fit their function, and when a complex manifests itself more than its environment allows, one talks then of an excess of feeling; its author is more-over seen as an impostor, or he is accused of not being serious, depending on the mood. But every person puts on an act, or else 'acting the fool is altogether relative'. Up to what point this is the case depends on the degree of intensity of the complex. At its climax, the complex is in the end capable, as I showed earlier, of sacrificing the whole individual to achieve its ends, but it is only that, a 'sacrifice'. The death of a person constitutes the nature of only one complex – the sexual complex. Every individual must disappear as such. In the case of an amoeba the whole 'personality' in fact literally disappears; in the case of human beings or other animals, only a fraction disappears (I cannot find another adequate word). But the instinct is always one of death, the annihilation of the personality, two individuals fused into one. This is how one can explain the numerous representations of the instinct as a destructive force, demonic, etc . . . This is also how the resistance of every personality to the sexual instinct can be explained; I do not imply here that two people who feel a sexual attraction wish to be constantly fused into one unit or anything like that. Sexual feeling is always tamed by other feelings; even during the sexual act, it is suppressed considerably, otherwise you would be facing a passionate killer or a martyr. I mean that, by destroying, the man wants to annihilate himself while the woman wants to be annihilated. One sees men as martyrs often enough. You also see often enough how cruelty towards others is linked to a person's own martyrdom. For example, 'Ivan the Terrible' who was also a martyr: after every action he did penance; he was also very pious. Indeed – I don't know! Maybe one should regard martyrdom here as 'feminine' nature, as a contradictory feeling!

Among very passionate artists like Wagner one must look beyond death for the culminating point of love. His heroes must die. Siegfried dies and so does Brunnhilde with him; it is thus that the domination of the idea of love is expressed! 'The race of gods has died away like a breath, I abandon the orphaned world; I now show the world the place of my most sacred knowledge':

No lands, no treasures,
No divine splendour,
No house, no court,
No princely pomp!
No obscure alliance,
No false treaty,
Neither the hard law
Of false custom!
Love offers to the lover
Only beatitude in pleasure as in sorrow!

It is when it is placed beyond death that a complex attains the sublime. I would have explained it here in the same way, even if I had not known the essence of the sexual act, and if I did not constantly have these numerous examples illustrating the 'wish for annihilation', the destructive instinct. In the *Vaisseau Fantôme* (Ghost Ship), the culminating point of love resides in death or beyond death. 'I will remain faithful to you until death!' These are my final impressions. You yourself of course know of enough situations where the man kills the woman and kills himself afterwards; or the other way round. Here is enough material for analysis! I must end this soon for classes begin tomorrow – *let us summarize therefore: the sexual instinct – an instinct which is there to renew the whole personality, a partial case of the transformation instinct which every isolated complex possesses! Sexual attraction –* attraction of similar people (people with the same nature – only partially so when people are less differentiated). Similar people, in the sense that 'what looks alike, comes together' and the 'opposites meet'.[8] A person who no longer likes smoking can understand a smoker, but not someone who does not know what smoking is. Nobody really knows what makes up an individual. A person consists of feelings and counter-feelings in different proportions. When the relationships are too similar between isolated complexes, they would disturb the oppressed part of the psyche, that is why people who are very much alike do not go well together. Both positive and negative emotions, but emotions that are nevertheless similar, can arouse sexual attraction. The 'negative' emotions can be explained by the fact that repressed feeling is more active. No! That is not even necessary! The man embraces, the woman is embraced, and that is why there occurs this remarkable phenomenon that you, for example, would not wish to say anything else than 'my baby', while your wife would most likely say 'our', if not 'my husband's young child'. It is you that you loved in the baby and your wife loved herself in you. And the phenomenon that dictates that one must continue to love the first image of the beloved, even when the love has died, needs to be emphasized; one loves one's ideal in the other; a short separation strengthens love because one prefers to remember the ideal image. But the ideal is nothing other than that which is deeply anchored in the psyche as a result of an infinity of circumstances. The similarity of ideals, emotions, and felt experiences arouses the attraction. Sometimes one ideal, sometimes another may feed the psyche, which explains the change in sexual taste. But the more ideals the lover has, the more lasting is the love. Some circumstances make some people more accessible to each other. I believe it is Turgenev who explains this: 'If a woman regrets something – one knows what will follow'. If you feel pity, that means that you put yourself in the same situation; the same complex fills you momentarily and similar complexes regulate sexual feelings. If they are two people of the same sex, a loving, light eroticism occurs; if they are not of the same sex, then the attraction goes deeper. This explains the sexual affection between a patient and her doctor who are in a psychic relationship. It is not the sexual feeling that is uppermost, otherwise one could choose any man for one's doctor. One goes to the doctor because one needs to be free of a complex, one confides in the doctor because one knows, or notices, his interest and sympathy; the interest corresponds to understanding, that is to possession of the same complex. Hence the sexual feeling. It is not at all necessary for one to react with a sexual complex. All sympathy between man and woman arouses sexual feelings. The sight of two magnificent grey eyes may accentuate the sympathy because those eyes by themselves are very eloquent, that is, they are linked to a certain powerful emotional complex, and perhaps express a certain mode of feeling. The sexual feeling aroused by the same complex disappears as soon as other complexes, which are no longer felt in common, besiege the psyche (besiege in the sense that they 'become more powerful').

Let us now examine the transformation of the sexual complex. Sexual feeling is the origin of a series of representations which we summarize as a sexual complex, in the narrow sense of the word. But as every strong complex provokes a sexual complex as soon as the partner feels it at the same time, it becomes part of the sexual complex itself. In this way, the most significant part of the psyche may become the sexual complex, and the magnitude of this cannot be assessed. In the broader sense of the word the totality of the sexual complex, hence the emotions felt for the lover, including all that has been felt simultaneously with him, must now (in the case of an unrequited love) be transformed in its entirety. The person to whom this is made known assumes great importance. If the transformation takes place between a man and a woman, the mutual feeling may provoke a new sexual attraction. Transformation may also take place in the form of artistic work; one is not then linked to a particular person and it is a safeguard against new loves.

Thus the sexual complex in the broad sense of the term can become a powerful motive force, especially in art, but that does not necessarily follow.[9] It does not follow when, for example, ideals press to be consolidated by a sexual transformation, when nature's charm is felt by a man in the shape of a woman, that is as a resonance of the ideal in a woman; it is in fact only the consequence of the instinct of transformation or the instinct of preservation of the self in every complex, that it also wants to be strengthened through the sexual act. *But it is not the sexual feeling which has become the motive force of art etc.; it is the instinct of transformation which every complex possesses, and since each aspect of the personality wants to make its presence felt, the sexual complex also possesses a transformation instinct; and the sexual act is but a particular aspect of this transformation whose function it is to establish a context that is new but also adapted to the same complexes.*[10] Considering its nature, sexual feeling does not need the transformation instinct, but it is present nonetheless; yet the transformation instinct needs the sexual feeling, the latter being a necessary component of the first; otherwise how would the combinations survive? They would end up dying.

As I have already said, complexes that necessitate transformation are not necessarily linked to the sexual complex; thus a painter who has just experienced a storm at sea can eternalize it in a painting without sexual feeling having anything to do with it; but if it intervened nevertheless, it is not the sexual feeling that would have made the artist paint: it is simply the 'complex gone wild which had to emerge, which needed to find full expression'. The sexual complex equally aroused would also be equally transformed. People like Marx, for example, who have dedicated their life to social problems, believe that the source of all feelings lies in socio-political relationships; according to this belief, all emotions, and thus science as well as art, should be modified by the influence of the new social order. Isn't this a huge exaggeration? We are totally ignorant of the cause of feelings, and it is impossible for us ever to know it!

One could at the most discuss the foundations of feeling; it is clear to me that the foundation, or the alpha or omega, of feeling is the transformation instinct, which could eventually be satisfied by the sexual act.

II

You see: I do not love you now, that is, not in the ideal sense – no, and this state is much more dreadful than death. Nothing matters to me ... The preservation of the species is more important than the preservation of an individual, we know that. Why don't you want to kill me, if you love me even though you know that I am a degenerate? But that does matter to me – and when I can explain that, I shall be free! I understand very well that you are older and that you have all the other respectable qualities, but one should not exclude the fact that in the circumstances a child can think rationally – on the contrary. And that is why I am taking the risk.[11]

As proof that everything converges towards the preservation of the species, you have given an example that could also very well serve as proof against yourself. The woman lived on in her two children; but why were they not identical to her? Why does love exist and not only coarse sexual attraction? Why are species which are more intellectually developed more discriminating in their choice? How can sexual feeling be diverted to something else, or rather, does this conform to the point of view that everything tends to promote the preservation of the species? I beg you, do not be impatient straight away! I do not want you to take this the wrong way. There is a fundamental difference between your concept and mine and if we are not in agreement, I will not be able to prove to you why some phenomenon or other seems to me to have a different cause, and that torments me. This is what I think. The final goal and problems of this kind – nonsense –! What strikes me as the highest form of unity that can be attained – is the power of inertia (*Beharrungsvermögen*) and the instinct of transformation. The preservation of the species is but a part of this instinct, and that is very important as it explains a lot of things. Wait a little! If you consider for a while the world of art, you see the following: plastic art represents first personal ideologies; this means that a warrior does not necessarily represent a girl but the ideal of a warrior etc. I have in front of me my little brother's drawings; I can send them to you for you to analyse. *It is one's own personality and immediate environment that one expresses; the more developed the person, the richer the personality*,[12] because it is more marked by the environment. A remark of Leonardo da Vinci is deeply embedded in my mind: he said (more or less) that every hand imitates involuntarily its own body forms; when I was still at the lycée, I had noticed that we girls drew only female figures while the boys preferred to draw men (we do not have mixed physical education classes). This could be explained by the context. In poetry too, we see objects expressed differently and one can say again that one is expressing oneself. It is difficult for me to prove this through German literature as I am not very familiar with its writers; in our culture on the other hand Gorky, the 'vagabond' (or whatever else you want to call him), describes a number of 'vagabonds' of this sort. Dostoyevsky, the hysterical epileptic, has only hysterical epileptic characters. Andreyev – 'madness and terror' – has only mad and terrible characters. Gogol, who brims with humour, has corresponding characters. But why go that far? I have recently experienced something weird myself. A girl of my age, and whom I did not know at all, for some strange reason asked to talk to me. She wanted to ask me several questions and I gladly promised to answer. (I knew that people's complexes are so different from mine that she would not be asking me anything dangerous.) These are her questions: have you ever felt that things you were saying were comprehensible only to you? etc . . . I do not know what each of us said; I explained to her in detail how we all end up telling our own stories, how we use the method of questioning eventually to reveal all, just in the way that was being demonstrated, how the complex makes use of all possible ways to get transformed. For us, this means that a part of the 'ego', that is the complex, wants to be assimilated and transformed, even if this contradicts the rest of our conscious contents; the young woman directed the conversation towards the Jews; after some time she quickly went back to the previous subject and said: 'You are somebody who thinks'.

And now for the last art form – music – that is again nothing but the 'personal expression' or rather more accurately the expression of the rhythm of a complex. 'In this connection', a small digression. I have thought a lot, of course, about *dem. praec. (dementia praecox)* which is characterized by strange stereotyped behaviour (such as getting up at regular intervals while it is possible to work perfectly well in between etc . . .).

I cannot say for sure, but I have a small hypothesis (cf. muscular contractions, tetanus as a result of too much excitement in one go). I do not think of feeling as a shock but as a series of waves; ordinary psychic life is like the still waters of a lake. When a boat goes across, you have a rhythmic series of waves which is like a fairly strong feeling; I have felt on innumerable occasions that an affect provokes a rhythmic movement: one walks up and down, one rubs one's hands together, one dances or sighs in a rhythmic sequence;[13] it is this that easily explains the opposite, that is, why it is so easy to walk or work to rhythm. If the interval between two wave crests is long enough, one can work very well in that time – I have, for example, had the experience of some stupidity annoying me considerably; I was nevertheless able partly to listen to the physics lesson, but each time the nasty business came back to my mind, I clenched my teeth and said: 'Go to hell!'. The complex could remain unconscious as far as *dem. praec.* is concerned, because consciousness requires a certain amount of light; only think of symbols!

A symbol is nothing else but a lateral association which has only a little of the feeling of the main association. And you can also see well enough that it is things which are over-loaded with affect that are symbolized, especially those that refer to sexuality. You will perhaps say: 'Sexual matters, certainly, because they are repressed'? But that would explain nothing. What does 'repressed' mean? And why are they 'repressed'? Is their emotional load positive or negative? Here yet again is a cardinal point. In itself every complex has a positive charge, but if we look at the psyche as a whole, the strongest complexes almost always have a negative charge – Why? It is simple – because the other complexes have a power of persistence and do not want to be annihilated by the stronger one. It is then that the whole of the psyche bristles with hostility towards a stronger complex. Do you think that amnesia occurs as a result, brought about by the force of the counter-representations? (repression). I hardly think so: a counter-representation need only itself become conscious – everything else does not have to become unconscious too (a law of physics: in every movement the force is equal to the resistance). When a mother loses her child, the 'repression' should incite her to think that 'the child is alive', and not induce a total amnesia or what is clearly the case in sexuality: when the contrasting representation brings about amnesia, the whole chain of associations should disappear, seeing that the resistance ought to decline or increase in proportion to the force (otherwise it would be impossible for a complex which is known to have a variety of characteristics to disappear); but we see that this is not the case, for symbols remain.

And now let us go back to the subject – You see that as regards sexual choice, one not only chooses people with the same nature but those who have the same ideals, that is people who can assimilate and transform the combination in question; as the ones whose instincts or ideals are not adapted to nature perish, only those are left whose ideals possess the necessary qualities for the preservation of the species. He who does not fit into this scheme is called disabled – *the more developed social life is, the more numerous are the ways*[14] of transforming the personality, up to a certain point, and that is when it is possible for the sexual component to take a back seat. This does not mean that sexual energy can contribute to a love of music or something of the sort, but that there is a common amount of energy, and the more of it is spent in frankly sexual transformation, the less of it is left for anything else, and vice versa. You can see this particularly clearly in women who are destined to find renewal specifically through sexual procreation: when this kind of transformation is dominant, the woman is more discriminating in her choice, and the more originality she has, the harder it will be for her to find a husband. As a woman is less able to rely on spiritual transformation because – at least temporarily – her fate is determined by sexual transformation and she is therefore not independent enough; we witness the well-known phenomenon of a woman looking for a man who can lavish attention on her; among the uncivilized this might perhaps manifest itself in the man espousing her feelings or instincts. You certainly know that one always finds similarities with the person one loves and vice versa. As psychic attraction causes sexual attraction, it is clear that some psychic feelings are closely linked to corresponding sexual emotions; especially where persons of the opposite sex are concerned.

All things considered, it is wrong to apply the term 'libido' (that is 'sexual feeling' in a limited sense) to art or science: the root of affectivity is not a special sexual feeling, but a power of inertia and an instinct of transformation which can eventually verge on the sexual side, in which case it would then be called 'libido'.[15] I would not attach so much importance to the form, if erroneous expressions did not so often lead to false ideas. *I must adopt an extreme position where you are concerned because you never admit, in the enthusiasm of your new theories, the possibility of non-sexual transformation.*[16] Thus, in the case of Mother, you cannot conceive of the simple fact that, though she does not have the least sexual affinity with her former lover, she cannot bear a caricature of him to live on in the noble part of her psyche. The same thing is true for me in my relationship with Prof. Bleuler, for whom I do not feel the least sexual attraction; the same goes for me as regards all colleagues for whom I have some esteem. It is far better to be not understood by people at all than to be misunderstood; the latter is a dreadful thing.

I hope that I haven't been writing in vain till gone one in the morning!

If you feel like throwing away the letter, let me rather have it back: I will work later on the ideas I have written out here.

Try carefully to understand me; during the treatment of hysteria, two separate things must be taken into consideration:

N. 1 Make it possible for the psycho-sexual component of the ego to transform itself (most of the time or always?) (whether this be by means of art or a simple reaction – as you wish); in this way that component is constantly weakened like a phonograph record going round and round. What's more, the feeling brings about corresponding innervations and the psyche does not exhaust itself by resisting them.

N. 2 Might it not be necessary perhaps, more often than it seems, to prevent as much as possible the excitement of a psycho-sexual expression by deflecting the feeling towards other components of the ego? It is dangerous to attach too much importance to the complex, to feed it with new representations; only an artist can live in this way, and even for him there are certain limits which are beyond his strength: in other words the rest of the psyche ends up being hostile to the complex.

As for me, my family has seen to it currently that, taken away from my studies, I am right in the middle of the complex again.

The desolation is once again limitless. Will I be able to come out of it safe and sound?

III

Do not act in the first flush of excitement: this principle of mine is a good one.[17] I am indeed very tired at the moment, but calm, so it seems to me. Yesterday's conversation seems to me like a bad dream, which continues to oppress me. Yes! Now the moment has come for me to react! Should I 'play the ambitious one'? Or the role of the righteous, offended woman? That would mean lying to myself and to you. Ah! If my whole being could tell me that I am right! And even then, it is terrible to me to hear you speak to me in this way. Still you must be aware that my 'unconscious' does not want to have anything to do with what your 'unconscious' rejects. Things are such that I can (indeed must) be frank, but not you. The fact that I abuse this outspokenness is for me a constant source of censure, but how can I act differently? The complexity of the situation makes me adopt the unnatural role of the man and you the feminine role. I am far from attributing some kind of absolute meaning to what has been said; I perfectly understand that you must offer resistance, but I also acknowledge that, for myself, resistance excites me. I am also very conscious of the fact that if it all depended on me, I would be resisting desperately with all my might. The word has raised a storm, a lot of nonsense has been written, and then rewritten all over again. I have just come back from my violin lesson and my heart is full of softness. O you! If only you knew how dear to me you are, without the least thought of the child.[18] Isn't the wish to bear your child really the wish to possess you at least in a smaller version? Isn't this the wish to offer to you, in the eyes of all, something special? Yes, if it were a bond of friendship that linked me to you! But you seek to stifle any strong feeling that you may feel for me. The result is that you are all diplomacy and lies. The result is that half-unconsciously you are looking for ways to divert me, by making me look again at Dr Binswanger's work, which is as clear as spring water. Must I explain it all to you? What's the use? First, you are probably aware of most of this and, secondly, you would undoubtedly be forced to deny it all. Previously you could discuss more abstract subjects with me, you would show me various things either at the laboratory or at your house, such as pictures or old books; these days anything that has no close relation to the sexual complex you call 'reading a paper' and you do not like that because the power of the complex is such that you are not fully master of it. I ask myself the question: are people always so stupid where they themselves are concerned, or is it that you do not want to admit it? But it would be remarkable with the analytical qualities that you have, that you should not have noticed the pathological rigmaroles you reserve for my benefit! Let us nevertheless go back to our conversation of yesterday. After an eternally long pause, which is even more noticeable in view of your well-known eloquence, you tell me the story of S.W. It is quite clear that the comparison supposes a similarity of situation, otherwise why would you come back to what is ancient history? It is obvious that in your mind, the young woman represents you and not me (*when you wished to talk about the refinement of your unconscious*). You say now that the young woman's unconscious (not yours) had a remarkably refined quality, and then there is the remarkable fact that you held the young woman in greater esteem than anybody else, and that you thought she was destined for you. But in the end the young woman began to tell incredible stories, which disappointed you and made you break with her. And this is supposed to be proof of the refinement of your unconscious? You might make others believe that! Not me, who thinks otherwise: you felt that 'the young imp' was getting to be dangerous for you and you called for help (cf. 'to have – a child', 'to put on a hat');[19] help came, though it took time to get through the fire. 'Yes,' you finally managed to say, 'a few years ago, I knew a similar woman; she too seemed to me like a goddess, but in the end she turned out to be just a flighty girl.'

I do not feel at ease talking to you like this. Yet what can I do? I cannot allow you to defend yourself by humiliating me. This is infinitely more terrible to me than if I were to die so that you could have peace. What must I do? I totally agree with you that we should never speak to each other again about the unconscious. I am going to Locarno, and hope that new sensations and time when I will not be seeing you will help to clarify the situation. At the moment my mind is on fire and I write mechanically. And then I have this idea: when at university I felt a justifiable rage, Miss Tloroff said that I had 'blood-spattered boys before my eyes'. The phrase is from *Boris Godounov*, Pushkin's celebrated work; it is an image which is often used when somebody is really furious. But why did this phrase come to my mind just then? Another follows immediately: 'yes, wretched is he who does not have a pure conscience', taken from the same monologue. You probably know that Boris Godounov was a Russian Tsar; though he only ruled for six years, his reign was beneficial to Russia, at a very troubled period. He was certainly not an ordinary person. But not being of the tsarist line, in order to seize power, he had to have the young heir to the throne (a child of nine) murdered. That child was the son of Ivan the Terrible, and his future could well be imagined. In Pushkin's tragedy, Boris Godounov is a very kind person. His real gifts are in proportion to his passion to rule.

Listen to his monologue: 'It is now six years that I have been on the throne and my soul does not know peace' etc . . . 'O my people! I wanted to obtain for you wealth and glory, win your love by looking after you, but I have had to renounce my folly: the masses do not understand the great when they are alive, they only respect the dead' . . .

It is then that the mention of blood-spattered boys and a bad conscience comes. Briefly, he died soon after in a popular uprising (a natural death; cf. what you say about death when it happens at the right time) and later his two children were murdered. I am evidently disturbed by not having a clear conscience, but it is only an impression, for I am not afraid. Fate takes its vengeance on the Tsar.

As a matter of fact, my crime would be that of borrowing *you* from your wife, but after all it is also my man that is being borrowed, and momentarily I do not care at all! Besides, what am I saying? I do not have the least desire to borrow you from your wife! 'It does not pay to frighten foxes, as is well-known; if you wish to protect your poultry-yard, watch over it well!' That is the devil whispering in my ear. That will do! This business is getting me down. My soul has lost its softness. The devil won't let me talk.

I am so tired of turning things over and over in my mind continuously! *Should I write this or should I not, as I do not want to read this letter again? And yet, I had to write it! For I cannot bear you to speak to me in this way: either we decide that we no longer discuss such areas, or if we do discuss them, I must respond to your remarks as I see fit.*[20] My wishes cannot of course change as a result of one conversation, because there needs to be a long period of conscious reflection for it to be effective. But my wish has never been formulated thus: 'I want to bear you a child'; for this means first of all: 'I agree to give you up for good'. And this seems possible[21] to me only in those isolated moments when I feel deeply offended by you; it is then that the desire to have a child by you dominates everything. But, otherwise, I cannot do it, and that is why I myself fight rather strongly against the complex. I am usually frightened by the thought that our relationship might no longer be as beautiful as happens with the most unselfish friendship. But at the same time there are moments when the fact that I will never have a child by you seems unbearable to me. When the time comes for me to take my final leave of you . . . then I do not know . . . But that is not yet for tomorrow; we do not know what fate reserves for us and I do not exclude the possibility that I may fall in love with somebody else; and that you have, where I am concerned, another destiny. It is the devil that makes me talk thus to you because just now the devil is oppressed. You would be highly mistaken if you believe that I correlate my happiness with a great destiny. I have never believed that my son was destined for me; I know too well that he will have his own life to live and that he belongs to me as little as I do to my parents. It is then that I realize[22] how alone I am. But one must not think of oneself;[23] the dark powers of destiny use us as they see fit, without worrying the least about the person's own wishes . . .

Notes

1 The extracts first appeared in French, translated from the German by Jeanne Moll, entitled 'Extraits inédits d'un journal' in *Le Bloc-Notes de la Psychanalyse*, 1983, No. 3, pp. 147–171, ed. Mario Cifali, Geneva. They are in three parts, most probably written at different dates. 'Love, death and transformation' was the title given by Jeanne Moll to the French translation. The German documents are in the private archives of the descendants of E. Claparède. The article also appeared in English in the *Journal of Analytical Psychology* in its January 2001 issue. Reprinted here by kind permission of *Le Bloc-Notes de la Psychanalyse*.

2 L. Binswanger published *Über das Verhalten des psychogalvanischen Phänomens beim Assoziationsexperiment* in 1907.

3 *Sabina Spielrein between Freud and Jung*, Paris, Aubier, 1981, p. 130.

4 In her letter to Freud of 13 June 1909 (in *Sabina Spielrein entre Freud et Jung* [*Sabina Spielrein between Freud and Jung*], 1981, Aubier, Paris, p. 130), S. Spielrein wrote that Dr Jung 'offered her the chance of collaborating in his first work *Über das Verhalten der Reaktionszeit beim Assoziationsexperimente*' (1905, *CW* 2).

5 These underlined words were crossed out in the original.

6 These sentences were crossed out in the original. Sabina Spielrein wrote above: 'I go back to our controversy' and with two blue dashes in the margin marked the importance of these lines and the following ones.

7 The whole of the preceding paragraph is marked with blue in the margin.

8 In French in the text, with the same orthography.

9 Heavily underlined with blue pencil.

10 Heavily underlined with blue pencil.

11 Underlined in blue pencil. The following paragraph is marked with a blue line in the margin.

12 Underlined in blue.

13 The same idea is expressed in the entry of 9 June 1906 (an unpublished 'black diary' which *Le Bloc-Notes de la Psychanalyse* intends to publish later).

14 Underlined in blue pencil.

15 Underlined in blue pencil.

16 Underlined in blue pencil.

17 The following pages are marked with a blue line in the margin (up to Locarno).

18 Bubi.

19 The same association, here added in between the lines, is quoted, page 131, in S. Spielrein's letter of 13.06.1909 to Freud in Carotenuto 1982, 'Sabina Spielrein between Freud and Jung'.

20 Underlined with a blue pencil.

21 Paragraph marked in blue in the margin up to 'the most unselfish'.

22 The following lines are also marked with blue in the margin.

23 She wrote 'sicht' [sight] instead of 'sich' [oneself] – a slip, no doubt, to repudiate this common bond.

Chapter 3

The letters of C.G. Jung to Sabina Spielrein

(Translated from the German by Barbara Wharton)

Dr C.G. Jung,   Burghölzli-Zürich

Lecturer in Psychiatry   20.6.08

My dear Miss Spielrein,

You managed well and truly to get to my unconscious with your biting letter. Such a thing could only happen to me.

On Monday I am engaged all day with Dr Jones.[1] However, I am coming into town on Tuesday morning and would like to meet you at 11 o'clock at the steamer landing stage on the Bahnhofstrasse. So that we can be alone and able to talk undisturbed, we'll take a boat out on to the lake. In the sunshine, and out on the open water, it will be easier to find a clear direction out of this turmoil of feelings. With affectionate greetings from your friend.

——◆——

Zürich, 30.6.08

My dear friend,

I must tell you briefly what a lovely impression I received of you today. Your image has changed completely, and I want to tell you how very, very happy it makes me to be able to hope that there are people who are like me, people in whom living and thinking are one; good people who do not misuse the power of their mind to dream up fetters but rather to create freedoms. As a result there awakens in me a feeling of beauty and freedom which has once more bathed the world and its objects in a fresh lustre. You can't believe how much it means to me to hope I can love someone whom I do not have to condemn, and who does not condemn herself either, to suffocate in the banality of habit.

How great would be my happiness to find that person in you, that '*esprit fort*[2] who never descends into sentimentality, but whose essential and innermost vital core is her own freedom and independence.

I look forward to seeing you again on Friday.

With warmest greetings, your friend.

———◆———

4.7.08

My dear friend,

What we discussed yesterday had a really releasing effect on me. The very *belief* that there are people who behave as they think, and who think only good things, is a relief which is so great that it compensates for many disappointments. Inwardly I feel calmer and more free. I would very much like to speak to you again next week, before you go to the Walensee.[3] Or if you are going to Wesen soon,[4] we could perhaps meet in Rapperswyl. May I ask you to write and tell me when you are going to W?

Warmest greetings from your friend.

———◆———

6.7.08

My Dear,

I found your letter yesterday evening on my return from Sch. I have to go into town on Tuesday morning to the district prosecutor's office, and could use this opportunity to meet you in the outer area of the Uto Quay at 10.30; from there you could come with me to the Burghölzli. In any case I shall be walking along the lake shore as far as Zürichhorn from 10.30 onwards. Unfortunately I have no time in the afternoon.

Affectionate greetings –

———◆———

22.7.08

My Dear,

Please do come to see me next Friday evening at 5.30. Unfortunately it is impossible for me to free a whole afternoon. Last week I had to attend two weddings and the chief[5] was spitting venom about it. So I am deeply annoyed. I have to work endlessly.

Affectionate greetings and goodbye till Friday, your friend.

———◆———

Dr C.G. Jung, Lecturer in Psychiatry   Burghölzli-Zürich

                                                        12.8.08

My dear friend,

Your letter gave me much pleasure and set my mind at rest. I was rather worried on account of your long silence. I was afraid something had happened to you, or that somehow the devil had had a hand in it. There are lovely things in your letter. I must admire your parents' truly great broadmindedness. For a mother, that is really a high achievement and one hardly to be expected. Tell your mother that I admire her for that. It will be easier for your father, for new outlooks and new life values come more readily to a man of ideas than to the natural conservatism of a woman. As you say in your letter, everything is fine and good; I rejoice at your happiness. This way your long desired and long feared stay in Russia will be easier. With me everything is trembling like a volcano: one minute everything is golden, the next everything is grey. Your letter came like a ray of sunshine through the clouds.[6] But your mother is quite right: you should get better notepaper; you do know that I dislike the 'botany tin' style* because of its lack of beauty. Even ugly clothes give me pain. You have given that up now, thank God.[7] Don't be angry with me for writing to you about such things again. I want you to be beautiful both inwardly and outwardly, for that alone is natural. No one who is not inwardly defective in feeling can love what is ugly and tasteless, and you are certainly not that! Your letter had a good effect on me; I realise how much more attached I am to you than I ever thought. I happen to be terribly suspicious, and always think other people are trying to exploit and tyrannise me. It is only with great difficulty that I can muster a belief in man's natural goodness, which I so often proclaim. That certainly does not apply to my feelings about you, however! I often think that the happiness that I want to give other people is begrudged me, or is returned to me in the form of hidden hostility, which is what has so often happened to me! All last week I was not really well, rather hysterical, and a convenient cold set in which sent me off to bed for a day. There your letter had a very good effect on my mood, so that since then my energy has significantly increased.

How do you like being in your home country again? Are you going into the steppes? And what did your old nurse say to you? Was she pleased to see how

---

*   This phrase is a literal translation of the German. Dr A. Plaut writes (personal communication, 2000): 'The word refers to a "Botanisiertrommel". I had such a thing as a child. It was made of tin, green, and hung around my neck, designed for collecting botanical specimens without squashing them. Quite a good idea. A "Trommel" ["drum"] that was oval in shape. A suitable educational present for a five year old.' Here the meaning seems to be 'parsimonious', 'useful' in a negative sense, 'merely functional'.

pretty you have become? We're reading here in the newspaper that cholera is rife in Rostov. Don't drink any unboiled water and don't eat any salads; you must be careful with uncooked fruit too because of the bacilli.

At the moment one of my patients is living at no. 6 xxxstrasse; Miss xxx,[8] a Polish woman. So be careful!

Recently I have had a great deal to do. Last week two American professors were with me, one from New York, the other from Michigan, then also another professor from New York, who is the president of the Lunacy Commission of New York State.[9] In addition a doctor from the Tübingen psychiatric clinic has been with me for three weeks[10] to get to know me, that is, my views and my methods.

On 23 August I am going on holiday. It will be best if you continue to send your letters to the Burghölzli; someone will send them on to me from there. I am urgently in need of a rest. First I'm going for a week to the Toggenburg[11] and will be walking with Riklin,[12] then a further six days to Schaffhausen to my wife and child.

When I return from holiday Prof. Freud will be coming for a few days.[13] On 28.6.1909 [the original date reads: 28 vi. IX; probably 28.9.08 is intended; trans.] I have to go on military service for five weeks. At present Prof. Bleuler is on holiday; so I have a lot to do, but I don't always do it with pleasure. I haven't got round to any scientific work at all recently. I hope that will improve in the winter.

Write to me again soon, so that I can see that you are happy and at peace.

I received the money safely. Thank you!

With an affectionate kiss from your friend.

———◆———

2.9.08

My Dear,

I like the small photograph best. You look your best in that one. So I will keep it, with many thanks.

In the meantime you will probably have received my last letter. Holidays are not favourable for long letters. One has literally to steal time from oneself to write.

Your detailed descriptions of your life delighted me very much. You write in a truly Russian way. I've now finished my tour in the mountains[14] and had glorious weather for it. Now the weather has turned really bad so that I'm having to postpone my planned bicycle trip from one day to the next. Don't stay too long in Russia, avoid everything that taxes you, physically and mentally, so that you can return to your studies with fresh energy.

With warmest greetings from your friend.

———◆———

Brugg, 28.9.08

Dear friend,

You can see from my mistake[15] that I often think of you. You will perhaps have thought of this or that reason for the fact that I have not written to you again for so long. However, you already know the reason: *Prof. Freud* was here for quite a long time.[16] At this meeting I really had an opportunity for the first time to see this great man in my world, out of his own milieu, and thus to understand him much more deeply than before. He is truly a great and good man who, by virtue of his wonderful knowledge of humankind and his experience of life, sees incomparably further than I do. You are right on that point. If I have previously only admired this man from a distance, now I have really come to love him. You will understand that I used the time with Freud to good effect. I clarified many areas for myself. In brief, it did me good.

At present I am on military service in Brugg for five weeks, that is, I am on service until 31 October. My address is still Burghölzli, however, for I shall be staying in Brugg only a few days; later we are going to the fortress in French-speaking Switzerland. I am hoping to have a thorough rest.

How are you? Are you living a peaceful life? What are you thinking about your future? I often worry about you now because of [. . .]

———◆———

4.12.08

My Dear,

I regret so much; I regret my weakness and curse the fate that is threatening me. I fear for my work, for my life's task, for all the lofty perspectives that are being revealed to me by this new philosophy as it evolves. How shall I, with my sensitive soul, free myself from all these questions? You will laugh when I tell you that recently *earlier and earlier childhood memories have been surfacing*, from a time (*3–4th year*) when I often hurt myself badly, and when, for example, I was once only just rescued from certain death by a maid.[17] My mind is torn to its very depths. I, who had to be a tower of strength for many weak people, am the weakest of all. Will you forgive me for being as I am? For offending you by being like this, and forgetting my duties as a doctor towards you? Will you understand that I am one of the weakest and most unstable of human beings? And will you never take revenge on me for that, either in words, or in thoughts or feelings? I am looking for someone who understands how to love, without punishing the other person, imprisoning him or sucking him dry; I am seeking this as yet unrealised person who will make it possible that love can be independent of social advantage and disadvantage, so that love may always be an end in itself, and not just a means to an end. It is my misfortune that I cannot live without the joy of love, of tempestuous, ever-changing love in my life. This daemon stands as an unholy contradiction to my compassion and my sensitivity. When love for a woman awakens within me, the first thing I feel is regret, pity for the poor woman who dreams of eternal faithfulness and other impossibilities, and is destined for a painful awakening out of all these dreams. Therefore if one is already married it is better to engage in this lie and do penance for it immediately than to repeat the experiment again and again, lying again and again, and repeatedly disappointing someone.[18] What on earth is to be done for the best? I do not know and dare not say, because I do not know what you will make of my words and feelings. Since the last upset I have completely lost my sense of security with regard to you. That weighs heavily on me. You must clear up this uncertainty once and for all. I should like to talk to you again at greater length. Could I for example speak with you next Tuesday morning between 9.15 and 12.00? [no question mark in original; trans.] Since you are perhaps less inhibited in your apartment, I am willing to come to you. Should Tuesday morning not suit you, write and tell me, otherwise I will come in the hope of getting some clarity. I should like definite assurances so that my mind can be at rest over your intentions. Otherwise my work suffers, and that seems to me more important than the passing problems and sufferings of the present. Give me back now something of the love and patience and unselfishness which I was able to give you at the time of your illness. Now I am ill [. . .]

———◆———

[Probably 1908]

Dear friend,

Tomorrow evening, Thursday, I shall be going to the theatre by boat around *6.40*. Since I have no idea where Scheuchzerstrasse is, I would be grateful if you would come with me. Will you wait for me at the Bellevue, that is at the tram-stop, at this time? Then we'll go straight there by tram or on foot, whichever suits you better. I hope the book reached you safely.
With best wishes.

———◆———

[Probably 1908]

My Dear,

Unfortunately I am busy on Wednesday until 7 o'clock. However, I am free at 6 o'clock on Thursday and on Friday from 5.30 onwards. If you send me no further word, I shall assume you will come on Friday.
Affectionate greetings from your friend.

———◆———

Küssnach b/Zürich,

12.9.10

Dear friend,

Although I have not yet finished your paper[19] I have already found passages in it which filled me with delight. The great trouble you took with the case has been richly rewarded by the outcome. I am somewhat critical of the presentation, in that your demands on the reader's attention and understanding are too high. The wine symbolism is thoroughly historical/mythical. On that point I must decidedly congratulate you. Laokoon is marvellous. You know the Laokoon monument, don't you? Deeply symbolic.

Until the next time, affectionate greetings and good wishes! Your friend.

——◆——

[Probably 9.1910]

My Dear,

Sincere thanks on behalf of my wife for the flowers.[20] That was very sweet of you. Affectionate greetings.

——◆——

[Probably 9/10.1910]

Dear friend,

I too have just recovered from a very severe attack of influenza. I was in bed from last Thursday. I am better now, but everything is an effort. Today I went back to work, but am still quite exhausted. Nevertheless I do have the strength to wish you a good recovery from the bottom of my heart. I am free on Thursday morning 9–11. On Friday 9–12 I have appointments which I cannot change. On Saturday 9–11 I am free again.

Please let me know whether you will be coming on Thursday or on Saturday. With affectionate greetings and best wishes for your recovery, yours.

——◆——

[Probably December 1910]

Dear friend,

Last Wednesday of course it did not cross my mind that you were already doing examinations[21] and so I waited for you. When you did not come I thought you were well and truly caught up with examination nerves.

So I will expect you next Wednesday at 9.00.

With affectionate greetings, your friend.

——◆——

[Probably July 1911]

My Dear,

Your detailed letter interested me very much, and I am very, very sorry that you have happened on an old swine who cannot distinguish between human and animal. That is too bad. One can see what stops men understanding psychoanalysis. Please get in touch with *Dr Seif*,[22] the nerve specialist. 21/1 Franz Josephstrasse, *Munich*. He is the president of the psychoanalytic society there. There you will be better received. Forgive me for keeping you waiting for my reply. At the moment everything has had to wait as I had to finish writing an article by the end of June.[23] I hope you will have a good reception there. By the same post you will receive separately the corrections of your paper,[24] *which you can* keep. The corrections have already been taken care of. I am excited about your new project.[25]
With affectionate greetings, yours very sincerely, Jung.

———◆———

Dr C.G. Jung,   Küsnach-Zürich

Lecturer in Psychiatry   Seestrasse 1003

                                                            8.8.11

My Dear,

I have unfortunately not yet been able to finish reading your comprehensive study[26] as the presence of Dr Seif, who is currently staying with me, has kept me from it. Nevertheless I have read so far with care that I can permit myself a provisional judgement. I am surprised at the abundance of excellent thoughts which anticipate various ideas of my own. But it is good that others see things the same way as I do. Your thinking is bold, far-reaching, and philosophical.[27] Hence the *Jahrbuch* will hardly be the right place for its publication. Either you can make a small independent book of it, or we could try to include your work in *Freud's 'Schriften zur angewandten Seelenkunde'* (papers on applied psychology). That would be the right place.[28] Various points of detail still need to be filled out. I hope grandfather Freud will have the same joy as I have over this fruit of your spirit.

Your stay in Munich does now seem to have been satisfactory in every respect.

Meanwhile I congratulate you most heartily on your paper.
With affectionate greetings, yours very sincerely, Dr Jung.
Tomorrow morning I am going away for three weeks.[29] My address remains *Küsnacht*.

———◆———

Dr C.G. Jung   [Probably 17/18.8.1911]

Lecturer in Psychiatry   Küsnach-Zürich, Seestrasse 1003

My Dear,

I can answer you only briefly as I am just at home between two trains and am going away again immediately.

Please get in touch with Dr Seif regarding the invitation to the Congress. I have sent the provisional programmes first to the sections. You should receive your invitation after Sep.1 Once again you are grumbling too soon.

Regarding accommodation apply to Dr K. Abraham,[30,31] Rankestrasse 24, Berlin W.

Best wishes for your stay by the sea. Your friend.

———◆———

Hotel Erbprinz, Weimar

[Probably 21/22.9 1911]

My Dear,

The enormous workload which running the Congress has meant must give you a good idea why I have not replied until today.

I see your situation clearly. I can hardly think that there is anything organically wrong with your foot, for the psychological situation is too powerfully and traumatically significant. Something in you was searching for a reason not to go to Weimar. In other words, you wanted to come with a certain phantasy/wish which you had to repress. You ought to have come in spite of that, however, for life demands sacrifices and self-denial, the subordination of stubbornness and pride to the rules of devoted love. Only when you seek the happiness of the other, will your own happiness be granted. I allow myself to write to you so frankly and to admonish you because, after long and solitary reflection, I have eliminated from my heart all the bitterness against you which it still harboured. To be sure, this bitterness did not come from your work, – for there is nothing in that which would be personally disagreeable to me – but from earlier, from all the inner anguish I endured because of you – and which you endured because of me. I truly wish you happiness from my heart, and it is with this feeling that I want to think of you. *But never forget that under no circumstances* must you retreat from an immediate goal which your heart considers good and reasonable. Each time that will mean a sacrifice of selfishness, of pride and of stubbornness, and it will seem to you as if you were losing yourself in the process . . . Only in the course of this mysterious self-sacrifice you will gain yourself in a new and more beautiful form and you will also as a result become a blessing and a source of happiness for other people. *So you should not have given up attending the Congress under any circumstances*; you made a grave error by doing so for which you immediately punished yourself. You ought to have sacrificed yourself. Your dissertations[32] were distributed as far as was possible.

Get well again now! Freud will certainly accept you. He has spoken several times of your dissertation, the best indication that it has made an impression on him. You do not need my recommendation.[33] Approach him as a great master and rabbi, then all will be well.

With affectionate greetings and wishes, yours.

———◆———

Dr med. C.G. Jung LL.D   1003 Seestrasse

Lecturer in Psychiatry   Küsnach-Zürich

[Probably beginning November 1911]

My Dear,

In these circumstances I must send you the paper[34] back immediately; I am sorry about it, since I have not finished it yet. In fact I was detailed to an exercise in the mountains[35] so that I lost all the time I had set aside for your work. *Please send me back your paper immediately*, when you have made the necessary use of it. I must certainly study it thoroughly, for there are so many important thoughts in it; I must be completely quiet in order to understand it all properly. Until now I have not had a moment's peace.

My dear, you are not to think that I retain any hard feelings towards you. I am just waiting for a few days' peace in order to read your work again *at one sitting*. If I am disturbed once more in the middle of it, I shall never reach a clear and conclusive understanding. I am sorry that you have been worried unnecessarily. I beg your forgiveness. Your work is on its way to you regis-tered as a valuable package[36] by immediate post.

Your news from Vienna is interesting – and distressing. Stekel[37] is enraptured but unscientific. Klages must have been impressed.[38] Why does he go to Vienna? Apart from Freud, Rank[39] and Sachs[40] there is little there that is serious. Please don't betray me.

Your ever devoted friend.

———◆———

Dr C.G. Jung   Küsnach-Zürich

Lecturer in Psychiatry   Seestrasse 1003

                                       13.11.11

My Dear,

At last I can send you the manuscript. When I went to send you the letter I suddenly realised that I did not have your address. (It was not on your last letter.) I received all your earlier letters while I was on military service.[41] Let me just say, by the way, that you can safely send your letters to me with the usual postage.

I would ask you again to send me the paper back straight away. In Part 2 of my work (have I sent you a separate copy of the first part?) I have made frequent references to your ideas.[42] I should like to do so with your new paper too. So that we are in harmony.

With affectionate greetings and apologies, your very devoted friend.

———◆———

Dr med. C.G. Jung LL.D   1003 Seestrasse

Lecturer in Psychiatry   Küsnach-Zürich

                                       24.11.11

My Dear,

Your news is very valuable to me. You partly confirm what I suspected. On the question of phylogenetic reproductions Freud will soon come over to my side, even if on certain more general philosophical questions he stands his ground. The difference between Vienna and Zürich will be clearly brought to light in Part 2, where I develop a genetic theory of libido.[43] I am rather worried about how Freud will take the corrections I am introducing into the theory of sexuality. The more I write in my own style, the greater becomes the danger of misunderstandings, for inwardly I am quite alien to the spirit of the Viennese school, though not to the spirit of Freud. If you will not betray me, I will show you a little snapshot: it reveals Freud in a spontaneous act which suggests the underlying cause of the fact that he has not gathered the best people around him in Vienna: a person (whom I also know) came to Freud. He had had endless affairs with women and was also neurotic. Freud said of him: 'X.Y. is interesting theoretically because he is really not entitled to have a neurosis' (that is to say, because he is living out his sexual instincts). There is an unspoken expectation that it is a fact that neurosis comes only from repressed sexuality. From this expectation Stekel was born. But here in Zürich we think that neurosis is a conflict, however one lives it out. You understand that this expression of opinion on Freud's part was a completely momentary act, which he would never raise to the level of theory: he is much too conscientious in his research for that. But the remark indicates a certain latent expectation. The fact that you think that *you* are not working along the right lines if I am not recognised means that you are still too closely bound up with me: you cannot judge my value or lack of value accurately. *You do not yet see who I am*, in the sense that you are not yet able to free your intuition from your personal prejudice. You will be set free only when you have completely cleansed your judgement. If you need to ask me anything about that, I will give you an answer.

I look forward to receiving your paper.

With best wishes, your friend.

————◆————

Dr C.G. Jung   Küsnach-Zürich

Lecturer in Psychiatry   Seestr. 1003

                                                     11.12.1911

My Dear,

Don't be so downcast. Your paper will go into the *Jahrbuch* if Prof. Freud wishes it.[44] I heartily *congratulate you on your success.*

The *Jahrbuch* for the second half of 1911, which went to print in the autumn, is complete. You will go to print in January, in the first issue of the 1912 edition. There you will appear in company with Frl. Grebelskaja's dissertation[45] and with my Part 2,[46] which I was unable to finish in time for the 1911 second issue. In addition, a very nice paper by Dr Nelken will be published.[47] I hope that the proofs will reach you promptly in February.

Have you met Silberer?[48] What is he like? His papers are good.

If only Steckel would not imagine himself to be a genius. His book on the language of dreams[49] is astonishing as far as the dream material he brings. The theoretical part however is thoroughly weak. His interpretation of dreams is quite one-sided. Moreover I am in an embarrassing position, as I was to bring out a discussion of it in the *Jahrbuch* and Freud does not want anything to do with it himself.

As soon as I have finished correcting the last paper for the *Jahrbuch*, which will soon be the case, you will be next.

With best wishes and greetings, your devoted friend.

Freud has told me some very good things about you.

————◆————

Dr C.G. JUNG   Küsnach-Zürich

Lecturer in Psychiatry   Seestr. 1003

                                                     23.12.11

My Dear,

According to your wish, the work was despatched to you a short time ago as a registered packet. *Deadline* is 31 Jan.1912. I would prefer it if you could prepare the paper so that it is ready for printing. Then give it first to Prof. Freud so that he can give his opinion of it. After that I will look through it and do any corrections that are necessary. With regard to your lecture I will let you have my advice in print: ask Rank for my lectures at Clark University;[50] there you will find how I basically set things out. The word association forms will be sent to you shortly.

Prof. Freud has spoken very flatteringly of you in his letters.[51] I congratulate you on this success, although there are other successes which I would wish for you much more.

With best wishes for the winter solstice, your devoted friend.

———◆———

Dr med. C.G. Jung LL.D   1003 Seestrasse

Lecturer in Psychiatry   Küsnach-Zürich

                                                     18.3.12

My Dear,

I did not know that Frl. Grebelskaja is in such difficult circumstances. She telephoned me recently to say that she was going away in a few days. I had to give her a certificate showing that her work is at the printers.[52] Her work is in press. Unfortunately I do not have the power to hurry the typesetter.

As I read your paper I find uncanny parallels with my own new work appearing in it which I did not at all suspect, for until then I had always read your title *incorrectly*: 'distinction' instead of 'destruction', and was puzzled about it. Now I find considerable parallels which show the results one gets if one goes on thinking logically and independently. Your work will be published *before mine* in the *Jahrbuch*. Your destruction wish is certainly correct. We desire not only the ascent but also the descent and the end. This thought is developed beautifully by Nietzsche and I say a lot about it too. (Stekel says that a death wish appears in all (?) dreams too. Certainly this wish is much more frequent than we think.) Stekel however has no overall conception. He is merely an interpreter. Do you not want to read his book? You would certainly enjoy it enormously![53] As a matter of fact I was involved in the formation of the lay association in Zürich.[54] Until now it has been a thriving concern.

I received your postscript.

With best wishes, your friend.

P.S. With regard to the word 'complex', this word is found in an old psychological work of *Bleuler* in the sense of a 'mass of images, feelings' etc. which, for example, constitute the 'I'. *That definition however has nothing in common with the present meaning of the concept* which I have introduced into psychology. (cf. Diagnostic Association Studies and Psychology of Dem. Praec.)[55]

————◆————

Dr med. C.G. Jung LL.D   1003 Seestrasse

Lecturer in Psychiatry   Küsnach-Zürich

                                                     25.3.12

My Dear,

You are upsetting yourself unnecessarily again. When I said there were 'uncanny' similarities, you again took that much too literally. I was intending it much more as a compliment to you. Your study is extraordinarily intelligent and contains splendid ideas whose priority I am happy to acknowledge as yours.[56] The death tendency or death wish was clear to you before it was to me, understandably! I am progressing only slowly with the manuscript since I am correcting style and expression at the same time. I express myself so differently from you in my work that no one could imagine that you had borrowed in any way from me. There is no question of it at all. With regard to the hidden interpenetration of thought, there are more lofty questions here which do not come into consideration in public life and of which, in any case, we know too little to be able to reckon seriously with them. Perhaps I borrowed from you too; certainly I have unwittingly absorbed a part of your soul, as you doubtless have of mine. What matters is what each of us has made of it. And you have made something good. I am glad that you are representing me in Vienna. The new work will *certainly* be misunderstood. I hope you will be able to represent my new ideas.

With affectionate greetings, your friend.

————◆————

Dr Med. C.G. Jung LL.D   1003 Seestrasse

Lecturer in Psychiatry   Küsnach-Zürich

                                      11.4.13

Dear friend,

Owing to a lack of material, I have never worked on the associations of morphine addicts. Have you much material of this kind? One case alone would hardly be typical.

I have just returned again from America.[57] It is for that reason that I am rather late answering your letter. I had no idea you were ill and am glad to hear that you have recovered.[58]

I have not heard of Frl. Aptekmann.[59] I am pleased to hear that Krauss[60] has found something good in my association studies. I cannot of course wait for the recognition of these men, but have meanwhile progressed further with the work.

I have left your long letter on the subject of my work unanswered, for I felt it would have needed half a book to reply to it. I could not manage that as I was then quite exhausted. So I did not reply at all. I was completely discouraged at that time because everyone was attacking me,[61] and in addition I was certain that Freud would never understand me and would break off his personal relationship with me. He wants to give me love, while I want understanding. I want to be a friend on an equal footing, while he wants to have me as a son.[62] For that reason he ascribes to a complex everything I do which does not fit the framework of his teaching. That is how he sees it, but I *never* recognise it. At the meeting in Munich I saw clearly that Freud is lost to me.[63] My inner struggles at that time absorbed me so much that I did not answer your letter. It is not that I am not open to criticism – but I know only too well that it is too extensive a matter for me to be able to explain it to you in detail. Too much has changed in me since I last saw you.

I wish you all the best.

I remain ever your friend.

———◆———

Dr Med. C.G. Jung LL.D   1003 Seestrasse

Lecturer in Psychiatry   Küsnach-Zürich

                                      24.8.13

Dear friend,

I read your letter with much interest and am glad to know how things are with you.[64] I wish you much happiness from the bottom of my heart. If you really love your child then certainly everything will be well. And why should you not love your child?

Where work is concerned, we are always in need of more careful analyses of Dem. praec. However, that is something beyond your reach, at least for the present.

What would be useful would be the analysis of literary characters such as I did in my libido work with Hölderlin, Nietzsche, etc. But it's difficult!

A *complete* bibliography of the psychoanalytic literature from 1909 onwards. For that the following would have to be researched:

Centralblatt for psychoanalysis.
International journal for medical psychoanalysis.
Jahrbuch.
Imago.
Journal for sexual science.
Journal of abnormal psychology and various other English and American periodicals.
English and American papers.
L'Encéphale.
Archives of neurology.
Journal for neurology and psychiatry.
Archive for general psychology
Psychotherapia (Russian).
Psiche (Italian).
It would be necessary to write to Holland, and also to various authors in different countries.
Journal for medical psychology and psychotherapy.
A huge task to collect all this material!
I would be glad if someone could do that carefully.
With best wishes and greetings, yours sincerely, Jung.

———◆———

[Probably end Dec. 1913]

I congratulate you on the happy event![65]

DR. MED. C.G. JUNG
KÜSNACHT/ZÜRICH

———◆———

Private letter to Dr S. Spielrein-Scheftel

2 bis, rue St. Léger. Genève, Chez Mme Roche

Dr. med. C.G. Jung LL.D   1003 Seestrasse

Lecturer in psychiatry   Küsnach-Zürich

15.4.14[66]

Dear friend,

Very many thanks for your friendly letter. Your fine ideas on ethics may be sure of general applause.[67] With regard to my resignation as editor of the *Jahrbuch*,[68] it is the result of so many painful experiences that I do not wish to speak of it. From the tone of the attacks that have been directed at me you may see what kind of tendencies are at work against me. The comparison with Stekel is a perfidious invention on the injustice of which the publisher Deuticke[69] can be most informative.

I am pleased that your little daughter is well. Long may she continue to thrive. I wish your work every success.

The tone of your letter touched me to the quick, for I can see that you too despise me. Respect for the human personality and its motives should not be undermined by psychoanalysis. Because I fight for that I suffer much.

Yours sincerely, Jung.

———◆———

Dr med. C.G. Jung LL.D   228 Seestrasse

Küsnacht-Zürich

31.5.16

Dear doctor,

The inductive method draws up laws based on a comparison of a series of facts. The deductive method infers the relationship of a fact to a general law. The introvert uses both methods. The extravert does so too, insofar as he can think. In that respect he is lacking, for his principle function is feeling, not thinking. He thinks according to the feeling principle, the introvert feels according to the thinking principle. It is very gratifying to know what a kind welcome my writings receive with you.

With collegial greetings, Dr. Jung.

———◆———

Internment of prisoners of war in Switzerland

The commandant of the English region   13 Sept. 1917

Dear doctor,

Unfortunately it is hardly possible for me to select a suitable case for you as I
have a great deal to do.

Your dream: I am still a figure in your unconscious, that is, I represent a
dimension in your unconscious which keeps hieroglyphs and such like at your
disposal, that is, clearly symbolic expressions which you have to decipher.
You know perhaps that I distinguish a personal unconscious (the domain of
the repressed personal contents) from an absolute or 'collective' unconscious.
The latter contains the primal images, that is, the developmental and historical deposits. The hieroglyphs are symbols of those. The new development
that will come announces itself in an old language, in symbolic signs. I must
frankly urge you to observe this language of signs in yourself. You can derive
a special insight from that, which can be of universal value, if the deciphering
is successful! I have long been occupied with this question of the psychic
contents of the collective and have found so many interesting things that they
have kept me awake at night.

With best wishes, Dr Jung.

———◆———

Dr C.G. Jung   228 Seestrasse

Küsnach-Zürich

10.10.17

Dear doctor,

With your hieroglyphs we are dealing with phylogenetic engrams of an historical symbolic nature. As it is a matter not of intellectual, but of irrational,
symbolic dimensions, your intellect suppresses and devalues these disturbing
engrams which now try to reproduce themselves in compensation for a too
one-sided intellectual attitude. You instinctively suspect (without knowing
it?) these parts of your unconscious. I cannot tell you any more about it in an
intellectual sense. I could only express myself irrationally and symbolically on
the subject, and for that you would punish me with disdain because that
wisdom would appear to you as ridiculous. Thus in your dream you fall
victim to German technical intellectualism and its brutal power, and you
must cry in vain for the sun, for the sun's golden magic, the greenness of
noon, and the scent of the earth. With what contempt people have treated the
libido work and intellectually torn it to shreds! They have bombarded it
intellectually, but it is nevertheless quite clear that a gothic cathedral and a

library of old manuscripts are nothing in the face of the thoroughly decisive power of a 28-cm. shell. Yes, my most respected lady, I have been slandered and mocked and criticised enough; that is why I am sticking to my runes and to all the pale skimpy little ideas at which I hinted in my libido work until people realise that they are sitting in a prison without air and without light – in a prison which, however, is perfectly satisfactory while they can snatch a breath of fresh air daily in the yard and find the sun filtering through the blinds sufficient. Now you really do want the sun and eternal beauty and the secret of the earth, you even demand it. But I mistrust your arguments, as one mistrusts Germany's pacifist ideas when it has been worshipping the god of war for years on end. I will not hand over my secret to see it trampled under foot by those who do not understand. A thick high wall has now been built round this garden, and I assure you that there is nothing behind it but those old familiar paltry ideas and 'superficial allegories' which were hinted at from a distance in the libido book. You see, *Freudian* theory goes much deeper, right into the glands, it is the most profound statement that can ever be made about human psychology. One cannot go any deeper than back to the mother's body. It is from there that the world is best explained. Everything else is superficial and 'unscientific', *a symbolic swindle built on repressed anal erotism.* You just have to know that ultimately everything comes from the mother's body, and that it is nothing but sexuality and its lamentable repression. Everything else is nothing but that. As a supporting hypothesis anti-semitism is worth recommending, and some more minor slanders. I am sending you by the same post a short paper[70] which is based on nothing and contains a string of arbitrary assertions which have arisen from a misunderstanding of Freud's teaching.

With best wishes, Dr Jung.

———◆———

30.11.17

Dear doctor,

Your comments are quite correct from the point of view of the psychology of instincts.[71] You are proceeding from the outset, in accordance with your type, on the view that there is only the instinct for the preservation of the species and for self-preservation, that is to say simply the instinct for the preservation of the species. That is a biological supposition which contains a certain average empirical truth. With this assumption, however, you do violence to the *psychology of the subject*, that is, that psychology which is orientated more or less exclusively towards the *ego* (Adler!).[72] It is inadmissible. We cannot allow a psychology based on biology simply to cut the throat of a psychology of the ego.

An orientation towards the ego precludes an orientation towards instincts, and an orientation towards instincts precludes an orientation towards the ego. A psychology of the ego has nothing at all to do with the self-preservation instinct for it is *not a psychology of instincts* but really a 'will to power'. You must read *Adler* or *Nietzsche*. *Nietzsche* for example, according to Freud's theory, would be nothing but repressed sexuality, whereas of course he is genuine. Is there any poet or thinker at all whose creativity did not spring from repressed sexuality? But the individuality of Nietzsche cannot be encompassed by contrasting him with, for example, Goethe. Thus *Freud's* theory is to that extent altogether incapable of understanding the subject. In fact it is suitable only for objects, not for active subjects. It is merely 'empirical', finding only moving objects, but no living subjects. It was this latter aspect that Adler perceived, but only this.[73]

With friendly greetings, yours sincerely, Dr Jung.

———◆———

Dr C.G. Jung   228 Seestrasse

                                                   Küsnach-Zürich

                                                   18.12.17

Dear doctor,

You have grasped the elements of type theory except for the problem of feeling.[74] You define feelings one-sidedly and arbitrarily as something conscious. If there are unconscious thoughts, there are also unconscious feelings ('so to speak!'). The feelings of the introvert are infantile/archaic/symbolic, because they are mainly of an unconscious nature. The extravert's own thoughts are similar. You are an intuitive extravert type.

Your conception of the unconscious seems arbitrary to me. It is not clear how you can practically distinguish between a side-conscious, a preconscious, a subconscious and an unconscious. Where do dreams come from?

Freud recognises the psychology of the ego in the same way as *Adler recognises sexuality*, but that is all. Adler is not to be ranked alongside Freud, otherwise you do violence to both.

With friendly greetings, yours sincerely, Dr Jung.

———◆———

Dr C.G. Jung   228 Seestrasse

                                                   Küsnach-Zürich

                                                   28.12.17

Dear Doctor,

You are perceiving the unconscious as wishes and thoughts that are not capable of consciousness.[75] But if these wishes are not capable of consciousness, how do you know about them? Moreover there are very many people to whom these wishes are by no means unconscious. In certain circumstances they are, like the rest, just below the surface. Freud's unconscious, as you correctly state, consists of the 'repressed': when the censorship is lifted, that is, when the repression is analysed, is there no longer an unconscious? Just a subconscious? I would make different distinctions: 1. a personal unconscious, consisting of *repressed* personal material, and 2. a collective unconscious, consisting of common archaic residues and recent combinations of these which represent 'possible' future contents of consciousness. As long as a personal censorship operates, the principles of repression psychology are valid. If the censorship is lifted, however, the energy valency of the psychic contents comes into play. Then the unconscious contents rise to the vicinity of consciousness in accordance with their energy valency.

The right interpretation (analytical or constructive, cf. *The Content of the Psychoses*, 2nd Edit.)[76] of a symbol is the one that brings out the greatest value for our life (a pragmatic view). Theoretically the symbol has debased as well as elevated meaning. For example, the Last Supper can be interpreted as a union in the spirit of Christ, and as archaic cannibalism (cf. Silberer: *Probl. Der Mystik* [*The Problem of Mysticism*]).[77] As long as personal repressions continue, so that we are not aware of our incompatible wishes, we must continue to analyse in a personal way as Freud does, without reaching the collective unconscious. What I designate as the collective unconscious is completely overlooked by Freud, that is, he interprets it as wholly personal, as merely repressed contents which could be got out of the way by understanding. Thus he remains completely rationalistic and biological and misses a quite essential part of real psychology. For that reason he conceives of morals as coming from outside the person, whereas human morality springs from an inner urge. Moreover he has never understood what is meant by a split in the libido itself. There is no excuse for interpreting the opposition of a – z in such a way that a is nothing other than the negation of z. a is something in and for itself, and so is z. Libido as energy always assumes the opposite. Without an opposite (high and low) there is no energy at all, and so every energetic process (and that includes the dynamism of the psychic) assumes the a priori existence of the opposites and is itself bipolar because it immediately brings with it two different states. Energy always strives to cancel itself out, and at the same time presses to manifest itself. But a manifestation is at the same time its own means of cancelling itself.

Your conception of symbol formation seems correct to me, although there are at times conscious influences in it.

With best wishes, yours sincerely, Dr Jung.

———◆———

Dr C.G. Jung

228 Seestrasse

Küsnach-Zürich

21.1.18

Dear doctor,

You are touching on something which belongs to the foundations of our culture. I find it very understandable that you cannot understand me, in spite of the fact that your dream is coming to your assistance.[78] I am underlining all the passages in your letter where you are thinking concretely and, *typically*, misunderstanding the symbol. Do not think that I am speaking against your music. Perhaps you are more a musician than a doctor. I don't want to argue in any way against your becoming a musician. But that question has nothing to do with the question of symbolism.

Your dream gives you the German as a representation of a person who acts in a concrete way and whose attitude is completely fixed on reality. Your earlier Russian attitude is that of an inactive dreamer. But with this later attitude a christification has taken place. Thus you are sandwiched between the German and the Russian attitudes, between the real and the unreal. That is precisely where the symbolic is found, as a common function of both. You probably live the symbol to a large extent without being conscious of it. For that reason your dreams think of bright spaces and green meadows. In relation to this world you have to be real, either a musician, or a doctor, or a wife and mother. But your task is not completed when you do that. Those are mere functions. *You have not thereby become yourself.* You are something different from those functions.

You are always trying to drag the Siegfried symbol back into reality, whereas in fact it is the bridge to your individual development. Human beings do not stand in *one* world only but between *two* worlds and must distinguish themselves from their functions in both worlds. That is individuation. You are rejecting dreams and seeking action. Then the dreams come and thwart your actions. The dreams are a world, and the real is a world. You have to stand between them and regulate the traffic in both worlds, just as Siegfried stands between the gods and men.

Do you understand that?

With best wishes, yours sincerely, Dr Jung.

———◆———

[Probably January 1918]

Dear doctor,

'Nebbich' as 'too bad', 'on the left' in a flippant tone is a contrasting association to the rest of the symbolic content; it follows that unconscious contents always contain pairs of opposites and consequently always express themselves in opposite forms. Something valuable through something worthless, or connected with worthlessness.

Do not forget that the Jew also had prophets. There is a part of the Jewish soul which you are not yet living, because you still have your eye too much on the outside. That is – 'unfortunately' – the curse of the Jew: the aspect of his psychology which belongs to him most deeply he calls 'infantile wish-fulfilment', he is the murderer of his own prophets, even of his Messiah.[79]

On the 6th floor instead of on the 4th means: higher up, a higher standpoint. Gegensätzlich [opposite] = 6 = 'sex', as Freud understands it.

You are orientating yourself by everything around you, by the visible world, so the inner world is chaotic. The inner world however comes with irresistible force and will take possession of you. You will experience a remarkable transformation.

I have just recovered from influenza.

With best wishes, Dr Jung.

———◆———

The Commandant of the xxx xxx Region,

Château-d'Oex   29 Nov. 1918

Dear doctor,

'Oore' certainly means 'ora' = pray.

'nabich' as an anagram of 'Sabina' is quite probable. The meaning is: 'pray to yourself', for your soul needs you to concentrate all your devotion on the central point of your being in order to find your one right path, the 'way'. You like to go away from yourself and you lose yourself by doing so. It is to this strong tendency to look to the outside that 'cannabis' relates.[80] That is of course 'cannabis indica', hemp, hashish, a narcotic which the orientals take to produce inner visions. Do you understand that?

With best wishes, yours sincerely, Dr Jung

———◆———

Dr med. C.G. Jung LL.D   228 Seestrasse

                                                                Küsnacht-Zürich

                                                                19.3.1919

Dear doctor,

Your dreams have a threatening character and show a murderous tendency because your conscious attitude is of a materialistic kind which kills the spirit. However the spirit will not let itself be killed but changes into an

unconscious force which can have murderous effects *of a magical kind* on all around. You should recognise the divine spirit and not deny it in that rationalistic way. You should acknowledge what you hold to be true and not speak the opposite; otherwise if you speak against your own conscience you are cursed. I hope it is not too late.
Yours sincerely Dr Jung.
P.S. A sum of 260fr has arrived at my address from a Mr *Seidmann* in Berlin. I do not know where the money has come from. I think it belongs to you. I am sending it to you today by mandate.
Yours sincerely, Dr Jung.
I wish your little daughter a swift return to health.

———◆———

C.G. JUNG. MD.LL.D

Seestrasse 228, KÜSNACHT-ZÜRICH   3.4.1919

Dear doctor,

Mistrust disturbs most the person who mistrusts himself. I do not know whether you mistrust yourself. My mistrust is aroused by the fickleness of the female spirit and its vain and tyrannical presumption. What you are calling 'killing Siegfried' is to me a rationalistic and materialistic razing to the ground. This razing to the level of banality belongs with the most amiable qualities of the female spirit. Your little daughter is quite safe when you do not want to kill the 'strange being' whom you call Siegfried.[81] For this being produces a harmful effect only when it is not accepted as a divine being but just as 'phantasy'. You have this being to thank for your suggestive influence. Your influence will be good and rich in blessing if you accept this being and worship it inwardly. *I wish your child everything that is good.* But I wish too that you would learn to accept 'Siegfried' for what he is. This is important as much for your child's sake as for your own. How you must accept Siegfried I cannot tell you. That is a secret. Your dream can help. Dreams are compensatory to the conscious attitude. *Reality and the unconscious are primary.* They are two forces that work simultaneously but are different. The hero unites them in a symbolic figure. He is the centre and the resolution. The dream contributes to life, as does reality. The human being stands between two worlds. *Freud's* view is a sinful violation of the sacred. It spreads darkness, not light; that *has to* happen, for only out of the deepest night will the new light be born. One of its sparks is Siegfried. This spark can and will never be extinguished. If you betray this, then you are cursed. What has Liebknecht to do with you?[82] Like Freud and Lenin, he disseminates rationalistic darkness which will yet extinguish the little lamps of understanding. I kindled a new light in you which you must protect against the time of darkness. That must not be betrayed externally and for the sake of external arguments. Surround this inner light with devotion, then it will never turn into danger for your little daughter. But whoever betrays this light for the sake of power or in order to be clever will be a figure of shame and will have a bad influence.

With best wishes, yours sincerely, Dr Jung.

———◆———

Dr med. C.G. Jung LL.D   228 Seestrasse

                                                            Küsnacht-Zürich

                                                            1 Sept. 1919

Dear doctor,

I have not replied until now as I have been in England for some time.

The love of S. for J. made the latter aware of something he had previously only vaguely suspected, namely of a power in the unconscious which shapes our destiny, a power which later led him to things of the greatest importance. The relationship had to be 'sublimated', because otherwise it would have led to delusion and madness (a concretisation of the unconscious).

Sometimes we must be unworthy to live at all.

With best wishes, yours sincerely, Dr Jung.

———◆———

Dr med. C.G. Jung LL.D.   228 Seestrasse

                                                            Küsnacht-Zürich

                                                            7.10.19

Dear doctor,

I congratulate you on your brother's success. That is very gratifying.

I cannot answer your question about types. I would have to write a book about it. Actually it has already been written. Your questions are answered there in detail. When I wrote it I had to cancel out the fundamental identity of extraversion and feeling, and of introversion and thinking. That was wrongly conceived and came from the fact that introverted thinking types and extraverted feeling types are the most conspicuous. Now I distinguish a universal introverted or extraverted attitude. Bleuler has an extraverted attitude. His most differentiated function is thinking. His feeling is introverted and archaic, relatively unconscious.

The schema is thus:

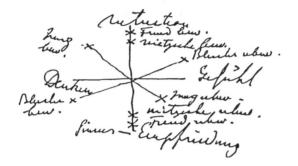

With regard to Freud I am not quite sure, as I don't know him well enough personally. His neurotic tendency accords with the schema however. It cannot be seen from the schema whether a person is introverted or extraverted, because it focuses on other aspects. Bleuler and Freud are extravert. Nietzsche and Jung introvert. Goethe is intuitive and extravert. Schiller is intuitive and introvert.

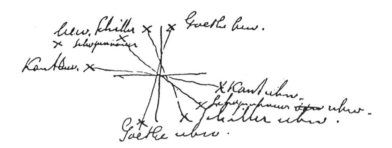

In general men are on the outer circle:

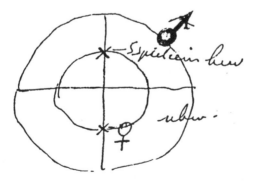

Probably you used to be much more extraverted than you are now.
Perhaps the schema will mean something to you.
With friendly greetings, yours sincerely, Dr Jung.

N.B.!

In the libido book[83] you will find a lot of material on the question of the transformation of libido; similarly in Silberer, *Problems of Mysticism*[84] who took up my ideas and worked further on them independently.

Notes

1 Ernest Jones (1879–1958), English psychoanalyst, biographer of Freud. For the visit to Jung mentioned here, see references in *Freud/Jung Letters*, ed. William McGuire, Hogarth Press and Routledge & Kegan Paul, 1974, (12.7.08, 18.7.08, & 11.8.08: 163, 164, & 166).

2 Free spirit.

3 Mountain lake between the cantons of Glarus and St. Gallen.

4 Place on the Walensee.

5 P. Eugen Bleuler; cf. Note 16, letters from S. Spielrein to C.G. Jung (in A. Carotenuto, *A Secret Symmetry*, New York, Pantheon Books, 1982).

6 S. Spielrein quotes this sentence in her letter to Freud of 10/20 June 1909 (section dated 11 June; in Carotenuto 1982).

7 cf. also a passage quoted to Freud by S. Spielrein from a letter to Jung, and her remarks referring to this in her letter to Freud of 10/20 June 1909 (section dated 13 June; in Carotenuto 1982).

8 At the request of the Jung family the name and address of the person in question have been omitted in order to safeguard her anonymity.

9 One of the guests from New York was Adolf Meyer from NY State Pathological Institute, who was also Professor of Psychiatry at Cornell University Medical School. Jung mentions this visit in his letter to Freud of 21.8.08 (*Freud/Jung Letters*: 169f. and footnote 1, ibid).

10 Wolf Stockmayer (1881–1933), analytical psychologist, at that time Assistant at the Tübingen University Clinic (*Freud/Jung Letters*, 12.7.08:164 & fn.4).

11 A region in the canton of St. Gallen.

12 Franz Riklin (1878–1938), Swiss psychiatrist; worked at the Burghölzli from 1902 to 1904 and together with Jung published 'The associations of normal subjects' in 1906 (in C.G. Jung, *Collected Works*, Vol. 2).

13 See Note 16 below.

14 See previous letter to S. Spielrein.

15 The mistake in the salutation cannot be completely explained: the 'n' in the middle of the word 'Freundin' ['friend'] has been added later and in all probability was written over another letter no longer visible. [Without the middle 'n', 'Freudin' might suggest 'Freud' and/or 'Freude' = 'joy'; trans.]

16 According to the note in the *Freud/Jung Letters* (23.9.08: 172), Freud was a guest of Jung from 18 to 21 September. During this visit Jung demonstrated to him the famous case of Babette (C.G. Jung, *Memories, Dreams, Reflections*, ed. Aniela Jaffé, Fontana, 1963: 149; cf. also Carotenuto, ibid, chap. 4).

17 cf. *Memories, Dreams, Reflections*: 24f.

18 S. Spielrein quotes this passage in her letter to Freud of 10/20 June 1909 (section dated 13 June; in Carotenuto ibid).

19 S. Spielrein's dissertation 'On the psychological content of a case of schizophrenia (*dementia praecox*)'.

20 S. Spielrein had probably sent her congratulations on the birth of Jung's third daughter, Marianne; cf. the last entry in her diary for September 1910 (in Carotenuto, ibid).

21 The first examinations took place on 9 and 15 December 1910, and the last in the

middle of January 1911 (see diary entries of 8 and 14 December 1910 and of 15 and 19 January 1911; in Carotenuto, ibid).

22 See Note 8, letters of S.Spielrein to C.G. Jung (in Carotenuto, ibid: 220).

23 cf. *Freud/Jung Letters*, 12.6.11: 426).

24 This must refer to corrections related to the publication of her dissertation which appeared in the *Jahrbuch* 3, 1 (August 1911).

25 The reference is to the paper 'Destruction as the cause of coming into being', which S. Spielrein completed during her stay in Munich, according to her diary entry of 7.1.1912 (Carotenuto, ibid: 40). The paper was published in English translation in the *Journal of Analytical Psychology*, 39, 2; April 1994.

26 See Note 25 above.

27 This remark, together with other comments made to S. Spielrein about 'Destruction as the cause of coming into being' (see letters of beg. Nov.1911, 13.11.11, 18.3.12, 25.3.12), is in marked contrast to the statement made by Jung in his letter to Freud of 1.4.12 (*Freud/Jung Letters*: 498).

28 The work did finally appear in the *Jahrbuch*, in the first half-year issue of Vol. 4 (Sep. 1912); cf. also S. Spielrein's comment in her diary, 7.1.1912 (Carotenuto, ibid: 41).

29 See *Freud/Jung Letters*, 19.7.11: 435.

30 S. Spielrein wanted to attend the Third International Psychoanalytic Congress in Weimar, 21–22 Sep. 1911.

31 See Note 6, letters from Freud to S. Spielrein (Carotenuto, ibid: 226).

32 See Note 19 above.

33 cf. S. Spielrein's letter to Jung, early 1911 (Carotenuto, ibid: 48).

34 S. Spielrein had sent Jung the manuscript of her paper on destruction in August. She probably needed it now to prepare her lecture for the Wednesday meeting on 29 Nov. 1911, at which she referred to a section of it (see minutes of the Vienna Psychoanalytic Society, ed. Herman Nunberg & Ernst Federn, Vol. 3, 1910–1911, Frankfurt am Main: S. Fischer,1979: 314–20).

35 cf. *Freud/Jung Letters*, 30.10.11: 452.

36 As is implied in Jung's next letter, there was a delay.

37 See Note 10, letters from S. Spielrein to Jung (Carotenuto, ibid: 220f).

38 cf. Note 4, letters from Freud to S. Spielrein (Carotenuto, ibid: 226).

39 See Note 18, letters from Freud to S. Spielrein (Carotenuto, ibid: 227).

40 See Note 19, letters from Freud to S. Spielrein (Carotenuto, ibid: 227).

41 Refers to the period from the end of September to 31 October 1911 (cf. *Freud/Jung Letters*, 4.10.11 & 30.10.11: 444 & 452).

42 Jung refers to Part 2 of *Transformations and Symbols of the Libido*, which appeared in the *Jahrbuch* 4: 1 in 1912, and in which numerous references to S. Spielrein's dissertation appear. (cf. Carotenuto, ibid Part 2, Chapter 2, Note 11).

43 With the differences alluded to here, Jung's numerous comments in the *Freud/Jung Letters* from November 1911 onwards on Part 2 of the libido work, and his later statement about the role of *Transformations and Symbols of the Libido* in his confrontation with Freud (*Memories, Dreams, Reflections*: 187–91).

44 cf. Jung's letter of the same date to Freud (*Freud/Jung Letters*, 11.12.1911: 470).

45 'Psychological analysis of a paranoid patient', *Jahrbuch* 4: 1 1912: 116–40.

46 *Transformations and Symbols of the Libido*, Part 2.

47 'Analytical observations on the phantasies of a schizophrenic', *Jahrbuch* 4: 1, 1912: 504–62.

48 See Note 26, letters from S. Spielrein to Jung (Carotenuto, ibid: 223).

49 See Note 10, letters from S. Spielrein to Jung (Carotenuto, ibid: 220).

50 'The association method', three lectures (1909). Two of the lectures ('The associ-

ation method' and 'The family constellation') are published in Vol. 2 of the *Collected Works*, one ('Psychic conflicts in a child') in Vol. 17.

51 See letters of 12. & 30.11, and 17.12.1911 (*Freud/Jung Letters*: 457ff, 468 & 472).

52 See Jung's letter to S. Spielrein of 11.12.1911 and Note 45 above.

53 cf. letter from S. Spielrein to Jung of late March 1911 (Carotenuto, ibid: 47–8).

54 In February 1912 a lay association for psychoanalytic endeavour was founded in Zürich (see Jung's communication to Freud of 15.2.12 (*Freud/Jung Letters*: 483 and fn. 1).

55 *Diagnostische Associationsstudien: Beiträge zur experimentellen Psychopathologie*, 2 volumes, Leipzig 1906 and 1909 (in *Collected Works*, Vol. 2); *Über die Psychologie der Dementia praecox: Ein Versuch* (in *Collected Works*, Vol. 3).

56 cf. S. Spielrein's diary entry of 26.11.1910 (Carotenuto, ibid: 35).

57 See Freud/Jung letters, 3.3.13: 545 & fn.1.

58 cf. Freud's letter to S. Spielrein, 20 Jan. 1913 (Carotenuto, ibid: 118).

59 cf. entry for September 1910 and Note 8, diary of S. Spielrein (Carotenuto, ibid: 17 & 218).

60 The reference must be to Friedrich Kraus who worked at the Charité (see Note 10, letters of Freud to S. Spielrein, in Carotenuto, ibid: 226); S. Spielrein had informed Freud of Kraus's approach to psychoanalysis (cf. Freud's letter to S. Spielrein, 9.2.1913, in Carotenuto, ibid: 119, and Freud's letter to Karl Abraham, 14.2.13 and Abraham's reply 3.3.13, in *Freud/Abraham Briefe 1907–1926*).

61 *Memories, Dreams, Reflections*: 191f.

62 cf. Carotenuto ibid. part 2, chapter 6, and the Foreword by J. Cremerius to the German edition of Carotenuto's book (*Tagebuch einer heimlichen Symmetrie*, Freiburg: Kore, 1986, also K.R. Eissler, 'Psychologische Aspekte des Briefwechsels zwischen Freud und Jung', *Jahrbuch der Psychoanalyse*, Beiheft 7, (Stuttgart-Bad Cannstatt: Frommann-Holzboog 1982), passim.

63 cf. letter from Jung to Freud of Nov. 1912 referring to the presidents' conference in Munich (*Freud/Jung Letters* 14. Nov. 1912: 520).

64 S. Spielrein was expecting a child.

65 Birth of Sabina Spielrein's daughter, Renata; cf. Freud's letter to S. Spielrein, 29 Sep. 1913 (Carotenuto, ibid: 121).

66 On the back of this letter is the fragmentary outline of a letter from S. Spielrein to Freud.

67 S. Spielrein had probably sent Jung the text of her lecture 'On ethics and psychoanalysis', which she had given in March 1914 to the Berlin group of the International Psychoanalytic Society (see Zeitschrift 2, 1914: 410).

68 Jung had resigned from the editorship of the *Jahrbuch* in October 1913 (see *Freud/Jung Letters* 27.10.13: 550).

69 Franz Deuticke among others published the *Jahrbuch* and the series *Schriften zur angewandten Seelenkunde* (Papers on Applied Psychiatry) edited by Freud.

70 See Note 17, letters from S. Spielrein to Jung (Carotenuto, ibid: 222) [The reference is to *Die Psychologie der unbewussten Prozesse* (Zürich 1917, the first edition of 'On the psychology of the unconscious', in *Two Essays on Analytical Psychology, Collected Works*, Vol. 7)].

71 cf. letter from S. Spielrein to Jung, 27.11.1917 (Carotenuto, ibid: 50–53).

72 See Note 18, Letters of S. Spielrein to Jung (Carotenuto, ibid: 222).

73 cf. letter from S. Spielrein to Jung, 3.12.1917 (Carotenuto, ibid: 53–6).

74 cf. letter from S. Spielrein to Jung, 15.12.1917, only parts of which have survived. Also letters from S. Spielrein to Jung, 3&4.12.1917.

75 cf. S. Spielrein's letters of 20&21.12.1917 (Carotenuto, ibid: 62ff).

76 Jung, *The Content of the Psychoses, Schriften zur angewandten Seelenkunde*, 3, Vienna & Leipzig: Deuticke, 2nd edition 1914 (in *Collected Works*, Vol. 3).

77 See Note 26, letters from S. Spielrein to Jung (Carotenuto, ibid: 223).

78 cf. letters from S. Spielrein to Jung, 6&7.1.1918 & 19.1.1918 (Carotenuto, ibid: 68–78 & 79–82).

79 cf. letter from S. Spielrein to Jung, 27/28.1.1918 (Carotenuto, ibid: 82–8).

80 Kannabich was also the name of a Russian psychoanalyst who was known to S. Spielrein. (See 'Russische Literatur' in *Bericht über die Fortschritte der Psychoanalyse* (*Report on the Advances in Psychoanalysis*) *1914–1919*, Vienna: Internationaler Psychoanalytischer Verlag, 1921: 356).

81 cf. the statement in S. Spielrein's letter to Jung, 6.1.1918. In this letter, and in the letter of 27/28.1.1918, S. Spielrein develops a discussion of the theme 'Siegfried – a threat to Renata', subsequently taken up by Jung.

82 The leader of the communist Spartacus League was murdered on 15.1.1919 together with Rosa Luxemburg.

83 *Transformations and Symbols of the Libido*, Part 1, *Jahrbuch* 3.1 (1911): 120–227, Part 2, *Jahrbuch* 4.1 (1912): 162–464.

84 See Note 26, letters from S. Spielrein to Jung (Carotenuto, ibid: 223).

Reference

Carotenuto, A. (1982) *A Secret Symmetry. Sabina Spielrein between Jung and Freud.* New York: Random House.

Chapter 4

Foreword to Carotenuto's *Tagebuch einer heimlichen Symmetrie*

Johannes Cremerius

(Translated from the German by Barbara Wharton)

This book documents the history of the tragic transference love between a patient and her analyst. Its unusual significance lies not in the arresting fact that the actors are C.G. Jung and Sabina Spielrein, but rather in what the book shows us of this transference–countertransference tragedy and its outcome: the analyst abandons the realm of phantasy and symbols; he becomes active, engages in affectionate behaviour and declares 'his' love to the patient. Its further significance lies in the influence which the experiences of all the participants exerted on the development of psychoanalytic technique. Sigmund Freud becomes the third actor in the drama as confessor to both Jung and Sabina Spielrein, and also as Spielrein's hoped-for comforter, protector and helper.

It is a terrible story, particularly in so far as it demonstrates the complicity of two men against the woman who has allowed herself to be seduced by one of them – and in the style of Victorian dual morality: when Jung wants to extricate himself from the relationship because a public scandal threatens (Sabina's mother, alerted anonymously to the 'affair' by Frau Jung, plans to call on Professor Eugen Bleuler, Jung's boss) to save his career and his marriage, both Jung and Freud condemn Sabina Spielrein and appeal to her reason and understanding: she must stand aside in favour of Jung's career and marriage. The book also recounts the complicity of two doctors of whom one (Jung) has committed a serious professional blunder, and the other (Freud), his teacher, protects his pupil against the injured woman. The letter which Freud writes to Sabina on 8.6.1909, after she has informed him of the matter, serves only one purpose, that is to protect Jung: he writes that he considers him incapable of frivolous and ignoble behaviour; she should subject herself to self-examination, suppress her feelings for Jung, and above all not resort 'to external intervention and the involvement of third persons' (Carotenuto 1982: 113f).

After Sabina Spielrein's second letter to Freud, however, – and after the rumour of the 'affair in analytical circles' began to spread and reached Freud's ears – he should certainly have insisted on clarification.

Instead he advises Jung not to go too far in the direction of contrition and reaction.

> Remember Lassalle's fine sentence about the chemist whose test tube had cracked: "With a slight frown over the resistance of matter, he gets on with his work." In view of the kind of matter we work with, it will never be possible to avoid little laboratory explosions. Maybe we didn't slant the test tube enough, or we heated it too quickly. In this way we learn what part of the danger lies in the matter and what part in our way of handling it . . .
>
> (McGuire 1974: 235; 18.6.1909)

When Jung then makes a full confession (in his letter to Freud of 21.6.1909) and Freud consequently realises how long he has been kept in the dark and how often he has been deceived, he writes to Sabina Spielrein on 24.6.1909 apologising for having made a mistake to her disadvantage. But this letter is a mere formality. The complicity continues. On 30.6.1909 he writes to his 'dear friend': 'I wrote Fräulein Sp. a few amiable lines, giving her satisfaction, and today received an answer from her . . . Don't find fault with yourself for drawing me into it; it was not your doing but hers. And the matter has ended in a manner satisfactory to all' (McGuire 1974: 238). Indeed for Jung it is satisfactory. In his reply of 10.7.1909 Jung thanks Freud for his help in the 'Spielrein matter, which has now settled itself so satisfactorily.' It has 'settled itself satisfactorily' for them both: neither Jung nor Freud has been damaged. The cynicism of this complicity from the point of view of the patient, who is sacrificed in a manner which severely disturbs and damages her, is shocking. For the destructive consequences he wrought by the way he ended the relationship Jung uses the words '*Spielrein-Angelegenheit*' ('the Spielrein matter') and '*erledigt*' ('dealt with'). (Note the double meaning of the latter word in German [and also in English, trans.]: to destroy, to kill.)

We can try to exonerate Freud, as Bettelheim does,[1] on the grounds that he was not officially informed by Jung but merely learned from rumour. On 9.3.1909 Freud writes to Jung: 'When Muthmann [a neurologist and psychoanalyst from Bad Nassau] came to see me, he spoke of a lady who had introduced herself to him as your mistress . . .' Jung replies immediately on 11.3.1909: 'The story hawked round by M. is Chinese to me.' This excuse might have been acceptable at the beginning, but not once Freud had received positive information. He had missed the opportunity to advise Jung how he could resolve the problem for and with the patient in the quickest and kindest way. Instead of this, both he and Jung were just glad that it did not lead to a scandal. They were both afraid of that: Jung was worried about his career and his marriage, Freud about the future of the psychoanalytic movement. He had thought of Jung as his direct heir: the 'man of the future', his 'crown prince' who, as his psychoanalytic work continued to expand, would act as the control centre for all the psychoanalytic ventures. He would have to establish contact between the different regional groups, and give advice and help when and where it was needed.[2] It was also important to Freud that Jung was an 'Aryan'. He feared that the spread of psychoanalysis might be hampered by the fact that he and his pupils were Jewish. These were all 'good' reasons – and they all led to the same goal: Jung continued his ascent in a highly respectable way, and his marriage remained intact; Freud retained his Aryan crown prince unblemished. Sabina Spielrein is left behind, sacrificed on the altar of science and power politics. Fame has no white wings, not even here.

Just how fateful this story was is hinted at in Jung's letter of confession to Freud of 21.6.1909, published in the volume of correspondence, in which he speaks for the first time of his 'guilt':

> Caught in my delusion that I was the victim of the sexual wiles of my patient, I wrote to her mother [Frau Spielrein had asked Jung for an explanation] that I was not the gratifier of her daughter's sexual desires but merely her doctor, and that she should free me from her. In view of the fact that the patient had shortly before been my friend and enjoyed my full confidence, my action was a piece of knavery which I very reluctantly confess to you as my father.
>
> (McGuire, ibid: 236)

It sounds all right, but let us remember that this letter reached Freud after Sabina Spielrein had already informed him on 10.6.1909 by sending him a copy of Jung's letter to her mother (see below). Remorse comes only after revelation.

What this letter does not mention, which came to light only in Carotenuto's book, is revealed in Jung's letter to Sabina Spielrein's mother – a veritable 'piece of knavery'. Frau Spielrein had become worried by an anonymous letter which Frau Jung – according to Sabina – was supposed to have written, and turned to Jung for help: he had 'saved her daughter' and would surely not want to 'undo' her now. She pleads with him not to exceed the bounds of friendship (Carotenuto 1982: 94). Jung's reply:

> I moved from being her doctor to being her friend, when I ceased to push my own feelings into the background. I could drop my role as doctor the more easily because I did not feel professionally obligated, for I never demanded a fee. This latter clearly establishes the limits imposed upon a doctor. You do understand of course, that a man and a girl cannot possibly continue indefinitely to have friendly dealings with each other without the likelihood that something more may enter the relationship. For what would restrain the two from drawing the consequences of their love? A doctor and his patient on the other hand can talk of the most intimate matters for as long as they like, and the patient can and should

expect her doctor to give her all the love and care she requires. But the doctor knows his limits and will never cross them, because he is paid for his trouble. That imposes the necessary restraints on him.

Therefore I would suggest that if you wish me to adhere strictly to my role as doctor, you should pay me a fee as suitable recompense for my trouble. In that way you will be absolutely certain that I will respect my duty as doctor in all circumstances.

As a friend of your daughter, on the other hand, one would have to leave matters to Fate. For no one can prevent two friends from doing as they wish. I hope, my dear and esteemed Madame, that you understand me and realise that these remarks conceal no baseness, but only experience and self-knowledge. My fee amounts to 10 francs per consultation.

I advise you to choose the prosaic solution since that is the more prudent one and creates no obligations for the future.

Here any comment is superfluous. Jung writes further:

I have always told your daughter that a sexual relationship is out of the question and that my actions were intended to express my feelings of friendship. When this occurred I happened to be in a very gentle and compassionate mood and I wanted to give your daughter convincing proof of my trust, my friendship, in order to liberate her inwardly. That turned out to be a grave mistake which I greatly regret . . . The headaches from which she suffers occur only periodically and are the result of unfulfilled desires, which unfortunately cannot be fulfilled by me.

But even that was not enough. Sabina Spielrein continues in her letter to Freud: 'I cannot bring myself to paraphrase no. 3 [she numbered Jung's letters to her mother 1,2,etc.]; I could only show it to you; it is even more insulting to me than no. 2' (Carotenuto 1982: 95).

If Jung wants to give the impression again of having become a victim of Sabina's passion and of having responded to her feelings merely out of friendship and sympathy, the four letters which are the only ones available from this year of love, speak another, unequivocal language:

On 26.4.1908 he invites her for a boat trip on Lake Zürich. On 30.6 he writes: 'Your image has changed completely . . . You can't believe how much it means to me to hope I can love someone whom I do not have to condemn, and who does not condemn herself either, to suffocate in the banality of habit.' He continues: he would be happy if he found in her someone whose essential vital core was 'freedom and independence' (Jung 2001: 173).

On 12.8 he writes:

With me everything is trembling like a volcano: one minute everything is golden, the next everything is grey. Your letter came like a ray of sunshine through the clouds . . . I realise how much more attached I am to you than I ever thought. I happen to be terribly suspicious, and always think other people are trying to exploit and tyrannize me. It is only with great difficulty that I can muster a belief in man's natural goodness, which I so often proclaim. That certainly does not apply to my feelings about you, however!

And on 4.12:

I am looking for someone who understands how to love, without punishing the other person, imprisoning him or sucking him dry; I am seeking this as yet unrealised person who will make it possible that love can be independent of social advantage and disadvantage, so that love may always be an end in itself, and not just a means to an end. It is my misfortune that I cannot live without the joy of love, of tempestuous, ever-changing love in my life.

(Jung 2001: 177).

He confesses that he must continually have love affairs with women and that they always end the same way, by his having to deceive and disappoint them. He mentions the 'last upset' between them, that is, there have been others. If we read Sabina Spielrein's diary alongside this letter, it begins to seem probable that the cause of the 'upsets' was always the same: Jung wanted a free love from his mistress, à la Otto Gross, untainted by bourgeois values, but he also wanted to remain in the safe haven and respectability of a bourgeois marriage. Sabina Spielrein perceived and understood this split in Jung: she knew that he wanted to live with her in a kind of heavenly paradise beyond reality where she would be merely the object of his phantasy, of his projection. The letter closes with a desperate appeal: 'Give me back now something of the love and patience and unselfishness which I was able to give you at the time of your illness. Now I am ill' (Jung ibid).

Sabina Spielrein finds other words (in her letter to Freud of 11.6): '. . . when we could linger for hours in wordless bliss, when he wept beside me, etc. etc. . . .' The projective nature of Jung's love becomes obvious: the two qualities *'freedom and independence'*, which he wishes Sabina possessed, are lacking in himself. He suffered from being entangled in an unhappy marriage, which he neither could nor would dissolve, and from his addictive dependence on love affairs – his 'daimon'. Even in his relationship with Freud he remains unfree and dependent: '. . . to ask you to let me enjoy your friendship not as one between equals but as that of father and son' (McGuire: 122, 20.2.1908). When years later he becomes conscious of this, he has to destroy the objects of his dependence, Freud and Sabina.

After reading the letter which Jung wrote to her mother Sabina Spielrein is deeply hurt. She writes to Freud: 'To suffer this disdain at the hands of a person whom one loved more than anything in the world for four, five years, to whom one gave the most beautiful part of one's soul, to whom one sacrificed one's maidenly pride, allowing oneself to be kissed etc, for the first and perhaps the last time in my life . . .' and later 'miserable good-for-nothing', 'let Siegfried die' – 'a kiss without consequences costs 10 francs'. But then she takes hold of herself: 'My dearest wish is that I may part from him in love' (Carotenuto: 93).

Here I will pause briefly to summarise what little is known about Sabina Spielrein's life: Sabina was admitted to the Burghölzli psychiatric clinic in Zürich in 1904 because of severe psychological disturbances of several years standing. There she was treated by Jung, who at that time was already familiar with some of Freud's writings. He had read *The Interpretation of Dreams* soon after its publication and cited it in his dissertation on occult phenomena in 1902. He was part of a team of whom the clinic director, Eugen Bleuler, wrote in 1904 to Freud that he and his colleagues had been using psychoanalysis for several years and had found a variety of applications for it. The team included two doctors who were to play an important role in the history of psychoanalysis, Max Eitingon and Karl Abraham.

But Jung's psychoanalytic knowledge was for the most part of a theoretical nature. When at nearly 30 years of age he met 19-year-old Sabina, his therapeutic experience of the psychoanalytic method was negligible. Jung speaks of his 'psychoanalytic test-case'. As so often happens when a doctor begins a treatment with therapeutic zeal and scientific ambitions – Jung was just at the point of obtaining his post-doctoral qualification and documented the 'case' as an aspect of his research – he achieved an astonishing success: ten months later the patient was able to leave the clinic, get an apartment in the city, matriculate in medicine at Zürich university, and study. Jung continued to treat her as an outpatient. In 1907, that is still in the course of the treatment, he presents the case at the International Congress for Psychiatry and Neurology as one of 'psychotic hysteria' and publishes it in the same year in his paper 'The Freudian theory of hysteria'.

From the spring of 1908, an unusual relationship developed between the two: a stormy love-affair ensued, alongside the continuing treatment and concurrently with joint scientific work. It ended dramatically in June 1909. In 1910 Sabina Spielrein resumed contact with Jung by letter. In May 1911 she obtained her doctorate with the work she had been doing with him, 'Concerning the psychological content of a case of schizophrenia', which was published in the same year, though under her name only, in the *Jahrbuch der Psychoanalyse* edited by Jung. After finishing her medical studies she fled from the dramatic entanglement with Jung, which continued unresolved even though Jung had distanced himself from her, first to Munich and then to Vienna. Here she is warmly received by Freud, attends his lectures, and is admitted to the Wednesday meetings.

From now on however she is restless and distraught. In 1912 she takes flight from her persistent 'love' for Jung in marriage, and in December 1913 gives birth to a daughter. She moves constantly from place to place, going to Berlin after spending nine months in Vienna, and then on to Munich. In 1911, during a short stay in Russia, she lectures on psychoanalysis in her home town, Rostov-on-Don, then we find her in Lausanne, Château d'Oex and Geneva until 1923. Here in 1921 she became Jean Piaget's analyst for 8 months. In 1923 she decided to return to her home and stayed there until her death. First she worked with Wulff as a training analyst at the psychoanalytic institute in Moscow, then she returned to her home town of Rostov, founded a psychoanalytic children's nursery there, and taught at the university until Stalin banned psychoanalysis in 1936. In 1937 her name was still on the membership list of the Russian psychoanalytic society.

Following the appearance of Carotenuto's book in Italy in 1980, Dr Ljunggren, a Swedish journalist, uncovered more precise details about the time and circumstances of Sabina's death.[3] While Carotenuto and other authors had assumed that she had perished in the confusion of Stalin's purge, Ljunggren was able to provide evidence that she was shot as a Jew with her daughters in 1941, by Germans who captured Rostov. Her husband had died just a few years earlier.

Following Jung's betrayal and the sudden collapse of all her hopes she kept herself free of hatred and destructiveness with dignity and great psychic strength. It seems that she sublimated her hate creatively in her essay 'Destruction as the cause of coming into being'. Freud's inability to accept her thesis of the existence of two instincts is perhaps due to the fact that he understood the concealed message that behind the abstract theory of destruction lay the actual destruction she had experienced.

Sabina takes care to ensure that Jung is not seen as a 'rogue' by Freud. She tries to interpret Jung's damaging infringement of his role as doctor as a phenomenon of transference and thus to exonerate him (McGuire: 228–9 and Sabina's letter to Freud of 12.6.09, in Carotenuto 1982); she stays true to her resolve to separate from Jung in a loving way. After 1910 she resumes contact with him until 1919 and tries to reconcile the two men who continue in a destructively hostile relationship to each other and who seek to make her an ally in their struggle. Freud writes to Sabina on 12.6.1914: '*If you stay with us . . . you must recognise the enemy in the other camp.*' Sabina's reply to Freud:

> In spite of all his wavering I like Jung and would like to lead him back into our fold. You, Professor, and he have not the faintest idea that you belong together far more than anyone might suspect. This pious hope is certainly not a betrayal of our society! Everyone knows that I declare myself as an adherent to the Freudian society, and J. cannot forgive me for that.
>
> (Carotenuto 1982: 112)

Sabina tries not to take sides: she becomes a member of the Vienna psycho-analytic society and of the Russian one, and she declares herself publicly as a member of Freud's group, publishing in its journals, while at the same time she remains in an intimate psychological exchange with Jung to whom she sends her dreams for interpretation (cf. Jung 1908–1919, 13.9.1917) and whose work she is translating into Russian. Freud asks enviously why she is not translating his works.

She is noteworthy in her time both as an analyst and as a scientist. Grant-ing her admission to the Wednesday meeting, Freud praises her intelligence: 'She is very bright and well organised; there is meaning in everything she says' (McGuire 1974: 494; 21.3.1912). After she has left Vienna Freud asks for her publications which ultimately appear in the official journals of the psycho-analytic society. In 1913 he tells her that he is thinking of including her name on the masthead of the *Journal of Psychoanalysis*. In Moscow too her work for the psychoanalytic institute is highly valued. She becomes a lecturer and conducts training analyses.

During the course of her life she publishes thirty psychoanalytic papers in German and in French. Of these two are particularly significant. The first, her dissertation, 'Concerning the psychological content of a case of schizo-phrenia'[4] written in collaboration with Jung, is a significant contribution to the understanding of the language of schizophrenics. Jung quoted it fre-quently in his work *Symbols of Transformation*, in the 1912 edition, and later in the 1952 edition. Her second work, 'Destruction as the cause of coming into being',[5] anticipates Freud's thoughts about the death instinct in *Beyond the Pleasure Principle* (1920).[6] Sabina is the first person to have presented the thesis that instinctual life is based on two opposing instincts, the life instinct and the death instinct. When she proposed this idea in the Wednesday meet-ing Freud rejected it. Twenty-five years later he tried to understand his rejec-tion of it: 'I remember my own defensive attitude when the idea of an instinct of destruction first emerged in the psycho-analytic literature, and how long it took before I became receptive to it' (Freud 1930a: 120). Federn in contrast recognised its significance straight away, as is clear from his review of her work.[7]

We are left with the question of why an analyst who was so distinguished in the early years of psychoanalysis is not well-known, why her papers are not cited. They are truly 'forgotten'. Her work on schizophrenia might have been forgotten because the psychoanalytic community was influenced by Freud's hostile separation from Jung.

Her second paper fell under the shadow of Freud's rejection of certain of Jung's mythological theories which he recognised in it: 'The lecture [S. Spiel-rein's] itself would give cause for criticism of Jung,' he declares on 29.11.1911 in the discussion at the Wednesday meeting which was energetically led by Tausk and Federn.[8] This is reinforced by the fact that in 1920, in *Beyond the Pleasure Principle*, he does not mention her work once. Even in 1930, speaking of his earlier resistance to the dual instinct theory, he does not recall that his resistance was first directed towards Sabina Spielrein.

How much in common have the enemies of today with the friends of yesterday! If Freud 'forgot' to mention Sabina Spielrein's contribution to psychoanalytic theory building in his later works, so Jung forgot Otto Gross's two-type theory (introversion/extraversion) in his work *Psychological Types*, published in 1921. If Freud allowed Gross's publications to be deleted from the bibliography of psychoanalysis, so Jung erased the acknowledgements of his thanks to Otto Gross from the later editions of his relevant works.

Jung's papers, 'The psychology of dementia praecox' (1906) and 'The significance of the father in the destiny of the individual' (1908), contain many allusions to the work of Otto Gross – particularly the latter which Jung wrote one year after he had ended his analysis of Gross. If Jung felt remorseful and guilty after the 'affair' with Sabina Spielrein had started, he still remained a wild adherent of his analysand and teacher, Otto Gross.

When on 31.1.1910, a good 6 months after Jung had broken off the relationship with Sabina Spielrein, Freud informed Jung that he was considering affiliating with a larger group working for a practical ideal, the 'International Fraternity for Ethics and Culture', Jung replies on 11.2.1910 very much in the spirit of Otto Gross:

> Do you think this Fraternity could have any practical use? Isn't it one of Forel's coalitions against stupidity and evil, and must we not love evil if we are to break away from the obsession with virtue that makes us sick and forbids us the joys of life? If a coalition is to have any ethical significance it should never be an artificial one ... I imagine a far finer and more comprehensive task for psychoanalysis than alliance with an ethical fraternity. I think we must give it time to infiltrate into people from many centres, to revivify among intellectuals a feeling for symbol and myth, ever so gently to transform Christ back into the soothsaying god of the vine ... and in this way absorb those ecstatic instinctual forces of Christianity for the one purpose of making the cult and the sacred myth what they once were – a drunken feast of joy where man regained the ethos and holiness of an animal.
>
> (McGuire 1974: 293–4)

It is an amusing reversal of roles: the discoverer and herald of instinct theory remained a bourgeois figure with strict moral judgements, a virtuous husband, while the admirer of Otto Gross who preached polygamy and sought free love was condemning instinct theory. Human contradictions abound. Just a year earlier Jung had written to Jones:

> We would do well not to trumpet the sexual theory about so much. I have various ideas in relation to that, especially regarding the ethical aspects

of the question. When you preach certain things publicly, I think you undermine civilisation and thus the incentive to sublimation ... An extreme position, such as Gross represents, is decidedly false and dangerous for the whole movement ... I make more progress both with *students and with patients when I do not put sexuality in the foreground.*

(Jung to Jones, 25.2.1909, in Jones II: 171/2)

Or is this letter simply a camouflage, in order to conceal what he is doing? He is still completely Otto Gross's pupil conducting an affair alongside his marriage, explaining to his lover that this cannot be anything serious or lasting, that he needs 'an ever-changing love'. He is there, but concealed. He is betraying his wife and Freud, because fundamentally he has not grown beyond his ideal, Otto Gross. He was the secret libertine with feelings of guilt which forced him into a dual existence.

Sabina Spielrein remains the victim even after the complicity between Jung and Freud against her has resolved into hatred of each other. She had ended up between the battle lines; she had tried to call a halt to the hate and destruction and had given as little heed to Freud's demand to align herself with him against Jung as she had to Jung's attempts to get her to take his side.

The documents upon which Carotenuto stumbled are unfortunately very incomplete and therefore allow only a partial insight into the events: Sabina's diary from the years 1909–1912 is incomplete; of her correspondence with Freud only two letters remain, and only the first is complete. Forty-six of Jung's letters to Sabina from 1908 to 1919 are extant. Carotenuto has examined them. He kindly placed at my disposal an Italian translation of thirty-one of the letters from which I have translated back into German. I found it striking that from the period between April 1908 and June 1909, the year of their love affair, only four of Jung's letters are available. One wonders if there were not more letters. It is hardly imaginable that a man so passionately in love should have written no letters in the long periods of separation, sometimes of several weeks, during Jung's holiday trips and Sabina's journey to Russia – Carotenuto gives no information about the reason for the incompleteness of the documents. The only complete item is the correspondence between Freud and Jung which has been available since 1974 in the volume of letters.

The incompleteness of the documents leaves room for the most diverse interpretations and free-ranging speculations. One of the first points of disagreement owes its existence to this very fact. When Carotenuto lectured about his book to the annual conference of the American Psychoanalytic Association on 18 December 1982, the main aspect of the debate was the assertion, in contradiction of Carotenuto, that Jung had had a sexual relationship with Sabina.[9] A year later Bettelheim too took up this argument forcefully against Carotenuto (Bettelheim 1983: 20). The letters we have to hand leave the whole thing open. But is that really the important point? Is not the point of view expressed here, that the sexual act itself is the fundamental trauma, just a part of that ancient, paternalistic over-valuation of the hymen? Are not disappointment, betrayal, humiliation and the abuse of trust, and the destruction of dignity and self-worth, of more consequence for a young girl to whom all this has happened?

I will now turn to the influence which the experiences of the participants had on the development of psychoanalytic theory and practice: The doctor/ patient relationship described here by Carotenuto seems to have opened Freud's eyes. If we follow the stages of the Spielrein tragedy, the dates on which Freud learned something fresh about Jung and Spielrein correspond with the dates on which he gained new insights into the dynamics of transference and countertransference.[10] If until now he had seen transference operating only in the patient's relationship to the analyst, he discovered after Jung's letter of 7.3.1909, in which Jung reports that an unnamed patient (Sabina) has kicked up a scandal for him because he would not give her a child, that the analyst too can be 'scorched by the love with which we operate – such are the perils of our trade' (McGuire 1974: 210, 9.3.09). After Jung has informed him obliquely of the relationship on 4.6, Freud's reply three days later shows how much he is preoccupied with the theory of the issue.

Such experiences, though painful, are necessary and hard to avoid. Without them we cannot really know life and what we are dealing with. I myself have never been taken in quite so badly, but I have come very close to it a number of times and had a narrow escape. . . . But no lasting harm is done. They help us to develop the thick skin we need and to dominate "countertransference", which is after all a permanent problem for us; they teach us to displace our own affects to best advantage. They are a 'blessing in disguise'

(McGuire 1974: 230–1, 7.6.09).

This is the first time the expression 'countertransference', which will later become a scientific term, appears in the psychoanalytic literature. Freud immediately recognises the great significance of the phenomenon and in March of the following year, at the second International Psychoanalytic Congress in Nuremberg, he speaks as follows on the subject in the context of a lecture, 'The Future Prospects of Psycho-analytic Therapy', which appears on p.1 of the *Zentralblatt für Psychoanalyse* in the same year: 'Other innovations in technique relate to the physician himself. We have become aware of the "counter-transference", which arises in him as a result of the patient's influence on his unconscious feelings, and we are almost inclined to insist that he shall recognise this counter-transference in himself and overcome it. . . . We have noticed that no psycho-analyst goes further than his own complexes and internal resistances permit.' Now – and from this we recognise the extent of his concern – he makes a suggestion for moderating this danger:

... we consequently require that he begin his activity with a self-analysis and continually carry it deeper while he is making his observations on his patients. Anyone who fails to produce results in self-analysis of this kind may at once give up any idea of being able to treat patients by analysis.

(Freud 1910d: 144f)

Two years later he mentions that it is part of the terms of the Zürich analytical school 'that they have laid increased emphasis on this requirement, and have embodied it in the demand that everyone who wishes to carry out analyses on other people shall first himself undergo an analysis by someone with expert knowledge' (Freud 1912e: 116). From whom did this requirement originate? Was it Jung himself who was drawing consequences from his disaster? The texts reveal nothing on the subject.

Sensitised by the Jung/Spielrein 'case', Freud is attentive from now on to similar occurrences among his pupils; he writes to Jung on 31.12.1911:

Frau C has told me all sorts of things about you and Pfister; I gather that neither of you has yet acquired the necessary objectivity in your practice, that you still get involved, giving a good deal of yourselves and expecting the patient to give something in return. Permit me ... to say that this technique is invariably ill-advised and that it is best to remain reserved and purely receptive. . . . I believe an article on "counter-transference" is sorely needed; of course we could not publish it, we should have to circulate copies among ourselves.

(McGuire 1974: 475–6).

The idea of concealing the article indicates Freud's anxiety. We may assume that above all he feared the reaction of the medical fraternity which colluded with Victorian double standards and would have regarded a doctor's becoming sexually aroused by a woman patient as a matter for the public prosecutor.

Freud speaks of countertransference one last time in 1915, and here again he seems to be referring to Jung. He mentions the example of an analyst who responds to his woman patient's transference love with a 'tendency to a counter-transference already present in his own mind'. This expresses itself in his pride at his 'conquest'. The analyst must recognise 'that the patient's falling in love is induced by the analytic situation and is not to be attributed to the charms of his own person' (Freud 1915a: 116f).

The fact that it took Freud so long to understand the relationship between Jung and Spielrein, or more precisely to understand Jung's part in it, is very closely linked to his concept of transference. Freud's idea of transference is wholly and completely endopsychic, that is, it exists outside the real relationship between people. It reproduces with 'unwished-for exactitude ... some portion of infantile sexual life, – of the Oedipus complex, that is, and its derivatives' (1920g: 18). The doctor is therefore 'introduce [d] into one of the psychical "series" which the patient has already formed' (Freud 1912b: 100) This ahistoric, automatic conception of transference drew Freud's attention finally to Sabina. What Jung reported of Sabina's behaviour (for example, her desire for children) was for Freud sufficient evidence that transference was at work (the oedipal relationship of the daughter to the father) and not really of an actual love story – particularly since Jung assured him that he had 'always acted the gentleman towards her' (McGuire 1974: 207, 7.3.1909) and that he was 'the most innocent of spouses . . . Such stories give me the horrors' (McGuire 1974: 212, 11.3.1909). Carotenuto too understands Jung's behaviour in this way. He interprets it as 'psychotic countertransference', since the patient is described as psychotic. Thus Jung is completely exonerated and his behaviour stands outside moral categories of judgement.

The other aspect which can contribute to our understanding of this is a historical one. Transference, which was described above as completely apersonal and ahistoric, was, in the early days of psychoanalysis, understood by Freud as the *woman's* infatuation with the male analyst. In the pioneering days of psychoanalysis, Breuer, Freud and many of their colleagues had experienced sudden declarations of love from female patients. It should be recalled that all Freud's case histories up to 1905 portray women. In failing to appreciate the social conditioning of these outbursts – women were above all the victims of a strict sexual morality and expressed in their 'hysterical' symptoms the unlived sexual life which was longed for but repressed – Freud hit upon the masculine desire and anxiety phantasies of his time as an interpretation of the phenomenon, phantasies which were expressed in the works of de Maupassant (a favourite author of Freud's), Schnitzler, Strindberg, and Wedekind among others. Woman is portrayed as 'Lulu', as a dangerous creature of instinct, who destroys the masculine world of order and intellect. As Jung writes to Freud on 4.6.1909: 'She was of course systematically planning my seduction' (McGuire 1974: 228). On this view of woman the two men are in agreement: the analyst, says Freud, must bring the 'woman who is in love with him' to the point at which she can 'give up her desires, and, having surmounted the animal side of herself, go on with the work of the analysis' (Freud 1915a: 163), or he must 'deny the patient who is craving for love the satisfaction she demands' (ibid: 165). In this early conception of transference the analyst is merely the victim of the patient: countertransference, that means the love which has been aroused in him by the woman, is something which 'arises in the doctor through the patient's influence on the doctor's unconscious feelings' (Freud 1910d: 144).

Jung follows the same track in seeking an explanation of his reaction to Sabina's falling in love with him and offers Freud three explanations for how his entanglement resulted from 'the patient's influence'. The first explanation is Sabina's own love for him. The second indicates the presence of a screen memory: 'then the Jewess popped up in another form, in the shape of my patient' (McGuire 1974: 229, 4.6.09) The third confirms the influence of another patient whom Jung was treating in analysis at the same time as Sabina, namely Otto Gross; he writes to Freud on 4.6.09: 'During the whole business Gross's notions flitted about a bit too much in my head. . . . Gross and Spielrein are bitter experiences. To none of my patients have I extended so much friendship and from none have I reaped so much sorrow' (McGuire 1974: 229).

What does Jung mean by the ideas of Otto Gross? Otto Gross, of whom Freud wrote to Jung on 18.2.08 that 'he [*Jung*] and Gross are the only original minds among his pupils';[11] the 'genius' admired by Jones and Stekel, propagated the idea of free, polygamous love and the living out of the sexual drive without restriction. Otto Gross called for a sexual revolution with the aim of rescuing today's world. At a gathering of revolutionaries in Vienna in 1918 he called for a state ministry to take on the task of weeding out the bourgeois – i.e. patriarchal – family and bourgeois sexuality. The fact that sexual life was confined to the orthodox forms of 'respectable' genital monogamy was to him as much of a tyranny as marriage itself. Desire was the only true source of value. And in his 'Soviet' article ('The basic idea of communism in the symbolism of paradise'), he explains that man can renew himself only by entering anew into the lost paradise of polymorphous perversity. He advocated and practised an orgiastic therapy which he called the 'cult of Astarte'. Here we can point to Gross as a forerunner of Wilhelm Reich.

Jung writes to Freud about Gross on 25.9.1907:

> Dr Gross tells me that he puts a quick stop to transference by turning people into sexual immoralists. He says the transference and its persistent fixation are mere monogamy symbols and as such symptomatic of repression. The truly healthy state for the neurotic is sexual immorality'
> (McGuire 1974: 90, 25.9.07).

At the end of this letter he condemns this way of thinking. But a few lines earlier he had confessed that his feelings differ from his thoughts: '. . . that I envy him [Eitingon] his uninhibited abreaction of the polygamous instinct. I therefore retract "impotent" as too compromising' (ibid). Compare this with the passage in Sabina's letter to Freud: 'He preached polygamy, his wife was supposed to have no objection . . .'(letter of 11.6.09). But Frau Jung was far from having no objection. It is clear from two later letters in 1911 and 1919 that these statements are merely acutely defensive explanations: On 21/ 22.9.1911 he writes to Sabina: '. . . bitterness . . . from all the inner anguish I endured because of you' – and only then does he add – 'and which you endured because of me.' Here it is clear that he holds to the reversal which Freud's concept assumes: the patient started it by falling in love with him, he merely reacted. Man is the victim of woman.

In reading this story a certain analogy with the story of Anna O. suggests itself. She was the patient with whom Breuer had for the first time tried out the basic form of the cathartic method, which was later to become the analytic procedure. She too fell in love with her therapist. Breuer threatened to succumb to this love. His wife 'rescued' him by offering him a choice: Anna O. or me. In contrast to Jung he decided in favour of his wife, before he became involved with the patient. Breuer's sudden, alarmed breaking off of her treatment plunged Anna O. into a severe crisis which forced her to live for years in an institution dependent on morphine. Sabina Spielrein did not succumb to an acute illness in this sense. For her the brutal destruction of her first love led to a protracted state of severe suffering. She wavered between 'forgiving him everything and murdering him' (letter to Freud, 10.6.1909, in Carotenuto 1986). From now on her life is restless and unsettled. In 1912 she writes in 'Destruction as the cause of coming into being', quoting Jung: 'A woman who, in today's society, abandons herself to passion soon leads herself to ruin' (Jung 1908, in Spielrein 1912: 155).

Freud's judgement on her seems problematic. He writes to Jung that a destructive drive is evident in Sabina Spielrein which is not to his liking, because he believes it is personally conditioned (McGuire 1974: 494). The date of this letter is 21.3.1912. In this same year the personal split between Freud and Jung became decisive. Freud could no longer deny that Jung was going his own way, and that much of what he was saying was directed not only against his theory but against himself. In June 1912 he reacts for the first time to this realisation. Instead of the hitherto accustomed form of address, 'Dear friend', Freud now uses 'Dear doctor'.

Only a few months before this realisation, in a phase of strong ambivalence, Freud spoke of Sabina's destructive drive, in other words turning the truth on its head despite knowing better. We have to understand this as just one of many attempts to rescue his 'crown prince', even at that late stage, as head of the psychoanalytic movement. He does the same thing here again as he did three years previously by reviving the complicity – Sabina Spielrein is the guilty party and she will be sacrificed.

Even the tone in which the two men talk about Sabina testifies to their continuing complicity: 'I'll gladly take Spielrein's new paper ["Destruction as the cause of coming into being"] for the first number of Jahrbuch 1912. It demands a great deal of revision, but then the little girl (!) has always been very demanding with me. However, she's worth it. I am glad you don't think badly of her' (McGuire 1974: 470; 11.12.1911). And on 1.4.1912: 'I was working on Spielrein's paper just before my departure. One must say: "*desinat in piscem mulier formosa superne*" ("What at the top is a lovely woman ends below in a fish" Horace). After a very promising start the continuation and end trail off dismally. Particularly the "Life and Death in Mythology" chapter needed extensive cutting as it contained gross errors and, worse still, faulty, one-sided interpretations. She has read too little and has fallen flat in this paper because it is not thorough enough. One must say by way of excuse that she has brought her problem to bear on an aspect of mythology that bristles with riddles. Besides that her paper is heavily overweighted with her own complexes. My criticism should be administered to the little authoress *in refracta dosi* only, please, if at all. I shall be writing to her myself before long.'

The woman he had loved passionately has become the 'little girl', the 'little authoress' is demeaned and her work disparaged. This is the work which foreshadows Freud's concept of the death instinct and thus contains a significant discovery. Freud participates in the collusion. He neither protests against Jung's tactless tone, nor does he oppose Jung's wish not to convey anything of his criticism to Sabina Spielrein. On 21.4.1912 he replies to Jung: 'Spielrein, to whom I was glad not to mention your criticism, came to say good-bye a few days ago' (McGuire 1974: 499).

There is a further analogy in that Freud's friendships with Breuer and with Jung respectively foundered around the time that their treatments of their respective patients broke down. Freud and Breuer split up finally in 1894 at the end of Anna O.'s treatment, Freud and Jung two years after Spielrein's. But the process which got going in the exchange of letters ('supervision') contributed substantially to the break. Freud writes to Sabina: 'My personal relationship with your Germanic hero has definitely been shattered' (20 1.13). And on 12.6.1914: 'Of course I want you to succeed in casting aside as so much trash your infantile dreams of the Germanic champion and hero, on which hinges your whole opposition to your environment and to your origins; you should not demand from this phantom the child you must once have craved from your father' [Carotenuto 1982: 122].

A further analogy is that the patient in question was the first case respectively for Breuer and for Jung and that both achieved a swift success – what Freud would later call a transference cure.

But the most striking analogy is that both, as victims of transference love, took on the greatest significance for the development of psychoanalytic technique. Anna O. discovered the value of talking freely and without conscious intention, and found the terms 'talking cure' and 'chimney sweeping' to describe it. She helps Breuer to discover the essence of 'rapport' and the effect of 'catharsis'. Sabina helps Freud to a deeper understanding of the nature of transference, to discover countertransference as a constituent of the psychoanalytic process, and to recognise the urgent necessity of finding an antidote to it. Freud finds it in the training analysis. But he also discovers something quite fundamental, namely that the analyst does not function in an impartial and objective way like a scientific observer: 'No psycho-analyst goes further than his own complexes and internal resistances permit' (Freud 1910d:144).

Is the sacrifice balanced by the gain? No! 'If knowledge hinders us from loving we must forego knowledge' (C.F. von Weizsäcker).

Notes

1 B. Bettelheim, 'Skandal in der Psychofamilie. C.G. Jung und seine Anima', *Tagesanzeiger*, Zürich, X/1983: 19–44.
2 E. Jones, *Das Leben und Werk von Sigmund Freud*, H. Huber, Bern-Stuttgart, 1962, Bd.2: 174.
3 M. Ljunggren, 'Sabina mellan Jung och Freud', *Expressen*, Stockholm, 1983:15.
4 *Jahrbuch*, 1911: 329–400.
5 *Jahrbuch*, 1912: 465–503; *Journal of Analytical Psychology*, 1994, 39, 2.
6 S. Freud, 1920g *Beyond the Pleasure Principle*, SE 18.
7 P. Federn, 'Sabina Spielrein. Destruktion als Ursache des Werdens'. *Zeitschrift*, 1913: 92–3.
8 *Protokolle der Wiener Psychoanalytischen Vereinung*, Eds. Hermann Nunberg und Ernst Federn, Bd. 3: 1910–1911 (Frankfurt am Main: S. Fischer, 1979): 314–20.
9 A. Carotenuto, *Trasgressioni*, Astrolabio, Roma, 1983: 121.
10 J. Cremerius, 'Die psychoanalytische Abstinenzregel. Vom regelhaften zum operationalen Gebrauch', *Psyche*, Frankfurt, 1984: 769–800.
11 M. Green, *Else und Frieda, Die Richthofen-Schwestern*, Kindler, München, 1976: 59.

References

Bettelheim, B. (1983) 'Skandal in der Psychofamilie. C.G. Jung und seine Anima'. Zürich: *Tagesanzeiger*, X/1983.
Carotenuto, A. (1982) *A Secret Symmetry. Sabina Spielrein between Jung and Freud.* New York: Random House.
—— (1986) *Tagebuch einer Heimlichen Symmetrie.* Freiburg: Kore Verlag.
Freud, S. (1910d) 'The future prospects of psycho-analytic therapy'. *SE* 11.
—— (1912b) 'The dynamics of transference'. *SE* 12.
—— (1912e) 'Recommendations to physicians practising psycho-analysis'. *SE* 12.
—— (1915a) 'Observations on transference love (Further recommendations on the technique of psycho-analysis)'. *SE* 12.
—— (1920g) *Beyond the Pleasure Principle. SE* 18.
—— (1930a) *Civilisation and its Discontents. SE* 21.
Jones, E. (1962) *Das Leben und Werk von Sigmund Freud.* Bern-Stuttgart: H. Huber. Vol. 2.
Jung, C.G. (2001) 'The Letters of C.G. Jung to Sabina Spielrein (1908–1919)'. *Journal of Analytical Psychology*, 46, 1, 173–199, and this volume, Chapter 3.
—— (1908) 'The Freudian theory of hysteria'. *CW* 4.
McGuire, W. (1974) (Ed.) *The Freud/Jung Letters.* London: Hogarth/Routledge & Kegan Paul.
Spielrein, S. (1912). 'Destruction as the cause of coming into being'. *Journal of Analytical Psychology*, 39, 2, 155–86.

Chapter 5

Burghölzli hospital records of Sabina Spielrein[1]

(Translated from the German by Barbara Wharton)[2]

| BURGHÖLZLI | HEREDITARY CONDITION | *Yes* | No |

NAME: **Spilrein, Sabina**

HOME TOWN:	PLACE OF RESIDENCE:	LAST RESIDENCE:
Rostov	**Rostov**	**Heller Sanatorium, Interlaken**

DATE OF BIRTH: **1885**[3]   STATUS: **single**   RELIGION: **israel**   PROFESSION:

No.	ADMIS-SION	DIS-CHARGED	CONDITION	DURATION OF ILLNESS	CLASS	PROVISIONAL DIAGNOSIS	DEFINITIVE DIAGNOSIS
8793	**17.8.04**	**1.6.05**	**improved**	**ca. 2 years**	**I**	**hysteria**	**hysteria**

N.B. Family members about whom there is no information or insufficient information, are to be indicated by ? Those who show no trace of disease are to be marked O

Family history of illness

No: 8793

Name: **Spilrein, Sabina**

Father: **Healthy [deleted], active, irritable, overwrought, neurasthenic, hot-tempered to the point of madness**

Father's father: **O**

Father's mother: **O**

Father's siblings: **(patient's uncle, aunt): number and illnesses: 2 brothers? 2 sisters? [deleted] nervous**

Mother: **Nervous (like patient) *hysterical!* Is a dentist. Has hysterical absences of a childish nature**

Mother's father: **O [deleted] senile dementia**

Mother's mother: **O [deleted] psychological state O**

Mother's siblings: **(uncle, aunt): number and illnesses: 3 brothers – nervous. numerous deceased**

Patients' siblings: **nervous**
3 brothers 1 brother nervous [deleted] 1 sister – died of stomach ailment

1 brother has hysterical fits of weeping, another suffers from tics and is very hot-tempered, the third is melancholic, very hysterical, and even does wrong in order to suffer

Children: **number, age and illnesses**

Close relatives:

NB: Organic and functional neuroses, psychoses, conspicuous characteristics, alcoholism, suicide, criminal activity, blood relatives, illegitimate birth, tuberculosis, diabetes

Burghölzli.

Belastet: <u>Ja</u> — Nein.

Name: *Spilrein, Sabina* .

Heimatort: *Rostow* , Wohnort: *Rostow* , Letzter Aufenthalt: *Heller'sches*
Geburtstag: *1885* Civilstand: *ledig* Religion: *israel* Beruf: / *Sanatorium Interlaken*

№	Aufnahme	Entlassen den / als	Krank seit	Classe	Vorläufige Diagnose	Definitive Diagnose
8793	I. 17 VIII.04	1.VI.05 geh.	ca 2 Mt	I	Hysterie.	Hysterie .
	II.					
	III.					
	IV.					
	V.					
	VI.					
	VII.					
	VIII.					

Datum:

Grösse .... cm. Statur .... Gewicht .... Ko.

Kopf

.... Umfang .... Form

Gesicht

Stirn

Nase

Mund

Zunge

Gaumen

Zähne

Kinn

Ohren

Augen

Haare

Bart

Brauen

Hals

Sprache

Gang

Reflexe

Besondere Merkmale

Nº 8793.

Name: _Spielrein, Sabina_

Vater: _gesund, lebt. nervös, überarbeitet, neurasthenisch. jähzornig bis zur Sinnlosigkeit._

Vater des Vaters: _0_

Mutter des Vaters: _0_

Geschwister des Vaters, (Onkel, Tante), Anzahl und Krankheiten derselben: _2 Br. ?_
2 Schw. } nervös.

Mutter: _hysterisch! nervös. (ähnlich wie Pat.) ist Zehnsüchtig. hat hysterische Absencen von südischem Charakter._

Vater der Mutter: _0 senil dement._

Mutter der Mutter: _0 psychisch 0._

Geschwister der Mutter: (Onkel, Tante), Anzahl und Krankheiten derselben: _3 Br. nervös. oder viel 4_

Geschwister: _3 Br. nervös. 1 Schw. an Magenkrank. 1 Br. hat hysterische Weitsprung, der andere Br. Tiquer, ablösig in III ist leidselig, schwer hysterisch, that auch Hamoleum geben._

Kinder:

Zahl, Alter & Krankheiten derselben:

Nebenlinien:

(Jung's handwriting)

1904, VIII, 17

Tonight at 10.30 patient is brought in by a medical police official and her uncle. Medical report from Dr. B. and Lublinsky. Pat. laughs and cries in a strangely mixed, compulsive manner. Masses of tics; she rotates her head jerkily, sticks out her tongue, twitches her legs. Complains of a terrible headache, saying that she was not mad, only upset, at the hotel, she could not stand people or noise. With private nurse in E II.

18. [8.1904]

Fairly quiet night. Expressed anxiety several times, demanded light. At one point said that she had two heads, her body felt foreign to her. This morning constant alternation of laughter and tears, jerking of the head, seductive glances. Complains about Dr. Heller.[4]

Anamnesis: Uncle Lublinsky ref. Patient was intelligent pupil, received gold medal at Gymnasium [grammar school; trans.]. Always rather hysterical. Ca. 3 years ago became more seriously ill. Has been in Interlaken with Dr. Heller for a month. Very dissatisfied there. Nothing had been done. She should have gone to Monakov.[5] But M. did not take her as she was too agitated.

(Being an old Russian Jew, he constantly gives only meagre and evasive answers, and in addition he does not have a good mastery of German.)

Today calmed down in the course of the day.

Pat. ref: As early as her first year very delicate and ailing. Had stomach pains. Later diphtheria, scarlet fever, measles, and angina a thousand times. Was a very precocious child, very sensitive. When ca. 5 years old went to Froebel infant school in Warsaw.

(Educated at home)

At the age of 10 went to Gymnasium in Rostov.

She lived with her family at that time. Many piano lessons. Attended the Gymnasium for 8 years. Did not work very hard at the G., but intellectually very advanced. Left the Gymnasium this year. Started Latin in class V. [2nd year at Gymnasium; trans.] Had singing lessons that year too. Did not like going to school, teachers are very stupid. Particularly enjoyed natural science subjects. Wanted to study medicine.

<u>Symptoms</u> from earliest childhood.

Could never watch someone being humiliated without falling into a pathological fit in which she finally had to masturbate. [The German word is 'schwitzen' = 'to sweat', which here seems to be used euphemistically for 'to masturbate'; trans.]

Family: Father merchant, marriage not unhappy. Mother: Practised as a dentist until 1 year ago, more for pleasure than from necessity.

Pat. loves her father 'painfully'. She cannot turn to her father, he does not really understand her, he says hurtful things to her. Because of her strong narcissism she cannot give in to her father, and when her father is then sad, she cannot talk to him and she is further deeply hurt. He has hit pat. and she has had to kiss his hand in return. (At this point numerous tics, grimaces and gestures of abhorrence.)

It finally emerges that the father has hit her several times on her bare buttocks, most recently in her 11th year, from time to time in front of her siblings. It takes a powerful battle to entice pat. to make this confession. At this point the tics are in keeping with the affect, as they express abhorrence and revulsion.

Insists several times she would and could never talk about it, and in any case did not want to be cured at all.

Is extremely sensitive, accuses the writer of not having the time to listen to everything, of not really being interested, of only pretending, etc.

Insists that if she had to say everything it would upset her so much that things would go really bad later. Then Ref. would see what would happen.

19. [8.1904]

Night quiet, demanded light only twice. Slept. Subjectively night was good.

Continuation of anamnesis:

3 years ago it happened that pat. said to her father that she could give up parents in favour of the company of other people. Big scene followed, father went wild and threatened suicide. There were often scenes like this, sometimes lasting for days.

It also distresses pat. that father insults and tyrannizes other members of the household. It pains her that he is unhappy, always talking about dying, etc. When he is kind to her she regrets that she behaves badly towards him. She is always afraid that one day he will kill himself.

She cannot say 'good morning' to her father, she cannot speak to him in French. This sense of shame has been there since childhood, 'when I see his *hand* I can't stand him'. She cannot kiss him. When she was chastised the peak of the experience was that her father was a *man*. Even now he occasionally makes indecent remarks.

Mother: A similar relationship with *mother*. Even during this last year mother tried to beat her in front of her brothers and her brothers' friends. Once when, at thirteen, her mother punished her, she ran away and hid in various places, doused herself with ice-cold water (winter!), and went into the cellar to catch her death of cold. This way she tried to torment her parents and kill herself. In her 15th year, she tried to starve herself to death in Karlsbad because she had made her mother angry.

1904, VIII, 20

Mother ref.: Always ill as a child, particularly with stomach complaints. Very precocious, intelligent, at 6 years old spoke German and French. Worked hard at the Gymnasium. As early as her 12th year had periods of apathy, brooded on the purpose of living, pitied all human beings. At 15 she realized the reason for living and started to learn. She wanted only the company of educated people. She wants to meet only good, clever people. Recently she fell in love with her old uncle who was a doctor. Mother listed all his faults for her, and as a result she was deeply disappointed and upset. The most recent outburst in the hotel was the result of her feeling that a recently admired doctor had let her down (Dr. Heller's assistant in Interlaken.)

As a child she played many mischievous pranks. Father used to be very strict with her.

She left Interlaken because the assistant had left.

1904, VIII, 22

During the discussions the tics appear at points in the conversation which have a particular connection with her complexes. Pat. is extremely sensitive, especially to any stimulation. Strict bed-rest therefore. No books, no conversation, no visitors. A doctor visits only once a day. The nurse goes into the room only once an hour for 5 minutes. During the first few days pat. is rather upset, and restless at night, is afraid, asks for the light to be put on. But has calmed down somewhat now.

Yesterday the medical assistant forbade her to leave her bed. Whereupon pat. made a point of getting up and declared energetically she would never obey, that she never wanted to get well, that she would behave badly. On being suitably coaxed by the writer she immediately returned to bed perfectly calm.

1904, VIII, 23

She had a big fright today. She felt as if someone were pressing in upon her, as if ['someone' erased] something were crawling around in her bed, something human (what ?). At the same time she felt as if someone were shouting in her ear. All the time she felt she was totally repulsive, like a dog or a devil. (Writes on a piece of paper the Russian word for devil (*cert*) [transcribed in print] (*tschort*). Her hands felt as though they did not belong to her.

Siblings: 3 brothers, 1 sister (deceased). Does not have an intimate relationship with her brothers. (Pat. is the eldest.) The sister was 6 years old when she died. She loved her sister 'more than anything in the world'. Pat. was almost 16 when the sister died (of typhoid). Her death left a terrible mark on her.

From the age of 7 or 8 pat. started to talk with a spirit.

From her mother she received a very religious upbringing. (God, angels; sins are recorded in heaven in red; a person is responsible for her sins from the age of 7.) As a child she was very pious and prayed a good deal. After a while God answered her in the form of an inner voice which spoke more through her feelings than in clear sentences. It seemed to her, however, that this inner voice was speaking to her in *German* (Russian is her mother tongue, at that time she was learning German). Gradually the idea came to her that the voice was not God but an angel sent to her by God, because she was an *extraordinary person*. With time she came to see the angel more as a good spirit who supported and guided her. At first the spirit spoke German too, later Russian. She often felt as though she understood the meaning of the words earlier ('than' deleted), before they were spoken.

1904, VIII, 24

On the evening of the 22.8, 10 pm. a tremendous noise. When the nurse (a replacement) was going to bed, the pat. demanded she should leave the room for 5 minutes. (Pat. probably had to relieve herself and was embarrassed to do so in front of the new nurse.) The nurse laughed and said, 'No', she was going to bed now. Whereupon the pat. replied 'perhaps she thought she was going to kill herself'. Pat. suddenly pulls off the curtain cord and while the nurse is trying to get it from her, she throws the nurse's watch on the floor, pours lemonade all over the room, pulls the bed apart, beats up the nurse, and then, wrapped in a blanket, sits in the armchair. When Ref. arrives she calmly and truthfully tells him what happened and goes to bed, completely quiet.

When she hears Ref. talking to the nurse outside the room, she asks him later, 'You didn't offend the girl, did you? Did you speak to her gently?' At the slightest sign of lack of respect or trust, she immediately retaliates with negativistic behaviour and with a succession of greater or lesser devilish tricks. Every conversation with her, aimed at obtaining information, is as difficult as walking on eggshells.

[Different handwriting]

IX. I. [1904] ['VIII. 29.' deleted][6]

Absence of the senior physician (since 27. VIII.). Yesterday (28. IX.) [actually VIII.] headache, getting worse. Tried to demand medication, which was refused. At night in bed, pulse 180, for that reason finally given morphine 0.015 [Gram; half the usual '*Dosis maxima simplex*'] in 2 doses, then good night.

Since then so-so. Out of bed a bit; no major foolish behaviour. Yesterday visit from mother, behaved badly with her 'against her (the pat.'s) will'. She felt it keenly when I said she had upset her mother. Wanted to write to tell her she was well but was not allowed to do so. So out of bed in the afternoon, but then calmed down. Today she read a letter from a girlfriend. Afterwards in a state of excitement, pulled down the curtain cord and tied it round her neck (not in a very dangerous manner). When it was taken away from her she pulled down the other cord. Then she took a medallion on a gold chain which she slid down her throat and then pulled up again. As she would not promise to stop this foolish behaviour, the medallion was gently but firmly removed, and a nurse was put with her, which annoyed her intensely; she stayed out of bed, headache (compresses); after several hours (8 o'clock) she became more approachable, and could be left alone; today no scenes or damage.

29th – bath day. Because of last night's upheavals she did not want to have a bath; this was granted, only she had to have one within the next three days. On the 30th she tried to negotiate about the 3 days, but I was prepared to go along with this only if she made certain promises; I said that I thought she would still go today. In spite of her denying this she went straight after my visit.

[Jung's handwriting]

[19]04, IX, 8

Has used the return of the senior physician to produce a few scenes. Among other things she climbed up the window grille in the corridor. On the evening of the 6.9. she tried with all her power to force the doctor to visit. On the 6th ['in the morning' erased] in the evening she sat for a long time in the doorway in her nightdress, just wrapped in a blanket; when no one took any notice of her, she ended up having a convulsive fit, and, completely exhausted, let herself be put back to bed. Quiet night. Yesterday afternoon and this morning completely calm.

[Typed]

[19]04. IX. 29[7]

The states of excitation have become less frequent recently. Pat. still uses her unoccupied hours for her childish pranks (suicidal gestures to drive the nurses crazy, running away, hiding, giving people scares, transgressing prohibitions.) After these excesses, sometimes a severe depressive reaction. Pat. has great insight into her condition but not the slightest inclination to improve it. She asks Ref. never to display the slightest sense of being at a loss about her but only the utmost fortitude and a firm belief in her recovery; that would be the only way for her to get better. Pat. has no attention span when she is reading by herself, but the doctor's mere personal presence can often enable her to concentrate for hours.

[There follows a receipt, pasted in, from the Heller Sanatorium, Interlaken. Made out to 'Miss Silberrein'. Dated 21 July. 'Received in advance 100 francs'. Signed B. Heller-Hirter. In addition 3 small drawings by the patient are shown:

1. A person under a shower with the caption 'Water treatment sanatorium'.
2. A woman lying down, a man either standing beside her or sitting on her, with the caption 'Electrocute'.
3. 2 people with a circle drawn round them who are labelled Dr. Heller and Dr. Hisselbaum. Next to them the word 'devil' in Russian script. This is possibly the piece of paper mentioned in the file on page 6 of the original Records.] [see entry for 23.VIII.1904]

[19]04, X, 10

Above drawing[8] was made by pat. in Interlaken; it shows Dr. Heller giving pat. electrical treatment. The position is a remarkably sexual one. Pat. reveals many other masochistic features: for example, the relationship with her father towards whom she feels a remarkable revulsion. The chastisements form the central complex. She constantly demands that the writer inflict pain on her, do something to hurt her, treat her badly in some way; we are never merely to ask something of her, but to command it.

[1904], X, 18

A few days ago pat. suddenly started to limp and this quickly got worse. P. finally ended up walking on the edge of her foot and complained of unbearable pain in the ball of her foot. An examination proved completely negative, merely an exaggerated hyperaesthesia in both feet. With a sly look she urgently demands treatment. Meekly stays in bed for two days. On the second day there is a profound abreaction, and on the third day the pain has completely gone. Analysing it reveals that pat. used a walk with Ref. (their first) as

04.IX.20. Die Aufregungen sind in letzter Zeit etwas seltener gewor-
den. Pat. benützt immer die unbeschäftigten Stunden zu ihren
kindischen Streichen (Selbstmordversuche, um die Wärterinnen
ins Bockshorn zu jagen, davonlaufen, sich verstecken, Leute
erschrecken, Verbote übertreten etc.) Nach den Excessen jewei
len starke depressive Gemüthsreaction. Pat. hat sehr grosse
Einsicht in ihren Zustand, aber nicht die geringste Energie,
danselben zu bessern. Sie bittet Ref. ihr ja nie die geringste Verlegenheit merken zulassen, sondern immer bloss äusser-
ste Energie & festen Glauben an ihre Heilung, das sei der
einzige Weg zu der dersemselben. Pat. hat sozusagen gar keine
Ausdauer, wenn sie für sich allein etwas lesen soll, bloss die
persönliche Gegenwart des Arztes kann sie fixieren, aber
dann sehr oft auf Stunden.

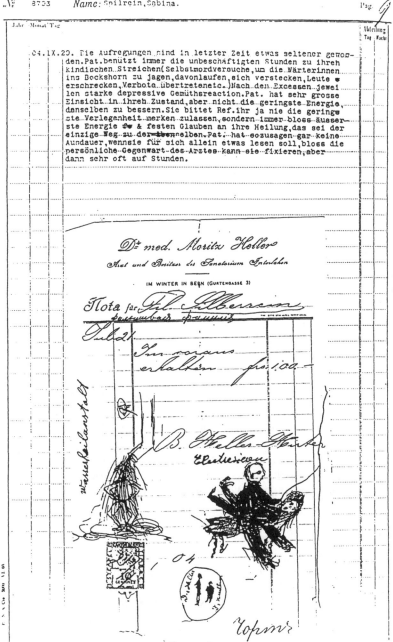

Dr med. Moritz Heller

Arzt und Besitzer des Sanatoriums Interlaken

IM WINTER IN BERN (GURTENGASSE 3)

an external cause for the pain in her feet. She developed unbearable pain in her feet for the first time after a particularly violent row between her parents. After that incident father stayed in bed for 2 days, sick with rage, neither speaking nor eating. On the second day, a relative visited who was not to know what had happened. Pat. had to ask father to get up, which was very embarrassing for her. The same evening the whole family went for a walk with their guest, and everyone behaved as though nothing had happened. Pat. however found this embarrassing charade very painful and would have given anything not to have had to go with them. During the walk her feet began to hurt so that she could not go out for a long time afterwards. Another time she developed pains when she had to travel abroad with her mother under various difficult circumstances, in order to visit Nothnagel for her hysterical stomach complaints; at that time she also had to stay with relatives she did not like. Pat. knows now that she gradually has to get used to a freer way of life; this thought came clearly into her consciousness for the first time during the walk outside the sanatorium. She is afraid of going out and of the future; so she tries to postpone going out as long as possible by means of the pain in her feet.

On the 16.10. ['Pat.' deleted] Ref. was absent all day. During this time pat. was very unsettled. The following day she reports that she constantly and with great longing imagines Ref. squeezing her left hand tightly until it hurts. She desires this painful treatment with all her strength. The next day she has a high grade hyperaesthesia in her left hand. 'I just want to feel pain,' pat. says calmly, 'I want you to do something really bad to me, to force me to do something that I am opposed to with all my being.'

Pat. entertains other patients by telling them fantastic tales about Mars. She insists that every evening she travels to Mars, on to which she projects all her contrasexual fantasies. On Mars people do not eat but are fed through osmosis. They do not procreate, but children quickly develop in the unconscious of individuals and one day appear ready made and without further difficulty. Maintains the correctness of this story in front of Ref. rather like a naughty child who does not want to give up a toy.

[1904] XI, 4

Owing to the absence of the senior physician, pat. left almost entirely to herself for the last week and much worse. Has many physical complaints, stabbing pains here and there, in her limbs, chest and head, tires easily, insists she cannot think, cannot follow the lecture at the clinic etc. Works very little, often stays in bed, torments the nurses, especially her own. The night before last she demanded a sleeping draught; if she did not get one she would create a scene during the night. Because of the threat of course nothing could be given to her. At 1 am she started to make a noise, would not let the nurse put her back to bed and resisted, kicking everyone. When the head nurse was called she stupidly dealt with the situation by forcing pat. back to bed. After that some peace. Unwell during the day, but went to the clinic, and afterwards stayed in the gallery as if nailed or glued to the wall – perhaps in expectation of Ref. (Bl [euler]) passing by. Let herself be taken to her ward, told the story of last night with remarkably little irritation, rather more complaining about her fate, improving remarkably during the account. Was not confident about the night, asked for a sleeping draught (Phenacet.) but did not take it in the end, perhaps someone had told her it would please me if she did not need it. Slept well from 11 pm (time of the draught being offered). This morning quite orderly. Made a correct diagnosis of epilepsy from a letter handed out at the clinic and correctly supported her diagnosis.

[1904, XI] 11

Asked to be permitted to go out by herself and this was granted. But as she had to have an exit card and to indicate the time she wanted to go out, she could not in the end make up her mind. She asked to go out in the evening at 9 o'clock. After that she did not mention it again. Went into the garden by herself, from there over the wall into the park and returned triumphantly. The day before yesterday she went to the park and left the attached note ('if I'm not back by tomorrow morning, it doesn't necessarily mean that I'm dead'), then came back after 5 minutes (having done nothing in particular, bad weather). Recently gives much less cause to be talked about than at the beginning of the month when she hid knives to annoy her nurse, or took possession of the gas workers' ladder on the ward, refusing to come down as long as they and the nurses were watching, etc. Enjoys putting obstacles in the ward corridor, (benches, etc.) for Ref. [Bleuler] to jump over, is pleased when he does so, but will not attempt the smallest jump herself; it would hurt the soles of her feet. Or she burns little holes in her handkerchief with a candle. Or she composes songs about the clinic doctors which she cannot recite for laughing. She breaks off writing a letter in order to write down, with her eyes closed, all the fantasies that go through her mind. In these associations the doctors again play a central role, and her favourite pastime, numerous pranks: 'Complex fantasy': always talking about Mars, but says she will not talk about it any more because no one believes her. Sometimes in a bad mood, complains that she cannot work, that living like this is useless. At other times she talks ostentatiously about suicide, saying that curtain cords should be returned to her room so that she can create a scene during the night. Demonstrates how she would strangle herself.

[1904] XI, 20

After return of Ref. (J) rapid deterioration, plays all kinds of pranks, torments the nurse so horribly that she has to be withdrawn from her. She pushes the stepladder around the corridor, scratching the floor, etc. Last night and this morning, after a walk, again painful abasia (inability to walk: trans.), fear of going into town. Yesterday evening and this morning refuses to eat, in order to starve herself to death. She says she desires with all her might to get ill, that she needs to be unconscious for at least 2 months, before she can get well again. Yesterday two crises with penetrating screaming which she has copied from a patient (Frau Stern). Has spontaneously admitted to masturbating which very much exhausts her.

[1904] XII[9]

Condition generally calmer and more balanced. If the pat. is not given the usual close attention for a few days, she becomes increasingly shut in and it is more and more difficult to get through to her. She then behaves very negativistically, complains about headaches instead of answering questions and insists that she has forgotten everything she wanted to say. Frequent enormously exaggerated and characteristically affectless demonstrations of hyperaesthesia of the feet and abasia. Once during a walk to Seefeld she expressed great disgust at shops, stuck her tongue out at them, etc. When she met a lady who spoke somewhat loudly, she copied her, with lively expressions of disgust. Later analysis revealed that at home a big family scene is connected with this. Her mother has the odd habit of having to buy everything she sees and can be talked into buying; every time she goes out shopping she brings home masses of things which no one needs but which are very expensive. She never has enough money on her to pay for everything and therefore has to borrow from relatives and then struggle to repay them from her household budget. Above all father must not know about this, so there is constant anxiety that father might find out about these dealings. From time to time when father gets a whiff of what is going on there is a huge row. Mother likes to play the great lady with her expensive acquisitions. Hence her disgust with ladies and shops.

[19]05, I, 8

With the New Year, marked decline, states of violent excitation, many gestures of disgust. In the night a great fright: there might be a cat or someone else in her room, someone was suddenly speaking in her ear. She felt something moving on her back like a snail and something grasped her side like a hand. When this mood is analysed the following is revealed:

On New Year's Day exactly a year ago, a big row at home (angry scenes with father). In connection with this she recalled a long sequence of such scenes, and finally, with great effort, scenes in which father had beaten her: when she was 13 years old, her father once threatened her with a beating; he took her into a special room and ordered her to lie down. She implored him not to beat her (he was trying to lift her skirt from behind). Finally he gave in, but he forced her to kneel down and kiss the picture of her grandfather and to swear always to be a good child. After this humiliating scene the boys were outside waiting to greet her.

Pat. emphasizes during this account her father's expressions which offended her sense of shame. Finally [after] a 3 hour analysis it transpires that since her fourth year she has experienced sexual arousal in connection with the beatings, she cannot hold her water, has to press her legs together, later even has an orgasmic discharge. In the end it was enough to see or hear her brother being beaten to make her want to masturbate, or someone had only to threaten her to make her immediately lie on her bed and masturbate. In recent years it went so far that the slightest hint could trigger off this impulse. She says that she only has to be laughed at, which to her symbolizes humiliation, to cause her to have an orgasm. When she saw a disturbed pat. being forcibly moved to another ward, she immediately experienced this irresistible urge. Basically all her expressions of disgust and her negative behaviour can be associated with this complex. She sees herself as a thoroughly bad and corrupt person, and feels therefore that she should not be allowed to be in the company of other people. When Ref. told her recently that she had to agree to regulations, 'agree' was perceived as 'submit'; it triggered the complex and caused her to masturbate. During the act, pat. wishes on herself all manner of torments; she pictures these as vividly as possible, in particular being beaten on her bare bottom, and, in order to increase her arousal, she imagines that it is taking place in front of a large audience.

[1905] I, 13

After the New Year the abasia had as its main reason the fact that she could not make up her mind to abreact this innermost and most important part of her complexes. The New Year only made the necessity of the decision clearer to her. At the same time the shifting of this complex would have meant the first step into the world which is always reacted to with abasia. After abreaction great relief, pains in her feet and headaches disappear.

Pat. now shows more initiative and demands regular useful activities. Behaves much more naturally.

[19]05, I, 29

Since the last abreaction substantial improvement. Still strongly emotional and unusually powerful expressions of feeling. At every stimulation of the complex she still reacts with her back, hands, tongue, and mouth, though significantly less so. She is now aware of it and hides her expressions of disgust behind her hands.

She recently tried associations with acquaintances and on this occasion it was shown that she could not say her complex trigger word 'to beat'. So she omitted it during the experiment.

Yesterday at my evening visit, pat. was reclining on the sofa in her usual oriental, voluptuous manner, with a sensuous, dreamy expression on her face. She did not really respond to questions and only smiled superficially. Then I told her something, and she suddenly laughed and said, now I can hear your voice double, I feel as if I had two heads, and that the whole of my left side were moving of its own accord.

She is now asked what was going on before I entered the room. Her head had felt very heavy. What was she doing that made her head feel so heavy? She had been reading Forel's 'Hypnotism': but the feeling could not have resulted from this. When Ref. opens the book to find the passage that triggered off the father complex, the pat. suddenly displays defensive movements and gestures of disgust, and indicates the passage in the book which she had just been reading: the pseudological story of Gottfried Keller, spec[ifically] the place where he describes how he is caned by other boys.

[Jung's handwriting]

[1905] IV, 28

In the last few weeks distinctly improved and increasingly calm. Now listens to lectures conscientiously and with interest (zoology, botany, chemistry, physics). Fluctuations in mood still occur from time to time, particularly in connection with letters from home.

[1905] VI, 1

Pat. is discharged. She now lives independently in town and attends university lectures.

Addendum to the patient's file

[Spielrein's handwriting]

Last Will.

After my death, I will permit only my head to be dissected, if it is not too dreadful to look at. No young person is to be present at the dissection. Only the very keenest students may observe. I bequeath my skull to our school. It is to be placed in a glass container and decorated with everlasting flowers. The following is to be inscribed on the container (in Russian): 'And let young life play at the entrance to the tomb and let indifferent nature shine with eternal splendour'. My brain I give to you. Just place it as it is in a beautiful vessel similarly decorated and write the same words on it. My body is to be cremated. But no one is to be present for this. Divide the ashes into three parts. Place one part in an urn and send it home. Scatter the second part on the ground over our biggest field. Plant an oak-tree there and write: 'I too was once a human being. My name was Sabina Spielrein'. My brother will tell you what is to be done with the third part.

Transcript of correspondence[10]

The letters date from the period 18 August 1904 to 7 July 1919.
The names under the date indicate the recipient.
Transcript correct to the letter but not to the line.
The copy book numbers in brackets [] indicate the letters which follow below.
The same applies to the comments on the style of writing.

[Nr. 59]

[Handwritten]

18.VIII.1904

Dr. med. Heller, Interlaken.

Dear Colleague,

Yesterday a Miss SABINA SPILREIN from Rostov, Russia, was admitted here. She declares that she was in treatment with you. We would be most obliged if you could send us a short report on the patient's behaviour.

Many thanks in advance

With best wishes from your colleague.

p.p. the Director

Dr. Jung Senior Physician

24.VIII.04

Mrs Spilrein, Hôtel Baur en Ville Zürich

Dear Madam,

Miss Spilrein wishes to have both her suitcases with her. Since your daughter is short of linen we would be most obliged if you would send us both her suitcases as soon as possible.

Yours sincerely the Director

p.p. Dr. Jung Senior Physician

27.VIII.04

Mrs Spilrein, Hôtel Bauer en Ville Zürich

Dear Madam,

In accordance with your daughter's wishes we are requesting you most courteously to bring her everything she has asked for in her letters to you. The remainder of her letters and books you can keep.

Yours sincerely the Director

Bleuler

[Nr 60]

10.IX.04

Mr Spielrein, Hôtel Baur en Ville, Zürich

Dear Sir,

You may visit your daughter tomorrow.

Yours faithfully the Director,

Bleuler

14.IX.04

Mr Spielrein, Universitätsstrasse 27, Zürich

Dear Sir,

Should you envisage having a dress made for your daughter in Zürich, we recommend that you arrange with your preferred seamstress to take the measurements. Otherwise, our resident seamstress at the Institution will take the measurements, but without the guarantee that the dress will fit particularly well.

Yours faithfully the Director,

Bleuler

[typed]

26.IX.04

Mr Spielrein, Rostov/Don, Russia

Dear Sir,

Your daughter's condition has not changed substantially recently, but a slight improvement is nevertheless noticeable. Her agitated states and childish jokes have receded somewhat so that there are now days which pass entirely uneventfully. We have now happily succeeded in stimulating Miss Spielrein's interest in scientific pursuits, so that she can be distracted for hours at a time from her pathological obsessions. During the morning she now participates with great interest in the examination of patients and in the afternoon she goes for walks with her nurse. Usually she uses this opportunity to play a few childish pranks, which however are of a harmless nature. Her nights are good on the whole; the night terrors have become significantly fewer. Her physical well-being is good, but she still tends to tire quickly. The deposit you paid will last until the end of September and we would now be grateful for an advance payment for the next quarter of 1,250 francs.

Yours faithfully the Director,

Bleuler

12.X.04

Mr Spielrein, Rostov-on-Don, Russia

Dear Sir,

In the interests of Miss Spielrein's treatment, we politely request your reply to your daughter's letter to you of 1.X. She eagerly awaits news from home. Her improvement continues, albeit somewhat slowly. At least there is the happy fact to report that Miss Spielrein has now decided to commence studying medicine next spring here in Zürich. On the whole she is much calmer and is now more able to concentrate on one task. She also goes for regular walks in our large grounds. Her physical condition is satisfactory.

Yours faithfully the Director,

Bleuler

25.X.04

Mr Spielrein, Rostov-on-Don, Russia

Dear Sir,

Please find enclosed two letters from Miss Sabina Spielrein. Your daughter's state of health is slowly improving. She has even been for accompanied walks outside the institution on a number of occasions. She is currently assisting one of our doctors on a scientific project, which she finds of great interest. She still displays little inclination or perseverance with regard to other tasks. She has decided to commence studying medicine here in Zürich next spring. She does not wish to go to another university as she has become familiar with the place. We consider it best that the patient remains here until then, although not necessarily at the institution, but at least within the city so that she can remain in contact with us. We strongly advise against a return to Russia for quite some time, and even a reunion with her family, before she has commenced her studies, would in our opinion be strongly contra-indicated. Your daughter needs to develop independence and self-reliance and must therefore remain unencumbered by all emotional anxiety for her family and all the restricting aspects of family life. This can only be achieved by her spending some time in a new and different environment where she can devote herself wholeheartedly to an absorbing activity. Your daughter too is of the opinion that these are the conditions necessary for her recovery.

The patient's physical condition is satisfactory.

Yours faithfully the Director,

Bleuler

28.XI.0

Mr N A Spielrein, Rostov-on-Don, Russia

Dear Sir,

I am happy to report that there have been no significant changes in your daughter's condition, which is something you might have assumed from reading her letters. Recently I was absent for three weeks as I had to attend military exercises. During this time her condition remained stable. Since then her improvement has continued, albeit slowly, as Miss Spielrein is unable to get accustomed to regular work. Unfortunately she still allows herself to become distracted by a whole range of different ideas. Nevertheless, she is much more able to focus clearly than she used to be. She has recently participated with some success at a social function given by Professor Bleuler. Her self-control has decidedly improved, but there are still days when she succumbs to her childish moods. It was during one of these moods that she wrote her recent letters to you. She admitted it to me immediately afterwards and sincerely regrets this unconsidered course of action. Her letters therefore do not imply a deterioration in her condition.

Her physical condition remains excellent.

We have not yet found anything which raises doubts about a recovery from her condition, but the treatment will still take a considerable period of time.

Yours faithfully the Director,

pp Dr Jung Senior Physician

[Nr 61]

6.1.05

Mr Spielrein, Rostov-on-Don, Russia

Dear Sir,

During December Miss Sabina Spielrein's condition remained stable throughout. The new year however, with its reminders of home, brought a serious state of agitation, but that has now receded. The patient still feels somewhat exhausted and has therefore requested her doctor to write to her parents on her behalf. As her memories of you agitate her greatly we are of the opinion that Miss Spielrein should not write to you directly over the next few months. In order to relieve her of this responsibility we have therefore forbidden her to write to her father. In spite of her recent disturbance the general progress in her recovery is satisfactory. Miss Spielrein now occupies herself almost daily with scientific reading and she has also commenced practical scientific studies in the anatomy laboratory.

She wishes to convey her fond greetings.

Yours faithfully the Director,

Bleuler

22.1.05

Mrs Spielrein, Rostov/Don, Russia

Dear Madam,

In spite of numerous difficulties Miss Spielrein is steadily improving. She recently worked herself into a state at the thought that she ought to send her father greetings on his birthday. It now seems that she has managed to send him a greeting, if only a modest one. This, though, caused her so much agitation that I have had to forbid any further letters to her father for the time being, as stated in our last report. This restriction has given her much relief, insofar as she is now able again to write home a short report on her state of health as she used to. We are therefore unable to commit ourselves to writing a regular weekly report, indeed our workload is simply too heavy to permit us to do so. Currently the patient is slowly being reacquainted with the city, walking with other people and dining with them. Yesterday she voluntarily joined the table of the assistant doctors at lunch, and this can be seen as a significant success. Recently Miss Spielrein has repeatedly expressed her wish to see her mother again. We have no objections to this very understandable request and even believe that a visit from her mother would be very positive. Madam, we therefore recommend that you perhaps come to Switzerland in the next few weeks. However, a meeting with other members of the family is not to be recommended for the time being. It is your daughter's wish, and we agree with her, that a visit should take place before April. We shall then use this opportunity to report to you in person on the health of your daughter.

We await your earliest reply in keenest anticipation.

Yours faithfully the Director,

pp Dr Jung Senior Physician

13.11.05

Mrs Spielrein, Rostov/Don, Russia

Dear Madam,

Assuming that you did not receive our letter of 23.I.1905 (we have not received a reply to it), may we reproduce it once more. In spite of numerous difficulties Miss Spielrein's condition is slowly improving. She recently worked herself into a state at the thought that she ought to send her father greetings on his birthday. It now seems that she has managed to send him a greeting, if only a modest one. Since she always becomes so agitated at the memory of her father we have had to forbid any further letters to her father for the time being. She will nevertheless send home reports on her condition from time to time. We are unable to commit ourselves to writing a regular weekly report, as requested by Mr Spielrein; indeed our workload is simply too heavy to permit us to do so. Your daughter has now improved so much that she voluntarily joins the table of the assistant doctors at lunch daily, and this can be considered a significant success. Recently Miss Spielrein has repeatedly expressed her wish to see her mother again. We have no objections to this very understandable request and even believe that it would be a good thing if you were to visit your daughter. The patient would then be able to unburden herself to you on different matters. We would also like to consult you person-ally about your daughter's illness . . . .[11] . . . . in the time since the date of this letter your daughter has continued to improve. She occupies herself for several hours daily with scientific studies. She is largely free of hysterical symptoms, and she can therefore be regarded as having recovered.

We sincerely seek your earliest reply.

Yours faithfully the Director,

Bleuler

[Nr 62]

18.IV.1905[12]

Miss Sabina Spielrein from Rostov-on-Don (Russia) has been resident at our institution since 17.VIII.1904. It is anticipated that she will spend some considerable period of time with us and plans to attend lectures at the university.

Dr Jung Senior Physician

[handwritten]

27.IV.1905

Medical Certificate

Miss Sabina Spielrein from Rostov/Don, resident at this institution and planning to matriculate at the medical faculty in the summer term, is not mentally ill. She was here for treatment for a nervous complaint with hysterical symptoms. We must therefore recommend her for matriculation.

The Director,

Bleuler

[typed]

23.V.1905

Mr Spielrein, Rostov/Don, Russia

Dear Sir,

I have been instructed by Miss Spielrein to write to you on her behalf and to inform you that her refraining from writing to you is due not to any lack of affection or gratitude towards you, but because she feels better and more relieved if she does not have continually to recall images and memories of home. As I have already explained to you in person, it is characteristic of your daughter's nervous disposition that she links all kinds of pathological obsessional fantasies with your person, and these worry and disturb her. Your daughter is therefore afraid lest you regard it as a lack of affection if she does not write to you. In order to calm her I promised that I would write to you to explain that she retains only feelings of love for you. Her situation now is most satisfactory. She attends lectures daily and with great interest. She regards it almost as a matter of honour to participate and to be punctual to the best of her ability. Her behaviour is admittedly still not quite normal, but is significantly better than it was during your last visit. We now believe that the time will soon come when your daughter will leave here to commence an independent life. We will talk to her about it and will inform you of your daughter's decision.

Yours faithfully,

Dr Jung Senior Physician

[handwritten]

31.V.1905

Mr Spielrein, Rostov/Don, Russia

Dear Sir,

Miss Spielrein has become extremely agitated at being expected to look after her brother. Owing to the weak state of her nerves she requires utmost forbearance to enable her to concentrate fully on her studies. In order to maintain her improved condition she must remain *absolutely free* of any obligations towards her family. Miss Spielrein has found herself an apartment which she is likely to rent as of today so that a move can be accomplished within the next few days.

Yours faithfully the Director,

Bleuler

[typed]

7.VI.05

Mr Spielrein, Rostov/Don

Dear Sir,

We hereby inform you that Miss Spielrein departed from here on 1.VI.05. Her new address is Schoenleinstrasse 7, Zürich. She has since visited me and has said that she likes her new apartment. Meanwhile, an uncomfortable and embarrassing situation has arisen: her brother's apartment is also in the vicinity and this raises the possibility that she might run into her brother quite frequently, which would be decidedly damaging to her state of health. Unfortunately, it was very difficult to find lodgings, otherwise she could have taken this factor into consideration when choosing her room. As we have already stressed to you on a number of occasions, for the sake of Miss Spielrein's health it is of the utmost importance that she has as little contact with her brother as possible. We would very much welcome it if you could persuade your eldest son to attend a university other than Zürich. At the same time, it is of great importance to your daughter's continuing improvement that all contact with the younger brother be curtailed as much as possible. Unfortunately we do not really know how this could be managed, but in the interests of the patient we very much hope that some solution can be found. When we recommended Zürich as a location for your son we were as yet unaware of the obsessional fantasies which are attached by our patient to her brother, otherwise we would have been more hesitant in recommending Zürich to you. We assume that your younger son is here only temporarily and we ask you to bear this in mind when you place your elder son elsewhere. Perhaps it would then be a good idea if both brothers were to rent the same apartment.

You will now be sending money directly to your daughter, but should you require some supervision in this matter I would be pleased to be at your service and to receive the money for Miss Spielrein on her behalf.

Yours faithfully,

Dr C G Jung Senior Physician

[Nr 63]

25.9.1905 [13]

Report on Miss Spielrein to Professor Freud in Vienna, delivered to Mrs Spielrein for use if the occasion arises.

Dear Professor,

The daughter of Mrs Spielrein, Miss Sabina Spielrein, student of medicine, suffers from hysteria.

The patient suffers significantly from a hereditary weakness, both father and mother being hysteric, especially the mother. A brother of the patient has suffered severely from hysteria from an early age.

The patient is turning twenty and her affliction appeared distinctly about three years ago. But of course her pathogenic experiences reach far back to her early years. By using your method I have analysed the clinical condition fairly thoroughly and with considerable success from the outset. The analysis has essentially established the following:

The physical chastisements administered to the patient's posterior by her father from the age of four until seven unfortunately became associated with the patient's premature and now highly developed sexual awareness. This sexuality came to be expressed by the patient from very early on by her rubbing her thighs together to commence an act of masturbation. Masturbation always occurred after she underwent punishment from her father. After a while the beatings were no longer necessary to initiate sexual arousal; it came to be triggered through mere threats and other situations implying violence, such as verbal abuse, threatening movements of the hands, etc. After a time she could not even look at her father's hands without becoming sexually aroused, or watch him eat without imagining how the food was ejected, and then being thrashed on the buttocks, etc. These associations extended to the younger brother too, who also masturbated frequently from an early age. Threats to the boy or ill-treatment of him aroused her and she had to masturbate whenever she saw him being punished. In time any situation which reflected violence aroused her, for example, being told to obey. As soon as she was alone she was plagued by obsessional fantasies; for example, she would imagine all kinds of torments. The same happened in her dreams: for example, she often dreamt that she was eating her lunch and simultaneously sitting on the lavatory and that everything was going straight out through her bottom; at the same time she was surrounded by a large crowd of people watching her; on another occasion she was being whipped in front of a great mob of people, etc.

Thus her situation at home naturally became untenable. After numerous severe disturbances she was brought to Switzerland about a year ago, first to a sanatorium. The doctor there however was no match for her frankly demonic moods and contrary behaviour. She drove everyone there to despair. Finally, the private clinic could no longer cope and she was brought to us here at the asylum. She initially harassed everybody, tormenting the nurses to the limits of their endurance. As the analysis progressed her condition noticeably improved and she finally emerged as a highly intelligent and talented person of great sensibility. There is a certain callousness and unreasonableness in her character and she lacks any kind of feeling for situation and for external propriety, but much of this must of course be put down to Russian peculiarities.

Her condition improved so much that she could commence studies last summer term. She suffers enormously whenever she meets with members of her family, something that the mother cannot quite comprehend, but which should be understandable on reading the above (Mrs Spielrein knows about the most important part of her daughter's complex).

During treatment the patient had the misfortune to fall in love with me. She raves on to her mother about her love in an ostentatious manner, and a secret perverse enjoyment of her mother's dismay seems to play a not inconsiderable part. Now in this distressing situation the mother wants to place her elsewhere for treatment, with which I am naturally in agreement.

Remaining at your service and most faithfully yours,

Dr Jung

[Nr 81]

19.XI.09

Miss S Spielrein, Scheuchzerstrasse 28, Room IV

Dear Madam,

The administration department has sent me your bill, duly stamped as paid as I had to send them the excess 5 francs. I cannot quite understand why they do not contact you directly, but am willing to be of service and hope everything is well. If you would care to send me 3,40 francs I will ensure that the two gratuities are paid.

1 enclosure

At your service with best wishes,

Bleuler

9.XII.09

Miss S Spielrein, Scheuchzerstrasse 28, Room II

Dear Madam,

I duly acknowledge receipt of 4,40 francs as an addition to your earlier payment. Following your request I have divided this sum equally between Melanie and the porter so that each has received 5,50 francs.

At your service with best wishes,

Bleuler

[Nr 116]

28.XII.1914

Madam Dr S Spielrein-Scheftel

c/o Mrs Kupferschmied, Seefeldstrasse 47, Zürich

Dear Madam Doctor,

We are more than willing to assist you in your studies to the best of our abilities. However, we do not have any morphine addicts at the institution at present and it is very seldom that we do, so I do not really know how we can help you. If you would like to discuss the matter with me please telephone for an appointment.

Yours faithfully the Director,

Bleuler

[Nr 152]

7.VII.1919

Madam Dr S Spielrein-Scheftel

Pension Jolimont, Les Marecottes sur Solvan

Dear Madam Colleague,

I probably do have the *Sancte de Sanctis*, in which case I will send it to you. As for the survey I must request you not to use our institution's address. As you know, psychoanalysis has many opponents and I must add that even the public prosecutor has looked into it once. It would be well not to draw public attention to ourselves in such a sensitive matter. In place of our clinic's address you can choose any pseudonym you wish.

I am glad to hear that your daughter is well and send you my best regards.

The Director,

Bleuler

Notes

1 These records were first published in *Luzifer-Amor, Zeitschrift zur Geschichte der Psychoanalyse*, Vol. 7, No. 14, 1994, in the article 'Sabina Spielrein. Jung's patient at the Burghölzli' by Bernard Minder. Reprinted in English by kind permission of *Luzifer-Amor* and the C.G. Jung Estate.
2 Translator's note: the original hospital records were written in note form, that is, pronoun subjects, verbs and articles are often missing; this style has been largely followed in the English translation except where more elaboration seemed necessary for clarity. The abbreviation 'pat.' is often used for 'patient'; 'Ref.' (short for 'Referent') indicates the writer, or occasionally the provider of the information (cf. the entry of 18.8.1904). The dates have been reproduced as they appear in the original, the figures in square brackets having been added, again for the reader's clarification.
3 The exact date of birth is not known. I was able to locate it in the Register of Aliens with the police in Lausanne.
4 Dr Heller ran a private sanatorium in Interlaken (Dr Heller's Sanatorium and Spa. Especially for nervous patients. Clinical treatment); cf. receipt in the patient's file page 9. This institution closed down during the thirties owing to lack of patients. The archive and patients' files have not survived (information obtained verbally from Prof. R. Keller (Aarau), grandson of Dr E. Grandjean, himself brother-in-law of Dr Heller).
5 Constantin von Monakov, a Russian émigré. Came to Zürich in 1866. Studied medicine. Assistant at the Burghölzli under Professor Hitzig. Qualified as university lecturer in neurology at University of Zürich. As well as his epoch-making work in the field of brain anatomy, he ran a private clinic with 10–12 patients.
6 This entry was made by hand by an unknown doctor (transcribed by Mrs Anke Wilke, Hanover).
7 The following entries in the patient's files were all typed, save those dated 28.1V.1905 and 1.V1.1905. Style and content point undoubtedly to Jung as their

author, with the exception of entries dated 4.XI.1904 and 11.XI.1904, which are probably by Bleuler.

8   See p. 91 of this volume p. 9 of original text.

9   No indication of day and year.

10 The official house correspondence from 1878 to 1932 exists in its entirety in duplicate in bound format. The years 1933 to 1945 are completely missing. From 1946 onwards the correspondence is filed in folders unbound. Apart from a few exceptions contained in patients' files, all letters sent to the clinic are missing.

11 The following five lines of text have faded and are illegible.

12 Recipient unknown.

13 This document is remarkable from several points of view and justifies the following extensive comment:

The date 25.9.1905: the first documented record of contact between Jung and Freud is Freud's response, dated 11.4.1906, to Jung's sending him his *Studies in Word Association* (McGuire 1974). This newly discovered letter is consequently to be considered as Jung's first documented attempt to get in touch with Freud. One would assume that a referral to Freud of all people would be significantly supported by the fact that the patient was being treated according to his 'method'. The fact however that the letter was written on official note-paper and nearly four months after her discharge from the Clinic, that is at a time when Sabina Spielrein had long been a private outpatient of Jung's, gives rise to the supposition that Jung was seeking to make contact with Freud (the use of the official clinic letterhead for correspondence regarding private patients is incidentally unique among the letters signed by Jung which have been preserved. At this time Jung held the position of deputy to Prof. Bleuler in his absence). It is also possible that Jung was acceding to the mother's wish, although he calls his letter a 'report'. From another point of view, the phenomenon of transference was not new (the mother wanted to withdraw her daughter from treatment because she had had the 'misfortune' to fall in love with her therapist). On the one hand he reports in his paper 'Association, dream and hysterical symptom' (1906) on a patient who had fallen in love with him and mentions Miss L. (another patient in the hospital) with similar emotional disturbances. A reading of these two patients' records dates the events to the spring/summer of 1905. On the other hand, Sabina Spielrein's records document her repeatedly 'falling in love' with at least two doctors (one an uncle and the other the assistant at the Heller Sanatorium). It is to say the least unusual to produce a 'report *for use if the occasion arises*' which contains detailed information on the patient's pathology and is finally 'delivered to Mrs Spielrein'. In the event the patient's treatment was not taken over by Freud. Sabina Spielrein stayed in Zürich and in treatment with Jung. The original of this document remained in the keeping of the Spielrein family. Sabina Spielrein quoted from it in her letter to Freud of 10.6.1909 (Carotenuto 1986: 100).

Chapter 6

Sabina Spielrein. Jung's patient at the Burghölzli[1]

Bernard Minder

(Translated from the German by Barbara Wharton)

The concept of hysteria at the Burghölzli Clinic and in the early publications of C.G. Jung

It was at the beginning of the 1880s that hypnosis and suggestion were introduced by Auguste Forel at the Burghölzli. In 1887 he had deepened his knowledge in these areas with Bernheim and Liébeault in Nancy. Forel's work on memory indicates that his psychological method was related ultimately to a biological model of human functioning. At the same time, however, his connection with the Nancy school indicated that his understanding of psychic life was a thoroughly dynamic one. The reservations he later held with regard to Freud's work lay in his lack of sympathy for the latter's libido theory and the development of infantile sexuality. In any event, both in the public arena, and in his medical work, he espoused the cause of the 'psychics'. From 1898 (till 1927) Eugen Bleuler took over the directorship of the Clinic. Evidence for Bleuler's connection with hypnosis is found in two of his works. In 'On the psychology of hypnosis' (1889) he describes his observation of himself under hypnosis, after he had been hypnotized by Forel among others. In 1894, in 'Opinions', he reports on six cases of incurable psychiatric patients whom he was able to release from severely restrictive symptoms by means of hypnosis and suggestion. The following quotation comes from that time (p. 17): 'In the course of 1000 hypnoses I have never had a disaster'. In contrast with Forel, Bleuler had a fundamentally different attitude to Freud's work. In 1896 in the *Munich Medical Weekly* he described Freud's book, *Studies on Hysteria*, as 'one of the most important publications of the last few years in the field of normal and pathological psychology'. The hospital records however give no indication of any clinical application of Freud's ideas before 1904.

In 1900 C.G. Jung took up his post at the Burghölzli Clinic, at a time therefore when this renowned clinic clearly represented the French school in the worldwide discussion of hysteria. So it is not surprising that these influences made their mark on Jung's works.

In several of his early works Jung expresses an opinion on the concept of hysteria. As I shall show in more detail below, in the section on the influence of Sabina Spielrein on Jung's treatment of hysterical patients, he had had little experience of this clinical syndrome in the early years of his employment at the Burghölzli. Uncertainty about the concept of hysteria is expressed in the Jung–Freud correspondence too. Thus Jung writes in his letter of 4.12.1906:

> 3. In practice, the concept of hysteria is still far from clear. Countless cases of mild *hebephrenia* still pass under the diagnosis of 'hysteria', and here the results are doubtful to bad, as I know from my own experience. (. . .) How little clarity reigns in this area is shown by a recent publication from the Heidelberg Clinic, where a case of *unquestionable* catatonia was asserted to be hysteria.
>
> (McGuire 1974:11)

In his time at the Burghölzli Jung published more than twenty works, among them his dissertation and his habilitation [his qualifying paper for becoming a university lecturer; trans.]. Alongside numerous smaller articles, his publications on the word association test occupy a large space. Thus the 'forgetting' of events particularly linked to unpleasant feelings is described as a completely typical phenomenon in hysterical patients ('Experimental observations on the faculty of memory', 1905); similarly, the 'misapprehension' of stimulus words in the experiment is seen as a pointer to repressed complexes ('The associations of normal subjects', 1904). With the following quotations from these works I will try to define the concept of hysteria as Jung then saw it.

In his paper of 1906, 'A third and final opinion on two contradictory psychiatric diagnoses', he writes as follows:

> Hysteria is a morbid condition, congenital or acquired, in which the affects are exceedingly powerful. Hence the patients are more or less continual victims of their affects. At the same time, however, hysteria generally determines only the *quantity*, not the *quality*, of the affects. The quality is given by the patient's character.
>
> (Jung 1906a, para. 464)

And further:

> Owing to the strength of their affects, hysterical persons are always their own victims; they do not belong to themselves, as it were, but to the momentary affect. Consequently, their actions are always being compromised by passing moods. We all know how much these can obscure our judgment and hinder reflection.
>
> (Jung 1906a, para. 475)

In 'The psychological diagnosis of evidence' (1905) he writes:

> Secondly, the experiment is important for psychiatric practice in that, especially in hysteria, in which as a rule the whole mental life is disturbed, it provides us with the most valuable indications for finding the pathogenic factor, since in hysteria a complex is always at work.
>
> (Jung 1905b, para. 754)

And from 'Association, dream and hysterical symptom' (1906):

> The complex has an abnormal autonomy in hysteria and a tendency to an active separate existence, which reduces and replaces the constellating power of the ego-complex. In this way a new morbid personality is gradually created, the inclinations, judgments, and resolutions of which move only in the direction of the will to be ill. This second personality devours what is left of the normal ego and forces it into the role of a secondary (oppressed) complex. A purposive treatment of hysteria must therefore strengthen what has remained of the normal ego, and this is best achieved by introducing some new complex that liberates the ego from domination by the complex of the illness.
>
> (Jung 1906b, paras. 861 & 862)

Here Jung goes into more detail regarding the dynamics of the origins of hysteria.

In other papers Jung expresses an opinion about individual symptoms of hysteria, as well as about the observations he has made in the context of his association studies which suggest a diagnosis of hysteria. In his dissertation in 1902 he describes somnambulism as 'a partial manifestation of severe hysteria' (Jung 1902, para. 5) and discusses the phenomenon of the splitting of consciousness in these circumstances. In a reply ('On hysterical misreading', 1904) to a criticism of his dissertation he writes:

> The reason why I attach particular importance to hysterical misreading is that it demonstrates in a nutshell the splitting off of psychic functions from the ego-complex, which is such a characteristic of hysteria, and consequently the strong tendency of the psychic elements towards autonomy ('*Tendenz der psychischen Elemente zur Selbstständigbeit*').
>
> (Jung 1904, para. 159; italics in original German but not in English)

In his 1903 paper 'On simulated insanity' Jung discusses among other things the question whether a psychic 'disposition to neutralize affects in a faulty or abnormal way coincides with hysteria':

> . . . according to Freud's theory of hysteria the two are identical. Janet

found that the influence of affects is seen most clearly in hysterical persons, and that it produces a state of dissociation in which the will, attention, ability to concentrate are paralyzed and all the higher psychic phenomena are impaired in the interests of the lower; that is, there is a displacement towards the automatic side, where everything that was formerly under the control of the will is now set free.

(Jung 1903, para. 318)

So much for hysteria as it is described in Jung's early works. As we know from the Jung–Freud correspondence and from his publications, his later interest while he was at the Burghölzli was centred chiefly on dementia praecox. Not least as a result of his clinical experience, as well as through his subsequent experiments with the galvanometer and the pneumograph, Jung tried to show analogies between hysteria and dementia praecox. I will return to his writings in the section on the influence exerted on Jung by his experience with Sabina Spielrein.

It was against this background that Sabina Spielrein entered the Burghölzli on 17 August 1904. In the next section Sabina Spielrein's anamnesis, the development of her illness, her hospitalization, and her treatment will be described in the light of the new material now available.

Sabina Spielrein: Jung's patient at the Burghölzli

Before we turn to Sabina Spielrein's hospital notes we must consider more closely the staff situation and the range of duties of the medical personnel in order to be able to evaluate the available material. In the table (see opposite) it is clear that not only in Jung's time at the Burghölzli (1900–1909), but from the opening of the Clinic in 1870, a very small number of doctors and of nursing staff had in their care a large number of patients. It easily follows that, taking into account the time-consuming responsibilities of writing reports, of liaising with the authorities, of further training and research projects, not forgetting contact with patients, very little time was left for keeping hospital records. Understandably the entries at the beginning of the hospitalization occupy most space. They comprise the taking of the history, the patient's physical condition, and the instituting of the first therapeutic measures. Later entries are as a rule brief. They include on the one hand particular incidents, reasons for transfer to other departments, medication, and descriptions of the course of the illness. An overview of the 2500 sets of notes of new admissions during Jung's time at the Burghölzli suggests that the foregoing description was the rule, at least for that time. Of course there are variations, determined on the one hand by the clinical picture – thus descriptions of dementing patients are briefer than those of hysterics – and on the other the duration of the hospitalization plays a substantial role.

From this point of view it is worth examining Sabina Spielrein's hospital notes as a first step.

Staff and patient populations 1870–1915

Year	Number of patients at 31 December	Admissions	Doctors	Care staff
1870	121	190	2	20
1875	251	271	3	40
1880	319	225	4	27
1885	329	295	4	49
1890	361	257	4	53
1895	364	219	4	56
1900	391	203	4	72
1901	360	236	4	84
1902	386	335	4	79
1903	380	303	4	91
1904	388	332	5	97
1905	379	340	5	96
1906	406	350	5	111
1907	410	294	5	109
1908	397	304	5	111
1909	374	379	5	104
1910	402	505	7	107
1915	399	591	10	109

Source: Audit Statements of the Clinic; Burghölzli Archive.

Anamnesis, development of the illness and diagnosis

Sabina Spielrein was in hospital from 17 August 1904 until 1 June 1905, that is for about nine and a half months. The hospital records contain a total of twenty-one entries, at first daily, later weekly, until the end of January 1905, with a few longer intervals in September (Jung being away on military service) and December (without any apparent reason). There follow just two further entries (April and July). At this point it should be noted that it is stated in the letter of 13 February 1905: 'She is largely free of hysterical symptoms, and she can therefore be regarded as having recovered'; consequently under the high pressure of work there was no reason for 'superfluous' documentation. This is made clear in the passage in the same letter in which the father's wish for weekly reports on her progress is refused.

The detail: the hospital records open with the usual cover-sheet (see Chapter 5). The entry 'Hereditary condition: yes' refers to the family weakness (as we shall see below). The surname is stated incorrectly as 'Spilrein' (instead of 'Spielrein'). For 'date of birth' only the year of birth is noted (which is unusual). The entry for 'Religion: israel' was the customary house-style for designating Jews. Of Heller's Sanatorium, which is entered as 'previous residence', more will be said later. For the rest, we learn from this first page the dates of her admission and of her discharge, the statement that she had been ill for about two years,[2] and that she was treated as a first-class patient, as well as the provisional and definitive diagnosis of 'hysteria'. On discharge the patient was described as 'better'. It is striking that there is no report on her physical condition. We might be inclined to put down this omission, together with the errors mentioned above, to the advanced hour (she arrived at 10.30 at night). But no documentation of her physical condition is given later either. Only in the entry for 18 October 1904 is mention made of an examination carried out in relation to pains in her feet: 'The examination proved completely negative, merely an exaggerated hyperaesthesia in both feet'. In the letters to her parents her physical health is mentioned briefly as good, even as excellent (26 September 1904 and 28 November 1904 respectively). Comparisons with the hospital records of other hysterical female patients who as such had a marked tendency to somatic symptoms and were therefore examined regularly for restrictions in their field of vision and tested with needles for dysaesthesias, make this circumstance striking. Also missing are her menstrual history and any notes on her menstrual periods.

The accompanying document on the hereditary weakness, which follows, was probably revised at least once. Besides the once more incorrectly spelt surname, it is striking that, apart from the two uncles on the father's side and the maternal grandmother, all the family members mentioned were at least psychologically strange (Chapter 5: 82). It is not possible to trace who provided the statements on which this information rests. At all events the family weakness seemed considerable, suggesting the diagnostic criteria for an hysterical illness. In what follows I shall complete the diagnostic picture of hysteria, using the hospital records as a baseline.

Family anamnesis

PATIENT ANAMNESIS

She was the first of five children. No information is available on the pregnancy and birth. In the hospital records her early childhood is mentioned in two places. According to the patient's statement: 'In my first year I was delicate and ailing. I had stomach pains. Later diphtheria, scarlet fever, measles, and angina a thousand times'. The mother's statement ran: 'As a child she was always ill, particularly with stomach complaints'. There is no information on any other more serious illnesses or hospitalizations. At school she gave the impression of a precocious, intelligent child. At five she entered a Froebel infant school in Warsaw where in all probability she enjoyed a broad education for five years, most of the time separated from her family. At six she was learning German and French. She took Latin as a further foreign language, and in addition singing and piano lessons. She was particularly interested in natural science subjects. According to her own statements she was not very hard working. But according to her mother she worked very hard at the Gymnasium. At that time she was living in the parental home. While she was at the Gymnasium she expressed the wish to study medicine. She left school a year before she entered the Clinic. There is a brief mention in the hospital records of her religious education: 'From her mother she received a very religious upbringing; (God, angels; sins are recorded in heaven in red; a person is responsible for her sins from the age of seven.) As a child she was very pious and prayed a good deal'.

The family situation

The family was well off, the father a businessman, the mother a dentist who, up to a year before her daughter's admission to the Clinic, had practised 'more for pleasure than from necessity'. As a foreigner her daughter must have been treated under a private tariff at the Burghölzli, at a cost of 1250 francs a quarter. Moreover Sabina and at least two of her brothers were able to study abroad.[3] The father is described as irritable, overwrought, neurasthenic and hot-tempered. It appears from various passages in the hospital records that he frequently or regularly hit his children, and addressed his daughter in an 'indecent' way which offended 'modesty'. The father's pathology manifests itself in more detail in numerous passages. Thus he repeatedly threatened suicide, and reacted to 'family upsets' by refusing food and withdrawing to bed. He was an 'unhappy' man. He also 'insulted and tyrannized other members of the household'. Sabina's relationship to her father was very ambivalent. Certainly 'she loved her father "painfully"' and felt sympathy towards him in his extreme states, and yet her relationship with him was clouded by a 'curious abhorrence'. She felt she was not understood by him and her symptomatology was given expression mainly in relation to him (she could not kiss him, could not say 'good morning' to him; see below). It is not clear from the records how much time the father spent at home. On the one hand Sabina was probably in Warsaw for five years (from the ages of 5 to 10); on the other hand we do not know how often the father had to be away on business.

The mother was described as an anxious hysterical woman who suffered, among other things, from 'absences of a childish nature'. A more precise description is to be found in the entry of December 1904:

> ... mother has the odd habit of having to buy everything she sees which she can be talked into buying; every time she goes out shopping she brings home masses of things which no one needs but which are very expensive. She never has enough money on her to pay for everything and therefore has to borrow from relatives and then struggle to repay them

from her household budget. [. . .] The mother likes to play the great lady with her expensive acquisitions.

The mother too hit her daughter on numerous occasions. The relationship with the mother seemed to have been rather more intimate. On the one hand the patient wanted her mother to visit her while she was in hospital, on the other hand the mother tried to protect her daughter from a relationship with Jung which threatened conflict (report of 25.9.1905). The marriage of the Spielrein parents is described in one passage as 'not unhappy'. This statement, probably made through the uncle 'Lublinsky', must be regarded as a glossing over of the situation. It is hardly credible that the personalities of both parties in this marriage as they are described could be 'happy' together. The mother had to try to hush up her financial escapades from her husband. 'Extraordinarily violent rows between the parents' are also described. The three brothers are all described as more or less odd psychologically (one was given to 'hysterical fits of weeping', another was 'very hot-tempered' and suffered from tics, and the third was 'melancholic, and severely hysterical'). She had 'no really intimate relationship with her brothers'. In contradiction to this is the wish, expressed in her 'Last Will' (Chapter 5: 96), to ask her brother what was to be done with the third portion of her ashes. We learn from the Clinic correspondence that the care of a brother, who was apparently living in Zürich at the same time as she was, was to be handed over to her; this idea was repeatedly rejected as inappropriate by the Clinic. The only sister died at the age of six from typhoid, when Sabina Spielrein was 16 years old. 'She loved her sister "more than anything in the world" (. . .) Her death left a terrible mark on her'.

Development of the illness before admission to the Clinic

A brief summary of the development of the illness is given in Jung's referral letter to Freud of 25.9.1905:[4]

> The patient is turning twenty and her affliction appeared distinctly about three years ago. But of course her pathogenic experiences reach far back to her early years. [. . .] The physical chastisements administered to the patient's posterior by her father from the age of four until seven unfortunately became associated with the patient's premature and now highly developed sexual awareness. This sexuality came to be expressed by the patient from very early on by her rubbing her thighs together to commence an act of masturbation. Masturbation always occurred after she underwent punishment from her father. After a while the beatings were no longer necessary to initiate sexual arousal; it came to be triggered through mere threats and other situations implying violence, such as verbal abuse, threatening hand movements, etc. After a time she could

not even look at her father's hands without becoming sexually aroused, or watch him eat without imagining how the food was ejected, and then being thrashed on the buttocks, etc. These associations extended to the younger brother too, who also masturbated frequently from an early age. Threats to the boy or ill-treatment of him aroused her and she had to masturbate whenever she saw him being punished. In time any situation which reflected violence aroused her, for example, being told to obey. As soon as she was alone she was plagued by obsessional fantasies, for example, she would imagine all kinds of torments; the same thing happened in her dreams: for example, she often dreamt that she was eating her lunch and simultaneously sitting on the lavatory and that everything was going straight out through her bottom; at the same she was surrounded by a large crowd of people watching her; on another occasion she was being whipped in front of a great mob of people, etc.

To complement this summary we learn from the hospital records that, as well as the compulsive urge to masturbate which followed actual physical blows and later any subjugating treatment, symbolized for example by laughter, she also 'could not hold her water'. 'She could never watch someone being humiliated without falling into a pathological rage in which she finally had to masturbate.' The conflicts between father and daughter took place not only on the level of physical power. 'When she was chastised, the peak of the experience was that her father was a *man*.' In connection with a remark about the role of parents in society the father reacted with '. . . a big scene, father went wild and threatened suicide. There were often scenes like this, sometimes lasting for days. [. . .] She is always afraid that one day he will kill himself'. Yet 'because of her strong narcissism she cannot give in to her father'. On several occasions the daughter adopted the father's reactions:

Once when, at thirteen, her mother punished her she ran away and hid in various places, doused herself with ice-cold water (in the middle of winter!), and went into the cellar to catch her death of cold; this way she tried to torment her parents and kill herself. In her fifteenth year she tried to starve herself to death because she had made her mother angry.

Furthermore, 'periods of apathy' are described 'as early as her twelfth year'. Somatic symptoms appeared too.

She developed unbearable pain in her feet for the first time after a particularly violent row between her parents. [. . .] so that she could not go out for a long time. Another time she developed pains when she had to travel abroad with her mother under various difficult circumstances.[5]

In addition, borderline paranoid states appeared:

From the age of seven or eight the patient started to talk with a spirit. [. . .] After a while God answered her in the form of an inner voice which spoke more through her feelings than in clear sentences. It seemed to her, however, that this inner voice was speaking to her in *German*. Gradually the idea came to her that it (i.e. the voice) was not God, but an angel sent to her by God because she was an *extraordinary person*. With time she came to see the angel more as a good spirit who supported and guided her. At first the spirit spoke in German too, later in Russian. She often felt as though she understood the meaning of the words earlier ('than' deleted) before she heard them.' . . . The ideas of grandeur, expressed above in her conviction that she was a special person chosen by God, are documented in other passages in the hospital records: 'She wants only the company of educated people. She wants to meet only good, clever people. [. . .] Did not like going to school, the teachers are very stupid.'

In addition, the 'Last Will' (Chapter 5: 96f) bears striking witness to this symptomatology.

These ideas of course had a background of reality. Both in her own estimation and in that of others she was described as very intelligent and precocious.

So much for the course of the illness as it is disclosed in the 'Burghölzli records'. What seems astonishing at this point is that in her situation she could complete her schooling at the Gymnasium with distinction. Finally it came to her admission to hospital:

Thus her situation at home naturally became untenable. After numerous severe disturbances she was brought to Switzerland about a year ago, first to a sanatorium. The doctor there however was no match for her frankly demonic moods and contrary behaviour. She drove everyone there to despair. Finally, the private clinic could no longer cope and she was brought to us here at the asylum.

(Jung's letter to Freud, 25.9.1905 Chapter 5: 105f and Chapter 7)

This passage is not quite correct. Referring to the same point, the statement in the hospital records reads: 'Has been in Interlaken with Dr Heller for a month. Very dissatisfied there. Nothing had been done. She should have gone to Monakov.[6] But M. did not take her because she was too agitated'.[7] Finally, after extreme behaviour at the Hôtel en Ville, she was brought to the Burghölzli in the late evening of 17.8.1904 with a diagnosis of hysteria backed by a report from Dr B.

Condition on entry and progress during hospitalization

I will collect together otherwise separate extracts according to their meaning and present them here in a connected way since, on the one hand, there is no real account of her condition on admission and, on the other, as was customary at that time, the symptomatology is descriptive and, in particular, was not organized according to symptom categories, for example following the AMDP[8] as it would be today. After that the treatment will be discussed in detail; see below.

Disturbances of consciousness and orientation were not in evidence. There were spasmodic disturbances in concentration (in the context of her 'depressive mood swings'; see below). Most prominent are the patient's compulsions which seem closely linked to her tics. 'When she saw a disturbed patient being forcibly moved to another ward, she immediately experienced this irresistible urge' [to masturbate; author]. These disturbances are also described in the correspondence: '. . . it is characteristic of your daughter's nervous disposition that she links all kinds of pathological obsessional fantasies with your person' (23 May 1905) and in the report to Freud already mentioned: 'As soon as she was alone, she was plagued by obsessional fantasies, for example she would imagine all kinds of torments; the same happened in her dreams . . . .' A true symptomatology of psychosis is not present. The illusions described in the following passages seem pathologically bizarre, but there is no suggestion that she believed that her experience was real in any external sense. 'She once said that she had two heads, and her body felt foreign to her [. . .] She felt as if someone were pressing in upon her, as though something were crawling around in her bed, something human. (What?) She also felt as if someone were shouting in her ear. All the time she felt she was totally repulsive, like a dog or a devil. [. . .] Her hands felt as if they did not belong to her. [. . .] She felt something moving on her back like a snail, and something grasped her side like a hand [. . .] she laughed and said, now I can hear your voice double, I feel as if I had two heads, and that the whole of my left side were moving of its own accord.' No ego-disturbances are documented. There are pronounced disturbances of affectivity. 'The patient laughs and cries in a strangely mixed compulsive manner. [. . .] alternating constantly between laughter, weeping, jerking of the head; seductive glances.' Disturbances of vitality affect and depressive episodes: 'After these excesses sometimes a severe depressive reaction'. From time to time she was unable to work, was quickly fatigued, and found no value in life. Anxiety attacks at night (frequently had to have a light at night), 'Fear of going out and of the future'. The most striking symptom was the tics. From the day of her admission and persisting throughout practically the whole of her stay at the hospital: twitching of the legs, sticking out her tongue, jerky rotation of the head, grimaces, defensive gestures. There is even a question of a seizure accompanied by twitching. 'They express abhorrence and revulsion.' 'The patient also reveals many masochistic features. [. . .] She constantly demands that the writer inflict pain on her, treat her badly in some way; we are never merely to ask something of her but to command it. [. . .] She desired this painful treatment with all her strength.' And finally in relation to her 'masturbation compulsion': 'During the act the patient wishes on herself all manner of torments; she pictures these as vividly as possible, in particular being beaten on her bare bottom, and, in order to increase her arousal, she imagines that it is taking place in front of a large audience'. In addition many physical complaints: 'Stabbing pains here and there, in the limbs, chest and head', painful hypersensitivity in the feet and hands, abasia, and headaches.

In several passages she is described as very 'sensitive': 'At the slightest sign of lack of respect or trust she immediately retaliates with very negativistic behaviour and a succession of greater or lesser devilish tricks'. This striking, partly infantile behaviour is given much space in the patient's records. There is no lack of description of various kinds of challenging opposition. Jung writes further on the subject in his report to Freud: 'There is a certain callousness and unreasonableness in her character, and she lacks any feeling for situation and for external propriety: but much of this must naturally be put down to Russian peculiarities'.

After an evaluation of the available material, and in accordance with the concept as it was understood at the time, the diagnosis would be correctly given as hysteria.[9]

The therapy

'By using your method I have analysed the affliction fairly thoroughly and with considerable success, from the outset.' This statement of Jung's in his report to Freud of 25 September 1905 is eminently significant. It indicates, together with other material, that Sabina Spielrein was the first patient on whom he practised Freudian psychoanalysis. As I shall show in more detail below, all hysterical patients admitted to the hospital before this date were treated, if at all, by hypnosis.

In relation to Jung's statement, however, a reading of the hospital records proves rather disappointing. The notes give hardly any indication of the 'method'.

The detail: 'Patient is extremely sensitive, especially with regard to any stimulation. Strict bed-rest therefore. No books, no conversation, no visitors. A doctor visits only once a day. The nurse goes into her room only once an hour for five minutes. [. . .] Yesterday the medical assistant forbade her to leave her bed, whereupon the patient made a point of getting up, and declared energetically that she would never obey, that she never wanted to get well, and that she would behave badly. On being suitably coaxed by the writer she immediately returned to bed perfectly calm.' In addition she was periodically forbidden to write to her mother, and later to her father. Promises were extracted from her to behave sensibly. She was forcibly put to bed. By means of these 'therapeutic' methods attempts were made in the first two months of her hospitalization to gain control of the patient's 'tricksterish behaviour', over which her caretakers in Interlaken had despaired. In the course of events the patient 'calmed down' to such an extent that the use of such force was given up, not least because it was recognized that the direct use of force, threats and disciplinary measures led to an accentuation of the symptoms which had their roots in childhood traumas connected with her parents' violence. Other methods, in the sense of behavioural and occupational therapy, are being tried out just a month after admission: 'We have now happily succeeded in stimulating Miss Spielrein's interest in scientific pursuits, so that she can be distracted for hours at a time from her pathological obsessions' (Correspondence, 26 September 1904). She was evidently admitted to lectures at the Clinic (cf. Hospital Records, entry for 4.11.1904), and later worked in the anatomy laboratory and took part in association experiments.[10] Even after her discharge the family were recommended to release their daughter from family duties of any kind and to help her to avoid contact with her brother who was then in Zürich.

From the physical point of view reference is made in two passages to the treatment of severe headaches: on one occasion, when it is accompanied by tachycardia, with morphine, on the other with 'compresses'.

At the beginning there was no question of cooperation from the patient. Massive resistances were in place: 'It takes a powerful battle to entice pat. to make this confession. [. . .] Every conversation with her aimed at obtaining information is as difficult as walking on eggshells'. When from time to time there was talk in these discussions of her parents' chastisements, she reacted violently. Jung notes in one passage: 'At this point numerous tics, grimaces and gestures of abhorrence'. As early as her second day in hospital Jung established a connection between the appearance of these disturbances and the trauma of parental violence hidden behind them. In the entry of 10 October 1904 he writes further: 'The chastisements form the central complex'. The direct axis to the early childhood sexual trauma remained hidden from him however till the end of November when the patient '. . . spontaneously admitted to masturbating'. There had been no lack of previous indications that the chastisements, as Jung formulated in his report to Freud in 1905, '. . . had unfortunately become associated with the patient's premature and now highly developed sexual awareness'. Thus it was a question of 'modesty' originating in her childhood; from the 'peak moment' in the chastisements when her father was a *man*. 'He still occasionally makes indecent remarks'. Even in relation to the Interlaken drawing (see Chapter 5: 91) Jung writes on 10 October 1904: '. . . it shows Dr Heller giving pat. electrical treatment. The position is a remarkably sexual one'. When the patient was finally able to talk about her masturbation compulsion, Jung recognized the roots of her symptoms: 'Basically all her gestures of revulsion and her negative behaviour can be traced back to this complex [sexual associ-ation to the physical trauma; present author]. She sees herself as a thoroughly bad and corrupt person, and feels therefore that she should not be allowed to be in the company of other people'. It seems highly astonishing to me that incest was never brought into the discussion, either by Jung, or later by Freud. Freud writes to Jung (27 October 1906): 'Infantile fixation of the libido on the father – the typical choice of object; anal auto-erotism'. In his lecture of 1907 Jung accepted this interpretation. It emerges from the hospital records that, as the patient slowly improved, she was increasingly able to analyse her childhood traumas with Jung and to accept them as an aetio-logical factor; it is also clear, however, that it was only the introduction of the sexual components after the turn of the year 1904/5 that brought about the conclusive result.

References to the work with dreams, however, are very scanty. As a com-parison: of the few hysterical patients, men and women, whom Jung treated in the hospital, only in two cases are analyses of dreams documented. One was published by Jung in his paper 'Association, dream and hysterical symp-tom' (there will be further discussion of this work below) and the other was the case mentioned in the letter to Freud of 2 January 1908.[11] Only the entry of 11 November 1904 suggests possible work on 'associative material': 'She breaks off writing a letter in order to write down, with her eyes closed, all the fantasies that go through her mind. In these associations the doctors again play a central role, and her favourite pastime, numerous pranks: com-plex fantasy', as well as the above-mentioned dreams with masochistic con-tent. Analyses of these associations or of the dreams are nowhere to be found in a concrete sense. It is a question of the occasional brief mention of 'the following analysis'. In the entry of 29 January 1905 (the last but three) Jung notes: 'Since the last abreaction substantial improvement. Still strongly emo-tional and unusually powerful expressions of feeling. At every stimulation of the complex she still reacts with her back, hands, tongue and mouth, though significantly less so'. And finally in the next entry three months later, shortly after Sabina Spielrein had taken up her studies: 'In the last few weeks distinctly improved and increasingly calm. Now listens to lectures conscientiously and with interest. . . .'

Evidently for the final months of her hospitalization Jung gave up docu-menting further developments in any detail. It is therefore not clear what the nature of the subsequent treatment was. The only thing that is certain is that she remained in treatment with Jung as an outpatient for another four years after she was discharged on 1 June 1905 as 'better'.

I will emphasize at this point the special status which Sabina Spielrein enjoyed as a patient. For a patient to attend lectures and take part in scientific 'in-house' experiments is unique in Jung's time at the Burghölzli. The missing (or undocumented) report on the physical condition of an hysterical patient is also very striking. She certainly enjoyed medical care which was out of the ordinary. One possible reason for this was surely her personality and the transference and countertransference situation with C.G. Jung; another lies in her role as an object of the spectacular success which flattered her therapist's confidence in such a timely way, occurring as it did parallel with Jung's achieving university lectureship (17 February 1905).

In the next section I will investigate the question of what influence this successful therapy exerted on Jung and on Bleuler's clinic.

The influence on the work of C.G. Jung and on the treatment of hysterical patients at the Burghölzli Clinic

Jung writes with justification in his letter to Freud (5.10.1906): 'I am still pretty far from understanding the therapy and the genesis of hysteria because our material on hysteria is rather meagre'. That meagreness is borne out by the figures given below.

In the first thirty years after the opening of the Clinic (1870–1900) six or seven patients on average per year, men and women, were hospitalized with a diagnosis of 'hysteria'. It should be observed in this context that the diagnostic key underwent numerous changes in the assessment reports at this time, so that 'pure hysterias' were diagnosed in only a few of the years in question. Hysteria was rather subsumed variously under 'periodic, primary or secondary insanity', 'simple psychosis', 'inherited idiopathic psychosis', 'inherited and constitutional psychosis', and others, and/or it appeared as a diagnostic component of other clinical pictures, for example 'hysterical epilepsy', 'hystero-epilepsy', 'hysterical madness', 'hysteria and imbecility', etc. This confusion in terminology is to be explained not through changes in clinical directors but as reflecting accurately the uncertainty regarding the concept of hysteria at that time. It is remarkable how few patients with such a diagnosis were hospitalized compared with numbers in France as reported in publications of exponents of psychiatry there. Furthermore the figures given in the annual statistics are not exact. A precise review of the hospital records archive yielded different figures (mostly one or two more patients per year, see Table below).

Newly hospitalized hysterical female patients in Jung's time at the Burghölzli

1900:	3 (0)	1905:	9 (3)
1901:	2 (2)	1906:	3 (0)
1902:	4 (1)	1907:	3 (0)
1903:	8 (1)	1980:	10 (2)
1904:	11 (6)	1909:	7 (0)

Numbers in brackets are those in treatment with Jung.

Source: Burghölzli hospital records.

These figures require further explanation. While he was at the Burghölzli Jung moved up the hierarchical structure as far as deputy clinic director and had therefore varying areas of responsibility. From 11 December 1900 to 31 March 1902 he was a second medical assistant; from 1 April 1902 to 30 September 1902 a first assistant; finally Jung went to France to the Salpêtrière (returning on 14 April 1903), and, as we shall see later, that was of great significance. After a period of voluntary status in the summer of that year, he again took up his duties as deputy to the senior physician until 18 April 1905. Finally from 19 April 1905 to 15 April 1909 he was effectively the senior physician.[12] This meant, among other things, that only from the spring of 1905 (as senior physician) was he authorized to care for outpatients, men and women. To put it another way: this shows that before Sabina Spielrein's admission to the Burghölzli he had had experience of treating only eight hysterical patients (apart from an unknown number during his time in France). After these introductory remarks I will now turn again to Jung's early publications.

In 1901 Prof. Bleuler commissioned Jung to carry out association experiments at the Clinic; research had been carried out in this field for some time, mostly in German psychiatry, Aschaffenburg deserving particular mention. At the same time German psychiatry was very much under the influence of the 'somatic' tendency at the end of the nineteenth century. Of course the 'psychic' tendency also had prominent representatives in Germany, for example Paul Julius Moebius. In the same year Jung was working under Bleuler on his dissertation 'On the psychology and pathology of so-called occult phenomena', which appeared in 1902. We can easily deduce from the bibliography of that work that Jung was principally orientated towards the writings of the French school which, following Mesmerism, tried to approach psychologically based mental disturbances chiefly through hypnosis and suggestion. With these at first sight contradictory tasks, Jung entered a field in which the opposites were far from resolved. The medical directorate of the Clinic had close links with the French school. Auguste Forel (director from 6.4.1879–15.4.1898) was on most familiar terms with Liébault and Bernheim, while later Eugen Bleuler (director from 16.4.1898–1927) was conversant with Janet (Jung himself was with Janet in 1902/1903). The 'flaw' in all this lay in the criticism that scientific criteria were not satisfactorily met by these approaches. With the help of experimental work the gap was to be bridged. The conflict was resolved: from Jung's paper 'The psychopathological significance of the association experiment' we learn:

> Although there is more interest in psychology as a subject nowadays among non-psychologists than there was a few decades ago, nonetheless the relative youth of experimental psychology does mean that in this sphere little has as yet been clarified, and there is a good deal of controversy over many aspects of the subject. [. . .] One wants to make

psychology a creed, the other a science. Understandably these entirely divergent tendencies are in conflict with and hinder each other. [. . .] So long as it is a matter of dogmas and axioms, which owe their existence to the *petitio* principle, one cannot hope for clarity, for each dogma entails a certain obscurity, as is well known. We are, therefore waiting for enlightenment from experimental psychology which, it is true, is still in its infancy yet can already look back on a rich harvest from the work in this field.

(Jung 1906c, para. 863)

In short, it was most important at that time to defend the position of the French school in this 'scientific dispute'. Freud's thinking was certainly taken into account, but it had no significance in clinical psychiatry at the Burghölzli. In Jung's dissertation Freud is cited only briefly and critically. Jung himself writes in *Memories, Dreams, Reflections*:

As early as 1900 I had read Freud's *The Interpretation of Dreams*. I had laid the book aside, at the time, because I did not yet grasp it. At the age of twenty-five I lacked the experience to appreciate Freud's theories. Such experience did not come until later. In 1903 I once more took up *The Interpretation of Dreams* and discovered how it all linked up with my own ideas.

(Jung 1973: 169–70)

This sequence of events is elucidated by Jung's publications. In his second paper of 1902, 'A case of hysterical stupor in a prisoner in detention' (incidentally his first case of an hysterical patient; Miss S.W. in his dissertation was not a patient), the work of Freud and Breuer receives a mere mention. He refers to the term 'hysterical conversion' as denoting the 'primary phenomenon in the genesis of hysterical symptoms' (Jung 1902, para. 298). In his next work, 'On manic mood disorder' (1903), there is no reference to Freud. In the same year 'On simulated insanity' appears. The following quotation comes from that work:

How far this [mental; present author] disposition to neutralize affects in a faulty or abnormal way coincides with hysteria is not easy to determine, but according to Freud's theory of hysteria the two are identical.

(Jung 1903, para. 318)

He contrasts Janet's position, which I will not go into in more detail here, with Freud's view. As I mentioned in my introductory remarks, Jung stayed with Janet during this year. In 1904, the year of Sabina Spielrein's admission to the Clinic, Jung published three papers: 'On hysterical misreading', 'A medical opinion on a case of simulated insanity', and, with Franz Riklin,

'The associations of normal subjects'. In this last paper there is only a brief mention of Freud, in relation to a subject who was able to complete an unconscious train of thought through 'free association'.

Let us now imagine where Jung stood at this point in time with his experimental work and his clinical experience. He had been working (together with Riklin) on his experiments for a good three years. In 1903 there followed, as Jung himself writes, his rediscovery of Freud's *Interpretation of Dreams*, through which he recognized its congruence with his own work. His early interest, as his dissertation shows, was focused on hysteria. His clinical experience of hysteria was meagre, as I showed above. His first published case was Godwina F. (hysterical stupor). Sabina Spielrein entered this situation at the Clinic in the autumn of 1904 as a very severe case of hysteria. For whatever motives, Jung began by trying out the Freudian 'method' on her. Using obviously quite useless disciplinary measures to begin with, then later working over childhood memories and related 'associative material', he reached such an improved situation in so short a time that Sabina Spielrein was able to take up her medical studies in the spring of 1905. This must have left a lasting impression on Jung. His rapprochement to Freud was strengthened by the circumstance that Sabina Spielrein's symptomatology was an expression of a sexual compulsion (with its roots in childhood trauma). Above all he found in Spielrein's symptoms confirmation of the mechanism of repression and support for the therapeutic approach resulting from it. As we know, however, this did not lead to an unconditional acceptance of the 'sexual trauma' postulated by Freud. Thus Jung writes in *Memories, Dreams, Reflections*:

> The situation was different when it came to the content of the repression. Here I could not agree with Freud. He considered the cause of the repression to be a sexual trauma, [and that did not satisfy me].
>
> (Jung 1973: 170)

> [phrase in brackets is in the original German but has been omitted from the English version; trans.]

In the Jung–Freud correspondence too, from its inception in 1906, this point remained a subject of discussion. From another point of view too the Sabina Spielrein case stood at the turning point of Jung's work. It was now a question not only of providing the French school with a scientific base, but of bringing the Freudian approach into clinical work; this began with Sabina Spielrein, and it obtained support for Freud's still very controversial views. Through the work of Auguste Forel the reputation of the Burghölzli was an outstanding one right across Europe. In these circumstances the risk of being the first clinic to clear the way for Freud's thought was considerable. This conflict, to which Eugen Bleuler as the director at that time saw himself exposed, is revealed in his (Bleuler's) ambivalent attitude to the psycho-analytic movement, as emerges in the Jung–Freud letters.

Briefly, Jung was prudent enough not to publish his spectacular case. Only in 1907, in a lecture, did Jung elucidate the fundamentals of Freud's thought by using Sabina Spielrein as an example. With good reason he was anxious not to depart from the path of 'scientific research' on which he had embarked. However, to return now to Jung's publications.

With regard to the papers which appeared in 1905 it is important to bear in mind that these were based on the experience and work of the preceding year. In 'Cryptomnesia' Jung presents among others the case of an hysterical woman patient, who in all probability is Sabina Spielrein. It is true that the hospital records do not contain the following observation, but as I have already shown in my introduction, Sabina Spielrein was one of the few hys-terical patients in treatment with Jung apart from Godwina F. (in 'A case of hysterical stupor in a prisoner in detention'). Looking through these other case notes we can only conclude that Sabina Spielrein is the patient described:

> Still more drastic examples are provided by hysteria, which is nothing other than a caricature of normal psychological mechanisms. Recently I had to treat a hysterical young lady who became ill chiefly because she had been brutally beaten by her father. Once, when we were out for a walk, this lady dropped her cloak in the dust. I picked it up, and tried to get the dust off by beating it with my stick. The next moment the lady hurled herself upon me with violent defensive gestures and tore the cloak out of my hands. She said she couldn't stand the sight, it was quite unendurable to her. I at once guessed the connection and urged her to tell me the motives for her behaviour. She was nonplussed, and could only say that it was extremely unpleasant for her to see her cloak cleaned like that. These symptomatic actions, as Sigmund Freud calls them, are very common among hysterics. The explanation is simple. A feeling-toned memory complex, though not present in consciousness at the moment, motivates certain actions from its invisible seat in the unconscious just as if it were present in the conscious mind.
>
> (Jung 1905a, para. 170)

And further:

> It may be that the majority of hysterical persons are ill because they possess a mass of memories, highly charged with affect and therefore deeply rooted in the unconscious, which cannot be controlled and which tyrannize the conscious mind and will of the patient. [and para. 172]: Anyone who has read Freud's dream analyses or, better still, has done some himself, will know how the unconscious can bedevil the most

innocent and decent-minded people with sexual symbols whose lewdness is positively horrifying.

> (Jung 1905a, paras. 176 & 172)

In 'The psychological diagnosis of evidence' (1905) we find:

> These [aspects of psychopathology; present author] are the principles of Sigmund Freud's ingenious psychoanalysis. Only when one has completely assimilated Freud's method is one able with any certainty to consider associations from a psychoanalytical point of view.

> (Jung 1905b, para. 761)

In 'An analysis of the associations of an epileptic' (1905) Jung refers briefly to Freud's work *The Psychopathology of Everyday Life* in connection with slips of the tongue. The third paper in the series of *Studies in Word Association*, 'The reaction-time ratio in the association experiment', contains in relation to Freud merely a few elucidations of his terminology, for example 'treatment of symptoms', 'censorship' and 'repression'.

In Jung's next paper, 'Experimental observations on the faculty of memory' (1905), Freud is cited for the first time in more detail in reference to his own observations, for example linking 'forgetting' and 'not wanting to remember' with repressed experiences associated with unpleasure.

> It is to the credit of Freud, and partly also of Breuer – as is probably well known – that they have amply demonstrated this fact (forgetting equated with repression) in hysterical patients. The validity of this can be doubted only by someone who has not himself tested Freudian psychoanalysis (para. 640). . . . These investigations [i.e. Riklin's] fully confirm the correctness of Freud's teachings on this point (para. 657).

> (Jung 1905c)

So far it is clear that Jung is supporting Freud's ideas with increasing enthusiasm. There is neither a direct contrast with his own work nor an incorporation of it.

In 'Psychoanalysis and association experiments' Jung now ventures to take this step. After again establishing his support for Freud's position in his introduction he comments: 'I may therefore be allowed to try to open up new avenues to Freud's body of knowledge' (Jung 1906d, para. 665). In this paper Jung presents the case of 'Miss E', who consulted him with a request for treatment by hypnosis on account of insomnia, inner restlessness and irritation. But: 'An attempt at hypnosis was frustrated because she could not keep her eyes fixed on anything. [. . .] I therefore carried out the association experiment with her' (Jung 1906d, para. 666). He compared psychoanalysis directly with this experiment:

Just as hesitating, faulty reproduction and all the other characteristic disturbances always occur in the association experiment whenever the complex is touched on, so in the analysis difficulties always arise whenever one gets close to the complex. In order to bypass these difficulties, Freud, as is well known, induces 'free associations'. [. . .] In this case I carried out psychoanalysis strictly on Freud's lines.

(Jung 1906d, para. 704)

I will not discuss the case itself here. In any event the treatment had a 'happy outcome'. Jung does not neglect to point out how he differs from Freud:

I therefore put the emphasis on arousing and strengthening of the will and not on mere 'abreacting', as Freud originally did. [. . .] It therefore gives me great satisfaction to draw attention to Freud's theories – at the risk of also becoming a victim of persistent amnesia.

(Jung 1906d, paras. 725 & 726)

Finally in 1906, in 'Association, dream and hysterical symptom', his seventh paper in this series, Jung goes a step further. This is the case of Mrs S, whose hospitalization of barely three months was unsuccessful. Here Jung compares not 'free association' but the analysis of a series of dreams with his association experiment, in order finally 'to apply our knowledge of the form and content of the sexual complex, gained in the two previous chapters, to the symptoms of the illness' (Jung 1906b, para. 845). As has already been mentioned, Jung emphasizes:

The interferences that the complex causes in the association experiment are none other than resistances in psychoanalysis, as described by Freud.

(Jung 1906b, para. 859)

So much for the significance of the Sabina Spielrein case in relation to Jung's attitude to Freud's ideas as it is expressed in his publications. Now it remains to answer the question of how far this experience had an impact on the treatment of hysterical patients from the point of view of the management of the Clinic. In that connection I should like to refer to my introductory remarks at the beginning of this section. There I drew attention to the connection of the Burghölzli with the French school. The hospital records made during Forel's time at the Clinic are very rudimentary. Thus only the odd reference to hypnosis is found in them. Eugen Bleuler laid down firm guidelines for organizing hospital records clearly. The first hysterical patient (presented as Miss E. in Jung's dissertation as a case of sleep-walking) to be admitted to the hospital (17.9–14.11.1898) after Bleuler took charge as director of the clinic had already been treated by means of hypnosis. Two quotations from the hospital records make this clear. In the entry of 26.10 we read:

> Treated with hypnosis since 22.10; after the first hypnosis slept the whole night, still well since then, headache quite mild [and on 7.11]: Through daily hypnosis the headache has consistently decreased.

Let it be mentioned at this point that with Miss E., as with most other cases, but in contrast to Sabina Spielrein, a detailed account of the patient's physical condition is given (see also Jung's dissertation, p. 6). The relatively small number of hospitalized hysterical patients, men and women, now allows us to follow the treatment they received.

Of the total of twenty-eight male and female patients with the diagnosis of hysteria who were hospitalized from the time when Jung took up his post there up to the admission of Sabina Spielrein, nine were evidently treated by means of hypnosis (according to the records). The small number of documented attempts at treatment is explained partly by the fact that in some individual cases their stay in hospital lasted only a few days, and partly because once the association experiments began in 1901 a new approach was found. It is important to note that in not a single case are 'free association' or dream analyses recorded. I examined Sabina Spielrein's hospital records in detail in the previous section. After her admission mention is made in only one set of records (up to April 1909 when Jung left his post) of hypnosis being used as a treatment. It is quite another matter with reports of the 'Freudian method'. From the spring of 1905 mention is made at first sporadically, and then frequently, of dreams and their analyses, and indeed not only with the few patients treated by Jung (among them being the two cases Jung published in his writings). With his first and impressive success following the 'Freudian method' Jung had effected the introduction of Freud's thought into the practice of the Clinic. It is understandable therefore, even if we reject Carotenuto's interpretation of the later relationship between Jung and Spielrein, that Jung writes in his letter of 4 June 1909: 'She was my psychoanalytic test-case as it were, and for that reason I hold her in special gratitude and affection'.

Summary

Treatment by hypnosis, as it was practised at the Burghölzli Psychiatric Clinic first under Prof. A. Forel from 1880, had its origins in the French school (Liébault and Bernheim, in Nancy; Janet, at the Salpêtrière in Paris). Hypnosis was vulnerable to the criticisms resulting from the conflict between the 'somatics' and the 'psychics' which had been levelled at it for almost a hundred years. The aim of the association experiments carried out by Jung from 1901 under the aegis of Prof. E. Bleuler was not least to be able to meet the criticism of a lack of scientific foundation. In the course of the association experiments Jung discovered the congruence between his observations of the complexes of hysterical female patients and the dynamics of the genesis of hysteria as postulated by Freud.

After a long history of illness and an intervening hospitalization in Interlaken in the summer of 1904, Sabina Spielrein (1885–1942; later the well-known Russian psychoanalyst) enters the Burghölzli Clinic. She is suffering from a severe form of hysteria with manifold symptoms. C.G. Jung takes on the patient's treatment in his capacity as deputy to the senior physician. Jung, who has little experience of hysterical patients at his disposal, puts himself to the test with Sabina Spielrein by using the Freudian 'method' for the first time. The result is decisive. Within less than six months the patient is free of her symptoms to the extent that she can take up the study of medicine in the spring of 1905. This highly impressive success was not without consequences for Jung's work.

Before Sabina Spielrein's admission, Freud was certainly acknowledged at the Burghölzli, but he exerted no influence there. Evidence for this is found particularly in Jung's publications before 1905, in which, if Freud is mentioned at all, it is only briefly and critically. After the 'Spielrein experience' Jung began to support Freud with increasing enthusiasm in his writings, and by that means secured an entry for his ideas into clinical psychiatry. Sabina Spielrein therefore stands at the beginning of the Jung–Freud relationship; she provided a key experience at a turning-point not only for Jung but for the whole Clinic – as 'a psychoanalytic test-case so to speak', as Jung wrote to Freud on 4.6.1909 (McGuire 1974: 228).

Notes

1 This article was first published in German in *Luzifer-Amor, Zeitschrift zur Geschichte der Psychoanalyse*, Vol. 7, No. 14, 1994, entitled 'Sabina Spielrein. Jungs Patientin am Burghölzli' by Bernard Minder. Reprinted in English in the *Journal of Analytical Psychology* in January 2001, Vol 46, 1, by kind permission of *Luzifer-Amor* and the C.G. Jung Estate.

2 This entry is obviously incorrect as the further anamnesis below shows.

3 By a decree of the Czar the admission of Jewish students to the universities in Russia was restricted. This led to a mass exodus of the Jewish intelligentsia (and of anti-czarist political activists). According to the student records at the turn of the century, Zürich provided a haven for a veritable Russian colony at that time.

4 This document is remarkable from several points of view and justifies the extensive comment given in Note 13 of Chapter 5. See also chapter 7.

5 Sabina Spielrein's 'foot' is interesting from several points of view. As we know from the Jung–Freud correspondence, and also from a lecture of Jung's in 1907, Sabina Spielrein used her foot to inhibit her defaecation in the context of her 'infantile perversion' (anal erotism, according to Freud). A quotation from Jung's lecture runs thus: 'The earliest symptoms occur between the third and fourth years of life. At that time the patient began to withhold her stool for as long as she could until she was forced by the pain to defaecate. Gradually she began to employ a

supporting procedure: she crouched in a squatting position on the heel of one foot and tried to defaecate in this position, while at the same time blocking her anus with her heel. She continued with this perverse practice until her seventh year' (Carotenuto). The 'painful foot' emerged again in 1911. From the letter from Jung to Spielrein (probably 21/22.9.1911) it appears that because of a 'painful foot' Sabina Spielrein was unable to attend the Weimar Congress (Carotenuto; cf. also Jung's interpretation of this phenomenon). In 1913 Sabina Spielrein herself published a paper with the title 'Self-gratification in foot-symbolism' (cf. Sabina Spielrein, 'Collected Writings').

6 Constantin von Monakov, a Russian émigré. Came to Zürich in 1866. Studied medicine. Assistant at the Burghölzli under Prof. Hitzig. Qualified as university lecturer in neurology at the University of Zürich. In addition to his epoch-making work in the field of brain anatomy, he ran a private clinic with 10–12 patients.

7 No transfer document either from the Heller Sanatorium or from Prof. Monakov has been discovered to date. The sanatorium report on Spielrein's one-month hospitalization in 1904, which Jung asked for in his letter of 18.8.1904, has not been preserved.

8 Association for Methodology and Documentation in Psychiatry.

9 In his 1907 lecture in Amsterdam Jung speaks of a 'case of *psychotic* hysteria', which one can accept as being in accordance with the symptomatology described in the hospital records. In the diagnostic key as it then stood at the Clinic, this finer distinction did not exist; that explains the absence of the word 'psychotic' from the cover-sheet of the hospital records.

10 There is no reference in the hospital records to Sabina Spielrein's having undergone an association test herself. It is nevertheless hardly likely that among the few hysterical patients who were in the hospital at that time she alone would be left out in this respect. We learn from the entry of 29.1.1905: 'She recently tried associations with acquaintances and on this occasion it was shown that she could not say her complex trigger-word "to beat". So she omitted it during the experiment'.

11 'At the moment I am treating another case of severe hysteria with twilight states. It's going well. She is a twenty-six-year-old student. The case is an uncommonly interesting one. I work almost exclusively with dream analyses, the other sources being too scanty. The transference dreams started very early in the most miraculous way, many of them are of somnambulistic clarity' (Jung to Freud, 2.1.1908).

12 On 7.3.1909, with an accompanying letter from Prof. Bleuler, Jung tenders his resignation from the Clinic on the grounds 'that I should like to devote myself more than previously to "scientific pursuits"'. In order to be able to do further work on his experiments, he asks in the same letter to retain his voluntary status. Three days later on 10 March 1909 these requests were granted by a motion of the directorate of the health authority through the executive body. Shortly before this Jung had approached the executive body with the request, accompanied by a letter from Bleuler, to be released from his duties as deputy to the senior physician in the clinical sector and instead to take over the running of the research laboratory. The request was granted subject to a few conditions. (Source: State Archive of the Canton of Zürich.) What is most interesting about this application for resignation is its date. On the same day Jung wrote a letter to Freud in which his resignation is not mentioned. The main subject of that letter is Sabina Spielrein (McGuire 1974).

References

C. G. Jung (1961). *Memories, Dreams, Reflections*. Recorded and edited by Aniela Jaffé. London: Fontana, 1973.

—— (1902) 'A case of hysterical stupor in a prisoner in detention'. *CW* 1.

—— (1903) 'On simulated insanity'. *CW* 1.

—— (1904) 'On hysterical misreading'. *CW* 1.

—— (1905a) 'Cryptomnesia'. *CW* 1.

—— (1905b) 'The psychological diagnosis of evidence'. *CW* 2.

—— (1905c) 'Experimental observations on the faculty of memory'. *CW* 2.

—— (1906a) 'A third and final opinion on two contradictory psychiatric diagnoses'. *CW* 1.

—— (1906b) 'Association, dream, and hysterical symptom'. *CW* 2.

—— (1906c) 'The psychopathological significance of the association experiment'. *CW* 2.

—— (1906d) 'Psychoanalysis and association experiments'. *CW* 4.

McGuire, W. (1974) (ed.) *The Freud/Jung Letters*. London: Hogarth/Routledge & Kegan Paul.

Chapter 7

A document. Jung to Freud 1905: A report on Sabina Spielrein

Bernard Minder

(Translated from the German by Barbara Wharton)

A recently discovered letter, dated September 25, 1905, proves that Jung's first attempt to get in contact with Freud had taken place earlier than it had been assumed on the basis of their published correspondence. The letter contains a brief case history of Sabina Spielrein's illness. It was addressed to Freud and handed over to Sabina Spielrein's mother who intended to remove her daughter from Jung with whom the girl had fallen in love. However, the letter was never passed on to Freud.

Introduction

In 1980, in *Diario di una segreta simmetria – Sabina Spielrein tra Jung e Freud*, Carotenuto published the diaries and letters of Sabina Spielrein which had been discovered in Geneva in 1977. In 1986 it became possible to supplement this material for the first time in German from the missing letters of C.G. Jung.[1] By means of these publications a pioneer of the psychoanalytic movement was brought into focus – someone who, almost exemplifying the fate of significant women of that time, had fallen into oblivion.

Sabina Spielrein was born in Russia in Rostov-on-Don in 1885. She developed signs of severe hysteria in early childhood. As a highly intelligent girl she was able to complete her schooling with great success, in spite of her psychological difficulties. In 1904 she was brought to Switzerland in a desperate state and was admitted to the Burghölzli Psychiatric Clinic on 17 August 1904. She remained an outpatient of Jung's until 1909. With the material he published, Carotenuto tried to claim that the transference/countertransference situation between Spielrein and Jung had developed in a sinister way.[2] The letter, which I published in an earlier paper (see Note 4, Chapter 6), contributes to a clarification of the relationship between Jung and Spielrein.

This letter is significant in another way too. It documents Jung's attempts to get in touch with Freud. When this letter did not fulfil his intention, Jung again made an approach and laid the foundation of their collaboration by sending Freud his *Studies in Word Association*. Apparently the previous report never reached Freud, since in his second letter to Freud, on 23 October 1906, Jung presents a brief sketch of the history of Sabina Spielrein's illness.[3]

This letter, signed by Jung, was found in duplicate form in the 'copy-book' of the Burghölzli University Psychiatric Clinic. From 1878 (the Clinic was opened in 1870) all the letters of the medical director which left the hospital were stored in duplicate; they were kept in their entirety, in bound format, until 1936. They contain the correspondence relating to male and female inpatients. A letter of a private nature rarely appears. Unfortunately only a few isolated examples of letters sent to the Clinic remain in preservation. The present letter is partly known to us from Carotenuto's work, but the date is there marked as an 'error' with the comment that the documented Jung–Freud correspondence began on 11.4.1906.

I am grateful to the relatives of Sabina Spielrein and to the medical director of the Burghölzli Clinic (Prof. Dr D. Hell) for permission to publish the letter.

The letter ('report')

Source: Burghölzli copy-books, Vol. 63; Burghölzli Archive.
Transcription accurate regarding text, but not regarding lines.

25.9.1905
Report on Miss Spielrein to Professor Freud in Vienna, delivered to Mrs Spielrein for use if the occasion arises.

Dear Professor,

The daughter of Mrs Spielrein, Miss Sabina Spielrein, student of medicine, suffers from hysteria.

The patient suffers significantly from an hereditary weakness, both father and mother being hysteric, especially the mother. A brother of the patient has suffered severely from hysteria from an early age.

The patient is turning twenty and her affliction appeared distinctly about three years ago. But of course her pathogenic experiences reach far back to her early years. By using your method I have analysed the clinical condition fairly thoroughly and with considerable success from the outset.

The analysis has essentially established the following:

The physical chastisements administered to the patient's posterior by her father from the age of four until seven had unfortunately become associated with the patient's premature and now highly developed sexual awareness. This sexuality came to be expressed by the patient from very early on by her rubbing her thighs together to commence an act of masturbation. Masturbation always occurred after she underwent punishment from her father. After a while the beatings were no longer necessary to initiate sexual arousal; it came to be triggered through mere threats and other situations implying violence, such as verbal abuse, threatening movements of the hands, etc. After a time she could not even look at her father's hands without becoming sexually aroused, or watch him eat without imagining how the food was ejected, and then being thrashed on the buttocks, etc. These associations extended to the younger brother too, who also masturbated frequently from an early age. Threats to the boy or ill-treatment of him aroused her and she had to masturbate whenever she saw him being punished. In time any situation which reflected violence aroused her, for instance being told to obey. As soon as she was alone she was plagued by obsessional fantasies, for example, she would imagine all kinds of torments; the same thing happened in her dreams: for example, she often dreamt that she was eating her lunch and simultaneously sitting on the lavatory and that everything was going straight out through her bottom; at the same time she was surrounded by a large crowd of people watching her; on another occasion she was being whipped in front of a great mob of people, etc.

Thus her situation at home naturally became untenable. After numerous severe disturbances she was brought to Switzerland about a year ago, first to a sanatorium. The doctor there however was no match for her frankly demonic moods and contrary behaviour. She drove everyone there to despair. Finally the private clinic could no longer cope and she was brought to us here at the asylum. She initially harassed everybody, tormenting the nurses to the limits of their endurance. As the analysis progressed, her condition noticeably improved and she finally emerged as a highly intelligent and talented person of great sensibility. There is a certain callousness and unreasonableness in her character and she lacks any kind of feeling for situation and for external propriety, but much of this must be put down to Russian peculiarities.

Her condition improved so much that she could commence studies last summer term. She suffers enormously whenever she meets with members of her family, something that the mother cannot quite comprehend, but which should be understandable on reading the above (Mrs Spielrein knows about the most important part of her daughter's complex).

During treatment the patient had the misfortune to fall in love with me. She raves on to her mother about her love in an ostentatious manner, and a secret perverse enjoyment of her mother's dismay seems to play a not inconsiderable part. In view of this situation her mother therefore wishes, if the necessity arises, to place her elsewhere for treatment, with which I am naturally in agreement.

Remaining at your service and most faithfully yours,

Dr Jung.

Discussion

The date of the document is remarkable in several respects. For one thing this is the first attempt by Jung to make contact with Freud. Furthermore the letter was written on the letterhead of the medical director three months after Sabina Spielrein had been discharged from the Burghölzli. What made Jung use the medical director's note-paper for his outpatient? The simplest explanation probably lies in the following circumstances.

From April 1905 Jung had occupied the position of a senior physician; as a result he had to deputize for Prof. Eugen Bleuler in the latter's absence. This was the situation at the end of September 1905.[4] As we learn from the letter, Spielrein's mother called on Jung with the intention of transferring her treatment elsewhere. She therefore found Jung at the Clinic and he used the note-paper which was conveniently to hand. This is an important point, because the use of the Clinic letterhead for outpatients seems to be unique; an inspection of all the letters in the Clinic archive signed by Jung confirms this.

The document bears the title of 'report'. It is not therefore a medical referral letter in the narrower sense. This is borne out by the phrase 'for use if the occasion arises'. This form of words suggests that Spielrein's mother was in an awkward position in relation to Jung. After all, the care her daughter had received under Jung during her nine-month stay at the Burghölzli had led to a dramatic improvement. After six months she was able to take up the study of medicine at the Clinic. Now 'if the necessity arose' she had to protect her daughter from a possible love relationship. Evidently she was not certain, for she intended to make use of the letter only 'if the occasion arose'. Why Sabina Spielrein remained in treatment with Jung after all, we do not know. In any event she never became Freud's patient.

The next question is why she should have been referred to Freud in Vienna of all places. After all Sabina Spielrein was living and studying in Zürich. It is possible that this accorded with a wish of the mother. Another more plausible explanation is offered by the following connection; Jung writes:

> By using your method I have analysed the affliction fairly thoroughly and with considerable success, from the outset.

Sabina Spielrein was the first hysterical patient of Jung's on whom he had used the Freudian 'method' (cf. note 2 of this chapter). Thus on the one hand it made sense for the patient (in terms of continuity of treatment), while, on the other, right at the beginning of a much hoped for contact with Freud, Jung could offer him an interesting case in the form of Sabina Spielrein. Later it was Jung again who laid the foundation of a mutually useful and fertile relationship by sending Freud his *Studies in Word Association* (see Freud's first letter to Jung, McGuire 1974).

Jung's report begins with the very unusual remark that it is to be handed over to Spielrein's mother. Clearly Jung was subordinating the medical duty of confidentiality to parental power. (The patient was at that time not quite twenty.) Some remarks on the family weakness follow, then a brief case-history of the illness and of his therapeutic approach (references to work with dream material) and of the progress of the treatment. The effect is to confirm fully the psychopathology as we know it from Carotenuto. What is new is that Jung was looking to Freud's approach for a bearing on the dynamics of the origins of hysteria. Astonishing here – as it is in the later correspondence between Jung and Freud – is the apparent recognition that the 'physical chastisements administered to the patient's posterior . . . had unfortunately become associated with the patient's premature and now highly developed sexual awareness'. Thus a 'trauma' is associated with 'sexual awareness', there is no question of 'sexual trauma'. The problem of incest is not even discussed later. Jung's understandable uncertainty in this area is illustrated partly by his statement that he had analysed the patient only 'fairly thoroughly', and partly by his somewhat awkward formulation of her 'character': 'much of this must of course be put down to Russian peculiarities'. His choice of the expression 'put down' is to be noted: here, it seems to stand for 'putting aside unresolved problems'. On the other hand, the assertion that callousness, unreasonableness, a lack of feeling for situation and for external propriety are Russian peculiarities has a disturbing effect on the reader.

At the end of the 'report' there is an answer to the question of how it came to be written at all. The patient had the 'misfortune' to fall in love with Jung and apparently acted with 'a secret enjoyment of her mother's dismay'. As we know from Jung's paper 'Association, dream and hysterical symptom' (1906),[5] this situation was not new to him. In that paper he reports on similar emotional disturbances in two patients who were hospitalized at the Burghölzli in the spring/summer of 1905 (as a reading of the hospital records shows), that is, before the visit from Spielrein's mother. The patient mainly under discussion in that paper underwent the association experiment and the information gained from that was compared with the analysis of her dreams. I will quote two dream analyses from the paper, dream no.5 and dream no.7:

> Here the black man has turned into a white figure; the burning house is the sexual complex. Miss L. [the other patient; present author] is a patient who has a crush on the author. She was, like the patient, taken ill because of an erotic complex. The patient therefore expresses through this person that she has fallen in love with the author. Thus the patient substituted the tender relationship with her mother, which is damaging to her energy, by the erotic relation to the doctor.
>
> (Jung 1906, para. 835)

> The patient desires a sexual relationship with the author, . . . but this is connected with the obviously deep impression made on her by my previous analysis, in which I ruthlessly destroyed her illusions.
>
> (ibid, para. 839)

Jung was therefore aware of the phenomenon of transference love and was able to establish a clear boundary in relation to these patients. But it is note-worthy that he then speaks of 'misfortune' in relation to Sabina Spielrein. It should also be mentioned at this point that Sabina Spielrein was the victim of similar emotional disturbances several times during the course of her illness. Whether in the end it was due to pressure from the mother, or because of a presentiment of the future development of his relationship with the patient, that Jung expressed himself as 'naturally in agreement' that she should be referred 'elsewhere for treatment', must remain an open question.

Notes

1 Carotenuto, A. (1986) *Tagebuch einer Heimlichen Symmetrie*. Freiburg: Kore Verlag.
2 The period of her hospitalization remained unknown until recently. Her complete hospital records were published within the context of my dissertation (1992), incorporated in *Luzifel-Amor*: see Chapter 6, n1. The significance of the 'Spiel-rein case' for Jung and for the Clinic was elucidated there.
3 McGuire, W. (ed.) (1974) *The Freud/Jung Letters*. Princeton, NJ: Princeton University Press.
4 Bleuler's application to the governing executive on 28.8.1905 for leave from 7.9. until 28.9.1905, Bleuler's return to duty on 28.9.1905; Burghölzli-Archive.
5 Jung, C.G. (1906) *Experimental researches. CW* 2.

Chapter 8

The Zürich School of Psychiatry in theory and practice. Sabina Spielrein's treatment at the Burghölzli Clinic in Zürich

Angela Graf-Nold

(Translated from the German by Barbara Wharton)

> If however it is well known that some geniuses perish by insanity, perhaps it is less clear to the doctors that, behind the appearance of some forms of hysteria and other mental disturbances, some geniuses, or at least talents, slumber and languish like a bird in a cage . . .
>
> (Forel 1889, author's trans.)

Admission

On 17 August 1904, at 10.30 at night, 19-year-old Sabina was brought to the Burghölzli 'Treatment and Care Institution' in Zürich by a medical police official and an uncle.[1] The time of day and the presence of the official suggest that the admission was an emergency.

It is not indicated who called the medical police, where she had been staying immediately beforehand, and what made her emergency admission necessary. Her previous place of residence is given as 'Heller's Sanatorium, Interlaken'. Yet a letter from C.G. Jung to Dr Heller in Interlaken, with the request for a short report on Miss Sabina Spielrein, who 'declares that she was in treatment with you', suggests that she did not come directly from there.

One thing is clear: C.G. Jung, the deputy to the senior physician at the time, admitted her. He checked the medical certificate given by a Dr B (which is not among the hospital records), and Lublinsky's statements (the maternal uncle who accompanied her, himself a doctor by profession), took a good look at the young patient, and questioned her about her situation.

She laughed and cried 'in a strangely mixed compulsive manner', noted Jung, and she had numerous tics, rotating her head in a jerky fashion, sticking out her tongue, and twitching her legs. She complained of a dreadful headache; she insisted that she was not mad but had just got very 'upset' at the hotel. Who or what exactly had upset her is not noted, only that she could not bear any people or any noise.

In this short entry Jung's objective approach, which is in accordance with scientific medical standards still valid today, and indeed in some ways exceeds today's standards, is striking: in differentiating between facts and fantasies, it allows the reader to reconstruct the psychodynamics of both the patient's symptoms and the doctor's reactions. Jung takes the medical certificates supplied by the other doctors (Dr B. and Lublinsky) into account,[2] observes without passing judgement, and questions the patient herself. Then a thorough examination follows, which in Sabina Spielrein's case is postponed until the following day.

Jung arranged for the young patient to be accommodated in the women's ward with a private nurse. Sabina was a private patient with a room to herself. Her parents paid 1250 francs a quarter[3] for her accommodation, a sum that corresponded exactly with the salary of the senior physician.[4]

The Burghölzli psychiatric institution 1870–1904 and the Zürich School of Psychiatry

Sabina Spielrein was thus one of roughly 400 patients in the palatial building complex on the Burghölzli hill which lay to the south of the city of Zürich covering 33 hectares. The hospital, which had been designed for 250 patients, was an exceptionally lavish construction if one takes into account the circumstances in Zürich at the time. It was completed in 1870 after six years.

From an administrative point of view it belonged to the recently founded University of Zürich and bore witness to the belief in progress of this young and aspiring university city. According to the maxim of Wilhelm Griesinger who had designed the clinic while he was Professor of Internal Medicine at Zürich University before taking over the direction of the Charité Clinic in Berlin, the slogan ran: 'Diseases of the mind are diseases of the brain'; in other words, progress in treatment was expected mostly from the newly developing brain research. The Burghölzli was considered to be a treatment centre for acute 'curable' cases, whereas the 'incurable' chronic patients were consigned to the Rheinau asylum, an old monastery on a remote island in the Rhine about 60km from Zürich, where they were 'cared for'.

In 1904, when Sabina Spielrein was admitted as a patient, the Burghölzli Clinic was under the direction of Eugen Bleuler. When he was elected to that post in 1898 as successor to Auguste Forel, he was the fifth director of the Burghölzli since its opening in 1870, and the first to come from the Zürich area and to speak the local dialect. He had had nearly 20 years' experience of running an asylum; for in 1886, at the age of 29, and at the instigation of Forel, with whom he had previously spent a year as medical assistant, Bleuler had taken over the running of the asylum at Rheinau where, with only one medical colleague, he had been responsible for the 500 'inmates' of that institution.

Auguste Forel: Hypnosis and the monistic 'identity hypothesis'

For his part, Forel had taken over the direction of the Burghölzli in 1879 at the age of 31, when its reputation was at a low point and none of his international colleagues was any longer competing for the post. His three predecessors, all of them renowned in brain research, had complained of too much work and had worn themselves out in quarrels with the influential administrator, a former locksmith, who had curtailed the responsibilities of the directors and taken over important decisions concerning personnel and organization.

Forel was well informed about the battles of his predecessors. Although a native of the French-speaking part of Switzerland, Forel had studied in Zürich and followed his psychiatry teacher, Bernhard von Gudden, the first director of the Burghölzli, who resigned after two years in 1872, as assistant at the psychiatric clinic in Munich, Germany. As a senior physician back in Zürich at the Burghölzli, he had witnessed the battles of his predecessor, the famous brain researcher, Eduard Hitzig. Forel would subsequently prove to be not only a passionate scientist and research worker but also an exceptionally influential and brilliant organizer. Before taking up his post he had, by means of a sit-in at the office of the relevant government official, achieved overall control of the medical administration over the heads of the management, something that all his predecessors had tried in vain to do.

He then organized the day-to-day running of the Clinic according to his own rigorous standards: he demanded of the doctors that they relinquish all private practice, and forbade them to accept gifts from [patients'] relatives; he allowed only a joint kitty for tips for nurses and attendants (Forel 1935). Under Forel, as with his predecessors, there were 'residential duties' for medical and care personnel: apartments were available for the director and the senior physician; assistants and trainee doctors had rooms; nurses did not have rooms of their own but slept on camp beds in the patients' rooms or in the corridors. Even married people had only one day a week off. As far as patients were concerned, their letters were censored and visits were supervised.[5]

In relation to the scientific work, Forel set up a laboratory for brain anatomy where he carried out investigations into animals' brains with the help of 'Gudden's Microtom' (in the development of which he had been involved as Gudden's assistant in Munich). He succeeded in 1886, with the help of his assistant Eugen Bleuler, in making the discovery that nerve cells are related to each other not through anastomosis (as had been assumed) but through simple touch; this was a revolutionary discovery for the future development of neurology, a discovery that had been made simultaneously by His and was later popularized as the concept of the 'neurone-theory'.

The capacity for precise observation was one that Forel owed to his first scientific passion – the study of ants. And precise observation was the capacity on which he put most value where his students were concerned.[6]

Forel's essential service to psychiatry lay above all, however, in the introduction of hypnosis as a therapeutic tool in day-to-day psychiatric practice, and in integrating it into his scientific theories. The change in his approach to psychiatry came with his young German wife, Emma Steinheil, whom he married in 1883. She 'made friends with several patients', as Forel points out, conducted a choir, visited patients and played music with them (Forel 1935). Under her influence he began to transfer his interest from brain research to his patients' suffering under the conditions of everyday life: the sweatshops of the newly established silk industry, the discrimination against unmarried mothers, and the temptation to drown their sorrows in cider. The book *De la Suggestion et de ses Applications à la Thérapeutique* (1884) by Hippolyte Bernheim, Professor of Internal Medicine at Nancy, had fascinated him so much that in 1885 he arranged for Bernheim to give him a week's personal induction into the technique, and immediately afterwards he began to experiment at the Burghölzli with both colleagues and patients. Forel's results were in some cases spectacular and supported him in his monistic view of the 'unity of brain- and mind-phenomena', that is, 'the essential identity of the conscious and unconscious states of our psychology'. He saw no real difference in essence between the anatomy and physiology of the brain on the one hand, and states of feeling and consciousness on the other; he proposed that it was the same phenomenon 'looked at now from the outside, now from the inside' (the identity hypothesis). With this hypothesis Forel freed hypnosis from the twilight of scientific charlatanry and made it a subject of serious scientific research and reflection. In 1889 he published his textbook on hypnotism which remained a landmark text for 30 years and went through repeated revisions (Forel 1889). Sigmund Freud, who had translated Bernheim's book into German in 1888, and had also visited Bernheim (with a recommendation from Forel), devoted a detailed and enthusiastic discussion to Forel's book (Freud 1889, *SE* Vol.1, pp. 91–102). In 1892 Forel founded the *Zeitschrift für Hypnotismus und Suggestionstherapie* (*Journal of Hypnotism and Suggestion Therapy*) to which Freud too contributed as a co-editor.

The identity hypothesis had far-reaching consequences, not only for psychotherapy but for all areas of life (as Forel constantly emphasized); it also applied to abstinence from alcohol which became one of his main concerns. When Forel was persuaded to abstain by his shoemaker, a member of a Christian lay organization for abstinence (Blue Cross), he noticed a striking improvement in his health and creativity (Forel 1935).[7] With unstoppable enthusiasm he communicated his own experience by initiating a social movement for abstinence.

His crowded schedule led to symptoms of chronic overwork (persistent ringing in his ears) which defied all attempts at treatment. He was clearly overburdened by all his activities in the field of abstinence: the founding of a treatment institution for alcoholics, directed by the shoemaker and independent of the state, the founding of an Order of Good Templars in Switzerland,[8] and, last but not least, his political lobbying in organizing a new law in connection with the setting up of alcohol-free restaurants in Zürich and restricting the number of licences for those which were allowed to serve alcohol. So in 1898, at the age of 50, he decided to give up the directorship of the Burghölzli and his professorship at the University of Zürich; he wanted to devote more of his energy to his research into ants – and to completing his book on the 'sexual question'. He regarded 'the sexual question' as an urgent problem of the time; he had the idea that 'the longing of the human soul and the social experiences of the different human races and historical periods could be reconciled with the findings of natural science and with the laws of psychological and sexual evolution which had come to light through these findings' (Forel 1935, Foreword).

In his book Forel battled in a very concrete and practical way against the Victorian taboos of his age; he discussed all the biological aspects of the act of procreation, as well as the (albeit inadequate) methods of contraception available at the time, and raised such modern social issues as full rights for women and equal status in law for illegitimate and legitimate children. The book appeared in 1905, at the same time as Freud's 'Three Essays on the Theory of Sexuality'.

Eugen Bleuler: Psychiatry and psychology

In succeeding Forel in 1898, Bleuler had undoubtedly taken on a difficult legacy: it is true that through his utopian vision of progress, and his passionate and effective commitment to his beliefs, Forel had opened up new perspectives for psychiatry; he had also built up its popularity and social relevance as a profession. But his optimism for progress collided in many ways with the restrictive conditions of the everyday running of the institution. And the total commitment (which finally overwhelmed Forel) was to prove too much for every one of his successors. For as a result of Forel's tireless activities, several new duties had been added to the already excessive list of tasks facing a director of the Burghölzli. It was part of Bleuler's job to be involved in the local and international committees of abstinence organizations and the supervision of the alcohol treatment centre set up by Forel. In addition there were numerous court reports and, further, an even greater involvement with the university had become necessary; for through Forel's intervention psychiatry had become an examination subject for students of medicine at Zürich, so that to the courses and lectures taken by the director of the Burghölzli had been added the administering of examinations and a more active collaboration in the Zürich medical faculty.

It is astonishing how uncomplainingly Bleuler – and his wife too – accepted these burdens. In 1901, as a 44-year-old bachelor, he married one of the most distinguished graduate philologists in Switzerland, the teacher and author Hedwig Waser.[9] The young Mrs Bleuler conscientiously put aside her academic and literary ambitions in favour of running social events for the hospital and organizing the 'federation of abstaining women'; she integrated her household, which soon included five children, into the society of the Burghölzli which now contained around 500 people. Often patients came to tea in the afternoon. A working day of 14–16 hours was the rule for Bleuler; even at night peace was not guaranteed: a staircase led from their apartment directly to one of the wards (Bleuler, M. 1951).

Bleuler seems to have been predestined to be an almost ideal successor to Forel, for he incorporated all the latter's essential and characteristic ideas: a tireless zeal for work, membership of the international movement for abstinence (from alcohol), the tradition of brain research, the mastery of hypnosis as a therapeutic instrument, as well as a strong belief in the kind of progress that embraced social, ethical and epistemological values and which was orientated towards the philosophy of 'scientific monism'.

In spite of all that, Forel would have preferred his senior physician Delbrück as his successor, and to the very end he could not reconcile himself to the government's choice of Bleuler (Forel 1935). This was not without significance for the 'Zürich school', for Forel continued to exercise great influence; he followed events at the Burghölzli in detail and commented on them in letters to pupils and colleagues worldwide; even in the numerous subsequent editions of his textbook on hypnosis he always referred to Bleuler and his colleagues in strikingly ambivalent terms.

There was nevertheless no doubt that Bleuler forged the worldwide reputation of psychiatry in Zürich, and that he provided, particularly through the special reception given to Freud, and the psychodynamically orientated descriptions of disease profiles, the essential impetus for the establishment of a distinctive school of clinical psychiatry in Zürich. The essence of these developments was that, compared with Forel, Bleuler's interest and orientation were more psychological: even as director of the Rheinau institution he had been interested in the spoken utterances of his psychotic patients and had kept notes on them (Bleuler, M. 1988). Moreover, as a bachelor he had lived very close to the patients, practically sharing their everyday life. From this experience he had become a passionate supporter of the 'active community' for residents of institutions; for he had realized that all activities which were experienced by the patient as meaningful had a powerful therapeutic effect. Every patient had to contribute to the running of the hospital according to his capabilities. The 'active community' as the central idea of Eugen Bleuler's therapeutic approach was publicized by his son Manfred Bleuler (psychiatrist and successor as director of the Burghölzli from 1942–1969) (Bleuler, M. 1951). In his textbook Eugen Bleuler identifies as 'the most important tools for treating the psyche' 'patience, calm, and inner goodwill towards the patients, three qualities that must be completely inexhaustible'

(Bleuler, E. 1916). He undoubtedly paid more than lip-service to this. Ludwig Binswanger too, who later served for a time as assistant to Bleuler, remarked in his memoirs 'that the spirit of unconditional acceptance of the person, of the healthy as well as the sick, which reigned in the hospital, was moreover the spirit of discipline, order and justice' (Binswanger 1957).

On this basis Bleuler largely succeeded in running the major state institution of the Burghölzli as a 'therapeutic community'. It was in accordance with this concept that doctors, care staff and patients should live in the hospital and form a residential community, and that – in the case of the doctors – their wives too should be integrated into the institution. Bleuler's wife, Hedwig, not only organized social events in the hospital, but also contributed to the scientific discussions, as did Jung's wife, Emma. At least occasionally they participated in the 'neurological-psychiatric referral evenings', which took place fortnightly in the Burghölzli and in the private neurology laboratory of Bleuler's friend and colleague, Constantin von Monakov (Abraham 1976: 62).

Constantin von Monakov (1853–1930) was a Russian émigré. With Forel's support he had obtained his post-doctoral qualification in 1885 at the University of Zürich with a thesis on brain anatomy, and had subsequently set up a private neurology laboratory in Zürich and a private neurology outpatient clinic; in 1893 he opened a private clinic for inpatients too, with the profits from which he financed his researches (Monakov 1970; Jagella, Isler, & Hess 1994).

Monakov was investigating the reaction of brain functions to injuries to certain areas of the brain; from this he developed a theory which explained the difference between immediate and long-term consequences of injuries, contrasting this dynamic view of brain-functioning (the Diaschisis theory) with the static localization theory. Bleuler, who was working on the classification of psychiatric disease profiles and was interested in the psychological treatment of psychic trauma, felt he had common ground with Monakov both in his neurological and in his philosophical and therapeutic ideas; by comparing and contrasting himself with Monakov he developed his theory of schizophrenia.

As director of the Rheinau hospital, Bleuler had developed the idea that a loosening of the association pathways in the brain underlay psychotic processes, and he now hoped to substantiate his hypothesis with psychological association experiments of the type that were being set up in other psychological and psychiatric institutions. When C.G. Jung took over the organization of the psychology laboratory and the direction of the association experiments in 1904, an enthusiasm for research developed at the discussion evenings which Monakov observed with both interest and scepticism: 'The clinical material from the Burghölzli was studied (especially by Jung, Maeder and Riklin) from the point of view of Freud's theories, and many symptoms of dementia praecox were interpreted with great conviction as Freudian mechanisms, even by Bleuler' (Monakov 1970: 244).

It is probable that the case of Sabina Spielrein was discussed here, and also that, later, she took part in the discussions. From this 'psychiatry/neurology society' the 'Freud club' broke away in 1907 – much to Monakov's disapproval; in addition to himself, as he emphasizes, doctors from the city and 'all kinds of "unclassifiable" ladies, and even students of both sexes' were attracted to the 'club'.[10]

Bleuler had been acquainted with Freud for some time. While still director at Rheinau he had reviewed Freud's translation of Bernheim's 'New Studies in Hypnotism' and Charcot's 'Policlinic Lectures'. In 1896 Bleuler published a review of *Studies on Hysteria* by Breuer and Freud in the *Munich Medical Weekly*: the book, with its five detailed case studies ('They could not publish more because, as almost always in such cases, sexual occurrences are revealed'), opened up a completely new perspective on psychological mechanisms and was indeed 'one of the most important recent publications in the field of normal and pathological psychology', even if, from the therapeutic and theoretical point of view, essential questions still remained unanswered – thus for example there was no sufficient explanation of how 'abreaction' worked and whether the 'cathartic method' was not based on suggestion (Bleuler 1896: 524ff).

C.G. Jung and the Burghölzli

When in October 1900, as a student in his final year, C.G. Jung applied for the post which was about to become vacant at the Burghölzli, there were – as is often the case – no other applicants. He took up his post in December 1900, as a trainee doctor on almost no pay – only 1000 francs a year. Looking back at this time in a seminar in 1925, Jung describes how at first his work at the Burghölzli caused him a considerable shock:

> For six months I was struggling desperately to find my way in [psychiatry] and was all the time more and more baffled. I was deeply humiliated to see that my chief and my colleagues [the senior physician and one assistant] seemed to be sure of themselves, and that it was only I who was drifting helplessly. My failure to understand gave me such feelings of inferiority that I could not bear to go out of the hospital. Here was I, a man with a profession which I could not rightly grasp. I therefore stayed in all the time and gave myself up to the study of my cases.
> (Jung Seminar 1925: 17 [cf. MDR: 146])

Then Jung began his doctoral thesis, 'On the psychology and pathology of so-called occult phenomena', in which he proposed to 'broaden our knowledge of the relations between hysterical twilight states and the problems of normal psychology' (Jung 1902, para. 35). In this work he focused on several cases of alterations in consciousness of various kinds which he had met in the hospital and which were reported in the literature, but principally on the 'case of somnambulism in a girl with poor inheritance (Spiritualistic Medium)', 'Miss S.W'. (the pseudonym for his cousin Helly Preiswerk), with whom he had experimented in his student days. In one passage in this work (in a rather unimportant connection), Jung refers to Breuer and Freud's *Studies on Hysteria*, and in two passages to Freud's *Interpretation of Dreams*; in general he presented his view of the unconscious which was orientated, appropriately enough in his student years, towards Schopenhauer and Eduard von Hartmann in particular, and also followed Pierre Janet and Théodore Flournoy especially closely. Flournoy's book on the trance states of a medium in Geneva, *From India to the Planet Mars* (1900), had deeply impressed him, and a friendship then began with Flournoy, the experimental psychologist from Geneva, which was to outlast his relationship with Freud. Jung's insight into the psychological circumstances relating to the onset of hysterical and particularly of psychotic symptoms soon released him from his uncertainty and stagnation: even the strange stereotypical movements or the 'meaningless' verbal expressions of the old psychotic patients suddenly took on a meaning once he had succeeded in determining the connection with their personal desires and conflicts. Thus he claimed this insight as his own personal discovery which he could share with no one:

> At that time there was no psychological viewpoint to be found in the field of psychiatry. A label was put on each case; it was said to be a degeneration here, or an atrophy there, and then it was finished – there was nothing more to be done about it. It was only among the nurses that any psychological interest in the patients could be found, and among them there were some very shrewd guesses offered as to the conditions presented, but the doctors knew none of this.
>
> (Jung Seminar 1925: 17)

This account may be understood as an over-compensation for his feelings of inferiority described above; Forel for one complained later about Jung's exaggerated pride in his discoveries[11] and, as far as Bleuler was concerned, his publications, as well as all the other colleagues who ever expressed an opinion about him, bear witness to his particular interest, understanding and commitment (cf. Ellenberger 1985: 893).

It seems though that for Jung the psychogenesis of psychiatric symptoms took on a personal meaning which was different from the significance they had for Forel and Bleuler. While for them a tireless sense of order and an optimistic belief in social and scientific progress seemed to play a predominant role, Jung was personally touched by the symptoms of individual patients; he writes in his memoirs:

> Through my work with patients I realized that paranoid ideas and hallucinations contain a germ of meaning. A personality, a pattern of hopes and desires lies behind the psychosis. At bottom we discover nothing new and unknown in the mentally ill; rather we encounter the substratum of our own natures.
>
> (Jung 1961: 148)

It is easy to see that he must often have felt misunderstood. An indication of this state of affairs is the fact that Forel and Bleuler often complained about the pressure of work and the overcrowding of the hospital, but never about the lack of time available to the doctors to devote to individual patients.

As at the time when Forel began his work at the Burghölzli in 1879 with 300 patients, when Jung began in 1900 only two experienced doctors (the director and the senior physician) and two inexperienced ones (an assistant and a trainee) had the care of some 400 hospital patients. As Ellenberger reports, Bleuler did a ward round three or four times a day; but it is easy to calculate how long he would have spent on these visits even if he had tried to make them more than mere sentry duty. It is true that a meeting of the medical team took place every morning at which individual patients were discussed. Nevertheless in these circumstances the direct personal relationship of the individual doctor with the individual patient must indeed have been the exception rather than the rule. A more intensive relationship with the patient, as Jung had observed, was rather the province of the nurses, male and female – who at that time were completely untrained.

It is consistent with the circumstances therefore that Jung complained about his work situation. On 6 October 1901, together with the medical assistant, Otto Diem, he addressed a letter to 'Director Bleuler, at the central medical office of the canton of Zürich' with a petition for the creation of a post for a third medical assistant. Jung and Diem justified their petition on five hand-written pages (in Jung's hand-writing) by pointing to 'the progress made in the scientific and humane treatment', the almost complete absence of all coercive measures such as the bed bath, the straitjacket, and the bed strap since 1895, and the essential, precise, but also laborious and painstaking examinations which were necessary 'to do justice to the requirements of modern science to only a limited extent'; they pointed out that in 1895 the number of staff had stood at 56, and in 1900 at 86, and drew attention to the rising numbers of admissions and discharges of patients, and to the increased work occasioned by court reports. Finally the creation of an additional post would be in the interests of the institution if it 'made the strenuous and responsible task of younger psychiatrists more personally satisfying'.[12] Bleuler supported the venture in a covering letter and the senior executive officer endorsed the proposal; but the canton government turned it down. As a result, Otto Diem resigned his post in February 1902. C.G. Jung, who was just finishing his dissertation, stayed and on 1 April rose to the position of first medical assistant. In May 1902, after completing his dissertation, he became engaged to 22-year-old Emma Rauschenbach, the daughter of a manufacturer, whom he had known from his youth. On 23 July he too tendered his resignation and was released on 1 October 1902.[13] Neither in *Memories, Dreams, Reflections* nor in any of the biographies of Jung is this resignation mentioned.

Jung was clearly planning to build his future, both professional and private, outside the Burghölzli. First he went to Paris to attend the lectures of Janet at the university there, to learn English at the Berlitz school,[14] to go to the theatre and to concerts, and among other things to meet his cousin Helly about whom he had just written in his dissertation (very critically and not altogether respectfully). She now had hardly any recollection of the time of her trances, and was very successful in her profession as a dressmaker in the workroom of a famous couturier.[15]

Jung married in February 1903 and moved into an apartment on the Zollikerstrasse in Zürich with his wife Emma, not very far from the Burghölzli. By May 1903 he was working at the Burghölzli again, deputizing for medical assistants who were away on military service.

Shortly after this, when the senior physician Ludwig von Muralt fell ill with tuberculosis and had to go on leave, C.G. Jung took over as his deputy too. Von Muralt's leave was extended several times, and Jung's plans to go to Basel as a senior physician seemed to be coming to nothing. Whether it was the indignation among the Basel clergy over Jung's dissertation that was so strong that he decided it was impossible, as Stefanie Zumstein-Preiswerk[16] believes – or whether it was because a German doctor by the name of Wolff had taken over the position of director at the mental hospital there: on 22 August C.G. Jung writes to his old friend Andreas Vischer about a 'Basel calamity' which had 'wrecked *for ever*' his 'academic career in Switzerland'. He continues:

> I might as well sit under a millstone as under Wolff who will stay up there immovably enthroned for thirty years until he is as old as Wille [Jung's tutor in psychiatry at Basel university]. For no one in Germany is stupid enough to take Wolff seriously, as Kraepelin has appropriately said, he is not even a psychiatrist. I have been robbed of any possibility of advancement in Basel now.[17]

Jung wrote this letter from a position which was indeed remarkable:

> I'm sitting here in the Burghölzli and for a month I've been playing the part of the director, the senior physician and the first medical assistant. All the personnel in question are away and I have amalgamated all the roles into one person. So almost every day I'm writing twenty letters,

giving twenty interviews, running all over the place and getting very annoyed. I have even lost another fourteen pounds in the last year as a result of this change of life, which otherwise is not a bad thing of course. On the contrary, all that would be fine (for what do we want from life more than real work?) if the public uncertainty of existence were not so great.[18]

Jung did not have to worry about 'real work' at the Burghölzli, and soon he was relieved of his 'public uncertainty': when the senior physician who was on sick leave finally resigned in September, Jung took over his position in October 1904 on a regular basis and moved into the senior physician's apartment in the Burghölzli with his wife Emma (who was expecting their first child in December). In his academic career too not much was standing in his way: four months later, in December 1904, he submitted his application for the post of lecturer at Zürich university.[19]

Anamnesis (August 1904)

In August 1904, when he was wrestling with the personal question of whether he should settle at the Burghölzli again or seek his professional future elsewhere, he was carrying the sole medical responsibility for all the patients; he therefore took the anamnesis of the newly admitted 19-year-old patient, Sabina Spielrein.

The nurse who had spent the night in her room reported that it had been fairly quiet; Sabina had merely expressed anxiety several times and had asked for a light. Once she said she had two heads, and that her body felt foreign to her. A similar experience of splitting was to occur again shortly before the end of the treatment.

The statements of the uncle, whom he questioned first, were evaluated by Jung as 'meagre and evasive'; he connected this, together with the uncle's insufficient command of the German language, to the fact that he was 'an old Russian Jew'. Which questions he evaded and in what way, and/or what was typical of an old Russian Jew in that, is not recorded. In any case Sabina's great agitation, which had led to the emergency admission the previous evening, is not clarified. Regarding Sabina's earlier history, Jung discovers that she was 'always rather hysterical'. She had been an intelligent pupil and had been prominent in her achievements. She had been ill for about three years. She had spent a month at the Heller sanatorium in Interlaken where she was very dissatisfied. 'She should have gone to Monakov, but he did not take her because she was too agitated'.

So it can be assumed that Monakov referred Sabina Spielrein to the Burghölzli: probably Uncle Lublinsky was consulted as the only relative; the entries on the clinic form relating to this were all later amended and elaborated.

Jung records the 'constant alternation of laughter and tears, jerking of the head and seductive glances'.

The anamnesis that Jung takes from Sabina Spielrein herself the following day is 'as difficult as walking on eggshells'. Nevertheless he obviously succeeds in breaking through the negativism of his patient 'in a powerful battle'. Jung's request to say 'everything' if she wants to get better was met by Sabina with the threat that, if she had to say everything, 'it would upset her so much that things would go really bad later. Then he would see what would happen'. 'She insists several times that she would and could never talk about it, and in any case does not want to be cured at all.'

Sabina seems to have given her somatic anamnesis and external details of her life without much of a battle. Her 'delicate' constitution was stressed ('stomach pains, angina a thousand times, precocious, sensitive').

'Precocious' seems to mean 'intellectual precociousness'. For Jung notes that 'Sabina did not work very hard at the Gymnasium but [was] intellectually very advanced'. At five she attended a Froebel infant school in Warsaw, more than 1000 km from Rostov-on-Don, her home town, and the family's last place of residence. It is not recorded whether that entailed her staying in a children's home and being separated from her family. After that she was taught at home until she entered a Gymnasium. She did not like it because the teachers were 'very stupid'. She also played the piano a lot and had singing lessons. Above all she was interested in the natural sciences and wanted to study medicine.

Zürich was then the 'Mecca of Russian women students' who, in the course of the political reforms in Russia, in particular the abolishment of serfdom in 1861, were gripped by a sense of a new era beginning and were striving for education and a new allocation of roles in society. A Russian university statute issued in 1863 excluded women absolutely from all higher education. A young Russian woman, Nadescha Suslova, the daughter of a serf, had enrolled at Zürich University and as the first woman student there – and as a fellow student of Forel – completed her studies and gained her doctorate in 1867 successfully and without hindrance. When this became known in Russian circles a whole stream of young Russian women poured into Zürich. In Zürich they lived together partly in 'Russian colonies' which were keenly involved in the political upheavals in their homeland (Bankowski-Züllig 1988). Among them was a strikingly large number of Jewish students, men as well as women, who to an extent were harshly discriminated against in universities in Russia.

Sabina was the eldest of five children of an obviously wealthy Jewish businessman. She had three younger brothers – a little sister, whom she loved 'more than everything in the world', died of typhoid at the age of 6, when Sabina herself was 16. Her mother was a dentist (whatever that meant at the time) but she had practised her profession only casually.

The parents clearly took the education of their daughter very seriously, although it is hardly thinkable that they were interested in changing the roles between the sexes – or indeed that they supported the ideals of the Russian revolution. For undoubtedly the relationships which held sway in the family were extremely patriarchal.

The real 'battle' that Jung fought and won with Sabina was to coax a 'confession' from her. And, as in the case histories in the *Studies on Hysteria* of Breuer and Freud, the confession is not about a reprehensible deed of her own but about being repeatedly shamed and anguished: she 'confesses' that her father has 'hit her several times on her bare buttocks, most recently in her eleventh year, from time to time in front of her siblings'.

It is possible to follow the process by which Jung wins the 'battle': he takes Sabina Spielrein through her ambivalence. As a result of his helping her to relate alternately to her own feelings and behaviour and to her father's, she succeeds for a moment in differentiating herself internally from him and in rediscovering her own congruence:

> *Pat.* loves her father 'painfully'. *She* cannot turn to him, *he* does not really understand her, *he* says hurtful things to her.
>
> Because of her strong narcissism *she* cannot give in to her father, and when *her father* is sad, *she* cannot talk to him and *she* is again deeply hurt.
>
> *He* has hit pat. and *she* had to kiss his hand in return.

'At this point,' observes Jung, 'innumerable tics and gestures of abhorrence occurred.'

After the 'confession' of her father's beatings, it strikes him that 'at this point the tics are in keeping with the affect. They express abhorrence and revulsion'.

That the tics disappeared after this is not the point. On the contrary, Jung established in the next few days that they 'appear at points in the conversation which have a certain connection with her complexes'. This remark refers to the association experiments in which Jung was then intensely involved together with Franz Riklin. At that particular time 'The associations of normal subjects' was being prepared, in which – according to Jung – the idea was to examine the influences on the association process of attention 'which by countless threads links the associative process with all other phenomena of the psychic and physical domain in consciousness' (Jung 1904, para. 4). Jung counted mimicked reactions to the stimulus word as indications of the presence of a 'feeling toned complex', that is, 'the sum of ideas referring to a particular feeling-toned event' (ibid. para. 167, fn.).

It should also be noted that Jung does not use hypnosis or suggestion (as Freud suggested in his *Studies on Hysteria*) to elicit the 'confession'; with Sabina Spielrein he works on the complex by accompanying her and participating with her in free association. In other words, he takes up a position in relation to the patient in which participation and observation are balanced.

But Sabina continues to battle with her negativism: 'she could and would never talk about it, and in any case did not want to be cured at all'. Jung met this resistance with remarkable benevolence, interpreting it as an expression of her sensitivity: 'Is extremely sensitive, accuses the writer of not having the time to listen to everything, of not really being interested, of only pretending, etc.' Jung himself thus showed how 'extremely sensitive' he was towards Sabina Spielrein.

On the following two days Jung continued the anamnesis with Sabina and also spoke to her mother. Sabina tells him more about her relationship with her parents and her brothers, in the course of which a truly shocking picture unfolds: three years before, that is when she was just 16, she had said: 'I could give up parents in favour of the company of other people' (by which she meant, in her youthful striving for independence, that her relation to other people was more important to her than her relations within the family). 'Hearing this, her father went wild and threatened suicide.' The father's suicide threats were present all the time as an instrument of power: 'it pains her that he is unhappy, always talking about dying. It also distresses her that he insults and tyrannizes other members of the household.' The fact that he insults and tyrannizes her is not reiterated; and the idea that sexual power too is involved in the chastisements is not directly pointed out, although Jung records: 'the peak of the experience was that her father was a *man*' and 'Even now he occasionally makes indecent remarks'.

The statement that a 'similar relationship' existed with the mother, as Jung writes, can be linked only in a general way to the relationship dominated by terror that prevailed with her father. 'Even during this last year her mother tried to beat her in front of her brothers and her brothers' friends.' Sabina's desperation had taken on extreme proportions even while she was still at school: 'Once when, at thirteen, her mother punished her, she hid and doused herself with ice-cold water in winter in order to catch her death of cold.' 'At the age of 15 she tried to starve herself to death' in Karlsbad[20] 'because she had made her mother angry.'

Jung seems to have questioned the mother about the history of Sabina's illness without at all confronting her with her daughter's statements. Mrs Spielrein focused (as had the uncle) above all on Sabina's intelligence and achievements (precocious, intelligent, German and French already at the age of 6, worked hard at the Gymnasium).[21] In similar vein was her statement that 'in her twelfth year Sabina had periods of apathy, and pitied all human beings'. But 'at fifteen she realized the reason for living and started to work'. She wanted the company only of good, educated and clever people. Her statement that Sabina had recently 'fallen in love with her old uncle, who was a doctor' sounds particularly strange ('in love' with Uncle Lublinsky who had accompanied her?). The mother had listed 'all his faults for her and as a result Sabina was deeply disappointed and upset'.

Whatever Jung has omitted from his notes, Mrs Spielrein must have left behind a very disturbed impression, so that he wrote 'hysterical!' on the cover sheet, underlined it, and noted 'hysterical absences of a childish nature'. However, if one studies the information about the family on the cover sheet (which is all amended and elaborated), and if one imagines Sabina's position in this family, one can understand the upset and despair which seized her when her mother tried to spoil even her love for her old uncle: one brother has hysterical fits of weeping, another has tics and is very hot-tempered, the third is 'melancholic', severely hysterical, and 'does wrong in order to suffer'. How was she to survive there when her father ('neurasthenic, hot-tempered to the point of madness' and constantly threatening suicide) tried to keep her with him?

Unusually for an anamnesis, the patient's religious upbringing comes into the discussion. It seems typical of Sabina's family relationships that the religious values (which were mediated above all by her mother) were geared towards deterrence and anxiety. 'Sins are recorded in heaven in red: a person is responsible for her sins from the age of seven.' Sabina's reaction seems however to have been more personal: from the age of 7 or 8 she 'started to talk with a spirit'.

> As a child she was very pious and prayed a good deal. After a while God answered her in the form of an inner voice which spoke more through her feelings than in clear sentences. It seemed to her however that this inner voice was speaking to her in *German* (Russian is her mother-tongue; at that time she was learning German). Gradually the idea came to her that the voice was not God but an angel sent to her by God because she was an *extraordinary person* . . . She often felt as though she understood the meaning of the words even before they were spoken.
>
> (Chapter 5: 88; original italics)

It is very likely that Jung was powerfully affected by this subject matter: as we know from his biography, his grandfather on his mother's side, a professor of theology, a specialist in ancient languages, and a leading clergyman in the reformed church in the university city of Basel, spoke with 'spirits'. In addition Jung knew from his own history the feeling of being an 'extraordinary person' which he first registered in the context of a minor humiliation (Jung 1961, p.39f.). Furthermore the fact that Sabina's 'spirit' spoke in a foreign language must have reminded him of Flournoy's medium Hélène, as well as of his cousin Hélène who, as he had described in his dissertation, had changed in her trances from a superficial young girl into a wise old man speaking in elevated language.

Diagnosis: Hysteria

Jung and Bleuler gave the diagnosis of 'hysteria' for Sabina – both at the beginning and at the end of her treatment. This diagnosis had previously only seldom been made at the Zürich clinic (Minder counts eight cases of hysteria with which Jung had had contact at the Burghölzli up to that time) (Minder 1992). Yet there was no doubt that hysteria was then something like the main paradigm for clinical psychiatric research. A 900-page monograph had just been published by Otto Binswanger, a doyen of German psychiatry (Binswanger 1904).

Both Bleuler and Jung had given special thought to the theme. In his dissertation Jung had explained many of the 'so-called occult phenomena' in the example of his cousin Hélène as hysterical symptoms. In doing so he had drawn particularly on the contemporary French psychiatric and psychological literature (Charcot, Janet, Binet, Flournoy) in which the 'hysterical' phenomena of somnambulism and of dual consciousness, as well as the 'automation' of various psychic functions (normally those lying just beneath the conscious will) and also spectacular 'achievements' (speaking otherwise unknown languages, 'clairvoyance') were discussed. Jung saw in the performances of his 16-year-old cousin as a spirit medium somnambulistic episodes in which she lived out her wishful adolescent dreams and enacted her barely conscious knowledge of relationships in romantic fantasies. The various 'subconscious personalities' represented different (partly suppressed) aspects of her past and reminded Jung vividly of Freud's investigations of dreams 'which uncovered the independent life of repressed thoughts'.[22]

In 1904, just as he began work with Sabina, Jung used a reply to a review of his dissertation, which had appeared in book form in 1902, to set out again his views on hysterical misreading, or rather of the 'hysterical process' in general. His patient's 'hysterical misreading' could be explained by the assumption of a split in consciousness and 'demonstrates in a nutshell the splitting off of psychic functions from the ego-complex, which is so characteristic of hysteria, and consequently the strong tendency of the psychic elements towards autonomy' (Jung 1904, para. 159). And more remarkably Jung attaches great importance to the discovery that: '[t]he analysis of the clinical picture is not [as the reviewer thinks] based on the French writers, but on Freud's investigations of hysteria'! (ibid, para. 165) Holding this point of view Jung was undoubtedly in agreement with his medical mentor and his chief, Eugen Bleuler, even if Bleuler's interest went in a more practical direction. Indeed in his textbook which appeared in 1916 Bleuler does not mention Freud's and Breuer's 'investigations of hysteria'. Nevertheless he states: 'Psychoanalysis, which makes diseased mechanisms accessible to consciousness and "abreacts" them, cures many cases' (Bleuler, E. 1916).

In his textbook on hypnotism of 1902, Forel too had cited Freud among a number of authors ('Charcot, Breuer, Vogt and many before them') who had produced evidence that even severe cases 'are generated through ideas and are disposed of through ideas' (Forel 1902: 136). And in another passage he states that in hysterical disturbances one must 'according to Freud's procedure, always look for earlier causative emotional trauma'. But he warned against 'any infringement of tact or propriety' through 'offensive questioning'. He also said that one should not 'construct a dogma out of an isolated occurrence as Freud does' (ibid: 168). Forel does not give the name 'sexual abuse' to the 'isolated occurrence' in question. Bleuler too speaks only in general terms about the psychogenesis of hysteria. He counts the 'hysterical syndrome', 'with its more moderate neurotic symptoms and striking psychic connections', among 'psychopathic reaction formations (situational psychoses)'. Above all he emphasizes the mixture of psychic and physical symptoms (twilight states, anaesthesias, hyperaesthesias, paralyses, convulsions, vomiting), all of which were produced through 'similar reactions in similar people' and at best were denoted as 'psychogenic'. Hysterics were 'emotional people' ('*Affektmenschen*') who in their given circumstances could not realize their aspirations in a normal way and in addition characteristically show 'a stronger capacity to split, or rather a greater incapacity to keep their suppressed strivings at bay' (Bleuler, E. 1916: 421).

In Forel's view hysteria does not present an isolated clinical picture but 'a complex of symptoms or a syndrome' which was based above all on 'pathological dissociation' (suggestibility and autosuggestibility). 'As a result of this, when consciousness has become restricted, intensely active, spontaneous somnambulistic links are formed which can drag the personality along with them and eventually divide into a dual ego, giving rise to the most wonderful phenomena, but also resulting in dramatic, hysterical lying and the dream-like lability of those patients' (Forel 1902: 138).

Forel had already found Charcot's theory of hysteria questionable; Charcot's 'stigmata' were to be valued not as diagnostic signs but rather as artefacts which as a result of powerful (auto)suggestibility had become fixated. In treatment, waking suggestion was much better than hypnosis, which was to be applied only with great caution. 'The old rule stands: friendly, consistent and firm.' It was important to win the cooperation of the hysterical patient and at the same time to inspire their respect: 'one must never mock them, and never show any mistrust, dislike or contempt towards them, otherwise one would greatly harm them' (ibid: p. 138).

Bleuler himself names as 'the most important psychic tools' patience, calm, and inner goodwill towards the patients, three qualities that must be inexhaustible (Bleuler, E. 1916: 389). His more concrete principles were as pragmatic as they were idealistic: 'To remove the basis of hysterical outbursts and other symptoms which have merely an attention-seeking nature by deliberately ignoring them', and 'to alter the conditions in which syndromes grew and were nourished', writes Bleuler. But above all 'if possible to create a purpose in life for the patients by taking account not only of external relationships, but also of the internal ones which have caused the patients to reject their sense of purpose in life' (ibid: 389).

For the often predominant wish to be ill must be overcompensated by positive strivings which assume health.

Treatment (September 1904 – June 1905)

Sabina Spielrein's treatment seems in many respects to have been a test-case for both Bleuler and Jung: a test-case for their new collaboration after Jung's resignation in 1903, and a test-case for Bleuler's idea of an institution as a therapeutic community in which everyone is occupied according to his ability and is supported with goodwill, patience, and calm; a test-case too for Jung's efforts, now newly supported by the association experiments, to understand 'what actually takes place inside the mentally ill' (Jung 1961: 135).

On 23 August Jung noted a remarkable experience that Sabina Spielrein had had in what was obviously a semi-conscious state: 'She felt as if someone were pressing in upon her, as if (someone) something were creeping around in her bed, something human. At the same time she felt as if someone were shouting in her ear.' And: 'All the time she felt she was totally repulsive, like a dog or a devil.' And especially: 'Her hands felt as though they did not belong to her.' This entry is neither interpreted nor commented on.

But on 5 January, when Sabina's condition had already greatly improved, and the decision had been made that she would take up her medical studies in Zürich in spring 1905, her condition suddenly deteriorated considerably and the symptom reappeared: 'In the night a great fright: there might be a cat or someone else in her room, someone was suddenly speaking in her ear. She felt something moving on her back like a snail, and something grasped her side like a hand.' Today many therapists would undoubtedly suspect flashbacks of night-time sexual infringements in relation to these descriptions (Herman 1981).

The 'analysis of the feelings' connected with this hallucinatory experience on 5 January 1905, as noted by the doctor treating her, reveals a memory of New Year's Day 1904 when 'there was a big row (angry scenes with the father)'. More precise facts are not given, only that 'many such scenes' took place, which Sabina described with 'great affect'. In particular there was a scene when she was already 13 years old and her father tried to beat her: 'he took her into a special room and ordered her to lie down; she implored him not to beat her (he was trying to lift her skirt from behind). Finally he gave in, but he forced her to kneel down and kiss the picture of her grandfather and to swear always to be a good child. After this humiliating scene the boys (her brothers) were waiting outside to greet her.'

According to this description the father's chastisements were humiliating rituals, taking place behind closed doors, and for that reason alone containing an undertone of sexual infringement. 'Her father's expressions which offended her sense of shame' also point in this direction. The reporter (C.G. Jung) notes regarding these that Sabina put particular emphasis on them in her accounts.

With what 'expressions' her father offended her 'sense of shame' is not recorded. But we might assume that he used insults of a sexual nature in connection with the command 'lie down'; these had the effect of making the young girl 'feel totally repulsive, like a dog or a devil'.

Later she acknowledged what Jung regarded as the most important fact: 'Finally after a three-hour analysis (!) it turned out that since her fourth year she has experienced sexual arousal.' She feels a pressure to urinate and has to press her legs together. We read that later she had an 'orgasmic discharge'. Finally it was enough to see or hear her brother being beaten for her to 'want to masturbate'; 'or someone had only to threaten her to make her immediately lie on her bed and masturbate.' Recently it had taken increasingly slight suggestions to awaken the impulse in her, for example someone only had to laugh at her, thus indicating her humiliation, 'to cause her to have an orgasm', as the doctor conducting the analysis – the style is Jung's – writes.

These formulations suggest that Jung certainly sees the sexual activity as being on Sabina Spielrein's side. At all events it is not clear from this passage that he holds the father responsible for his daughter's confused feelings through his beatings of her, and through his offences against her sense of shame. For as the passage subsequently shows, she undoubtedly suffered much from the complex 'to which basically all her expressions of disgust and her negative behaviour could be traced'. 'She sees herself as a thoroughly bad and corrupt person and feels therefore that she should not be allowed to be in the company of other people.' Any suggestion of forced submission triggered the complex, and caused her to masturbate. And, 'during the act, pat. wishes on herself all manner of torments; she pictures these as vividly as possible, in particular being beaten on her bare bottom and, in order to increase her arousal, she imagines that it is taking place in front of a large audience'.

His analysis of this 'act' leaves the impression that Jung was not paying attention to the drama as a whole but was focusing on the 'lustful' patient. In that context it should be stated that Jung's lengthy analysis (lasting many hours) took place in January 1905 before he became personally acquainted with Freud, and before the publication of Freud's 'Three essays on the theory of sexuality'; Jung's focus on 'infantile sexuality' anticipates Freud's change of focus after he turned away from the seduction theory.

It should also be pointed out that Jung's analysis did not explain at all what he was at first trying to explain: the remarkable and alarming hallucinatory experience that something/someone was creeping about in her bed.

Whatever the analysis of Sabina's 'core-complex' had produced and whatever conclusions were to be drawn from it, the malicious spectators of whom she was so afraid did not include Bleuler. On the day following Jung's lengthy analysis, Bleuler personally wrote a letter to the father who demanded a regular weekly progress report from Sabina.[23] Miss Spielrein's condition was stable, reported Bleuler. The New Year, 'with its reminders of home', had however brought a 'serious state of agitation', which had now receded. Nevertheless she was still feeling exhausted and had asked her doctor to write to her parents on her behalf. 'As her memories of you agitate her greatly,' continues Bleuler, 'we are of the opinion that Miss Spielrein should not write to you directly over the next few months. In order to relieve her of this responsibility we have therefore forbidden her to write to her father.'

For the rest, her recovery was proceeding well:

> Miss Spielrein now occupies herself almost daily with scientific reading and she has also commenced practical scientific study in the anatomy laboratory.[24]

> She wishes to convey her fond greetings.

> Yours faithfully, the Director,

> Bleuler.

Thus on doctor's orders the father's control over his daughter was massively restricted by Bleuler himself. Mr Spielrein was compensated for this severe curtailment of his power only by the satisfaction that 'Miss Spielrein' was engaged in 'practical scientific studies', which must have flattered his ambition.

Mr Spielrein, who was paying a considerable sum for his daughter's treatment, may have pictured her recovery somewhat differently. Bleuler's letters to him which have been preserved are all worded in such a way as to give a strangely mixed impression of disapproval and painstaking friendliness. In September Mr Spielrein had been in Zürich to visit his daughter; and even then he must obviously have realized that he could no longer behave as freely with her as he imagined. 'Dear Sir, You may visit your daughter tomorrow', runs the terse text of a letter sent by Bleuler to his hotel. A few days later Bleuler is worrying about a dress Mr Spielrein wants to have made for his daughter. Bleuler wants the dressmaker commissioned by Mr Spielrein to take Sabina's measurements personally, so that the dress will fit properly. Mr Spielrein's visit to the Burghölzli on 11 September 1904 is not mentioned in Sabina's hospital notes. Three days earlier, on 8 September, Jung notes that Sabina 'used' his return (after a week's absence) 'to produce a few scenes': thus for example she climbed up the window grille in the corridor and forced him to pay her an evening visit; she sat in the doorway in her nightdress, wrapped in a blanket, and when no one took any notice of her she finally had a convulsive fit and let herself be taken back to bed 'completely exhausted'. Next, Bleuler writes again to Mr Spielrein in Rostov-on-Don: his daughter's condition had not essentially changed, but 'a slight improvement' was noticeable and some days pass quite peacefully. 'Happily' they had now succeeded 'in stimulating Miss Spielrein's interest in scientific pursuits so that she can be distracted for hours at a time from her pathological obsessions. During the morning she now often participates with great interest in the examination of patients and in the afternoon she goes for walks with her nurse.'

She uses this opportunity to play 'childish jokes of a harmless nature'. Sabina's night terrors had been discussed with her father; Bleuler writes that they have become significantly fewer. Physically too she is well, though still easily tired. Finally he asks for payment of fees for the next quarter.

In an entry in the hospital notes for 29 September Jung enumerates some of Sabina's 'childish pranks of a harmless nature': 'suicidal gestures to drive the nurses crazy, running away, giving people scares, transgressing prohibitions, etc.' She sometimes feels depressed after these excesses and has insight into her condition but not the slightest inclination to improve it. She asks him (Jung) not to show the slightest doubt about her recovery. Jung also remarks that Sabina has no powers of concentration when left to read on her own, but 'the doctor's mere personal presence can often enable her to concentrate for hours'. Jung must therefore sometimes have spent hours with her.

Two weeks later Bleuler again approaches the father: 'In the interests of Miss Spielrein's treatment' he is requested to answer the letter which she wrote to him on 1 October. She is slowly getting better, and happily she has decided to begin her medical studies in Zürich next spring.

Mr Spielrein who, according to Sabina's reports, was accustomed to react with a total breakdown of communication even to minor conflicts, must have experienced Bleuler's demands as meddling with his paternal rights, and as insulting and presumptuous. Was it not his affair whether and how he answered his daughter's letters, and also whether and where his daughter studied? Many of the Russian women students reported on the great battles they had with their fathers to be allowed to study abroad. And Mr Spielrein, who kept his daughter under such tight control and responded to her wishes for independence at 16 years with threats of suicide, must have suffered a serious crisis as a result of the increasing impertinences from Zürich.

Unfortunately it is not known whether or how Mr Spielrein replied to his daughter's letter and to the director's. At all events Bleuler did not give up. On 25 October he forwarded to Mr Spielrein two letters from Sabina; this meant that no private communication from the father to Sabina could take place while she was under the protection of the clinic. Bleuler knew how to mitigate his presumption *vis-à-vis* the father with news of Sabina's slow improvement: she was already going for accompanied walks outside the institution. In addition, he reports, she is 'currently assisting one of our doctors[25] on a scientific project which she finds of great interest'. Bleuler again mentions her decision to study medicine in Zürich, and makes it clear that there is no question of her returning to Russia. 'And even a reunion with her family, before she has commenced her studies, would in our opinion be strongly contraindicated,' writes Bleuler.

> Your daughter needs to develop independence and self-reliance and must therefore remain unencumbered by all emotional anxiety for her family and all restricting aspects of family life. This can only be achieved by her spending some time in a new and different environment where she can devote herself wholeheartedly to an absorbing activity. Your daughter too is of the opinion that these are the conditions necessary for her recovery.

That was indeed a new and unfamiliar tone for Mr Spielrein; it is hardly to be supposed that he liked it, although he may have been flattered by the Swiss doctors' confidence in his daughter's scholarship. Sabina must also have felt bad in her new role in relation to her father. Had she betrayed him? Shown him up, disregarded him? Would he survive, when previously he had always threatened suicide? How will he tolerate her letters? Will she herself survive if she stands up to him?

Mr Spielrein's reaction to Bleuler was apparently a letter in which he stated that he had concluded from Sabina's letters in October that there had been a massive deterioration in her condition; possibly he also threatened to demand her discharge and transfer. On 28 November C.G. Jung took up the correspondence with the father 'on behalf of the director' in order to excuse Sabina's letters and to hold out the prospect of her recovery: fortunately there had been no such alteration in his daughter's condition as he seemed to have concluded from her letters. Since he, Jung, had returned from his three-week military service, her recovery had progressed. 'Miss Spielrein' could now concentrate much better. Recently she had participated 'with some success' at a social function at Prof. Bleuler's. Of course there were also days when she succumbed to her childish moods; it was in one of those moods that she had written her recent letters. 'She admitted it to me immediately afterwards and sincerely regrets this unconsidered course of action. Her letters therefore do not imply a deterioration in her condition.'

This statement is in direct contradiction to the remarks recorded in the hospital notes: in November 1904 Sabina's condition took another severe turn for the worse in connection with Jung's absence, although Bleuler's goodwill, patience and calm 'were quite inexhaustible': 'Owing to the absence of the senior physician, pat. left almost entirely to herself for the last week and much worse,' writes Bleuler on 4 November. 'Has many physical complaints, insists she cannot think and cannot follow the lecture at the clinic etc' [the lecture in clinical psychiatry]; she demanded a sleeping draught, and then threatened to 'create a scene' in the night if she did not get it. Indeed she did start making a noise at 1.00 a.m. When the nurse tried to get her back to bed she resisted by kicking her: 'When the head nurse was called she stupidly dealt with the situation by forcing pat. back to bed. After that some peace.' So Bleuler apparently did not object to being fetched by the head nurse at 1 o'clock in the morning to take control of the situation! During the day Sabina had been unwell; she did go to the clinic [the clinical lecture], but afterwards remained clinging to the wall as if nailed there, perhaps in the expectation that Bleuler would pass. He then took her back to the ward, got her to tell him what happened the previous night, and noticed how she seemed to get considerably better as she did so. Nevertheless she still asked for a sleeping remedy but did not take it, because, as Bleuler comments, perhaps someone had told her that he would be pleased if she did not take it. Bleuler also states that she 'made a diagnosis of epilepsy' from a letter handed out at the lecture 'and supported it correctly'. A week later Bleuler's entries report dramatic suicide threats; she hid knives, and left behind 'farewell letters', took possession of the gasworkers' ladder on the ward and put obstacles [benches] in the corridor 'for him to jump over'. She enjoys watching Bleuler jump, but 'will not attempt the smallest jump herself: it would hurt the soles of her feet', Bleuler states. She composes songs which she cannot recite for laughing, and in which 'the hospital doctors[26] play the main parts'.

She complains that she cannot work, that life is pointless, and again talks openly of suicide; she wants the curtain cords to be returned to her room so that she can 'create a scene during the night' and demonstrates how she will try to strangle herself with them.

On 20 November Jung notes that there has again been a 'rapid deterioration' following his return: 'all kinds of pranks', 'torments the nurse so horribly that she has to be withdrawn', 'kicks the stepladder around the corridor', 'scratches the floor'. She refuses to go into town, complains of pains in her feet, refuses to eat in order to starve herself to death, 'says she desires with all her might to get ill, that she needs to be unconscious for at least two months before she can get well again'. In October, before his three-week absence, Jung had grappled intensively with Sabina's 'father complex'.

In October he pasted a bill from the Heller sanatorium, where she had been before her admission to the Burghölzli, together with some sketches of Sabina's, into the hospital notes. Most striking was this drawing: a female person, lying in helplessness and panic, on whom a man is sitting. 'It is Dr Heller giving a patient electrical treatment. The position is a remarkably sexual one' Jung writes, and continues: 'Pat. reveals many other masochistic features, for example her relationship with her father towards whom she feels a strange disgust. The chastisements form the central complex.' Even from him she constantly demands that he 'inflict pain on her, treat her badly in some way'; he was 'never merely to ask something of her, but to command it'. The remarkable treatment given by Dr Heller had obviously re-awakened for Sabina a situation of being violated. Jung links Sabina's drawing to her relationship with her father – however, he does not bring out the father's sadism and the sexual connotations of his behaviour, nor Sabina's helplessness and panic, but only her masochism.

Another theme in October is provided by the pains in Sabina's feet, which were thoroughly 'abreacted' after a day's bed rest. The analysis revealed a connection with an unpleasant walk after a row between her parents: afterwards 'the father stayed in bed for two days sick with rage, neither speaking nor eating'. When a relative then arrived on a visit, Sabina had to ask her father to get up, and also to go for a walk, so as to behave as though nothing were wrong. It was then that the pains in her feet started, so that for some time she could not walk. In addition, when she had to travel with her mother to Vienna 'in various difficult circumstances' she got the same pains. Sabina now knew that she must gradually accustom herself to a freer life. 'She is afraid of going out and of the future; so she tries to postpone going out as long as possible by means of the pain in her feet.'

Finally Sabina's Mars fantasies also form a theme. She entertains other patients by telling them 'fantastic tales about Mars'.

> She insists that every evening she travels to Mars, on to which she projects all her contrasexual fantasies. On Mars people do not eat but are fed through osmosis. They do not procreate, but children quickly develop in the unconscious of individuals and one day appear ready-made and without further difficulty.

Jung seems to have found Sabina's fantasy stories rather annoying; he comments that she maintains the correctness of this story with him 'rather like a stubborn child who does not want to give up a toy'. Had Sabina given Jung Flournoy's *From India to the Planet Mars* to read, and then tried to impress him with similar stories?[27] Or was Mars the safe fantasy world contrasting with her real situation?[28] Bleuler too knew about Sabina's Mars stories, but she clearly did not want to elaborate further on them with him 'because no one believes her', as Bleuler comments in November 1904.

On 22 January 1905, on behalf of the director, Jung approaches Mrs Spielrein personally with his report, asking her to visit Zürich. He explains to her too that Sabina has to be forbidden to write to her father since she has recently become so agitated over sending him birthday greetings. A weekly report such as the father wants is impossible on account of the burden of work on the doctors. 'The patient' is now slowly getting used to the city again, going for walks, and eating with other people. 'Yesterday she voluntarily joined the table of the assistant doctors at lunch, and this can be seen as a significant success.' For the rest she would very much like to see her mother again, a wish that even the doctors support. 'A meeting with other members of the family is not to be recommended for the time being.' He will then be able to report to her verbally on her daughter's state of health.

It can be assumed that Mr Spielrein, as a Jewish father, could in no way accept that only his wife was welcome to take part in conversations with his daughter and her doctors. And for Mrs Spielrein too her position must have been rather uncomfortable.

When no reply had been received from Mrs Spielrein after three weeks, Bleuler tried again, copying Jung's letter partly word for word, partly with small but not insignificant alterations. Her visit was important because Sabina would then be able to unburden herself on various matters. Apart from that, her recovery was progressing; she now 'voluntarily joins the table of the assistant doctors at lunch daily'. And: 'She is largely free of hysterical symptoms and she can therefore be regarded as having recovered.'

It can be assumed that Mrs Spielrein did come. In the hospital records, however, there is no mention of her visit.

An entry in the hospital records on 29.1.1905 comments on Sabina Spielrein's inability to say the trigger word 'beat' while taking part in the association experiments with acquaintances; in addition, she went into a kind of daze with the same strange feeling in her head as she had felt on her first night at the Burghölzli: on an evening visit Jung found the patient lying on the sofa with a remarkably 'sensuous dreamy expression on her face'. When he said something she suddenly laughed and said: 'Now I can hear your voice double, I feel as if I had two heads, and as if the whole of my left side were moving of its own accord.' Jung's enquiry revealed that Sabina had fallen into this state while reading Forel's book on hypnotism. When he picks up the book 'to find the passage that triggered off the father complex' she suddenly makes her defensive movements and gestures of disgust and points to the passage in which Forel illustrates the phenomenon of 'suggested false memory' with an anecdote from an autobiographical tale by the Swiss author Gottfried Keller. Keller describes how as a 7-year-old boy he had made up a false story in which he accused four older boys at his school of kidnapping him and beating him to make him call the teachers names and use foul language. Was it the trigger word 'beat' in this story which was the crucial factor, or was she tormented by doubts about the accuracy of her memories? At all events she soon seemed to recover. Three months later, on 29 April 1905, Jung commented: 'In the last few weeks distinctly improved and increasingly calm. Now listens to lectures conscientiously and with interest (zoology, botany, chemistry, physics). Fluctuations in mood still occur from time to time, particularly in connection with letters from home.'

All the more remarkable, it seems, is Jung's unaddressed medical certificate, apparently meant for the university authorities: Miss Sabina Spielrein from Russia has been at the clinic since 17.8.1904; she will probably remain here some time longer and intends 'to attend lectures at the university'. Undoubtedly this certificate hardly encourages confidence; Jung stresses the length of time she has already spent in hospital and leaves her intentions for studying vague and even dubious.

It was Bleuler who, a few days later, gave Sabina Spielrein the backing she needed to enrol at the university as a regular student by giving her a clear certificate. 'Miss Spielrein, resident at this institution and planning to matriculate at the medical faculty, is not mentally ill,' states Bleuler. 'She was here for treatment for a nervous complaint with hysterical symptoms. We must therefore recommend her for matriculation.'

The discharge

On 1 June 1905 Sabina Spielrein was discharged. 'She now lives independently in town and attends lectures' we read in the hospital records.

A week before her discharge, on 23.5.1905, Jung had again written to her father to assure him on Sabina's behalf that it was not from lack of love or gratitude that she was refraining from writing to him, but because 'she feels better and more relieved if she does not have continually to recall images and memories of home'. Furthermore it is 'characteristic of her nervous disposition' that she 'links all kinds of pathological obsessional fantasies' to his person. It is not clear what conscious or unconscious intention underlay Jung's addressing the father in this way. Was he forced by Sabina, who worried intensely about her father's rage? Did he himself feel obliged to 'explain' the situation in this way? Was it merely to propitiate the father in order to win his support for Sabina's studies? Admittedly 'her behaviour was still not quite normal', Jung continues, but it was time for her to leave 'to commence an independent existence. We will talk to her about it and will inform you of your daughter's decision'.

Mr Spielrein, who was surely hardly accustomed to wait on his daughter's decisions, immediately sent the eldest of her three brothers to study in Zürich – and in her newly won independence Sabina again felt pursued by family demands. Obviously Bleuler saw it that way too. The day before her discharge he wrote to her father: 'Miss Spielrein has become extremely agitated at being expected to look after her brother.' If she is to remain in her improved state she must be 'absolutely free of any obligations to her family'. The last letter to the father from the Burghölzli comes significantly from Jung. A week after Sabina Spielrein's discharge, on 7.6.1905, Jung gives the father her new address, which unfortunately is near her brother's apartment, and asks him to find other lodgings for the brother since it is of the utmost importance for his daughter's health 'to have as little contact with her brother as possible'. The 'brother complex' was not explicitly discussed in the hospital records, but the brothers seem to have functioned as substitutes for the father. 'When we recommended Zürich as a location for your son we were as yet unaware of the obsessional fantasies which are attached by the patient to her brother, otherwise we would have been more hesitant in recommending Zürich to you,' writes Jung. In addition he asks him to send money direct to his daughter now. 'But should you require some supervision in this matter I would be pleased to be at your service and to receive the money for Miss Spielrein on her behalf.'

It is striking that Jung does not refer to Bleuler's letter of 31 May, which would have been quite enough to keep Mr Spielrein's demands within bounds. There was undoubtedly in Jung's directives – in contrast with Bleuler's clear statements – a violation of boundaries: Did he really think that the father would find another lodging for the brother? And why is he 'at his service' to receive money for Sabina on her behalf?

Did that not mean that he was tending – in place of the father – to take control of her instead of supporting her independence? Had Jung really understood Sabina's father complex, if he was so eager to assume guardianship of her in financial matters? How much did he really value her capabilities? Was her discharge from the hospital really a release into freedom?

Sabina Spielrein at least seems to have fought her own battles over her freedom. On 24 April 1905, the day before the start of lectures, she began to keep a diary in Russian, which she hid from Jung. She was worried about studying and 'awaited this happy moment' in a state of 'somehow deathly darkness'.

> My head aches, I feel sick and weak. I don't believe in my strengths, in fact I don't believe in anything. Jung is going along the corridor. Soon he'll come in here: I must hide the book so as not to let him see what I'm doing, but why don't I show him? The devil alone knows!
>
> (Wackenhut & Willke 1994: 185f)

At the university especially she felt isolated from her fellow students; she felt she was 'much more thorough, more serious, with a more developed critical capacity, more independent . . .'. Yet she doubted her capacity to work in a scientific way.

> First, will my health allow me to? And most important of all: will I be talented enough? Meanwhile life without science is unimaginable to me. What would be left for me without science? Marriage? The thought fills me with dread: sometimes my heart aches for tenderness, for love, but it is only a deceptive, fleeting, superficial moment which hides the most pitiful prose . . . I wish I had a good friend, to whom I could bare my soul, I want the love of an older person who could love me and understand me as parents love their child (spiritual affinity). And for me it is as if my parents were not parents at all . . . But that story is too well known for me to want to describe it.

And without warning she continues: 'If only I were as wise as my Jung[a]! Damn! I just want to know whether anything can be made of me,' she asks, and says: 'And how stupid it is, that I'm not a man: they have it so much easier with everything. It's outrageous that the whole of life goes their way. I won't be a slave!'

A month later, on 8 June 1905, a week after moving into her own apartment, and the day after Jung's letter to her father, she is not at all concerned about her brother's proximity but she is anxious about being close to people:

> Somehow I'm afraid to get close to people. I fear for my freedom. The only thing I have now is my freedom, and I'm protecting this last treasure with all my strength. I cannot bear the tiniest criticism of my personality, not even in the form of a simple instruction: it feels like a punishing sermon . . .

Nevertheless:

> Only from Jung can I tolerate everything. It is unbelievably painful to me when he reprimands me. I want to weep, to implore him to stop, because I feel my personality being suppressed, but on the other hand I can't resist him at all.

> (ibid: 186)

No doubt Jung had moved Sabina deeply. To him she had confessed her shameful secrets, her hidden thoughts and feelings. And it was probably thanks to his patience, and his intense devotion to and enthusiasm for the emotional life which she experienced from him that 'life without science became unimaginable for her'.

It was Bleuler, however, not Jung, who laid down the outlines of her treatment. Her treatment was in accordance with ideas that had already been introduced at the Burghölzli by Forel: she was treated as a victim of severe traumatization. Her substantial symptoms were diagnosed as 'hysterical', and 'hysteria' (a controversial term at that time, as it is now) was seen as a 'traumatic neurosis' in the sense of Breuer and Freud. Notwithstanding all the changes that the concept of 'traumatic neurosis' has undergone in the last hundred years, the essential therapeutic principle described by Bleuler is still valid: to treat patients with patience, calm and inner goodwill, and to create an environment which prevents the patients' acting-out and promotes their resources and talents.

What was unusual in Sabina Spielrein's case was how unreservedly Bleuler stood up for her; she could rely on his unwavering backing for her apparently almost hopeless struggle for independence from her father and from her whole family by whom she felt literally 'possessed'. In spite of her 'childish pranks', her tormenting of the nurses, and her continuing threats of suicide, Bleuler invited her not only to lunch with the doctors but to his own home; he admitted her to his lectures, involved her in the ongoing psychological research, and finally recommended her unconditionally to be enrolled at the university to study medicine. No doubt Bleuler's demanding principle that Sabina's acting out of tyrannical and violent impulses be met with goodwill and forbearance, and that at the same time she be respected as a future colleague and co-worker, reached the limits of what was tolerable to doctors and nurses, and to other patients at the clinic.

Compared with Bleuler's, Jung's attitude to Sabina and his engagement with her was as intensive but much less consistent. Although Sabina made it clear to him that she had been traumatized since her early childhood, it remains unclear whether and how Jung comprehended her traumatization. However we may judge his analysis and his conclusions today, the result of his ambitious scrutiny of Sabina's complexes was that the trauma as well as the perpetrator faded into the background. A close relationship developed between them which would later prove to be as powerful as it was critical.

It is easy to understand why she awaited the 'happy moment' of her discharge in a state of 'somehow deathly darkness'. Her situation seemed almost hopeless: at 20 years old, and with serious social anxieties, how would she, a Russian Jewess, manage to integrate herself into a society which was foreign to her in nearly all its aspects? How would she not only cope with the demands of the university but at the same time take on a role there as a woman pioneer among medical students? How would she separate from her father and family despite the fact that she had no one to stand by her and would remain in economic dependence?

She was discharged as 'recovered', not as 'cured'. She had a place as a student in Zürich, and she took pleasure in studying. But she was not yet 'free'. Who would give her support in the future, and would she find someone to love her 'as parents love their child'?

Notes

1   All details of Sabina Spielrein's stay at the Burghölzli in Zürich have been taken (when not otherwise indicated) from the hospital records published by B. Minder in *Luzifer-Amor. Zeitschrift zur Geschichte der Psychoanalyse* (1994), 14.
2   Patients could be admitted to the hospital only with a medical certificate dated not more than two weeks previously; certificates from doctors related to the patient were not valid. Only addicted persons could be admitted of their own volition [Forel, A. 1894, Bleuler, E. (1916) 4th edition, 1923: 162].
3   Letter from E. Bleuler to Mr Spielrein 26.9.1904.
4   Zürich State Archive, government resolution 20.10.1904.
5   Organizational rules, Annual Report, Burghölzli Mental Hospital, 1869–1905.
6   Adolf Meyer (1866–1950) who, as Director of the Johns Hopkins University in Baltimore, played a leading role as a mentor in American psychiatry, was a former doctoral candidate of Forel's and remained in active contact with him all his life; in 1893 he reported to Forel on a course in psychiatry which he was giving to students:

I get the doctors to enact the part of a group of patients and I direct the proceedings. In the course of the demonstration they must not use any technical language; the description of clinical observations must be expressed in concrete terms without recourse to pseudo-psychological or pseudo-physiological paraphrases.

One semester and several clinics after I worked at the Burghölzli, that was all the psychiatry I brought back with me to America. I must say it is now proving to be a good foundation and I hope that in time I will progress far enough to call myself your pupil without your having to protest at such presumption.

7 The frequent correlation between alcoholism, venereal disease and mental illness led Forel to the hypothesis that alcohol, even in small doses, causes damage to the germ cells ('blastophthoria'), with specific damage to the mental and physical health of the next generation. He acknowledged (1924) that this hypothesis is not proven (Meier, Rolf 1986: 82).

8 The International Order of Good Templars (IOGT) was founded in the USA in 1851 as a pioneer organization for abstinence from alcohol and for the community of nations; in 1892 Forel founded a Swiss section, and in 1906 the National Order of Good Templars (IOGTN), which still exists.

9 Hedwig Bleuler-Waser (1869–1940): 'Lebensrückblick', in *Schweizer Frauen der Tat* Bd.2 ('Looking back over my life', in: *Swiss Women of Action*, Vol 2).

10 Monakov recalls particularly a very crowded meeting at which 'Bleuler and his wife were so enthusiastic about psychoanalysis that they were even celebrating the movement in verse and where a medallion of Freud was passed round' (Monakov 1970: 244).

11 'Jung and Maeder analysed a paranoid woman with confused speech whom I had treated earlier at the Burghölzli hospital; I had partly uncovered the meaning of the madness behind her apparent speech confusion . . . I had already presented such patients, and other similar ones, in my clinic at the beginning of the nineties and drawn attention to elliptical speech patterns' (Forel, *Hypnotismus*, 6th edition, 1921: 233).

12 Letter 6.10.1901, Zürich State Archive.

13 Letter of resignation 23.7.1902. Minutes of senior executive meetings 1902, Zürich State Archive.

14 C.G. Jung to Andreas Vischer (undated letter, kindly lent by S. Zumstein-Preiswerk).

15 As Jung said in retrospect in 1925, he had missed the point of the situation: his own connection with it. 'The girl had of course fallen hopelessly in love with me, but I paid very little attention to it and none at all to the role I was playing in her psychology' (Jung 1925, Seminar).

16 Zumstein-Preiswerk: personal communication.

17 Letter to Andreas Vischer, 22.8.1904 (kindly lent by S. Zumstein-Preiswerk).

18 ibid

19 C.G. Jung to Andreas Vischer 12.12.1904: 'Then I completed my doctoral thesis which now lies before the faculty' (letter kindly lent by S. Zumstein-Preiswerk).

20 In her childhood diary 1895–98 (Wackenhut & Willke 1994) Sabina describes a trip with her mother to Berlin and Karlsbad. She complains that she is completely responsible for her mother who is 'too nervous' to cope alone. The incident mentioned here is not reported in the published diary.

21 The fact that academic achievement had been extremely important to her parents

is also evident from the diary entries 1895–98, which were checked by her father (Wackenhut & Willke 1995).

22 Jung, C.G. 1902: 86 (78?). In the footnote to this passage Jung refers to the *Studies on Hysteria* by Breuer and Freud.

23 When Sabina was at school her father made her keep a diary regularly and he used to check it. The diaries have been partly preserved and were published in 1994 in German translation (Wackenhut & Willke 1994).

24 Sabina Spielrein, as has been shown, worked in the *psychology* laboratory at the Burghölzli; it seems that Bleuler described her as working in the *anatomy* laboratory in order to prevent her father doubting the seriousness of her medical activities.

25 Franz Riklin and Jung were working at that time on 'The associations of normal subjects'.

26 In addition to Bleuler and Jung, from 1 October 1904 Carl Abraham (1881–1924) had also become part of the team.

27 The reference is to an article about the medium Hélène Smith, who among other things spoke the Martians' language.

28 Jung's notes on Sabina's 'Mars fantasies' are reminiscent of another patient with a moon fantasy whom Jung treated privately in 1910 and often made a subject of discussion: the girl, from a cultured family, heard voices, refused food and no longer spoke; at 15 she had been 'seduced by her brother and abused by his school-friends'. Jung writes; from that time she became increasingly isolated and hid away from people, until at the age of 17 she was admitted to the clinic in a catatonic state. In her fantasies she lived on the moon with women and children in a 'sublunar dwelling', threatened by a vampire. After much resistance and several dramatic relapses she came to realize 'that life on earth was unavoidable' and 'resigned herself gradually to her fate' (Jung/Jaffé 1962: 150ff. For the implications of Jung's interpretation of this case cf. Höfer 1993: 307 & 312–18).

References

Abraham, H. (1976) *Karl Abraham. Sein Leben für die Psychoanalyse*. München: Kindler.

Bankowski-Züllig, M. (1988) 'Zürich–das russische Mekka'. In *Verein Fem. Wissenschaft*, ed. Zürich: efef.

Bernheim, H. (1884) *De la Suggestion: des Applications à la Thérapeutique*. Paris: Doin.

Binswanger, L. (1957) 'Erinnerungen an Eugen Bleuler'. *Schweizer Med. Wochenschrift, 35/36*, 1112f.

Binswanger, O. (1904) *Die Hysterie*. Wien: Hölder.

Bleuler, E. (1892) Review: Bernheim, H, 'Neue Studien über Hypnotismus, Suggestion und Psychotherapie'. Transl. by Sigmund Freud. *Müncher Med. Wochenschrift, 39*, 431.

——(1896) Review: 'E. Breuer, S. Freud: Studien über Hysterie'. *Münchner Med. Wochenschrift, 43*, 524f.

——(1923/1936) [1916] *Textbook of Psychiatry*. Engl. ed. A.A. Brill. London: Allen & Unwin.

Bleuler, M. (1951) 'Geschichte des Burghölzlis und der Psychiatrischen Universitätsklinik'. In *Zürcher Spitalgeschichte*, 2: 377–425.

—— (1988) *Vorwort zu Bleuler E.* [1911]. Tübingen: Ed. Discord.

Breuer, J., & Freud, S. (1895) *Studies on Hysteria. SE* 2.

Carotenuto, A. (1982) *A Secret Symmetry.* New York: Pantheon Books. [*Diario di una segreta simmetria. Sabina Spielrein tra Jung and Freud.* Rome, 1980].

Ellenberger, H. (1985) *The Discovery of the Unconscious.* London: Allen Lane/The Penguin Press.

Flournoy, T. (1900) *From India to the Planet Mars. A Case of Multiple Personality with Imaginary Languages.* Foreword C.G. Jung, and Commentary M. Cifali, ed. and introd. S. Shamdasani. Princeton, NJ: Princeton University Press, 1994.

Forel, A. (1889) *Der Hypnotismus und die Suggestive Psychotherapie.* Stuttgart: Enke, 1902, 4th ed. English translation of 5th ed. by H.W. Armit: publ. 1906 by Rebman of London & New York.

—— (1937) *Out of my Life.* New York, 1937. [*Rückblick auf mein Leben.* Zürich, 1935.]

—— (1968) *Briefe/Correspondence.* Ed. H. Walser. Bern: Huber.

Freud, S. (1889) Review of Auguste Forel's *Hypnotism. SE* 1.

Herman, J. L. (1981) *Father–Daughter Incest.* Cambridge, MA & London: Harvard University Press.

Höfer, R. (1993) *Die Hiobsbotschaft C.G. Jungs. Folgen sexuellen Missbrauchs.* ('C.G. Jung's Message to Job. Consequences of Sexual Abuse'). Lüneburg: zu Klampen.

Jagella, C., Isler, H., & Hess, K. (1994) '100 Jahre Neurologie an der Universität Zürich (1894–1994); Constantin von Monakov (1853–1940). Hirnforscher, Neurologe, Psychiater, Denker'. *Schweizer Journal für Neurologie und Psychiatrie, 145,* Supplement.

Jung, C.G. (1902) *On the Psychology and Pathology of so-called Occult Phenomena CW* 1.

—— (1904, 1906) *Diagnostische Assoziationsstudien. G. W* 4.

—— (1911/1912) 'Wandlungen und Symbole der Libido' ('Transformations and Symbols of the Libido') *Jahrbuch für psychoanalytische und psychopathologische Forschungen,* eds. E. Bleuler & S. Freud. I (Teil 1), II (Teil 2).

—— (1913) *The theory of psychoanalysis CW* 4.

—— (1961) *Memories, Dreams, Reflections.* Recorded and edited by Aniela Jaffé. London: Fontana, 1973.

—— (1989) 'Analytical Psychology'. Notes of the Seminar given in 1925 by C.G. Jung. Edited by W. McGuire. Princeton NJ.: Princeton University Press.

McGuire, W. (1974) (ed.) *The Freud/Jung Letters.* Princeton, NJ.: Princeton University Press.

Minder, B. (1994) [1992] 'Sabina Spielrein: Jungs Patientin am Burghölzli Zürich'. *Luzifer-Amor. Zeitschr. f. Geschichte der Psychoanalyse 7,* 14, 55–127. [Med. Diss. Universität Bern]. *Journal of Analytical Psychology, 46,* 1, and this volume, Chapter 6.

Monakov, C. V. (1970) *Vita mea. Mein Leben.* Eds. A.W. Gubser & E.W. Ackerknecht. Bern: Huber.

Wackenhut, I. & Willke, A. (1994) *Sabina Spielrein. Missbrauchüberlebende und Psychoanalytikerin* ('Sabina Spielrein, Survivor of abuse and psychoanalyst'). Diss. Med: Fak. Med: Hochschule Hannover.

Chapter 9

Comments on the Burghölzli hospital records of Sabina Spielrein

Coline Covington

On the basis of accepting the historical accounts of his patients as literal, Freud hypothesized his seduction theory and rooted pathogenic behaviour in the trauma of the past. Freud's 'cathartic method' of analysis enabled the patient to recover traumatic memories from the unconscious and to restore a cognitive link between the past and the present. The relation between memory and trauma had become a matter of debate and speculation since 1872 when Charcot's treatment of hysterics by means of hypnosis at the Salpêtrière Hospital in Paris first received wide attention within scientific and medical circles. In 1885 Freud became Charcot's apprentice. During this time Janet was also demonstrating how hypnosis could be used to reveal the repressed psychological trauma that underlay hysteria. By 1888 Janet had published several cases of hysteria. Four years later Freud finished the translation of Charcot's lectures and presented his own view of hysteria in a footnote:

> The core of a hysterical attack, in whatever form it may appear, is a memory, the hallucinatory reliving of a scene which is significant for the onset of the illness . . . the content of the memory is as a rule a psychical trauma which is qualified by its intensity to provoke the outbreak of hysteria in the patient or is the event which, owing to its occurrence at a particular moment, has become a trauma.
>
> (Freud 1886–1899: 137)

Three years later, in 1895, Freud wrote, 'Hysterics suffer mainly from reminiscences'. Taking a step further from the moral and physical traumas that Charcot and Janet had hypothesized as causing hysteria, Freud postulated that hysteria was more specifically linked to the trauma of seduction or sexual assault. 'Reminiscences' were expressed in the form of distorted memories. It was only after 1897, when Freud had to abandon his seduction theory, that the roots of hysteria were further extended and 'psychologized' as resting in purely psychic events, i.e. the repressed sexual fantasies of childhood.

From this brief history, we can see how the view of the aetiology of hysteria gradually shifted from external factors to internal, psychological ones. I would like to suggest that this theoretical shift can also be seen in Jung's treatment of Sabina Spielrein, and to explore some of the reasons why this may have occurred.

Jung evolved his own theory of hysteria that combined personal, historical experiences and associations with innate psychological ones (what he initially described as 'primordial images' and later defined as archetypal) in his idea of the complex. Ten years after Freud had written 'Hysterics suffer mainly from reminiscences', Jung wrote, 'in hysteria a complex is always at work'. He describes hysteria as a morbid condition, congenital or acquired, in which the affects are exceedingly powerful. Hence the patients are more or less continual victims of their affects. At the same time, however, hysteria generally determines only the quantity, not the quality, of the affects. The quality is given by the patient's character.

(Jung 1906a, para. 464, quoted in Chapter 6: 112)

Jung does not specifically trace the root of the complex that is 'always at work' in hysteria to memory. However, what Jung describes here is how memory (or the idea represented by the memory and stored in the complex) becomes dissociated from affect when it is traumatic. This dissociation leads in turn to somatization of the affect.

When Sabina Spielrein was admitted to the Burghölzli and interviewed by Jung on the evening of 17th August 1904, he gave her the diagnosis of a hysteric. Jung reports in her notes, 'Patient laughs and cries in a strangely mixed, compulsive manner. Masses of tics, she rotates her head jerkily, sticks out her tongue, twitches her legs. Complains of a terrible headache, saying that she was not mad, only upset, at the hotel, she could not stand people or noise' (Chapter 5: 85). Today, Sabina might well be diagnosed as psychotic. Furthermore, she was referred to the Burghölzli because she could not be treated at the Heller Institute where she had been previously. We then see throughout the hospital notes how difficult Sabina's behaviour was and how much she tried to create havoc around her to get attention and especially to provoke the doctors and staff of the hospital to punish her. In her fear of being abused, she became the abuser. Jung notes: 'At the slightest sign of lack of respect or trust, she immediately retaliates with negativistic behaviour and with a succession of greater or lesser devilish tricks' (ibid: 88). What is also apparent in the hospital notes is how Sabina's behaviour was managed and controlled by a consistently firm and non-punitive approach in which it was made clear that she would not receive attention for her misbehaviour. After the first few days following her admission, during which 'strict bed-rest' was prescribed, Jung writes:

Yesterday the medical assistant forbade her to leave her bed. Whereupon patient made a point of getting up and declared energetically she would never obey, that she never wanted to get well, that she would behave badly. On being suitably coaxed by the writer she returned to bed perfectly calm.

(ibid: 87)

Sabina's outbursts diminished considerably during her first few weeks at the Burghölzli, while the difficulties she experienced in being left became manifest. This was first noted on 29th August, when Jung writes:

Absence of senior physician (since 27th August). Yesterday (28th August) headache, getting worse. Tried to demand medication, which was refused. At night in bed, pulse 180, for that reason finally given Morphine . . . then good night.

(ibid: 89)

A month later, Sabina's growing attachment to Jung is noted. On 29th September, he writes:

Patient has great insight into her condition but not the slightest inclination to improve it. She asks Ref. never to betray the slightest sense of being at a loss about her but only the utmost fortitude and a firm belief in her recovery; that would be the only way for her to get better.

Pat. has no attention span when she is reading by herself, but the doctor's mere personal presence can often enable her to concentrate for hours.

(ibid: 90)

Sabina's determination not to improve her condition indicates how frightened she was not only of separation but also that if she got involved with Jung, she would be abused. The effects of the next separation are reported on the 16th October when Jung had been absent all day. He writes:

During this time patient was very unsettled. The following day she reports that she constantly and with great longing imagines Ref. squeezing her left hand tightly until it hurts. She desires this painful treatment with all her strength. The next day she has a high grade hyperaesthesia in her left hand. 'I just want to feel this pain', patient says calmly, 'I want you to do something really bad to me, to force me to do something that I am opposed to with all my being'.

(ibid: 92)

Sabina's transference onto Jung of her 'painful' love of her father is clearly evident here. What is also evident is how she uses her desire to suffer something 'really bad' in order to defend herself against being involved in a loving relation with Jung and in this way she tries to repeat her relationship with her abusive father.

The hospital notes give us some indication of how Sabina was managed. Doctors and care staff were on call at all hours and lived on the premises with their families. As Graf-Nold points out, Bleuler had successfully established what would be considered today a residential therapeutic community (Chapter 8: 149). Bleuler's three 'tools for treating the psyche' – 'patience, calm, and inner goodwill towards the patients' (ibid: 148) – were undoubtedly important ingredients in enabling Sabina to trust that no one would abuse her and in contributing to her impressive progress.

Nevertheless, we are given very little idea of what exactly went on between Sabina and Jung, nor do we learn much about his particular therapeutic approach. Jung was at the start of his career and was experimenting for the first time in applying Freud's concepts to his work. At the same time, we know that Jung was already familiar with the phenomenon of the transference (chapter 5, note 13: 109) and would most probably have been aware of Sabina's unfolding erotic transference to him. In his interview with Sabina's mother, Jung is informed of Sabina's previous erotic transferences – some time before she had fallen in love with her uncle, a doctor, and subsequently with another doctor – both had disappointed her (ibid: 109). In both cases it seems clear that Sabina had been repeating her relationship with her father – to the point of rejection. In contrast, Jung was able to accept Sabina's erotic transference, while it was more difficult for him to differentiate himself from her transference projections due to his own emerging transference.

The roots of Sabina's erotic transference to Jung can be seen in her hateful relations with both her parents as described in the hospital records. Her sadomasochistic relationship with her father seemed to revolve around the shame she experienced with him, her misbehaviour, the excitement and relief she derived from his physical beating of her, and her anxiety about her father's depression and periodic threats of suicide. Jung notes:

> She cannot turn to her father, he does not really understand her, he says hurtful things to her. Because of her strong narcissism she cannot give in to her father, and when her father is then sad, she cannot talk to him and she is deeply hurt. He has hit patient and she has had to kiss his hand in return.
> (At this point numerous tics, grimaces and gestures of abhorrence.)
> (ibid: 86)

Sabina recounts to Jung, with a further display of tics, how her father had hit her on her bare buttocks until she was aged 11, at times in front of her siblings. He later notes:

Three years ago it happened that patient said to her father that she could give up parents in favour of the company of other people. Big scene followed, father went wild and threatened suicide. There were often scenes like this, sometimes lasting for days. It also distresses patient that father insults and tyrannizes other members of the household. It pains her that he is unhappy, always talking about dying, etc. When he is kind to her she regrets that she behaves badly towards him. She is always afraid that one day he will kill himself.

(ibid: 86)

Sabina's father is portrayed as a masochistic tyrant, using his depression to manipulate his daughter (and no doubt other members of the family) – when Sabina suggests that she would rather live without him, he threatens suicide. We can see here the conflict that Sabina faced in her relation with her father – to leave him effectively meant she would be killing him. She could only either stay with him (and continue in this hateful way of relating) or leave him and suffer intolerable (and pathological) guilt. There was no separation between father and daughter. Just as Sabina was searching for a mother in her father, he too was searching for that in her. We can see how this was later repeated in the transference and counter-transference with Jung. It is not surprising that Sabina would have insisted that the only way for her to get better was for Jung to show the 'utmost fortitude and a firm belief in her recovery'. Sabina's identification with her father is also evident in the records. She is controlling, provocative, and punitive towards the doctors and the nurses, threatening to commit suicide and forming hysterical symptoms when she is crossed or left.

Sabina's relationship with her mother seemed to be similarly tumultuous and sado-masochistic. Jung notes:

Even during this last year mother tried to beat her in front of her brothers and her brothers' friends. Once when, at thirteen, her mother punished her, she ran away and hid in various places, doused herself with ice-cold water (winter!), and went into the cellar to catch her death of cold. This way she wanted to torment her parents and kill herself. In her 15th year, she tried to starve herself to death in Karlsbad because she had made her mother angry.

(ibid: 87)

Just as Sabina, like her father, retaliates against her mother by threatening to kill herself, she also punishes herself in this way. Jung writes: 'She sees herself as a thoroughly bad and corrupt person, and feels therefore that she should not be allowed to be in the company of other people' (ibid: 95). She is only able to establish relations with others through painful treatment and the manipulation of guilt. This is evident in her provocative behaviour towards the hospital staff, whom she constantly challenges to punish her and thereby confirm her in her narcissistic guilt. Sabina's conviction that she is a 'bad and corrupt person' both explains and reinforces the abusive treatment she receives from her parents. In order to be loved, Sabina conforms to the expectations she imagines her parents have of her – punishment and humiliation, particularly at the hand of the father, then become associated with sexual excitement.

The only other specific information we are given about Sabina's mother is when Jung records her behaviour during a walk when Sabina showed 'great disgust at shops, stuck her tongue out at them, etc' (ibid: 94). Jung discovers,

> [h]er mother has the odd habit of having to buy everything she sees and can be talked into buying; every time she goes out shopping she brings home masses of things which no one needs but which are very expensive. She never has enough money on her to pay for everything and therefore has to borrow from relatives and then struggle to repay them from her household budget. Above all father must not know about this, so there is constant anxiety that father might find out about these dealings . . .
>
> (ibid: 94)

Sabina's mother is what in today's jargon would be called a 'shopaholic' – her compulsive need to buy everything presumably gave her narcissistic gratification, in playing 'the great lady with her expensive acquisitions', as well as trying to extort love from her family through her showering of presents and her constant need for loans. Sabina, as witness to this, must have felt her mother's emptiness and her mother's attack against her father who could not satisfy her. Sabina's own disgust 'with ladies and shops' (ibid: 94) indicates her own identification with her mother's self-hatred and her homosexual solution in wanting to eschew what is feminine in order to obtain her mother's love and to try to satisfy her where her father had clearly failed.

From Jung's account of Sabina, we can see how much she needed to find a mother who would make her feel wanted, and a loving father. The impression we have of Jung's treatment of Sabina was that he, much like Bleuler, was patient, calm and supportive – he made Sabina feel wanted and accepted. He did not respond punitively to her 'devilish tricks' but was able to provide her with some form of benign superego which she had been unable to experience in her life. In 1917, Sabina acknowledges what Jung gave her when she wrote to him, 'In practice what matters is less precise classification than one's intuitive understanding of the patient, because practical psychotherapy is a healing art. We agree on that point. We need scientific findings only as points of reference' (quoted in Cifali 1988/2001: 132). Sabina's view accords with Jung's understanding and approach to treating hysteria in which, he writes, 'a complex is always at work' (Jung 1905b, para. 754, quoted in Chapter 6: 113). A year later, in 1906, Jung elaborates this idea in his paper, 'Association, dream and hysterical symptom'. He writes:

The complex has an abnormal autonomy in hysteria and a tendency to an active separate existence, which reduces and replaces the constellating power of the ego-complex. In this way a new morbid personality is gradually created, the inclinations, judgments, and resolutions of which move only in the direction of the will to be ill. This second personality devours what is left of the normal ego and forces it into the role of a secondary (oppressed) complex. A purposive treatment of hysteria must therefore strengthen what has remained of the normal ego, and this is best achieved by introducing some new complex that liberates the ego from domination by the complex of the illness.

(Jung 1906b, paras. 861–2; see Chapter 6: 113)

Here Jung's description of the autonomy of the complex and its threat to the ego can perhaps be seen as a forerunner to Otto Rank's work on 'the double' in 1914 when he postulated that it originates as a form of defence against the destruction of the ego.

Five years later, Freud, in his essay, 'The "uncanny"', links the idea of the double with the compulsion to repeat, 'proceeding from the instinctual impulses and probably inherent in the very nature of the instincts – a compulsion powerful enough to overrule the pleasure principle, lending to certain aspects of the mind their daemonic character . . .' (Freud 1919: 360–1).

Jung's 'purposive treatment of hysteria' specifies that the ego must be strengthened 'by introducing some new complex that liberates the ego from domination by the complex of the illness'. In this case Jung's view of repetition compulsion – or the complex 'always at work in hysteria' – is that it served as a defence against an undeveloped or insufficiently strong ego. Seen from this perspective, the emphasis Jung (and subsequently Janet) placed on the therapeutic relationship makes sense in terms of enabling the patient to experience a different object in the present which can then be internalized so that the ego structure can be strengthened and altered, allowing it to let go of its old defences. In the importance Jung gives to processes of identification and internalization, we can also see early links to object relations theory and the notion of the corrective emotional experience. It is the introduction of 'some new complex' which Jung cites as the curative factor – this over and above the uncovering and working through of trauma that Freud argued enabled patients to differentiate from their past.

Jung's early work on word association gave him the means to uncover the complex. The hospital records suggest that Jung administered the word association test in his treatment of Sabina and indicate that she in turn applied the test to other patients at the Burghölzli. Jung notes on 29th January 1905:

Since the last abreaction substantial improvement. Still strongly emotional and unusually powerful expressions of feeling. At every stimulation of the complex she still reacts with her back, hands, tongue, and mouth, though significantly less so. She is now aware of it and hides her expressions of disgust behind her hands. She recently tried associations with acquaintances and on this occasion it was shown that she could not say her complex trigger word 'to beat'. So she omitted it during the experiment.

(Chapter 5: 95f)

Through the use of these trigger words, Sabina's memory of abuse could come out and she could give vent to her rage, with the result that her need to somatize her affect and to act out her abusive past in such a compulsive manner was considerably reduced. Jung, like Freud, recognized the personal historical aetiology of hysteria and demonstrated, in Sabina's case quite dramatically, the symptom relief that could be achieved through the recovery of repressed memory. But it was through his work on word associations that Jung later came to view the complex as derived from or as a manifestation of an archetypal constellation, which included not simply personal associations but also archetypal or collective ones. Although Jung was undoubtedly aware of Sabina's transference towards him, we do not know to what extent, if any, he interpreted the transference. He seems to place more emphasis on the importance of establishing a 'new complex' in the treatment to liberate 'the ego from domination by the complex of the illness'. In this way Jung shifts the locus of treatment away from the recovery of the past in order to separate from it towards a more purposive or homeostatic view of therapy. From this viewpoint symptoms are regarded not so much as historical artefacts but as indicating an imbalance in the psyche that needs to be corrected. This shift would also be consistent with Jung's apparent discomfort with his patients' transference and his own counter-transference. For example, in a report, dated 25th September 1905, addressed to Freud and delivered to Frau Spielrein 'for use if the occasion arises' (the report was never sent on to Freud), Jung writes, somewhat defensively, about Sabina's erotic transference: 'During treatment the patient had the misfortune to fall in love with me' (Chapter 5: 106).

While Jung was grappling with Sabina's 'father complex' and effectively acting in *loco parentis* himself in relation to Sabina, we also do not know to what extent, if any, Jung was able to view Sabina's erotic transference as a repetition of her relation with her father. In her diary entry of 25th April 1905, following her first day at medical school, Sabina wrote:

To me, life without science is completely senseless. What else is there for me if there is no science? Get married? But that thought fills me with dread: at times my heart aches for tenderness, love; but that is but a deceptive, passing, external display that hides the most pitiful prose. The price is subjugation of the personality. . . . No! I do not want such love: I want a good friend to whom I can bare my soul; I want the love of an older man so that he would love me the way parents love and understand their child (spiritual affinity). But my parents – they are not it – If only I were as wise a human being as my Junga! ... And how stupid that I am not a man: men have it easier with everything. It is a shame that everything in life goes their way. I do not want to be a slave!'

(Quoted from Brinkmann & Bose 1986; see Chapter 10: 194)

Sabina reveals her longing for someone who will be a parent for her and not a partner – she still looks for her father's love in Jung (i.e. she is still attached to a father in her mind who prizes scientific achievement above all else and who makes her feel bad about herself as a woman – she envies men their ease in life and equates marriage with subjugation). While Bleuler protects Sabina from contact with her father and we have the impression that he can see how destructive this relationship is for Sabina, there is not this same sense with Jung. Jung refers to Sabina's father complex but we are left with the question as to whether Jung was able to help Sabina to separate from her father and the extent to which he could help her to understand her underlying need for a mother.

In an unpublished letter to Freud, written in June 1909, Sabina reveals her own fear of discovering her maternal transference in her eroticized search for a mother in men as she recounts her dream, '. . . A few months ago I had to forgo the wish to write to you because in the dream you had female breasts . . .' (quoted from Wackenhut & Willke: 200–202; see Chapter 10: 207). In writing about Sabina's drawings of the electrical treatment she had received from Dr Heller, Graf-Nold also questions Jung's response. She writes,

> Jung links Sabina's drawing to her relationship with her father – however, he does not bring out the father's sadism and the sexual connotations of his behaviour, nor Sabina's powerlessness and panic, but only her masochism.
>
> (Chapter 8: 166f)

Was Jung unable to talk about Sabina's father's sadism – and her sadism – because he could not know about his own father complex and his hatred of his father? Jung's failure to see the maternal transference underlying Sabina's erotic transference to the father would also suggest his fear of his feminine self as well as his fear of knowing about his own lack of a mother. Jung became entangled in Sabina's erotic projections towards him as a mother – and became a mother to her – because he too was searching for a mother. In December 1908, in a state of desperation, Jung wrote to Sabina urging her not to seek revenge on him while at the same time revealing his own transference to her as his mother. He writes:

I am looking for a person who understands how to love, without punishing the other person, imprisoning him or sucking him dry. . . . Give me back now something of the love and patience and unselfishness which I was able to give you at the time of your illness. Now I am ill.

(Chapter 3: 38)

Towards the end of 1908, Sabina writes from Zürich in an unpublished letter to her mother in Rostov:

Just recently Jung finished his paper that created such a stir, ('The significance of the father in the destiny of the individual'), in which he shows that the choice of the future (love) object is determined in the first relations of the child with his parents. That I love him is as firmly determined as that he loves me. He is for me a father and I am a mother for him, or, more precisely, the woman who has acted as the first substitute for the mother (his mother came down with hysteria when he was two years old); and he became so attached to the (substitute) woman that when she was absent he saw her in hallucinations, etc., etc. Why he fell in love with his wife I do not know . . . Let us say, his wife is 'not completely' satisfactory, and now he has fallen in love with me, a hysteric; and I fell in love with a psychopath, and is it necessary to explain why? I have never seen my father as normal. His insane striving 'to know himself' is best expressed in Jung for whom his scientific activity is more important than anything in this world. . . . An uneven dynamic character coupled with a highly developed sensibility, a need to suffer and to be compassionate 'ad magnum'. . . . If you could only hide in the next room and hear how concerned he is for me and my fate. . . . Then he starts reproaching himself endlessly for his feelings, for example, that I am something sacred for him, that he is ready to beg for forgiveness, etc. . . . Remember how dear daddy was apologizing to you in exactly the same manner! . . . He suffered through many nights thinking about me. . . . He felt responsible for my fate . . .

(Chapter 10: 203)

Sabina makes it clear here how she has come to understand the link between Jung and her father (or whom Jung represents for her in her transference) and, similarly, whom she represents for Jung (in his transference). What is also painfully evident is Jung's own need to make his hysterical mother better and his feeling of responsibility towards her, as he expressed towards Sabina. For both Jung and Sabina, their erotic transferences served to mask their depression and to protect them from knowing about their respective need for a mother.

From later material and accounts of her life, it seems that Sabina recovered but was not cured. While she was able to find a more benign and loving father in Jung, Sabina's contempt for her mother and her desire to have father to herself served to defend her against knowing about her need for a mother and to perpetuate her sado-masochistic attachment to her father. Jung's ambivalence towards his own father and authority figures may also have been his way of defending himself from knowing about his need for a father who could help him to separate from his mother and who could enable him to know about his need for a loving mother. Lacking this internal father, Jung was unable ultimately to provide this for Sabina. Soon after his treatment of Sabina, Jung suffered from what seems to have been a psychotic breakdown. Following this episode, Jung continued to exhibit compelling erotic transferences to his women patients (to the point of including Toni Wolff in his domestic household) in which he would replicate his childhood relationships – his intense relationship with his nurse and more distant one with his mother, and his desire to eliminate his father altogether so as not to have to know about his own need for a father who would love him and his mother. What perhaps also remained unresolved, for both Sabina and Jung, was their guilt about their hatred towards these depressed parents, which made them feel unduly responsible for them and made separation from them unbearable.

We can see how Jung's developing theoretical approach accommodated this aspect of his own self-denial – in his work with Sabina he repudiated more and more the idea of repetition compulsion and repeating the past. In its place, he postulated his idea of the complex and its inherited or archetypal features. In changing the emphasis onto conflicts derived from constitutional deficits, was Jung in fact trying to protect his internal objects from his own hatred? Viewed in this light, Sabina's concept of the death instinct (her thesis, 'Destruction as the cause of coming into being'), which she formulated in discussion with Jung, can be seen to be her way of understanding her aggression and hatred as stemming from an innate drive or impulse as opposed to resulting from her experience of relationships. For Sabina, love was associated with destructiveness and perhaps this was how she maintained her attachment to her own masochistic father in her mind.

From Freud's correspondence with Sabina following her marriage to Dr Paul Scheftel in June 1912, it is clear that Sabina had approached him with a view to continuing her analysis. In his letter to her, dated August 1912, Freud writes:

> So you are a married woman now, and as far as I am concerned that means that you are half cured of your neurotic dependence on Jung. Otherwise you would not have decided to get married. The other half still remains; the question is what is to be done about that. My wish is for you to be cured completely . . . We had agreed that you would let me know before 1 Oct. whether you still intend to drive out the tyrant by psychoanalysis with me. Today I would like to put in a word or two about that decision. I imagine that the man of whom you say so many nice things

has rights as well. These would be badly prejudiced by treatment so soon after your marriage. Let him first try to see how far he can tie you to himself and make you forget the old dreams. Only what remnant he fails to clear up belongs properly to psychoanalysis. Meanwhile, it might happen that someone else will turn up who will have more rights than both the old and the new man put together. At this stage, it is best for analysis to take a back seat.

(Carotenuto 1982: 116–17)

While Freud encourages Sabina to enjoy her new married life and the prospects of motherhood, he also recognizes that her analysis has not effected a complete cure – she had not finished her analysis. At the same time we cannot help but wonder here if Freud, aware of the intensity of Sabina's transference towards Jung and the ensuing difficulties in that analysis, might not also have been relieved at this course of events.

Although Jung and Sabina were aware of the power of repetition compulsion, they were unable to fully analyze their respective struggles to overcome their past and not to repeat it. In a letter dated 1st September 1919 Jung writes to Sabina:

The love of S. for J. made the latter aware of something he had previously only vaguely suspected, namely of a power in the unconscious which shapes our destiny, a power which later led him to things of the greatest importance. The relationship had to be 'sublimated', because otherwise it would have led to delusion and madness (a concretization of the unconscious). Sometimes we must be unworthy to live at all.

(Chapter 3: 57)

Jung does not link the 'power in the unconscious which shapes our destiny' to the repetition compulsion. He is nevertheless clear that 'the relationship had to be "sublimated"' and not acted out. But we are left with the impression that 'sublimation' was the only way Jung knew of to try to resolve and overcome the powerful forces that had emerged between Sabina and himself in the transference and counter-transference. Jung is also clear about how much he benefited from his analysis of Sabina. What perhaps neither Jung nor Sabina was able to understand and work through was the unconscious neurotic guilt that lay behind their 'painful love' and how this was to go on haunting them in different ways throughout their lives.

References

Carotenuto, A. (1982) *A Secret Symmetry: Sabina Spielrein Between Jung and Freud.* New York: Random House.

Cifali, M. (1988/2001) '*Une femme dans la psychanalyse, Sabina Spielrein: un autre portrait'*. *Le Bloc-Notes de la Psychanalyse*, 1988, 9: 253–65/'Sabina Spielrein: A woman in psychoanalysis, another picture'. Translated from the French in *Journal of Analytical Psychology*, 2001, *46*, 1.

Freud, S. (1886–1899) *SE* 1: 137.

—— (1886–1939) *The Standard Edition of the Complete Psychological Works of Sigmund Freud*. London: The Hogarth Press and the Institute of Psycho-Analysis, 1953–1974.

—— (1919). *The "Uncanny"*. London: Penguin Freud Library (14).

Graf-Nold, A. (2001) 'The Zürich School of Psychiatry in theory and practice: Sabina Spielrein's treatment at the Burghölzli Clinic in Zürich'. *Journal of Analytical Psychology*, *46*, 1, and this volume, Chapter 8.

Jung, C.G. (1904) 'Burghölzli Clinic Hospital Records of Sabina Spielrein'. *Journal of Analytical Psychology*, *46*, 1: 15–42.

—— (1908–1919/2001) 'The Letters of C.G. Jung to Sabina Spielrein'. *Journal of Analytical Psychology*, *46*, 1.

—— (1973) 'Experimental researches'. *CW* 2.

Lothane, Z. (1999) 'Tender love and transference: Unpublished letters of C.G. Jung and Sabina Spielrein'. *International Journal of Psychoanalysis*, *80*, 6: 1189–1204, and this volume, Chapter 10.

Minder, B. (2001) 'Sabina Spielrein: Jung's patient at the Burghölzli'. *Journal of Analytical Psychology*, *46*, 1, and this volume, Chapter 6.

Tender love and transference: Unpublished letters of C. G. Jung and Sabina Spielrein

Zvi Lothane

This article is reprinted here by kind permission of the *International Journal of Psychoanalysis* where it was first published in 1999, Vol. 80, Part 6: 1189–1204. The Discussion, however, was specially written for this edition.

The author dissents from the widely accepted interpretation that the relationship between Sabina Spielrein and Carl Jung in the years 1904–1910 included sexual intercourse and constituted an ethical breach of the doctor–patient boundary during ongoing treatment. Spielrein declared that her treatment ended with her discharge from the Burghölzli hospital as Jung's patient in 1904–1905. Jung maintained he 'prolonged the relationship' in order to prevent a relapse and also referred to it as a friendship. Materials published in 1994 (letters, drafts, diaries, hospital chart) and unpublished letters recently found by the author in the Claparède archive in Geneva shed new light on previously published documents and interpretations by Carotenuto that have dominated the secondary literature since 1980. The new materials provide a more nuanced view of the Spielrein–Jung relationship and point to the function of non-erotic love in the therapeutic relationship. A new look at the Freud–Jung correspondence about the Spielrein–Jung relationship shows that Jung's perception that a sex scandal was initiated by Spielrein was due to Jung's misreading of rumours concerning another woman; the episode had no ill effect on the relationship between Freud and Jung.

In many European languages, the word 'love' means both a personal attachment of affectionate, benevolent liking as well as passionate erotic desire for another person. In any given situation, only the context tells us which kind of love is meant; and sometimes even the context leaves us in uncertainties. This is the case in one of the most famous love knots in the history of psychoanalysis, the relationship between Sabina Spielrein (1885–1941) and Carl Gustav Jung (1875–1961), the nature of which is still being debated in the literature.

A brief overview of the present state of scholarship about the Spielrein–Jung relationship should be helpful to understand the revisions proposed in this contribution. Until 1980, Spielrein was but a citation in Freud's footnotes

(1900: 131; 1911: 80; 1920: 55) and a topic in The Freud/Jung Letters (McGuire 1974). In 1977 Carlo Trombetta, the biographer of Edouard Claparède, Freud's champion in Geneva, told the Jungian Aldo Carotenuto of a cache of Spielrein's German diaries and letters he had discovered in Geneva. In 1980 Carotenuto published them in Italian, in his book *Diario di una Segreta Simmetria – Sabina Spielrein tra Jung e Freud* (*Diary of a secret symmetry – Sabina Spielrein between Jung and Freud*), translated into English in 1982 and followed by a corrected German version in 1986, which included hitherto unpublished letters from Jung to Spielrein. Carotenuto's work set the trend of the voluminous secondary literature up to and including Kerr (1993). New ground was broken with the publication by Bernard Minder (1993, 1994) of Spielrein's hospital chart and other documents. Also in 1994, a German doctoral dissertation was defended by Wackenhut and Willke in Hanover that included additional unpublished Russian (in German translation) and German diaries and letters of Spielrein. The documents made public in 1994 shed new light on the story itself and on the state of the controversy surrounding it. They point to a need to disentangle facts, as presented in written statements left by the protagonists, from the various interpretations of such facts, to reappraise the claim that Carotenuto and Kerr have 'reconstructed the Jung–Spielrein relationship in sufficient detail' (Gabbard & Lester 1995: 72), and to advance new insights in the light of information presented here and supported by additional unpublished documents I examined in the Claparède archive in Geneva. The new data offer a more accurate and nuanced perspective on that relationship.

The period in question, from 1904 to 1911, can be divided into four phases: A. 1904–1905 inpatient treatment; B. 1906–1908 the deepening friendship; C. 1909–1910 the erotic-sensual relationship; D. 1911 and beyond: the epilogue.

A. Inpatient treatment (1904–1905)

1904

On 17 August 1904, 19-year-old Sabina Spielrein, who had come to Zürich with her mother from Rostov-on-Don, was transferred from a private psychiatric hospital to the Burghölzli Cantonal Asylum headed by Eugen Bleuler. She became Jung's patient, was diagnosed as suffering from hysteria, and Jung '"analyzed the clinical condition almost completely with the help of [Freud's] method and with a favorable result"' (Lothane 1996). Jung was 'then living with his wife and two children in a flat in the main building of the Burghölzli' (McGuire 1974: 4 fn1). According to Minder (1994), Spielrein was not an average patient but was accorded special status: she was spared a physical examination and was invited by Jung to participate in his famed association experiments, both as subject and research assistant. Thus, from the start Jung and Spielrein established strong professional and personal bonds, as reflected in excerpts from the hospital chart that follow.

Toward the end of 1904, Jung handles well Spielrein's behaviour on the ward: 'as a child she played many mischievous pranks' (Minder 1994: 101), documents Jung; now, 'in response to even the slightest hint of lack of respect or trust [from staff], she takes instant revenge in the form of totally negativistic behaviour and a series of bigger or smaller devilish tricks' (p. 103); 'childish pranks (suicidal gestures in order to drive the nurses crazy . . .). Begs the writer [Jung] never to act baffled but always display the utmost fortitude and firm belief in her recovery, because this is the only way to achieve it' (pp. 104–105; my translation).

1905

On 8 January Jung notes a

> marked deterioration. . . . Exactly a year ago around New Year's Day there was a big scandal at home (angry scenes with father). In this connection, a long series of similar scenes and finally scenes of being beaten by the father, retold with great emotion: when she was already 13 years old, father threatened her with beating; led her into a room, ordered her to lie down; she asked him politely not to hit her (he was about to lift her dress from behind) whereupon he relented but forced her, on her knees, to kiss the portrait of the grandfather and to swear always to strive to be a well behaved child. . . . At the end of a three hour long analysis it emerged that in connection with those beatings, already at the age of four, she experienced sexual excitation. . . . She states that sometimes it is enough if someone laughs at her, which to her symbolizes submission, to cause her to experience orgasm.
>
> (Minder 1994: 109)

On 29.1.1905 Jung writes in the chart: 'since the last abreactions considerable improvement' (p. 110).

On 17.4.1905, while still living at Burghölzli, she applied to Zürich University medical school. In her Russian diary, on the eve of her first day at the university, Spielrein described her anticipatory emotions 'of that happy moment' as 'killingly sinister', and her head as 'bursting from nausea and weakness' (entry of 24.05.1905, Brinkmann & Bose 1986: 215; Wackenhut & Willke 1994: 177; henceforth abbreviated as B&B and W&W, respectively). She felt overwhelmed by the impression of her first day at university on 25 April:

> I have been afire with interest and now I have a contrary feeling that weighs heavily upon me! I feel isolated from the other students . . . it is

impossible to open up to these children. I feel myself more thorough, serious, critically evolved, independent, . . . [W]ill I be able to work scientifically? . . . To me, life without science is completely senseless. What else is there for me if there is no science? Get married? But that thought fills me with dread: at times my heart aches for tenderness, love; but that is but a deceptive, passing, external display that hides the most pitiful prose. The price is subjugation of the personality. . . . No! I do not want such love: I want a good friend to whom I can bare my soul; I want the love of an older man so that he would love me the way parents love and understand their child (spiritual affinity). But my parents – they are not it – If only I were as wise a human being as my Junga! [an affectionate Russian-sounding form of Jung]. . . . And how stupid that I am not a man: men have it easier with everything. It is a shame that everything in life goes their way. I do not want to be a slave!

(B&B 1986: 215–16; W&W 1994: 177).

According to her Zürich University medical school transcript (Swales 1992), Spielrein matriculated on 17.4.1905 and on 27.4.1905 she submitted to the admissions office the required medical certificate:

27.IV.1905

Medical certificate

Miss Sabina Spielrein from Rostov-on-Don, residing in this Asylum and planning to matriculate for the summer semester at the Faculty of Medicine, is not mentally ill [i.e., psychotic]. She was admitted here for treatment of nervousness with hysterical symptoms. We have no reservation in recommending her for matriculation.

The Directorate: Bleuler

(Minder 1994: 118–19; my translation; cf. Chapter 5: 103)

It is important to note that even though Bleuler endorsed Jung's diagnosis of hysteria, three years later Jung (1908) would arbitrarily change it to hysterical psychosis while Carotenuto, going one better than Jung, misdiagnosed Spielrein as a schizophrenic, both views no longer considered tenable. She was discharged on 1 June 1905 and moved to a pension in downtown Zürich.

Former inpatient and now enthusiastic freshman medical student Spielrein continues to describe in the Russian diary her trials and triumphs as she progresses in her medical studies and grows both emotionally and intellectually, as her friendship with Jung deepens:

The only thing I now possess is my freedom and I defend this ultimate prized possession of mine with all my strength. I cannot bear even the smallest judgment of my personality, and even when given in the form of a simple instruction it can turn into a stinging sermon . . . it gets me into a rage. (I do not know why this happens.) I can take anything only from Junga. . . . To-morrow I am going to the medical library and will borrow [Eduard von] Hartmann's '[Philosophy of] The Unconscious', which I accidentally saw in the catalogue. Since I saw this book at Junga's, I believe it is worth reading.

(W&W, Russian diary, entry of 8.6.05: 178, 179)

In addition, Spielrein paints a moving portrait of her bond with Jung in a letter to her 'mamochka' (term of endearment in Russian = mummy) of 26.8.05:

Dear Mamochka,

I am now somewhat tired but completely at peace. I am deliriously happy as never before in my life. At the same time it hurts and I would like to cry from happiness. You have probably guessed that the cause of all this is Junga. I visited him today. He comforted me about Remi [a woman patient at Burghölzli under Spielrein's care]; in his opinion, he tells me, her condition has improved markedly and he advises me not to ask for the return of the money I had spent on her but to ask for it from the charitable society; on the other hand, the society could use this money to help another person, and so forth in this vein. We broached this subject after Junga told me that I should not be wearing a hat with holes in it and that I should also have my shoes mended. I replied that I had run out of money, but that I had already received so much that I could not ask my parents for more. Thereupon he compelled me to tell him what I had spent the money on. Then he made a proposal to make me a loan of 100 francs and write you about it. But as I objected vigorously, he forced me to accept 10 francs from him for the hat and the repair of the shoes. How do you like this tip? I was so ashamed I wished the earth should swallow me, but you cannot win an argument with this man. On the other hand, I was delighted that he had done a good deed and I did not want to hamper his efforts. Do not breathe a word to him about it. Strange how it is somehow pleasant to be an object of his 'charitable attentions' and have him spend money on me. Naturally, I shall soon pay him this money back, but he does not know this as yet. So there, you can see what kind of a person he is, my Junga. When I left the Professor [Bleuler] today I felt like one condemned to die, but he [Jung] restored my faith in my abilities and made me so happy! He is coming to visit me on Friday (1st of September) at 3 o'clock. If only I could only learn to cook borscht before then! Today Jung and I went on rounds at our Hospital. There is a number of women for whom I am an object of admiration! But sleep is getting the better of me, I am going to bed. I was so excited that I forgot to convey to him your apology about the gift you sent him; but did not forget to tell him how I scared you when I had presented you Remi's letter to me as his letter and he said I should not have tortured you in this manner . . .

[misdated as 26.8.08 in W&W: 187; my translation].

Such is a maiden's heart, or as Spielrein says, 'the psychology of so-called modest girls, to which category I also belong' (Carotenuto, 1982: 4); and such is her transference onto Dr Jung, who acted as medical school teacher, mentor, and guardian *in loco parentis*.

On 25 September 1905 Jung composed a 'Report about Fräulein Spielrein to Professor Freud in Vienna, delivered to Frau Spielrein for possible use' (Minder 1993, 1994). It ends with this conclusion: ' "In the course of her treatment the patient had the *bad luck to fall in love with me*. She continues to rave blatantly to her mother about this love and her secret spiteful glee in scaring her mother is not the least of her motives. Therefore the mother would like, if needed, to have her referred to another doctor, with which I naturally concur" ' (Lothane 1996: 205; my italics; cf. Chapter 5: 106). It seems that the main purpose of the report was to reassure Mrs Spielrein, who had her own relationship with Jung. At any rate, the report never reached Freud but an idea was planted in both mother and daughter that would materialize in 1909 when Freud was consulted under very different circumstances.

On Spielrein's own showing, her treatment with Jung ended with her discharge from the hospital in 1905, as she would state in her letter of 11 June 1909 to Freud: 'Four and a half years ago Dr. Jung was my doctor, then he became my friend and finally my "poet," i.e., my beloved. Eventually he came to me and things went as they usually go with "poetry" ' (Carotenuto 1982: 93). Like others influenced by Carotenuto, I at first also believed that 'poetry' was a euphemistic code-word for the 'physical act of possession' (Carotenuto 1982: 219), or sexual intercourse. If it ever occurred, which I doubt, it is implausible that it would have been consummated at Burghölzli. Even Gabbard and Lester (1995), who regard the Jung–Spielrein relationship as a boundary violation, as a 'pervasively boundaryless relationship that characterized the years *following the analysis*' (p. 72; my italics), suggest that the 'tempestuous love affair' occurred after the formal doctor–patient relationship was dissolved.

B. The deepening friendship (1906–1908)

It was Jung who created the impression that he both continued to treat Spielrein after her discharge from Burghölzli and combined this care with friendship. The correspondence between Freud and Jung started in 1906 and in his second letter (23 October 1906) Jung for the first time anonymously mentions Spielrein: 'I am currently treating an hysteric with your method. Difficult case, a 20-year old Russian girl student, ill for 6 years' (McGuire 1974: 7).

There are no details about place, frequency, and treatment issues, while the complaint that she is difficult is ambiguous: what are those difficulties now? None is hinted at in Spielrein's diary entries either preceding or following this letter. Three years later, on 7 March 1909, Jung would mention Spielrein as

> a woman patient, whom *years ago* I pulled out of a very sticky neurosis with unstinting effort, [who] has violated my confidence and my friendship in the most mortifying way imaginable. She has kicked up a vile scandal solely because I denied myself the pleasure of giving her a child. I have always acted the gentleman towards her . . . I nevertheless don't feel clean, and that is what hurts me the most because my intentions were always honourable. . . . Meanwhile I have learnt an unspeakable amount of marital wisdom, for until now I had a totally inadequate idea of my polygamous components despite all self-analysis.
>
> (McGuire 1974: 207; my italics)

Note that Jung is speaking of Spielrein as a patient in the past who is now demanding to be given a child.

Jung admits two motives for continuing his unstinting efforts on behalf of his prized ex-patient, as stated in a letter of 4 June 1909: (1) 'She was published in abbreviated form [in 1908] in my Amsterdam lecture of blessed memory'; (2) *'Es war mein psychoanalytischer Schulfall sozusagen, weshalb ich ihr eine besondere Dankbarkeit und Affektion bewahrte'* (*Freud–Jung Briefwechsel*, McGuire 1974: 252) – it was, so to speak, my *psychoanalytic* text-book case, wherefore I offered her my special gratitude and affection' (my italics; compare with McGuire 1974: 228: 'She was, so to speak, my test case for which reason I remembered her with special gratitude and affection,' omitting 'psychoanalytic'). Moreover, Jung rationalized his self-sacrificing efforts on behalf of Spielrein:

> Since I knew from experience that she would immediately relapse if I withdrew my support, I prolonged the relationship over the years and in the end found myself morally obliged, as it were, to devote a large measure of friendship to her, until I saw that an unintended wheel had started turning, whereupon I finally broke with her. . . . I need hardly to say that I have made a clean break. Like [Otto] Gross, she is a case of fight-the-father, which in the name of all that's wonderful I was trying to cure *gratissime* (!) with untold tons of patience, even abusing our friendship for that purpose. On top of that, naturally, an amiable complex had to throw an outsize monkey wrench into the works.
>
> (McGuire 1974: 229)

True, Jung received no payment but Spielrein's mother, on her visits to her daughter in Zürich, gave him a number of gifts, as described in the mother's letter. But Jung made no clean break: he was mixing friendship with an ambiguous therapy without a fee. It is an ethical dilemma just as weighty as mixing ongoing therapy with a sexual relationship.

I previously misread the letters of Bleuler to Spielrein (Minder 1994) as showing payments Spielrein made to Burghölzli in 1909 for outpatient therapy (Lothane 1996: 207). In reality, these payments had nothing to do with therapy. Minder has confirmed (personal communication) that he too was mistaken when he wrote that Spielrein 'remained Jung's outpatient until 1909' (Minder 1993: 114).

1906

In another letter to Jung, copied that year into her German diary, Spielrein is filled with gratitude because Jung's letter, 'as dumb as it sounds, made her feel 20,000 tons lighter'; she also expresses her admiration for Jung's 'colossal intelligence and character' and for his

> lecture, which was wonderfully beautiful (not only in the scientific but also in the ethical sense). There you were, able to create so much enthusiasm and feeling – how is it possible? *You are endowed with a wonderful potential energy and you could achieve much more than you actually do.* – If you could only know how ethically beautiful you were then (when you treated the patients with so much care and love)! . . . I was completely transformed, soft and warm towards people. Even though I went home in a flood of tears, I was calm and strong in my decision – one doesn't need anything else, it all comes from poetry [my italics]. . . . I love you too much, and therefore perhaps I imagine something that is not there (or perhaps it is there?) (for example, that you despise me, that you do not want that I should stalk you, etc.). Each time that causes me emotional storms and self-torture. . . . For this reason I wanted to leave Zürich for at least three years, but I have found no better university. . . . What do you think? Should I try to leave you alone for three years?
> (German diary, 29.8.06, W&W: 205–207; B&B: 218–219; my translation)

This poetry, contrasted with the aforementioned dreary prose, is not yet of the nature of loving and sensuous, erotic, ecstatic exchanges that would occur in 1909; it is rather an adoring kind of love-cum-hero-worship for teacher and parent-surrogate in an inspired, highly intelligent, and highly idealizing young person. Even if one allows that it is nourished by an erotic current, no erotic crossing of boundaries is discernible here. In the same letter she also confesses to Jung that

> lately my conscience has not been clean because for the whole time I had been in a state of mute despair and my head turned completely stupid

from constant studying. I did nothing but create scandals and was chock-full with mischievous fantasies and played the wildest antisocial tricks (when one speaks of scandals, it feels as if there is a little animal in one's back on the left side). In the end I brought to the hospital a small syringe and a little KCN [potassium cyanide] and would spray anyone who spoke to me. The KCN was for effect only, because the syringe was filled with water.

(W&W: 206)

This description could have easily reminded Jung of the ways Spielrein had behaved during her hospitalization.

In two entries that follow, Spielrein avers that 'she has never met a human being in whom intelligence (even if different from yours) is united with such a moral strength, character, and idealism' and, 'since his [Jung's] letters bring her so much joy, to keep writing to her even if she does not answer', for his letters 'from time to time stimulate the better part of her personality so that at a moment of weakness she can think of him [Jung] and become stronger'. Medical student Spielrein then launches into a lengthy disquisition on various philosophical concepts, including those of the philosopher Ernst Mach on sensations and the biologist August Weismann on the immortality of unicellular organisms.

1907

In a letter to Freud of 6 July, Jung distorts Spielrein's quoting a Russian poem by giving it a starkly salacious reading

a hysterical patient told me a poem . . . about a prisoner . . . [who] opens the cage and lets his beloved bird fly out. . . . She admits that actually her greatest wish is to have a child by me who would fulfil her unfulfil-lable wishes. For that purpose I would naturally have to let 'the bird out' first.

(McGuire 1974: 72)

It is not clear when Spielrein told the poem, however Jung speaks of her as still being his patient but without giving further details. However, Jung misses the young woman's real deep maternal longing for a child, hers and his 'Sieg-fried' child, and its transference nature. Neither does he let on that he is up to his neck in a complex friendship with his former inpatient.

1908

On 11.5.1908 Spielrein passed her preliminary medical school examinations and in August would leave to spend a long-awaited summer with her family in

Rostov-on-Don. The German reissue of Carotenuto (1986: 189–197) contains eleven letters and fragments from Jung to Spielrein written in 1908, published for the first time and excerpted here in my translation. In these letters Jung sets up various encounters with Spielrein (the last one on 22.VII.1908), signs as 'your friend,' and speaks of his feelings for her. On 20.VI.08: 'How great would be my happiness to find in you a human being that is an "*esprit fort*", not given to sentimentality but whose essential and innermost vital core is her own freedom and independence' (p. 190; cf. Chapter 3: 33f). On 12.VIII.08:

> Your letter made me happy and calm. I was somewhat worried by your long silence. . . . I must express my admiration for the great personality of your parents. . . . As per your letter, everything is good and lovely; I delight in your happiness. In this way your long-feared visit in Russia will be so much easier. My own mood swings like a volcano, now everything looks golden, now it looks grey. Your letter was like a ray of sun through the clouds.
>
> (pp. 191–192; cf. Chapter 3: 35)

The following, hitherto unpublished letter from Jung, presented here for the first time, is unclearly dated: 27.VIII.1908 but bears a postal stamp of 19.8.1908. The date could not be 27.VII.08, because at that time Spielrein was still in Zürich. It is addressed to:

> Fräulein stud. med. Sabina Spielrein
> pr. adr. Herrn N. Spielrein
> Rostow o/Don
> Russland
>
> Russian postal stamp: Rostov Don 19.8.08
> (place name illegible) 27 VIII 08.

Meine Liebe!

Ich habe soeben Ihren freundlichen Brief erhalten und daraus den Eindruck empfangen, dass es Ihnen in Rostow nicht ganz wohl ist. Ich begreife. Ich bin Ihnen für Ihre lieben guten Worte dankbar. Ich bin jetzt wieder ganz ruhig. Die Ferien haben meine Nerven ganz beruhigt. Ich mache jeden Tag eine grosse Bergtour, meistens ganz allein. Das thut mir sehr gut. Die Complexe ordnen sich so allerichtig ein, dass man wieder klar sieht. Es kommt für Sie immer ein grosses Plus von Freundschaft heraus und ein herzlicher Wunsch, dass Ihnen Ihr Leben gelingen möge mit einem Minimum von Unzweckmässigkeiten und den damit verbundenen Schmerzen. Verlieren Sie nie die Hoffnung, dass ein Werk, das mit Liebe gethan wird, zu einem guten Ende führt. Ich kann Ihnen heute nur ganz kurz schreiben, da ich EBEN sehr müde von einer grossen Tour nach Hause gekommen bin. Schreiben Sie mir immer ins Burghölzli. Mit herzlicher Liebe Ihr J.

To Miss medical student Sabina Spielrein, care of Mr. N. Spielrein

My Dear One!

I have just received your friendly letter and got the impression that you are not entirely well in Rostov. I understand. I am grateful to you for your good and kind words. I am now quite calm again. The vacations have calmed my nerves considerably. Every day I take a long walk in the mountains, mostly all by myself. That does me a great deal of good. The complexes are getting all straightened out and one can see clearly again. You have come in for a great bonus of friendship along with the heartfelt wish that your life should be successful and with a minimum of goals that serve no purpose and the pain connected with them. Never lose the hope that work done with love will lead to a good end. I can only write a short letter today because I have JUST returned home very tired from a long walk. Please keep writing to me at the Burghölzli. With heartfelt love Your J[ung].

(my translation)

In stark contrast to the aforementioned letter to Freud of 6 July 1907, the expression 'work done with love' surely does not mean sexual love but a loving relationship of mutual respect, friendship, and sympathy, a message from one soul mate to another, a manifestation of psychological and spiritual connectedness. Jung is suffering emotionally and the strain is showing. He is also hinting to Spielrein that her dream of a life with him can never be fulfilled. Was Spielrein still in treatment with Jung or were they friends, ambiguously mixing sympathy and supportive therapy of sorts?

The undated Russian letter that follows, sent by Mme Spielrein from Rostov to her daughter, could have been written in 1908 after Jung's letter of 27 August 1908, for it refers to the daughter's departure and a letter from Jung to her:

Rostov, (?) 1.9.1908

Dear Sabinochka!

I cannot find peace after your departure and I do not know where to write. I was unable to rest for a moment, got busy cleaning the rooms so as not to have time to think about myself. At night I thought of you and him, and after having lost all hope of receiving any news, and when my suffering for you reached a climax, I suddenly received a letter addressed to you. I was so upset I could not read a word. I ask you a thousand times to forgive me for opening the letter, but I opened it because you would have let me read it anyway and I had to know what it held for you, because my entire mood depended on it. His letter calmed me down. It expresses deep friendship, lightly coloured by something else, which is quite natural. He often thought of you, of the cholera, of your soul. He is probably in the throes of a conflict and his counsel to you and to himself is not to let the feeling of love grow but to suppress it, though not to kill it completely. Have I got it right? He who is able to do it will be victorious, or else will be out in left field. I am sure he will be victorious. He writes that this is necessary for the sake of the loved ones, that is, his wife and children. And what about you? Perhaps I got it wrong? Anyway, I like the tone of his letter very much, especially the limits within which he places you and himself. It seems to me that it could not be any better. You have in him a person devoted to you, with a touch of love (more than that is not permitted and you have to remain content with that), a person for whom you have profound respect and appreciation, which you also have from him, and what more do you need? You should be happy because it is more than you had wished for. Had you wished to cause him to divorce his wife, then it would be a different matter, but if not, then you must not go any further. The important thing is to realize that he could be taken, but it is not worth it. You cannot have it better than the way it is. Do not torment yourself, suppress your feelings so that they do not make you suffer and continue meeting him as a friend. He also needs you, but he is not suffering, on the contrary, he is getting better. Please, please, do not tell him I opened the letter. As far as the jam is concerned, tell him that you brought along fruit for him but were unable to bring more. Rent a lavish apartment, invite him and write to me with all the details. You can talk to him about love but remain unyielding, you only stand to gain from it. For the time being, do not hide your feelings . . .

(original provided by Idéfilm, Stockholm; my translation)

The defining quality of their relationship at this time seems to be a mutually supportive friendship, tinged, as her mother correctly intuits, with erotic feelings and fantasies. This view is also expressed in a letter from Spielrein to Freud dated 13 June 1909 where she mentions in passing that she became aware of Jung's liking for Freud '1½ or 2 years ago, when there was still no question of a closer erotic relationship between us [i.e., herself and Jung]' (Carotenuto 1982: 100), i.e., a time going back to 1908, when the unpublished letter of Jung of 27 August 1908 was sent.

Let us now turn to the undated, unpublished Russian letter from Spielrein to her mother, sent from Zürich to Rostov. It probably dates from the end of 1908, for in it Spielrein cites a paper recently finished by Jung and listed in his letter of 27 November 1908: 'My wife is about to be confined. . . . The material for the first number [of *Jahrbuch für psychoanalytische und psychopathologische Forschungen*] is now complete [containing my paper] 'The significance of the father in the destiny of the individual.' (McGuire 1974: 179). It is amazing how much Spielrein has grown since 1905:

Dear Mamochka,

I am unable to write because, anyway, it is impossible to communicate important matters in a letter. One would have to say so much. Unfortunately, Zürich is so far away from Rostov. I cannot send you his letters because it is too risky, and to tell all is too long and too tiring. Were I able to make a firm decision, I would be living in an enchanted kingdom; as it is, I get exhausted thinking and there is no point in it, because *ducunt volentem Dei, nolentem trahunt* which means, the gods guide the willing and grind the unwilling to dust [actually, in Seneca the Younger: *ducunt volentem fata (= fates), nolentem trahunt*]. Just recently Junga finished his paper that created such a stir, 'Über die Rolle des Vaters im Schicksaale [sic] des Einzelnen,' in which he shows that the choice of the future [love] object is determined in the first relations of the child with his parents. That I love him is as firmly determined as that he loves me. He is for me a father and I am a mother for him, or, more precisely, the woman who has acted as the first substitute for the mother (his mother came down with hysteria when he was two years old); and he became so attached to the [substitute] woman that when she was absent he saw her in hallucinations, etc, etc. Why he fell in love with his wife I do not know . . . Let us say, his wife is 'not completely' satisfactory, and now he has fallen in love with me, a hysteric; and I fell in love with a psychopath, and is it necessary to explain why? I have never seen my father as normal. His insane striving 'to know himself' is best expressed in Jung for whom his scientific activity is more important than anything in this world . . . An uneven dynamic character coupled with a highly developed sensibility, a need to suffer and to be compassionate '*ad magnum*' [to the fullest]. You can do to him and get from him anything you want with love and tenderness. Twice in a row he became so emotional in my presence that tears just rolled down his face! If you could only hide in the next room and hear how concerned he is for me and my fate, you would be moved to tears yourself. Then he starts reproaching himself endlessly for his feelings, for example, that I am something sacred for him, that he is ready to beg for forgiveness, etc. I cannot quote the exact phrases for it is a bit sentimental, but you can well imagine everything. Remember how dear daddy was apologizing to you exactly in the same manner! It is unpleasant for me to quote all those self-reproaches he addressed to himself, because we are both either equally guilty or not guilty. Look, how many female patients have been to see him and, without fail, each one of them would fall in love with him but he could only act as a physician because he did not love in return! But you know how desperately he struggled with his feelings! What could one have done? He suffered through many nights thinking about me. We also considered the possibility of separating. But this solution was rejected as not feasible because we are both living in Zürich. . . . He felt responsible for my fate, and howled as he pronounced these words . . . he did not want to stand in the way of my happiness, . . . and he had reasons to fear for my future (in case we separated). – This conversation took place almost two weeks ago and we both felt literally tormented, unable to utter a word, etc. The heart to heart talk came to an end. *Ducunt volentem Dei, nolentem trahunt.* We stood still, in the most tender poetry. . . . Let tomorrow bring darkness and cold! Today I shall offer my heart to the sun! I shall be gay! I shall be young! I shall be happy, that's what I want! [the four last statements are grammatically masculine, as if they depicted Jung's mood]. Then I get a post card and a letter in one day, that I should not be sad, and last Friday he came again. Poetry again, and as usual, will I ever in my life forgive him what he had concocted with me; he did not sleep the night, became exhausted; he cannot fight it any longer. – But by the same token, I should also be saying: will he ever forgive me for what I have done to him! The difference is that I know that for him scientific activity is above all else in life and that he will be able to bear everything for the sake of science. . . . The question is only how my intellect is going to relate to this whole story and the trouble is that the intellect does not know how to relate. I should not be writing about him and his family but about me. The question for me is whether to surrender with all my being to this violent vortex of life and to be happy while the sun is shining, or, when the gloom descends, to let the feeling become transferred to a child and science, i.e., the scientific activity that I love so much? Firstly, who knows how this story will end? 'Unknown are the ways of the Lord.' Anyway, today's youth looks at these matters differently and it is very possible that I will fall in love again and will have success, i.e., I will find myself a husband. – But don't you forget that this is still very far in the future and therefore, do not worry. *So far we have remained at the level of poetry that is not dangerous, and we shall remain at that level, perhaps until the time I will become a doctor, unless circumstances will change.* –

I am only writing to you now because I cannot feel happy without a mother's blessing, that is, without you approving my actions and that you should delight as long as I am well. And afterwards? In the best of cases, we cannot say what will happen afterwards and where happiness is awaiting us. Consider the latest example. One of Jung's patients, in her attempt to get over her love for him, took to the mountains and became infatuated and sexually involved with a young man. She is now with child and the man who seduced her turned out to be a most small-minded person and abandoned her forthwith. Now she cannot stand him and in desperation wanted to end her life, and would have done it, had Junga not saved her once again. . . .

(my translation from the Russian manuscript in Spielrein's handwriting and italics)

Can we take this letter at face value or should we suspect that Spielrein is dissembling and hiding the 'real truth' from mother? In this letter to mother, 'poetry' suggests tender embraces and reveals a profile of a strong, principled woman, who in the three years since 1905 has become mature beyond her three-and-twenty years, insightful about herself and about her friend. She also suggests that she and Jung have not overstepped the boundaries of sympathy and tender love to consummate sex.

A heart-rending note is struck by Jung on 4.XII.08:

I regret a great deal and regret my weakness and curse fate that is menacing me. . . . You will laugh when I tell you that lately I am constantly flooded with **early childhood memories** [Jung's boldface] . . . Will you forgive me that I am who I am? That I am thereby offending you and forgetting my duty as physician towards you? . . . My misfortune is that I cannot live without the joy of stormy, ever-changing love in my life . . . Since the last scene I have completely lost my sense of security towards you. . . . I need definite agreements so that I do not need to worry about your intentions. Otherwise my work will suffer, and that seems to me more important than the momentary problems and suffering in the present. Give me at this moment something back of the love and patience and unselfishness that I was able to give to you during the time of your illness. Now I am the sick one . . .

(Carotenuto 1986: 195–6; cf. Chapter 3: 37f)

The roles were reversed: the former patient was requested to act as therapist.

C. The erotic-sensual relationship (1909–1910)

We do not know what Spielrein did in 1909 that was so different as to make Jung feel so threatened that he decided to turn to Freud on 7 March 1909 with a report about her 'vile scandal' (McGuire 1974: 207). But she did nothing different, as she describes a rather innocent encounter in the following unpublished fragment of a Russian letter to mother:

Dear Mamochka:

Truly miracles happen in this world. No more, no less, without intending to, I managed to hypnotize Junga. How did it happen? He came to me 5 minutes earlier than agreed upon. Knocks and I answer 'Ja!' He enters and I am greatly embarrassed because I did not expect it was him and I stand there with my hair half-loose, comb in hand. . . . He sat down on the couch and promised he would not look, even though I had known in advance that 'not looking' to him means he covers his face with his hands and peeps through the spaces between the fingers. I had to make do with this situation. – I hurried to finish getting dressed, put a red shade over the lamp and walked over to him. We greeted each other . . . [as if] after a long separation . . . Then, as always, he launched into long speeches about him not having slept all night thinking about me, him wanting me to be happy forever, etc. . . . I tell him that such speeches are a disturbance right now, that I love him anyway, and if one day we have to part then that will be that, but now I am not thinking of anything and I am fine. Then he kisses me and bawls. 'Was ist?' and he immediately glows with happiness. I am a mother for him, he a father, for me, the best of all possible worlds! But the best of all, he had the idea to make me a new hairdo: he pulled the comb out of my hairdo and loosened my hair, whereupon he became jubilant that I looked like an Egyptian woman(!) . . .

(my translation)

The wheel started turning following an anonymous letter sent by Jung's wife and another one by Spielrein's mother to Jung, prompting Jung to send the latter his oft-cited arrogant letter (Carotenuto 1982: 93–4), perhaps in an attempt to forestall Spielrein's revenge. As Minder suggests, it is noteworthy that on that same day, Jung 'tendered his resignation from the [Burghölzli] Hospital, accompanied by a letter from Bleuler, on the grounds that "he would like to devote himself more than before to scientific activity"' (Minder 1994: 125; cf. Chapter 5: 134). Perhaps Jung feared Bleuler's condemnation, had there been a 'scandal'. In his reply two days later, on 9 March 1909, Freud says:

I too have bad news of the woman patient through whom you became acquainted with the neurotic ingratitude of the spurned. . . . When Muthmann [a pro-Freud Swiss psychiatrist] came to see me, he spoke of a lady who had introduced herself to him as your mistress. . . . To be slandered and scorched by the love with which we operate – such are the perils of our trade, which we are certainly not going to abandon on that account.

(McGuire 1974: 210)

But that woman was not Spielrein! Jung, in the meantime, continued to claim that Spielrein was

of course, systematically planning my seduction which I considered inopportune. Now she is seeking revenge. Lately she has been spreading a rumour that I shall soon get a divorce from my wife and marry a certain girl student, which has thrown not a few of my colleagues into a flutter. What she is now planning is unknown to me. Nothing good, I suspect, unless perhaps you are imposed upon to act as a go-between.

(McGuire 1974: 228–9)

While falsely accusing Spielrein, Jung maintained a total denial of his own involvement and actions.

In a letter of 30 May 1909 Spielrein asked Freud to see her, whereupon Freud entered the fray as a skilful negotiator. In a letter of 18 June 1909 he reassures his friend that he suggested to Spielrein a more appropriate, endopsychic resolution of the matter (*'eine würdigere, sozusagen endopsychische Erledigung der Sache,' FJB:* 259), where 'endopsychic' suggests to Spielrein she had imagined something that did not really happen, stemming from her own inner turmoil and transference. The term endopsychic is nicely defined by Freud when he interprets superstitions and paranoid ideas as: *'nothing but psychology projected into the external world,* [i.e.] the obscure recognition (the endopsychic perception, as it were [added in 1907, Strachey]) of psychical factors and relations in the unconscious' (Freud 1901: 258; Freud's italics).

Interestingly, in a footnote in the Dora Case (1905a: 100) Freud invokes 'endopsychic resistance' to explain her forgetting of dreams, alongside 'endopsychic perception' and 'endopsychic defense.' The next important use is in the Schreber Case where 'endopsychic perceptions . . . [are] the basis for the explanation of paranoia' (Freud 1911: 79). But who was imagining what?

That year, Spielrein quotes in her diary one more unpublished letter to Freud (W&W 1994), quite moving in content and tone. It is not clear whether it was eventually sent out. It is undated and addressed to 'S. g. H. P.' (possibly: *'Sehr geehrter Herr Professor'* = dear Professor Freud). She says it is 'her long-promised last one . . . after she had received 2 letters' from Freud, i.e., it would fit between Freud's second letter of 8.6.1909 and his third one of 24.6.1909, but this is far from certain. A few excerpts follow:

Why now? The first time you were beautifully represented in a dream. A few months ago I had to forgo the wish to write to you because in the dream you had female breasts, old as Prof. Forel and ugly, to boot. But you were enormously cunning. We came to you with the brother (Dr. Jung); you paid attention to the brother and none to me. I will admit that after I received your first two letters I was happy with my dream: it did not seem right judging by its nature. History remains silent about the third one.

Now comes today's dream. I am in the hospital and hear you and Dr. Jung talking in the next room. Should I leave, since you are about to come into the room where I am? No, I continue with my work, I might even be able to make fun of both of you in the end. You come in and I feel that you have this thought about me: 'So this is the beauty he wanted to see on a par with my daughter?' I see myself in the mirror and feel ashamed because I do not find myself beautiful at all. I fear that you interpret every move of mine as having a sexual meaning. I feel dumb and do a few tricks. All I know is that Dr. Jung is very friendly towards me but not you. Soon you retire to the other room. I look at your face and see that it is young, handsome, and enormously likable. I feel sick, the heart and the throat are cramping up, I have to put a compress on my head; why won't he listen to me? Why does he think so poorly of me? . . . You can see how a young person is working through your letters in the depth of her personality. Firstly, my dream tells me that your better personality is now visible on the outside (in this respect my unconscious never deceives me), and secondly, the dream shows me that I am not indifferent to what you think of me; in my excitement, I forgot that you do not know me at all, that instead of sending you evidence I merely stated that it was so. Naturally, you think it is all my fantasy and whatever goes with it! . . .

You can show this letter to Dr. Jung . . . but do not betray to him my little qualm: when he is sure that one believes in his honesty, then this becomes a mighty prop for the better part of his personality, especially given his proclivity to be so proud and so labile in his affects. . . . I am in no way his enemy . . . I see him as my oldest little baby upon whom I have bestowed so much effort that can now live independently; if I speak to you of him in this manner it is because you love him: when I decided to write to you I did not yet know that he had told you anything. You know that for a fact! . . .

I agree fully with the theorem in 'The significance of the father in the destiny of the individual.' I am only surprised that a relatively short time ago Dr. Jung wanted to convince me that I could love anybody else exactly like him. I had to write him a long epistle (I still have it) to show that there is no accident here, that one loves similarities in the [love]-object, that therefore one first loves one's own family and then always discovers similarities in the beloved. Doesn't it sound funny, that my mother wants to take my beloved from me for the third time? Before Dr. Jung I was infatuated with two men (I was not yet ripe for love). They both liked me a great deal, but since I was still a child, both the first and the second hero fell in love with my mother head over heels.

(W&W: 200–2; my translation)

Some commentators have previously viewed both Jung's and Freud's handling of the situation as less than honest (Bettelheim, in Carotenuto 1982;

Cremerius in Carotenuto 1986; Lothane 1987, 1996). But the new documents have paved the way for a new look at the Freud–Jung letters that has led me to a different conclusion. Without being confrontational, in his letter of 7 July 1909 Freud even-handedly applies 'endopsychic' qua transference not only to Spielrein but to Jung as well, implicitly characterizing Jung's reaction to Spielrein's transference as a reciprocal mirror transference of his own, now renamed countertransference:

> Such experiences, though painful, are necessary and hard to avoid. . . . I myself have never been taken in quite so badly, but I have come very close to it a number of times and had a narrow escape. . . . But no lasting harm is done. They help us develop the thick skin we need and to dominate our 'countertransference' which is after all a permanent problem for us; they teach us to displace our own affects to best advantage. They are a 'blessing in disguise'.
>
> (McGuire 1974: 230–1)

Barron and Hoffer (1994) believe that the Spielrein episode inspired Freud to discover countertransference. Perhaps Freud was also thinking of the days as hypnotic-cathartic therapist and recalling an early experience of 'the personal emotional relation between doctor and patient' he would revisit in 1925, when a patient he was treating with the hypnotic-cathartic method 'woke up . . . [and] threw her arms around my neck. . . . I was modest enough not to attribute the event to my own irresistible personal attraction, and . . . grasped the nature of the mysterious element that was at work behind hypnotism' (Freud 1925: 27). Or was he thinking of Anna O.'s treatment by Breuer and Breuer's ignorance of erotic transference and countertransference? Or the lessons he learnt from Dora (Freud 1905a): 'I did not succeed in mastering the transference in good time' (p. 118); 'I was deaf to the first note of warning, thinking I have ample time before me . . . the transference took me unawares' (p. 120); and finally, 'I promised to forgive her for having deprived me of the satisfaction of affording her a far more radical cure for her troubles' (p. 122). Clearly, Freud had the benefit of age and of his greater clinical experience and once again, as in the triangle of Anna O., Breuer and himself, he was the detached and objective observer.

The interpretation worked and external events conspired favourably as well. On 21 June 1909 Jung was able to give Freud

> the good news . . . of my Spielrein affair. I took too black a view of things. . . . she turned up at my house and had a very decent talk with me, during which it transpired that the rumour buzzing about me does not emanate from her at all. My ideas of reference, understandable enough in the circumstances, attributed the rumour to her. I wish to retract this forthwith. Furthermore, she has herself freed herself from the

transference in the best and nicest way and has suffered no relapse (apart from a paroxysm of weeping after the separation). . . . Although not succumbing to helpless remorse, I deplore the sins I have committed, for I am largely to blame . . . naturally Eros was lurking in the background. Thus I imputed all the other wishes and hopes entirely to my patient without seeing the same thing in myself. . . . Caught in my delusion that I was the victim of the sexual wiles of my patient. . . . [and] in view of the fact that the patient had shortly before been my friend and enjoyed my full confidence, my action was a piece of knavery which I very reluctantly confess to you as my father. I would now like to ask you a great favour: would you please . . . [tell] her that I had fully informed you of the matter, and especially of the letter to her parents [in Carotenuto 1982: 96–7] which is what I regret most. . . . [Y]ou and she know of my 'perfect honesty' [English in the original]. I ask your pardon many times for it was my stupidity that drew you into this imbroglio.

(McGuire 1974: 236–7; my italics)

Jung's admission of his own transference, his endopsychic 'ideas of reference', exonerates both him and Spielrein. The conclusion is that it was not only Spielrein who was a victim of endopsychic perceptions, defences, and projections, but Jung as well, and more so than the woman: he was the one who under the pressure of fear, guilt and shame fabricated the fiction that Spielrein had orchestrated a scandal. But he mixed Spielrein up with another woman: there was no scandal except in his own mind.

The real 'scandal' started with the intervention of Spielrein's mother, as the daughter sums it up in her diary on 11.9.1910, completely in keeping with Jung's account of it:

We came to know each other, we became fond of each other without noticing it was happening; it was too late for flight; several times we sat in 'silent embrace.' Yes, it was a great deal! Then my mother intervened, conflict arose between her and him, then between him and me. I simply could not break with him under such circumstances. A few months later, when I was feeling stronger, I caught up with him after his lecture. At first he wanted to hurry away, because he thought I was his bitter enemy and perhaps feared a scandal. The foolish child. I reassured him, told him that I did not want 'to start' anything with him, that I had come because he was very dear to me, because I wanted to see him as a fine, noble person and therefore wanted to confront him with his horrid behavior toward my mother and me. His manner changed at once; he showed deep repentance, talked about a malicious person who had been telling tales about us . . . Well, we parted as best of friends.

(Carotenuto 1982: 11–12)

By 10 July 1909 Jung was once again able to report to Freud: 'I want to thank you very much for your kind help in the Spielrein matter, which has now settled itself satisfactorily' (McGuire 1974: 240). On 24 June 1909 Freud finally declared the case closed by making a gesture of reconciliation towards Spielrein that is both gallant and honourable:

> I have today learned something from Dr. Jung himself about the subject of your proposed visit to me, and now see that I had divined some matters correctly but that I have construed others wrongly and to your disadvantage. I must ask your forgiveness on this latter count. However, the fact that I was wrong and that the lapse has to be blamed on the man and not the woman, as my young friend himself admits, satisfies my need to hold women in high regard. Please accept this expression of my entire sympathy for the dignified way in which you have resolved the conflict. Yours faithfully, Freud
>
> (Carotenuto 1982: 114–15).

The record strongly suggests that in 1909 Spielrein and Jung had engaged in 'poetry', Spielrein's shorthand for sensual exchanges such as touching, holding, kissing, looking into each other's eyes and swooning romantically. Was there a public scandal? No. Did Jung suffer any consequences? No. What Jung dreamt up as a scandal turned out to be no more than a storm in a teacup. One further conclusion: Spielrein caused no trouble between Freud and Jung, for they broke up over doctrinal differences regarding the libido theory, fought in the arena of the Schreber Case (Lothane 1997a).

Interestingly, the 'poetry' continued for quite some time even after the tempest subsided. We can believe Spielrein to be truthful in her diary entry dated 21 September 1909: 'Friendship. Can it alter so suddenly? Mother says it is impossible for my friend and me to remain friends once we have given each other our love. A man cannot contain pure friendship in the long run. If I am nice to him he will want love' (Carotenuto 1982: 6). Here love means sex, but apparently Spielrein has been heeding her mother's admonitions all along. Only two days later, after she decides to 'ask for [her] dissertation back from Prof. Bleuler and send it to [her] friend, . . . a perfidy that tormented [her] constantly,' she writes in her diary:

> The most important outcome of our discussion [about the dissertation] was that we both loved each other fervently again. . . . Then he became more and more intense. At the end he pressed my hands to his heart several times and said this should mark the beginning of a new era. What could he have meant by that?
>
> (Carotenuto 1982: 8–9).

Towards the end of 1909 Spielrein contemplated the idea of leaving Zürich and moving to Heidelberg, as seen in Bleuler's letter of recommendation of 16.10.1909 typed on Burghölzli stationery, and reproduced in its entirety for the first time:

> The undersigned certifies that for the past two months Fräulein Sabine [sic] Spielrein has worked as a medical clerk [roughly equivalent to the German 'Famulus'] in this psychiatric hospital. She is somewhat nervous but has worked diligently. Otherwise I also know her to be a young woman of good reputation, highly intelligent and greatly interested in science, and I am therefore very pleased to recommend her matriculation at Heidelberg University. (Signed) Prof. Bleuler
>
> (my translation)

As she told her mother, the move was unthinkable; the resolution in Zürich was reached in due course.

1910

While working with Jung on her dissertation, Spielrein writes in her diary on 11.9.1910:

> My love for my friend overwhelmed me with a mad glow. At some moments I resisted violently, at others I let him kiss every one of my little fingers and clung to his lips, swooning with love. So this is I, usually the soul of pure, clear reason, allowing myself such fantasies.
>
> (Carotenuto 1982: 11)

These fantasies are a mix of 'poetry' and recollections of what used to happen. But now her resolve is:

> well, then, I shall try to become fond of someone else, if that is still possible. I want to be loved and respected by him, I want to unite my life with his . . . It is not easy to give up the thought of the baby boy, my longed-for Siegfried, but what is to be done?
>
> (p. 13)

One more poetry is described in an entry of 9.11.1910:

> Yes, the stronger poetry probably occurred a week ago Tuesday. He said then that he loves me because of the remarkable parallelism in our thoughts; sometimes I can predict his thoughts to him; he told me that he loves me for my magnificent, proud character, but he also told me he would never marry me . . . I felt like a mother who only wanted the best for him.
>
> (p. 33)

In December of that year Spielrein presented the written medical school examinations.

D. The epilogue (1911)

On 20 January Spielrein passed her examinations and on 9 February defended her doctoral dissertation (Swales 1992: 16) which her instructor Jung published in the *Jahrbuch* that year, in the same volume in which Freud published his essay on Schreber. On 11 October Frl. Dr Spielrein began attending the meetings of the Vienna Psychoanalytic Society (Nunberg & Federn 1974) and on 27 October Freud wrote to the second woman member of the Vienna Society:

> Dear Frau Doktor, As a woman you have the prerogative of observing things more accurately and of assessing emotions more closely than others. . . . Our last evening [of 25 October, Nunberg & Federn 1974: 293–8] was not exactly a glorious one. . . . I fully appreciate your attitude and look confidently to the future. I have been doing that, after all, for many years and under much more difficult circumstances. I hope that you will feel quite at home in our circle. With cordial greetings, Freud
>
> (Carotenuto 1982: 115)

Spielrein proved herself to be a keen observer in two other areas. During a discussion at the Vienna Psychoanalytic Society (8 November 1911) on time-lessness and the unconscious, she spoke of 'the fact that a recent experience tends to be replaced by one from infancy' which she related to 'the perversions (inversion, bisexuality), infantile theories of sex, and the regression to ideas of that sort in dementia praecox' and then invoked 'the Mothers,' from Goethe's *Faust*, ideas congenial to Tausk (Nunberg & Federn 1974: 302–303). During the next meeting (15 November), after a presentation by Reik on death and sexuality, Spielrein said 'that she has dealt with many of the problems discussed today in her paper "Destruction as the cause of coming into being"' (Spielrein 1912), while Stekel spoke of the 'destructive instinct' (Nunberg & Federn 1974: 316–7). These ideas about the fusion of anaclisis, sexual instincts and aggressive instincts prefigure Freud's future dual instinct theory, in which sexual and ego instincts are pitted against the death instinct, Freud's synonym for aggressive drives in *Beyond the Pleasure Principle*, where Freud (1920: 55) acknowledges his indebtedness to Spielrein, this great psychoanalytic pioneer.

DISCUSSION

In English we have the concepts of love and like. In other languages, love refers to either (1) love writ large, called agape, caritas, filia, sympathia, or (2) lust, i.e., libido, later called by Freud the id, thus a term covering both love as sexual desire and sexual pleasure, and love as attachment, later called by Freud the ego (Lothane 1982, 1986, 1987a, 1987b, 1987c, 1988, 1989, 1997b, 1997c, 1998a). In the psychoanalytic literature a distinction is made between the common word 'libidinous', having strong sexual desires, and 'libidinal', the technical term pertaining to Freud's libido theory of the neuroses, expounded in his *Three Essays on the Theory of Sexuality* (1905). The conflict between these two kinds of love, the asexual and the sexual, runs like a crimson thread through two millennia of misunderstanding and persecution in the West. And where there is love there is always conflict, moral conflict; thus, love and ethics are inseparable for the human condition (Lothane 1994, 1998b, 1999).

Once religion condemned sex as a sin of the flesh and the work of the devil, women and men were accused of sinful sexual excesses, convicted as witches and warlocks and burnt at the stake. As far as the influence of psychoanalysis on society is concerned, by redefining sexuality as a natural phenomenon, as the energy of sexual instinctual drives, as set forth in his canonical *Three Essays* (1905b), Freud took the sting of sin out of libido and destigmatized the varieties of human sexual expression, thus promoting a new spirit of tolerance.

When Jung started treating Spielrein with 'Freud's method' in 1904 he had mastered the method as set forth in the *Studies on Hysteria* (1895) and *The Interpretation of Dreams* (1900). With the aid of Freud's method Jung was able to trace Spielrein's current disorder to early childhood traumas, as outlined in the *Studies*, and combine it with an analysis of her complexes by his association experiments, the latter based on the central assumptions formulated in the *The Interpretation of Dreams*. He would have complemented Freud's method, I submit, by measures later authors would call rational and cognitive therapy, corrective emotional experience, behaviour modification, and the like.

By the time Freud and Jung began their correspondence, Freud had published his sexual aetiological theory of the neuroses and finished defining the libidinal theory of transference (1905a, 1905b). In the correspondence we find a counterpoint of three discussions: the case of Spielrein, the case of Schreber (Lothane 1997a), and a polemic about the libido theory, that finally led to their break-up. Thus, in his second letter (of 23 October 1906), Jung restates his '"reservations about [Freud's] far-reaching views"' (McGuire 1974: 7) on the sexual aetiology of the neuroses and, for the first time, reports on Spielrein anonymously, to which Freud responds (on 27.10.1906): '"You certainly did not show too much reserve and the "transference," the chief proof that the drive underlying the whole process is sexual in nature, seems to have become very clear to you"' (ibid: 8). On December 6 Freud elaborates:

> You are probably aware that our cures are brought about through the fixation of the libido prevailing in the unconscious (transference), and that this transference . . . provides the impulse necessary of understanding and translating the language of the ucs.; where it is lacking, the patient does not make the effort or does not listen when we submit our translation to him. Essentially, one might say, the cure is effected by love [*eine Heilung durch Liebe*, healing through love, *FJB*, p. 13]. And actually transference provides the most cogent, indeed, the only unassailable proof that neuroses are determined by the individual's love life [*Liebesleben*]
>
> (McGuire 1974: 12–13)

This healing through love is ambiguous. To be sure, the libidinal transference love travels in one direction only, from patient to doctor, with the analyst functioning as an unmoved mover, as an objective translator of the patient's dreams and desires, both conscious and unconscious. There is no room here for the doctor's erotic transference. But since in the *Three Essays* Freud (1905b) differentiated libidinal attachments rooted in the '"sensual current"' from attachments reflecting the tender, or '"affectionate current"'(Freud 1905b: 207), implicitly affirming their independent lines of development, we ask: in the above passage, do the locutions 'love' and 'love life' mean sexual or id-love only, or nonsexual, i.e., ego-love as well? Whereas a work entitled 'three essays on the theory of love', i.e., realistic, non-transference, non-erotized love based on mutual attachment, liking, and sympathy, was never written by Freud (although the subject would be discussed in a number of his sociological essays in the 1920s and 1930s), a beginning is hinted at in the above letter and more is said in the epochal *Studies on Hysteria* (1895). There Jung would have read the following lines in Freud's chapter on 'The psychotherapy of Hysteria', where Freud delineated a dyadic, i.e., reciprocal, model of therapeutic interaction (Lothane 1997b) between the analysand and analyst based on shared love, language, memory, meaning, and interpretation of meaning:

> The procedure is laborious and time-consuming for the physician. It presupposes great interest in psychological happenings, but personal concern for the patient as well. I cannot imagine bringing myself to delve into the psychical mechanism of hysteria in anyone who struck me as low-minded and repellent, and who, on closer acquaintance, would not be capable of arousing human sympathy; whereas I can keep the treatment of a tabetic or rheumatic patient apart from personal approval of

this kind. The demands made on the patient are not less. The procedure is not applicable at all below a certain level of intelligence . . . The complete consent and complete attention of the patients are needed, but above all their confidence, since the analysis invariably leads to the disclosure of the most intimate and secret psychical events.

(Freud, 1895: 265–6)

In German, human sympathy is another synonym for love writ large, as in the title of the work by Max Scheler (1923). And Freud elaborates further on the reciprocal roles of patient–student and doctor–teacher:

we make [the patient] himself into a collaborator, induce him to regard himself with the objective interest of an investigator, and thus push back the resistance, resting as it does on an affective basis. . . . This is no doubt when it ceases to be possible to state psychotherapeutic activity in formulas. One works to the best of one's power, as an elucidator (where ignorance has given rise to fear), as a teacher, as the representative of a freer or superior view of the world, as a father confessor who gives absolution, as it were, by a continuance of his sympathy and respect after the confession has been made. One tries to give the patient human assistance, so far as this is allowed by the capacity of one's own personality and by the amount of sympathy that one can feel for the particular case. . . . Besides the intellectual motives which we can mobilize to overcome the resistance, there is an affective factor, the personal influence of the physician, which we can seldom do without . . .

(Freud 1895: 282–3)

These passages, reflecting a dyadic model of love writ large, inspired Jung's treatment and analysis of Spielrein at the Burghölzli, as he said, using Freud's method. The question is whether he paid equal attention to Freud's discovery of the troubling phenomenon of transference later in that same chapter. Among the complications of this procedure Freud lists the third, transference: ' "If the patient is frightened at finding that she is transferring on to the figure of the physician the distressing ideas which arise from the content of her analysis." This is frequent, and indeed in some analyses a regular occurrence. Transference on to the physician takes place through a *false connection*.' (Freud 1895: 302). Freud makes it clear that in order analytically to overcome the patient's resistance in the attempt to explore the meaning of 'erotic trains of thought', the patient's cooperation becomes a personal sacrifice, which must be compensated by some substitute for love. The trouble taken by the physician and his friendliness have to suffice for such a substitute' (Freud 1895: 301), where 'substitute for love' stands for non-erotic friendliness, support, and a respectful concern for the patient's needs and vulnerabilities. Acknowledging the reciprocal nature of the process potentially implies that healing through love also means the care and ego-love given by the analyst to the patient. 'I say', emphasizes Freud, 'it is almost inevitable that [the patient's] personal relation to [the doctor] will force itself, for a time at least, unduly into the foreground. It seems, indeed, that an influence of this kind on the part of the doctor is a *sine qua non* to the solution of the problem. . . . Where I caused damage, the reasons lay elsewhere and deeper' (ibid: 265). The concept of counter-transference is foreshadowed here in those otherwise unclear words, 'I caused damage,' and it was given that name at the Second Psycho-Analytical Congress at Nuremberg (30 and 31 March 1910), less than a year after the alleged 'scandal', where Jung could have entertained retrospective reflections as he heard Freud speak about 'other innovations in technique [that] relate to the physician himself':

We have become aware of the 'counter-transference' which arises in him as a result of the patient's influence on his unconscious feelings, and we are almost inclined to insist that he shall recognize this counter-transference in himself and overcome it. Now that a considerable number of people are practising psycho-analysis and exchanging their observations with each other, we have noticed that the psycho-analyst goes no further than his own complexes and internal resistances permit; and we consequently require that he shall begin his activity with a self-analysis and continually carry it deeper while he is making his observations on his patients. Anyone who fails to produce results in a self-analysis of this kind may at once give up any idea of being able to treat patients by analysis.

(Freud 1910: 144–5)

Freud's words may have reminded Jung of having written to Sabina in 1908: 'You have come in for a great bonus of friendship along with the heartfelt wish that your life should be successful . . . Never lose the hope that work done with love will lead to a good end' (Jung in his previously unpublished letter of 1908). Perhaps Jung was harking back to his unresolved counter-transference to Sabina during the days at Burghölzli where not only she, but he, too, 'had the misfortune' of falling in love with her. He might have recalled Freud's struggles with ambitions, emotions and actions towards Dora. The only difference here was the following: that in Spielrein's case, during her stay and treatment at Burghölzli, it was not her erotic so much as her aggressive transference that came to the fore, as manifest in the course of the illness and documented in the clinical chart. But Jung's loving attention, devotion, and perseverance helped Spielrein overcome her neurosis. But I argue that the hospital period and the post-discharge period need to be considered separately instead of being lumped together, as has been done by countless commentators.

Thus, by 1908–1909, when Spielrein was no longer in treatment with Jung it was Jung who despite his protestations was the one who now sued Spielrein for attention, friendship and sympathy, justifying this in his own mind as a mix of free treatment and support for a fragile ex-patient, a set of emotions that blossomed into erotized affection. At that time Jung was in his early thirties, married with two children, while Spielrein, ten years his junior, was aroused to her first adult experience of passionate love. One can wonder if Jung was in the throes of '"the inhibitory influence of certain psychical complexes"' (Freud 1912: 180) and that he formulated once again as the conflict between the '"sensual current and (. . .) the "affectionate current (. . .): . . . Where they love they do not desire and where they desire they cannot love. They seek objects which they do not need to love, in order to keep their sensuality away from the objects they love, in accordance with the laws of "complexive sensitiveness" [Jung's term]' (Freud 1912: 183).

Jung loved his wife; he made it clear he would never leave his wife for Spielrein and found another solution to what he termed his polygamous tendencies. Spielrein desired, wanted to marry Jung and have a child by him but realized the futility of her dream and instead married Dr Paul Scheftel to live through, only to experience the vicissitudes of that marriage, as would be learned later.

But let us return to our concern with the difference between sexual and nonsexual love. From this perspective, the later monadic libido-psychological model of the *Three Essays* may be seen as a detour from the early ego psychology of love. The return to ego psychology in Freud's Schreber analysis (1911) came to fruition in 'On narcissism: an introduction'. In the latter work, the 'antithesis between ego-instincts and sexual instincts, to which we were forcibly led by analysis of the transference neuroses', (Freud 1914: 79), caused Freud to define the 'anaclitic' or 'attachment' type of love-object choice, directed at the mother as the provider of 'the vital functions of self-preservation' (ibid: 87), such that 'a person may love . . . (a) the woman who feeds him, (b) the man who protects him, and the succession of substitutes who take their place' (ibid: 90), i.e., the vital survival value of anaclitic, or attachment, love in men and women alike. Thus, the concepts of ego-instincts and the anaclitic type of love-object choice support the argument that Freud had an ego-psychological, relational model in place from the start but that it was temporarily overshadowed by his libido theory (Lothane 1997a). When Fairbairn proclaimed that 'libido is the function of the ego' and that 'the ego, and therefore libido, is fundamentally object-seeking' (1963) he was not introducing a new object-relations point of view: he was debating with Freud on metapsychology. From the start, Freud was aware that both libidinal and anaclitic currents are found in transference, and this methodological approach continues in his later writings.

Thus in Freud's Socratic dialogue, when the 'Impartial Person' (actually, Obersanitätsrat Durig) asks him: 'But how about the special personal influence that you yourself have after all admitted against the resistances?' Freud replies:

This personal influence is our most powerful dynamic weapon. It is the new element which we introduce into the situation and by means of which we make it fluid. The intellectual content of our explanations cannot do it ... The neurotic sets to work because he has faith in the analyst and believes him because he acquires a special emotional attitude towards the figure of the analyst. ... [the] use we make of this particularly large 'suggestive' influence [is] not for suppressing the symptoms – this distinguishes the analytic method from other psychotherapeutic procedures – but as a motive force to induce the patient to overcome his resistances. ... the emotional relation with the patient ... is, to put it plainly, in the nature of falling in love ... [that] grows exacting, calls for affectionate and sensual satisfaction, ... it has taken the place of the neurosis and ... our work has had the result of driving out one form illness with another.

(Freud 1926: 224–6)

Clearly, transference can be a boon and a bane. Freud separates the dividends resulting from benevolent bonds of love from the dangers of bondage to erotic demands in the transference. In his last revisiting of these themes Freud writes:

The relation of transference ... has an opportunity for a sort of after-education of the neurotic; but at this point a warning must be given against misusing this new influence. However much the analyst may be tempted to become a teacher, model and ideal for other people, he should not forget that this is not his task in the analytic relationship [. . .] In all his attempts at improving and educating the patient the analyst should respect his individuality [p. 175]. . . It is only when we are mindful of this caveat that we as analysts can serve the patient in various functions, as an authority and a substitute for his parents, as a teacher and educator; and we have done the best for him if, as analysts, we raise the mental processes in his ego to a normal level, transform what has become unconscious and repressed into preconscious material and thus return it once more to the possession of his ego.

(Freud 1940: 181)

The lessons of love are learned, repressed, and relearned in every generation (Lothane 1998). Freud's original message, powerfully restated by Ferenczi (1988) and Balint (1965), is now gaining acceptance among analysts.

In a recent contribution J. Novick and K.K. Novick write:

Freud was the foremost among a wide array of social scientists who explored human love and sexuality. He provided not only a theory, but also a method for investigating the most intimate of human emotions with relative objectivity. Through the method of psychoanalysis and the phenomenon of transference, Freud and those who followed him could describe the sources, range, variety, transformations, derivatives, perversions, and sublimations of love. But all this knowledge and theory construction was based on psychoanalytic observations of the *patient*. Very little was said about the analyst's reciprocal love for the patient. In contrast with the volumes written about love and sexuality in the patient, there has been, with a few notable exceptions (Ferenczi, Searles, Weinstein, Coen, Kernberg, Gabbard, Lothane, Charles), very little discussion of the analyst's love for the patient. Some of the reasons for this relative neglect can be construed as conceptual, ethical, and practical.

(Novick & Novick 2000: 189; emphasis in the original)

And they conclude: 'Implicit in our presentation is the assumption that psychoanalysis can be both a cognitive–affective restoration to a path of progressive development and a growth-enhancing developmental experience for both patient and analyst' (ibid: 214). The positive lesson of the Jung–Spielrein relationship is that both protagonists have exemplified and taught us the importance of reciprocal, realistic, objective, altruistic love as an essential ingredient in the therapeutic alliance and in analytic treatment.

Acknowledgements

I am deeply grateful to Mme and M. de Morsier of Geneva for their kind permission to publish the materials used in this article from which I was permitted to take notes in their gracious home in 1998. Spielrein's personal link to Claparède was forged via his marriage to a woman of a background similar to Spielrein's, the Jewish-Russian Hélène Spir, daughter of philosopher A.A. Spir. Along with Piaget and de Saussure, Spielrein was a member of the Geneva Psychoanalytic Society founded in 1920, with Claparède as President (Spielrein 1922). Spielrein's papers, stored in the home and office of Claparède, were given by his widow and daughter after his death to the late distinguished Genevan professor of neurology Dr Georges de Morsier, who then beqeathed them to his son and daughter-in-law, Mme Hélène de Morsier. The documents cited here thus come from the 'Archives privées de feu le Professeur Georges de Morsier, Fonds Edouard Claparède.' I am also grateful for the help given to me by psychologist and historian Dr Fernando Vidal of Geneva University, who first told me about the existence of the Willke & Wackenhut dissertation of 1993/1994, completed under Professor Wolfgang U. Eckart, Chair of the Institute for the History of Medicine at Heidelberg University, who also provided me a copy of that dissertation. That dissertation contains previously unpublished materials not included in Carotenuto (1982, 1986) (see Chapters 6 and 7 of this volume). Portions of these materials were previously published in Brinkmann & Bose (1986) and Cifali (1983).

ADDENDUM 2003

In March of this year I began my discussion following the screening of Elisabeth Márton's film, *My Name was Sabina Spielrein* (2002), at the weekly meeting of the New York Psychoanalytic Society by asking the members of the audience for a straw vote on the question: how many of you believe that Spielrein and Jung consummated a sexual relationship and how many do not. Roughly half voted yes and half voted no. While not rigorously scientific, this result points to a stubborn psychological fact: while seeing is believing, believing is also seeing, people tend to believe as dictated by their own emotions, projections, and transferences. The new findings presented in my chapter in this book suggest the verdict of *non liquet* (= not clear), and, at the very least, raise reasonable doubt regarding the sexual nature of the Spielrein/Jung relationship. Our judgment should really be guided by what the protagonists never tired of asserting themselves: that there was no sex. In the final analysis the question is whether we believe their testimony or not. I choose to believe them, and not out of prudery, but because in those days people saw premarital sexual relations, especially as applies to Spielrein, differently than we do today; moreover, because unconsummated sexual desire was even more poignant and more romantic than consummated sex. However, the sexual myth has died hard, providing sensational material for a number of theatrical productions and a plethora of articles in the popular press and professional journals.

There is one more facet to this story that has hitherto gone unnoticed (Lothane 2003). While Spielrein dreamt of marrying Jung and having his child, Jung had no intentions of leaving his wife, had children, and declared to Spielrein his need for romantic extramarital affairs, food for his creative soul. Thus Jung was faced with a choice: (a) either to view the Spielrein episode as his extramarital relationship, acceptable to some but objectionable to others on legal, moral, or religious grounds, but then an emotional problem of his own and perhaps requiring a therapeutic analysis, which, like Freud, he never undertook; or (b) to define his relationship with Spielrein as a misconduct, a boundary crossing, a case of sexual abuse, a violation of psychoanalytic ethics in the context of ongoing therapy, even though Spielrein was clear that therapy was terminated with her discharge as inpatient at Burghölzli while Jung continued to equivocate about her status as patient. While Jung presented both these aspects to Freud, i.e., as himself suffering from polygamous tendencies, a sign of both intrapsychic and interpersonal conflicts in the marriage, he consistently preferred to discuss the relationship in his letters to Freud, both before and after identifying Spielrein by name, as a problem of Spielrein's as his patient in therapy, not as his personal problem or conflict of his own. Clearly, it was easier for him to place the blame on Spielrein, even to admit to a therapeutic error, than to personal pathology, and this strategy could well be motivated by pride. Freud dutifully followed suit, acting both amused and avuncular, and ultimately offering support to both Spielrein and Jung. It is also speculated that this biased choice on Jung's and Freud's part yielded an unexpected benefit: it enabled Freud to invent a new name with which to exorcise the demons of erotic complications in therapy: countertransference, the counterpart to the patient's transference.

Tipping the scales in favor of the myth of a transference/ countertransference boundary crossing has also yielded benefits to a number of spokesmen and audiences amongst the living. Some analysts, e.g., the late Johannes Cremerius and others, have found here an opportunity to vent righteous indignation at Jung's alleged transgression, perhaps a defence amongst analysts who have either experienced such temptations or yielded to them. The myth has also inspired a sizable feminist literature, especially in Germany, in which Spielrein is presented as a victim of sexual abuse by Jung, forever the evil seducer, who wielded undue male power over the allegedly hapless and helpless woman. Even if one were to doubt the veracity of Spielrein's assurances to her mother that there was no sex, there is no such compelling reason to doubt the strength of her character, or her being Jung's equal in strength of character, if not stronger, or to distrust her when she claimed that both she and Jung were equally responsible. No, Sabina Spielrein was no victim of Jung's nor he a victim of her seduction. They respected each other's strength, valued their mutual attachment, love and friendship, and the intellectual stimulation they provided for each other. As a result, they bequeathed upon us a number of seminal ideas: the method of treating patients with psychotic disorders, the role of aggression and masochistic suffering in love relations, the feminine side of man and the masculine side of woman, and by Spielrein, original contributions to the emerging field of child psychoanalysis.

Various authors have also speculated wildly about Spielrein's alleged masochism as the cause of her being another kind of victim: her staying in harm's way, rather than joining the safety of being with her relatives in Moscow (including her now famous niece, the late Menikha Isakovna Spielrein), to allow herself to be murdered, along with her two daughters, in the 1942 massacre of the Jewish population in the Zmeiov Ravine on the outskirts of Rostov, after the city was retaken by the German invader. One might similarly speculate and attribute masochism to Freud for not leaving Vienna in time, were it not for the huge ransom for his escape to London that was paid to the Nazis by Princess Marie Bonaparte. I believe that Spielrein's masochism also remains unproven: very few people knew what the Nazis held in store for the Jews. In clinical as well as applied psychoanalysis, one should pay careful attention to historical circumstances before rushing to interpret. This caution has guided not only my attempt to understand the motives and actions of Sabina Spielrein and Carl Gustav Jung but also my purpose to rehabilitate them.

References

Balint, M. (1965) *Primary Love and Psycho-Analytic Technique*. London: Tavistock Publications.

Barron, J.W. & Hoffer, A. (1994) 'Historical events reinforcing Freud's emphasis on "holding down the countertransference"'. *Psychoanalytic Quarterly, LXIII*: 535–40.

Brinkmann, E. & Bose, G. (1986) *Sabina Spielrein. Marginalien*. Berlin: Brinkmann & Bose: 215–23.

Carotenuto, A. (1982) *A Secret Symmetry – Sabina Spielrein Between Jung and Freud*. New York: Pantheon Books.

—— (1986) *Tagebuch einer Heimlichen Symmetrie*. Freiburg/Breisgau: Kore.

Cifali, M. (1983). 'Sabina Spielrein. Extraits inédits d'un journal'. *Le Bloc-Notes de la Psychanalyse, 3*: 147–70.

Fairbairn, W.R.D. (1963) 'Synopsis of an object-relations theory of the personality'. *International Journal of Psycho-Analysis, 44*: 224–5.

Ferenczi, S. (1988) *The Clinical Diary of S. Ferenczi*. Ed. J. Dupont. Cambridge, MA: Harvard University Press. [Originally written in 1932.]

Freud, S. (1895) *Studies in Hysteria. SE* 2.

—— (1900) *The Interpretation of Dreams. SE* 4.

—— (1901) 'The psychopathology of everyday life'. *SE* 6.

—— (1905a) 'Fragment of an analysis of a case of hysteria'. *SE* 7.

—— (1905b) *Three Essays on the Theory of Sexuality. SE* 7.

—— (1910) 'The future prospects of psycho-analytic therapy'. *SE* 11.

—— (1911) 'Psycho-analytic notes on an autobiographical account of a case of paranoia (dementia paranoides)'. *SE* 12.

—— (1912) 'On the universal tendency to debasement in the sphere of love (contributions to the psychology of love II)'. *SE* 11.

—— (1914) 'On narcissism: an introduction'. *SE* 14.

—— (1920) *Beyond the Pleasure Principle. SE* 20.

—— (1925) *An Autobiographical Study. SE* 20.

—— (1926) 'The question of lay analysis'. *SE* 20.

—— (1940) *An Outline of Psycho-Analysis. SE* 23.

Freud, S. & Jung, C.G. (1974) *Briefwechsel*. Frankfurt/Main: S. Fischer.

Gabbard, G. & Lester, E. (1995) *Boundaries and Boundary Violations in Psychoanalysis*. New York: Basic Books.

Jung, C. G. (1908). 'Die Freud'sche Hysterietheorie'. *Monatschr. Psychiat. Neurol., XXIII*: 310–22.

Kerr, J. (1993) *A Most Dangerous Method*. New York: Knopf.

Lothane, Z. (1982) 'Dialogues are for dyads'. *Issues in Ego Psychology, 5*: 19–24.

—— (1986) 'La realltà d'amore, l'amore della realltà'. In Il Foglio e l'Albero. Milano: Spirali/Vel.

—— (1987a) 'Love, seduction, and trauma'. *Psychoanalytic Review, 74*: 83–105.

—— (1987b) 'The primacy of love: Love ethics versus hermeneutics'. *Academy Forum*, The American Academy of Psychoanalysis, *31*, 1: 3–4.

—— (1987c) 'Love and destructiveness'. *Academy Forum, 31*, 4: 8–9.

—— (1988) 'Freud: amore, seduzione e trauma'. *La Cifra, 1*: 291–302.

—— (1989) 'The nature of love'. *Academy Forum, 33*, 1, 2, Spring/Summer: 2, 11.

—— (1992) 'The human dilemma: heterosexual, homosexual, bisexual, "holosexual"' *Issues in Ego Psychology*, *15*: 18–32.

—— (1994) 'The revival of ethics'. *Academy Forum*, *38*, 1, 2: 4–6.

—— (1996) 'In defense of Sabina Spielrein'. *International Forum of Psychoanalysis*, 5: 203–17.

—— (1997a) 'The schism between Freud and Jung over Schreber: Its implications for method and doctrine'. *International Forum of Psychoanalysis*, *6*, 2: 103–15.

—— (1997b) 'Freud and the interpersonal'. *International Forum of Psychoanalysis*, 6: 175–84.

—— (1997c) 'Omnipotence, or the delusional aspect of ideology, in relation to love, power, and group dynamics'. *American Journal of Psychoanalysis*, *57*: 25–46. [Also in C. Ellman, & J. Reppen, eds., *Omnipotent Fantasies and the Vulnerable Self*. Northvale, NJ: Aronson.]

—— (1998a) 'The feud between Freud and Ferenczi over love'. *American Journal of Psychoanalysis*, *58*: 21–39.

—— (1998b) 'Ethics, morals, and psychoanalysis'. *Dynamische Psychiatrie* (Dynamic Psychiatry), *31*: 186–215.

—— (1999) 'Ethics in psychiatry and psychoanalysis. Psychopathology'. *International Journal of Descriptive Psychopathology Phenomenology and Clinical Diagnosis*: *32*, 3: 141–51.

—— (2000). Tenero amore e transfert: lettere inedite tra C. G. Jung e Sabina Spielrein. *Studi Junghiani*, 6:97–121.

—— (2001). Zärtlichkeit und Übertragung – Unveröffentliche Briefe von C. G. Jung und Sabina Spielrein. In: Krager, A., Knellessen, O., Lettau, G. & Weismüller, C. (Hg.). *Sexuelle Übergriffe in Psychoanalyse und Psychotherapie*. Göttingen: Vandenhoeck & Ruprecht, 2001.

—— (2001). Nezhnaia liubov i transfer: neopublikovannyie pis'ma K. G. Iunga i Sabiny Shpil'rein. *Vestnik psikhanaliza* (Spetsvypusk, Nr. 1), pages 87–106.

—— (2003). Nachwort. In: Traute Hensch (Hg.): Sabina Spielrein Tagebuch und Briefe. Die Frau zwischen Jung und Freud Gießen 2003: Psychosozial-Verlag/ Edition Kore, pp. 249–278.

McGuire, W. (1974) (ed.) *The Freud/Jung Letters*. Princeton, NJ: Princeton University Press.

Mahony, P., Bonomi, C. & Stensson, J. (eds.) (1997) *Behind the Scenes: Freud in Correspondence*. Oslo: Scandinavian University Press.

Márton, E. *Ich hieß Sabina Spielrein My name was Sabina Spielrein* (2002). Original version German, produced by Helgi Felix/Idé Film Felixson AB.

Minder, B. (1993) 'Jung an Freud 1905: Ein Bericht über Sabina Spielrein'. *Gesnerus*, *50*: 113–20.

—— (1994) 'Sabina Spielrein. Jung's Patientin am Burghölzli'. *Luzifer-Amor*, *14*: 55–127.

Novick, J. & Novick, K. K. (2000) 'Love in the therapeutic alliance'. *Journal of the American Psychoanalytic Association*, *48*: 189–218.

Nunberg, H. & Federn, E. (1974) *Minutes of the Vienna Psychoanalytic Society*. New York: International Universities Press, Vol. III.

Scheler, M. (1923) 1. *Wesen und Formen der Sympathie Der 'Phänomenologie der Sympathiegefühle'* 2. *Vermehrte und durchgesehene Auflage*. Bonn: F. Cohen.

Spielrein, S. (1911) 'Über den psychologischen Inhalt eines Falles von Schizophrenie (Dementia praecox)'. *Jahrbuch psychoanal. psychopathol. Forschungen, 3*: 329–400.

—— (1912) 'Die Destruktion als Ursache des Werdens'. *Jahrbuch, 4*: 465–503.

—— (1922) Report on the Geneva Psychoanalytic Society. *Int. Z. ärztl. Psychoanal., 8*: 234–5.

Swales, P. J. (1992) 'What Jung did not say'. *Harvest Journal of Jungian Studies, 38*: 30–7.

Wackenhut, I. & Willke, A. (1994) *Sabina Spielrein. Missbrauchüberlebende und Psychoanalytikerin. Eine Studie ihres Lebens und Werkes unter besonderer Berücksichtigung ihrer Tagebücher und ihres Briefwechsels.* (Sabina Spielrein. Survivor of abuse and psychoanalyst. A study of her life and work with particular reference to her diaries and letters.) Inaugural-Dissertation, Medizinische Hochschule Hannover, Germany.

Chapter 11

'In league with the devil, and yet you fear fire?'

Sabina Spielrein and C.G. Jung: A suppressed scandal from the early days of psychoanalysis

Sabine Richebächer

(Translated from the German by Barbara Wharton)

> 'The past is never dead. It is not even past.'
>
> (William Faulkner)

From its opening in 1838 the Baur en Ville Hotel on the Paradeplatz in Zürich has been one of the most elegant houses in the city. On 17 August 1904 there is a great commotion there: the daughter of the wealthy Jewish merchant Naphtul Spielrein from Rostov-on-Don is making such a fuss that she has to be admitted to the Burghölzli psychiatric clinic.

Accompanied by a medical police official and her uncle Lublinsky, and with a medical report from Dr Bion and from Lublinsky, the young Russian woman is brought to the Burghölzli at 10.30 in the evening. She is not mad, she insists, she has just got upset at the hotel; she cannot stand people or noise. Meanwhile she is laughing and crying in a strange mixture, rotating her head, sticking out her tongue, jerking her legs and complaining of a headache. After the admission procedure she is put into ward E11 with a private nurse. 'A fairly quiet night' is the comment in the patient's notes the following day. After a morning with still more commotion there is a further comment: 'calmed down in the course of the day' (Chapter 5: 85).

The Burghölzli

The cantonal treatment and care institution for the mentally ill, the Burghölzli in Zürich, developed under its directors Auguste Forel (1879–1898) and Eugen Bleuler (1898–1927) into an internationally recognised centre for the young science of psychiatry. In his early years Auguste Forel made his mark in the field of microscopic brain research; later he became interested in questions relating to body/mind problems. Like Freud in his early years, Forel shared an interest in hypnotism which he used first with the attendants, and later with the patients too.

In 1898 Eugen Bleuler took over the direction of the clinic. His chief interest was in schizophrenia, or dementia praecox as it was then called. Bleuler had been following Freud's work since the beginning of the 1890s and was impressed by the fact that, with the help of the so-called Freudian mechanisms, 'the whole chaotic jumble could be understood logically, that is affectively' (Bleuler 1910: 660).

With the opening of an important, and at that time progressive, psychiatric institution for its concerns, Freudian psychoanalysis was awakened like the Sleeping Beauty: it became clinically and scientifically presentable on an international scale. The collaboration between Vienna and Zürich lasted about seven years, from 1906 until about 1912/1913, when the tragic break between Freud and Jung occurred. The history of this eventful and mutually stimulating association is documented, among other ways, in 360 letters exchanged by Freud and Jung during those years. One of the chief architects, and the dynamic centre, of the rapid development of the psychoanalytic movement in those years was Carl Gustav Jung.

C.G. Jung

C.G. Jung came from an impoverished protestant pastor's family. He was born on 26 July 1875 in Kesswil, in the Canton of Thurgau. His father was Pastor Johann Paul Achilles Jung; his mother Emilie Preiswerk came from the Basel bourgeoisie. In 1879 the family moved to a district near Basel. There in Basel Jung attended the Gymnasium and also studied medicine.

When the vacant post of second medical assistant at the Burghölzli is announced at the beginning of December 1900, the only applicant is C.G. Jung from Basel. He obtains the position with a salary of 1000 francs per year together with free accommodation (according to the minutes of the senior executive for 1900; 1988 S 322.2 Zürich State Archive [StAZ]). Under Eugen Bleuler, Jung becomes acquainted with Freud's theories and uses them in elaborating independently on scientific topics. In the summer of 1902 he receives his doctorate of medicine at the University of Zürich with his dissertation 'On the psychology and pathology of so-called occult phenomena'. Subsequently he spends six months in Paris. After his marriage in February 1903 to Emma Rauschenbach from a wealthy industrial family from Schaffhausen he settles in Zürich again.

While there was lively theoretical discussion of Freud's theories at the Burghölzli, the clinical application of psychoanalysis was not undertaken until 1904 – according to Bernard Minder (Chapter 6: 133) who was permitted to see the hospital records at the Burghölzli. Freud's new explanatory model of human mental life, based on depth psychology, was built on the analysis of dreams, a self analysis, and his clinical work with hysterical patients. He worked in private practice with an intensive treatment method involving up to five or six hourly sessions per week.

In the Burghölzli mental asylum in those days, however, a large number of very seriously ill patients were confined without any treatment. For example in 1904, the year of Spielrein's hospitalisation, five doctors were responsible for 388 patients. The diagnosis of hysteria, moreover, was seldom used at the Burghölzli, and these patients were treated – if at all – in the tradition of the French psychiatric school of Nancy: that is, with hypnosis and suggestion.

Now the young Russian woman who was brought to the Burghölzli on 17 August 1904 was educated, gifted, wealthy, and she spoke German; she was also not as ill as the other patients. For Jung she was a real stroke of luck: at last he had a patient on whom he could try out the Freudian method. It was also her good fortune to end up at the Burghölzli where there was an interest in the new treatment method of psychoanalysis. She had arrived in an environment where people took her seriously, and stimulated her to scientific activities and to reading. The release from the over-excited and drama-ridden climate of the family did her good. The conversations she had with Jung according to the Freudian method made sense to her. Thus she quickly calmed down and only a few weeks later she was helping her therapist with a scientific project.

This course of events shows that Sabina was in no way the seriously ill patient that present day analysts – for example Carotenuto, Bruno Bettelheim, or Max Day – would have us believe. Sabina was able to make use of the situation at the Burghölzli and to develop a perspective which corresponded with her inclinations and her gifts. In this way she was able quickly to overcome her developmental crisis.

However, we would not expect to find a wealthy young Russian woman of that period as a patient in the Zürich asylum, but somewhere in a private clinic. The fact that Sabina Spielrein came to be at the Burghölzli is due to a chain of coincidences.

Who was Sabina Spielrein?

Until 1980 the Russian Jewish doctor and psychoanalyst Sabina Spielrein was represented in the psychoanalytic literature by four footnotes in the works of Freud. Of her life, her significance, and the part she played in pioneering psychoanalysis nothing was known; and her articles, numbering over thirty, on psychoanalytic theory, on child analysis, and on technique, lay dormant in old journals.

In 1977 – in the course of renovation work at the Wilson palace in Geneva, which had formerly housed the Psychological Institute of Geneva – a cardboard box was found containing highly interesting material from the early years of psychoanalysis. Aldo Carotenuto, a Jungian analyst, was informed of this find and immediately recognised its significance. In fact it contained among other documents the correspondence of Sigmund Freud and C.G. Jung with Sabina Spielrein, and also Spielrein's diaries from 1909 to 1912. In 1980 Carotenuto published this material – with the exception of Jung's letters – in Italian. In 1986, in the first German edition, it was possible – thanks to the publisher Traute Hensch – to publish Jung's letters for the first time too. Carotenuto's book was a stimulus for further research. Since then portions of documents about and by Sabina Spielrein have been published unsystematically, in extracts, in different countries, and in different languages.

No document is innocent, and every age reads documents in a new way. At that time, twenty years ago, the discovery of a love affair between Jung and Spielrein guaranteed excitement: the interest was further heightened by the initial ban on publishing Jung's letters to her. Yet the fact that Sabina Spielrein was an independent person, herself very gifted and creative, that she published numerous theoretical and clinical papers and operated at several important psychoanalytic centres, was thus obscured. Sabina Spielrein belonged indeed among the very first pioneers – as far as the international dawning of the psychoanalytic movement was concerned.

Sabina Spielrein was born on 7 November 1885 in Rostov-on-Don, the first child of the wealthy Jewish merchant Naphtul Spielrein and his wife Eva Marcona Lublinskaya. Rostov lies on the Black Sea, somewhat to the east of the so-called Jewish settlement belt which was created around 1800, with the issuing of a law by the Russian government, between Riga in the north and Odessa in the south. The subsequent founder of Israel, Chaim Weizmann, writes thus:

> Rostov on Don in southern Russia is the gateway to the Caucasus. The Jewish community there was small and exposed to the same chicaneries which bedevilled life for the Jews in the settlement area. But the material conditions were in general more favourable. The district was richer, the competition less, and if a family – like my wife's – belonged to the class of so-called 'guild merchants' it enjoyed particular privileges – that is, as Jews – and as a result its existence was assured.
>
> (Weizmann 1953: 112f)

The marriage of Naphtul Spielrein and Eva Lublinskaya was arranged by their parents, according to Jewish tradition. Sabina's father came from Warsaw. When he emigrated to Rostov he russified his name Naphtul Aronovitsch Spielrein to Nikolai Arkadjevitsch Spielrein. He ran a business in animal feed and made a considerable fortune. In Rostov he was known for his strong personality and for his original ideas.

Sabina's mother Eva came from a family of distinguished rabbis in Jekaterinstadt. She was allowed to attend the Christian Gymnasium and studied dentistry as one of the first women in Russia to do so. Eva Lublinskaya practised her profession until 1903 'more for pleasure than from necessity'.

Apart from their eldest daughter, Sabina, the couple had three sons: Jascha (Jan, Jean), Sanja (Isaak, Oscar), and Milja (Emil); a little daughter, Milotschka (Emilia) died in 1901 from typhus.

In the Spielreins' 'sugar-cake style' rococo palace in the Pushkinkaya, one of the great streets of the city, Eva Lublinskaya ran a household with numerous servants appropriate to her status. As the accounts of 11-year-old Sabina show, special value was placed on the children's education: there was a nursemaid; a private tutor who prepared the children for the Gymnasium; and in addition a music teacher. The children were brought up to be multilingual, speaking Russian, German, English, French. Sabina Spielrein writes: '[Papa] speaks French with me and Jascha, and German with Sanja; and we, that is Jascha and I, speak German with each other' (Wackenhut & Willke 1994: 128).

From the autumn of 1896 Sabina Spielrein attends the Empress Katherina II eight-grade Gymnasium for girls; she also has piano and singing lessons. She learns ancient Hebrew independently, 'so as to read the Bible in the original'. 'Up to the age of thirteen I was extremely religious; in spite of numerous contradictions I perceived, in spite of my father's derision,' we read in her diary (Diary 1909–1912 in Carotenuto 1982: 23). As is usual for children of her age, Sabina has her *best friends*; at 13 she enters puberty; at 15 she falls in love with her history teacher: 'I was looking for a friend to whom I could bare my soul' (Carotenuto 1982: p.25).

Around her sixteenth year a change sets in: 'Later I withdrew completely from other people; when I was in the sixth grade, after the death of my little sister, my illness began. I took refuge in isolation [. . .]' (ibid: 24).

In 1904 Sabina Spielrein finishes at the Gymnasium with the highest honours, the gold medal. But what is to happen to her now? Sabina would like to study medicine; her grandfather, Rabbi Mark Lublinsky, had given her his blessing as a doctor. As a Jew and as a woman, however, she can find no place to study in Russia. And marriage, the possibility of becoming like a Russian *Effi Briest* (a Novelle by Theodor Fontane), does not enter into her consideration. So immediately after leaving school she goes to stay with relatives in Warsaw. Sabina is now 18 years old. She does not know where to go, either with herself or in life. She falls into a serious psychological state which from a present-day developmental perspective we would call an adolescent crisis. At that time, around 1900, this standpoint was not yet considered by psychology and psychoanalysis. The situation with the young woman at home eventually becomes intolerable and the parents feel themselves constrained to seek help abroad. Eva Lublinskaya goes with her brother, who is himself a doctor, and with Sabina, to Switzerland.

In the summer of 1904 Sabina Spielrein is taken into hospital in Interlaken, to Dr Heller's Sanatorium and Spa, specialising in nervous disorders. There are difficulties there. At her own request she leaves after four weeks. She is taken to Zürich, to Professor Constantin von Monakov (1853–1930).

Monakov was a naturalised Russian, an associate professor of brain anatomy at the University of Zürich, and in addition founder and director of the Institute of Brain Anatomy and of the local outpatient clinic for nervous disorders. He declined to treat Sabina Spielrein: 'But M. did not take her,' we read in Sabina Spielrein's hospital notes, 'because she was too agitated.' In this highly charged situation there was no other help for it, and Sabina came to the Burghölzli. Here C.G. Jung takes over her treatment. At this time he is standing in for the registrar L. von Muralt who is on sick leave in Inner Arosa (cf. minutes of the senior executive officer 1904.1556.S 322.2, StAZ).

The official hospital records

Sabina Spielrein's official hospital records are housed today in the Zürich State Archive. They comprise thirteen pages of hand-written and typed entries by Jung and two entries by Bleuler. This document was transcribed at the beginning of the 1990s by the Swiss psychiatrist Bernard Minder and published together with the relevant correspondence within the framework of his dissertation (1992/1994).

The cover-sheet of the hospital records has been completed by Jung and contains the usual information: name, place of birth, place of residence, civil status. Religion is given as 'israel'. We have the admission date, 17 August 1904, and the discharge date, 1 June 1905; beside the latter date is the comment 'improved'. Under 'provisional diagnosis' is entered 'hysteria'; the 'definitive diagnosis' also gives 'hysteria'. The patient is admitted to the Class 1 part of the hospital – as was stipulated for foreign visitors at that time. In addition the cover-sheet shows quite a number of peculiarities: the patient's name is wrongly spelt; under *date of birth* only the year of birth is given; no information at all is given about her *somatic status*.

What had happened here?

Now on that 17 August we find a difficult situation: it is late in the evening; the young person is beside herself; and Jung says of the old uncle: 'As an old Russian Jew he constantly gave quite meagre and evasive answers, and in addition did not have a good mastery of German.' Who therefore could have given the information?

The fact is that the omission of, or variation from, the usual procedures, mentioned above, were not remedied later either. The patient had, if you like, infected the clinic at her first encounter with it, and the chaos is now there; accordingly she has a quiet night.

Regarding her treatment Jung writes: 'Pat. is extremely sensitive, especially to any stimulation. Strict bed-rest therefore. No books, no conversation, no visitors. A doctor visits only once a day. The nurse goes into the room only once every hour for 5 minutes (Chapter 5: 232). Bed-rest, protection from all distractions, visits forbidden: those were Jung's therapeutic measures for his new patient; they correspond with the state of knowledge at that time and they proved successful. From the middle of October Jung was going for walks with Sabina Spielrein: first in the park of the Burghölzli, later in the district of Seefeld. Therapeutic consultations took place regularly; once Jung notes a 'three-hour analysis'. And Sabina Spielrein was stimulated to meaningful activity in the Burghölzli, to reading and to scientific work. At the end of October Bleuler informs her parents: 'She is currently assisting one of our doctors on a scientific project, which she finds of great interest. She still displays little inclination or perseverance with regard to other tasks' (Chapter 5: 233).

Theatres of the mind

'All the world's a stage, and all the men and women merely players'; thus writes Shakespeare on behalf of us all in *As You Like It*. With the metaphor of the theatre as a stage for our psychic tragedies and comedies, I should make it clear that each of us is both author and actor in our own drama and also in the dramas of others. Sigmund Freud expressed it thus:

> [. . .] that each individual, through the combined operation of his innate disposition and the influences brought to bear on him during his early years, has acquired a specific method of his own in his conduct of his erotic life . . . this produces what might be described as a stereotype plate (or several such), which is constantly repeated – constantly reprinted afresh.
>
> (Freud 1912, 'The Dynamics of Transference': 99f)

In psychoanalysis the sometimes amazing repetition of what is past and forgotten during the course of our life's drama is called *transference*. Transference contains a whole variety of emotional colourings: it encompasses positive, tender feelings as well as negative, hostile attitudes, and conscious and unconscious components. The creator of this stereotype plate or script is a naïve, childlike aspect of the ego. In an adult world in which the rules of childhood do not hold and are not understood, this ego-aspect stages anew its own personal scenarios of unbearable psychic conflict and emotional pain, but also its gratifications and comedies. It can *also* be an expression of a search for better, life-enhancing solutions.

If we consider Sabina Spielrein's hospital records from the point of view of the development of relationship dynamics, or transference, we can distinguish three phases.

Phase 1: In the first few week a chaotic transference predominates: she is defiant; she makes threats; she is always up to mischief; and she tries – with some success – to get everyone in the clinic worked up. We must bear in mind, however, that we are talking about a very young person. When Sabina Spiel-rein is admitted to hospital, she is 18 years old, and she does not yet have a stable personality. In Jung's time it was not yet considered in psychoanalytic circles that adolescence was a distinct developmental phase. When we read the hospital notes, the adolescent colouring of the turbulent events fairly leaps off the page. At the end of September Jung makes the following entry:

> The states of excitation have become less frequent recently. Pat. still uses her unoccupied hours for her childish pranks (suicidal gestures to drive the nurses crazy, running away, hiding, giving people scares, transgressing prohibitions.) After these excesses, sometimes a severe depressive reaction. Pat. has great insight into her condition but not the slightest inclination to improve it. She asks Ref. never to display the slightest sense of being at a loss about her but only the utmost fortitude and a firm belief in her recovery; that would be the only way for her to get better.
>
> (Chapter 5: 90)

On the wider stage of the clinic things are gradually becoming calmer. The young Russian woman has settled in in an orderly fashion. She is using the clinic as a place where she has an opportunity to get a clear sense of her interests. As early as October Bleuler is able to convey the 'happy fact' to the father 'that Miss Spielrein has now decided to commence studying medicine next spring here in Zürich' (Chapter 5: 100).

Furthermore Sabina Spielrein has made a special, indeed a unique, place for herself at the Burghölzli. She is helping Jung with his association experiments for his post-doctoral thesis; she is present at the examination of patients, and is involved in diagnoses; she sits with the doctors at table and attends a social event at Bleuler's. We can well imagine that all this contributed enormously towards raising the young woman's self-esteem.

Phase 2: In proportion as the uproar on the clinic level dies down, the therapist increases in significance. Sabina Spielrein gains confidence and now develops a father transference. Until her thirteenth year she was frequently beaten by her father and tormented with suggestive remarks. In a concrete way she now demands that Jung inflict pain on her. She admits quite calmly: 'I just want to feel pain, I would like you to do something really bad to me, to force me to do something that I am opposed to with all my being' (Chapter 5: 92). Jung resists this bid.

According to the Control of Residents and Foreign Visitors for the City of Zürich (Zürich State Archive V.E.c.100., Periode 1901–1933), at the end of November 1904 Jung moves with his wife Emma from his apartment at 198 Zollikerstrasse into hospital accommodation at 31 Lenggstrasse, Burghölzli. At that time his wife is heavily pregnant and at the end of December the couple's first child, a daughter Agathe, is born. These reality details regarding her therapist are unlikely to have remained hidden from his attentive patient.

Whether and how these circumstances, which must have preoccupied her very much, came to be spoken about in her treatment, we do not know.

Phase 3: The hospital records show that Sabina Spielrein does not let things get her down, and that she is now venturing forward into the difficult terrain of sexuality. The fact that she can speak about it all from the heart brings relief; the pains in her head and her feet disappear. 'Pat. now shows more initiative and demands regular useful activities. Behaves much more naturally' (Chapter 5: 95).

With the arrival of sexuality the transference changes yet again, moving this time on to an adult, erotic/sexual plane. At the end of January Jung writes: 'Yesterday at my evening visit pat. was reclining on the sofa in her usual oriental, voluptuous manner, with a sensuous, dreamy expression on her face. She did not really respond to questions, but only smiled superficially' (Chapter 5: 96). We see how the young woman is practising, experimenting, how she is giving rein to her feminine charms.

From *today's* point of view this constellation offers a good therapeutic opportunity of working with Sabina Spielrein on her problems. Nearly a hundred years ago, things looked different to the 29-year-old Jung. He is doing his utmost for his patient; he would like to help her by means of the new psychoanalytic treatment. And now he sees himself faced with a woman who is gifted, who is openly emotional, and who is seductive.

When Spielrein grips C.G. Jung on an adult, erotic level he seems to lose his balance. The way he describes his patient here is highly ambivalent and opens up a view on to a new stage-set, which this time belongs to the therapist: a set furnished with a *fin-de-siècle* vision of the mysterious, sensuous, voluptuous orient. On this stage there stands the figure of a woman, seductive and dangerous.

Let us think: like the other pioneers of psychoanalysis Jung was not prepared or protected by training or by a personal analysis from the emotional turbulences of treatment and of contact with the unconscious. Not until 1923 was the first systematic training programme for psychoanalysts set up in Berlin. Before that people just got by somehow, and learned as best they could from experience. The early Viennese psychoanalysts could of course talk to Freud. Would Jung, rather isolated as he was in Zürich, have considered that in his unforeseen situation with Spielrein? The fact that the requirement of a personal analysis for future psychoanalysts goes back to Jung bears witness to his having been haunted by the matter and to his giving it much thought.

The appearance on Jung's stage of the oriental woman really marks the end of the patient's records. After that there is just a short note on 28 April which says that the patient is distinctly improved and is now listening to the lectures conscientiously and with interest.

Medical studies in Zürich

The next thing we can say with certainty is that on 17 April 1905 Sabina Spielrein registered personally at the office of the University of Zürich for matriculation in the medical faculty. She was given the matriculation number 15546, and had to pay seventeen francs for office and writing charges. She rented a room in one of the numerous lodging houses in the Platten quarter which among the people of Zürich was know as the 'Russian colony'.

There was nothing unusual at that time about people from Russia studying in Zürich. Most of them came from the Baltic, from Poland, the Ukraine, and the Caucasus. There were political/historical reasons for this. The policy of the Russian regime towards people of different nationalities living on Russian territory was really aimed at discriminating against non-Russian religions and nationalities; as a result of this, being Jewish qualified both as a religious adherence and as a nationality.

The beginnings of women's studies in Switzerland were determined to a large extent by Russian women. When in 1865 Nadescha P. Suslova approached the new liberal University of Zürich, then only 30 years old, with a request to study, the academic governing body decided to risk an experiment with women's studies. The graduation regulations were subsequently interpreted in such a way that in 1867 Suslova was able to graduate as a doctor of medicine: an event which caused quite a sensation in the Russian press. Thus Zürich was one of the first European universities to legalise women's studies. Once Suslova had discovered Zürich as a place for women to study, numerous Russian women followed her example.

As the daughter of a wealthy Rostov guild-merchant Sabina Spielrein had privileges above most of her fellow-students. This is what Chaim Weizmann has to say on the subject:

> For it was in Geneva – fifty years ago – that I got to know my wife. I first met her in the company of a small group of Russian Jewish girls, school friends of hers from her home town, Rostov-on-Don. Like many of her generation she had come to Geneva to study medicine because the universities of her own country were closed to her. Nevertheless the little group of young women to which Vera Chatzmann belonged differed markedly in appearance, behaviour, and in their approach to life from the great majority of Jewish women who were then studying at Swiss universities. They were different from and much more attractive than their fellow countrywomen from the Jewish settlement area, and they were less concerned with revolutionary politics. Not that they were politically indifferent, but they studied more enthusiastically and spent less time in public meetings and endless discussions than the average Russian student abroad so frequently did.

> (Weizmann 1953: 112)

Beside the proverbial poverty of most of these women students, the secluded life-style of the Russian colony was characteristic of the second so-called wave of Russian women immigrants in Zürich from around 1902 to 1914. And while the relationship between the Swiss students and the Russian women students had meanwhile lost some of its tension, the attitude of the general public in Zürich towards these foreign women remained ambivalent if not negative.

The press contributed towards the cementing of prejudices: 'Our little Switzerland is bristling with an over-abundance of secret societies, clandestine groups and committees', we read in the *Neue Zürcher Zeitung* in 1907 (16 December 1907: 2). And the conservative *Berner Volkszeitung* warns: 'These fearful sirens seduce our immature young men by subduing them in a frenzy of passion and then spur them on to desperate acts.'

Confusion of tongues or the language of tenderness and the language of passion

At the beginning of her studies Sabina Spielrein is still living in the Burghölzli. How might things have been for her at this time? She is living apart from her family and away from home, in a distinctly foreign culture; she faces the prospect of leaving the shelter of the clinic for an uncertain independence. Searching for lodgings is a difficult task for a Russian woman: she has to grapple with government officials, produce the necessary papers, etc. All that cannot have been easy for a spoilt young woman raised in a comfortable home.

On the first day of her studies Sabina Spielrein notes: 'Hell! I've been to the university. Such a mountain of impressions that I haven't the patience to describe them. I liked the Professor of Zoology, Lange, very much. I was burning with interest, but now the reaction has set in and I'm feeling miserable again!'

She attends lectures in botany with Schinz; osteology with Felix; systematic physical anthropology (morphology of the human races) with Martin; and anthropometrics with practical experiments on living people. She is also studying the behaviour of men and of women in groups, and genetic and racial development; under Bleuler she covers general and specialised psychiatry.

Sabina Spielrein will complete her studies successfully. It is not easy for her; learning and concentration come hard. Reading her letters and diaries one gets the impression that she has to struggle frequently with severe mood swings, with doubts and despondency. And then there is the matter of Jung. Her relationship with him had changed; it had become more complex, shifting between a therapeutic relationship, an idealised teacher/pupil relationship, a friendship, and a love-affair.

For C.G. Jung too, 1905 is an important year. In the middle of February the medical faculty of Zürich accepts his post-doctoral thesis and he receives his lecturer's licence in psychiatry at the beginning of the summer term 1905. Once granted, the licence is valid in the first instance for the duration of six terms. At the Burghölzli Jung's career too is making headway. At the beginning of April the director of the Burghölzli cantonal mental asylum writes to the Zürich health authority:

> Dear Sir,
>
> By the same post you will be receiving a letter of resignation from the registrar, Dr L. von Muralt. Unfortunately there is nothing left for it but to accept it. If I may make a suggestion, I would like to ask you to thank him appropriately on his retirement; he has devoted more than ten years' faithful service to Rheinau and the Burghölzli.
>
> Further I should like respectfully to request that Dr C. Jung from Basel, who has stood in for him until now, be selected to fill his post. An advertisement would make no sense in the present circumstances.
>
> Most respectfully yours,
>
> Bleuler.
>
> (3 April 1905, S 322.2 StAZ)

The senior executive officer complies with Bleuler's request and appoints C.G. Jung to the post of registrar on 18 April (cf. minutes of senior executive officer 1905.543.S 322.2, StAZ). In this position Jung is now permitted to treat private patients. He is 31. He is successful and could be very contented – if it were not for the Spielrein matter.

The relationship between Jung and Spielrein is continued or perhaps resumed after her discharge from the clinic. Whether regular therapeutic sessions took place at this time it is hard to say. Mrs Spielrein is kept informed about all developments through letters by her daughter; at some point she feels things have got out of hand and demands that her daughter be transferred to another therapist. On 25 September 1905 Jung writes a 'report on Miss Spielrein to Professor Freud in Vienna, delivered to Mrs Spielrein for use if the occasion arises'. This is Jung's first attempt to contact Freud. In the report we read: 'By using your method I have analysed the clinical condition fairly thoroughly and with considerable success from the outset' (Chapter 5: 105).

Meanwhile the page has turned. Jung continues: 'During treatment the patient had the misfortune to fall in love with me. [. . .] Now in this distressing situation the mother wants to place her elsewhere for treatment'(Chapter 5: 106). The words Jung uses leave open what kind of distress and whose distress is in question here. He seems somewhat shaken; he may be doubting himself and his therapeutic competence. In this situation he turns to the experienced

50-year-old master. But Freud never received this letter, because it stayed in the Spielrein family and was never sent to him.

Six months later Jung sends Freud a copy of *Studies in Word Association* (1906) representing his own work and that of other Burghölzli doctors. This time he gets through. Already in his second letter to Freud, Jung spells out his difficulties in detail: 'At the risk of boring you, I must abreact my most recent experience. I am currently treating an hysteric with your method. Difficult case, a 20-year-old Russian girl student, ill for 6 years' (McGuire 1974: 7).

Jung does not tell Freud that he has known the patient for over two years, that she is a private patient, that she is living independently in the city and successfully studying medicine. In comparison with other Burghölzli patients she is not so ill. So perhaps the case is difficult because the therapist is erotically involved? Jung's presentation is at any rate one-sided.

Freud is interested: 'I am glad to hear that your Russian girl is a student; uneducated persons are at present too inaccessible for our purposes' (McGuire 1974: 8). In the lively exchange that now develops between the two men, Spielrein is present – without her name being mentioned, and without Freud suspecting that it is always the same patient about whom Jung is consulting him. The correspondence with Freud must have taken the place of a personal analysis and of supervision for Jung.

In May 1908 Spielrein passes her preparatory examination in anatomy and physiology at Zürich University. At the end of June she is invited by Jung to a boating party on Lake Zürich. On the same day he writes to her:

My dear friend,

I must tell you briefly what a lovely impression I received of you today. Your image has changed completely, and I want to tell you how very, very happy it makes me to be able to hope that there are people who are like me, people in whom living and thinking are one; [. . .] You can't believe how much it means to me to hope I can love someone whom I do not have to condemn, and who does not condemn herself either, to suffocate in the banality of habit.

(Chapter 3: 33)

About two weeks later Sabina Spielrein notifies the authorities that she is leaving Zürich. On the residents' control form, under the heading 'Where are you moving to?' it merely says 'Away from Zürich'. Jung's concerned letter reaches her in Russia.

My dear friend,

Your letter gave me much pleasure and set my mind at rest. I was rather worried on account of your long silence. [. . .] How do you like being in your home country again? [. . .] And what did your old nurse say to you? Was she pleased to see how pretty you have become? We're reading here in the newspaper that cholera is rife in Rostov. Don't drink any unboiled water and don't eat any salads; [. . .] I received the money safely. Thank you! With an affectionate kiss from your friend.

(Chapter 3: 35)

In the autumn Spielrein is back: it was one of several attempts to get away from Zürich and from Jung. In the following months: mistakes, confusion, turmoil. In her diary Spielrein writes, looking back: 'Altogether, my love brought me almost nothing but pain; there were only single moments, when I rested in his arms, in which I was able to forget everything [. . .]' (11 September 1910, in Carotenuto 1982: 13).

At the beginning of December 1908 Jung writes:

My dear, I regret so much; I regret my weaknesses and curse the fate that is threatening me. [. . .] My mind is torn to its very depths. [. . .] Will you forgive me for being as I am? For offending you by being like this, and forgetting my duties as a doctor towards you? [. . .] Give me back now something of the love and patience and unselfishness which I was able to give you at the time of your illness. Now I am ill.

(Chapter 3: 37)

The roles have switched: now the therapist turns to his patient/pupil/friend with a plea for help. Spielrein writes to Jung:

You are trying to suppress all the stronger feelings you have towards me. As a result you are surviving on mere diplomacy and lies. Should I make everything clear to you? What would be the point? [. . .] Earlier you used to be able to discuss more abstract topics with me, you showed me different things in the laboratory or at home, things connected with pictures or old documents; now you call everything that is not narrowly connected with the sexual complex 'giving a lecture'; this seems annoying to you because the complex is so powerful that you are not quite master of it. I don't know: are we always so stupid when it comes to ourselves, or do you just not want to admit it; it would be striking, though, if, with your analytic capabilities, you had not noticed what kind of 'patient stories' you reserve for me. [. . .] I don't feel quite comfortable when I speak to you like this. And yet: what am I to do? [. . .] I'm going to Locarno now and hope that the new impressions and the longer time when I don't see you will give me a more sensible perspective on things – at the moment I am quite stupid [. . .].

(Wackenhut & Willke 1994: 247f)

The matter reaches a crisis when rumours circulate in Zürich and in Vienna about an affair Jung is having with a patient. Jung suspects Spielrein of being the instigator and brings the relationship to an abrupt end. It seems that Jung was urged at this time by the clinic directorate to leave the service. It is documented that in a letter of 7 March 1909 Jung requests the senior executive officer for release from his post of registrar from 15 April (cf. minutes of senior executive officer 1909.467.S 322.2, StAZ). Jung seems to be in great distress. On the very same day he telegraphs Freud and also writes him a detailed letter. The important step he has just taken, of resigning from the clinic at short notice, is not even mentioned. Jung's theme is again Spielrein:

> [. . .] a woman patient, whom years ago I pulled out of a very sticky neurosis with unstinting effort, has violated my confidence and friendship in the most mortifying way imaginable. She has kicked up a vile scandal solely because I denied myself the pleasure of giving her a child. [. . .] But you know how it is – the devil can use even the best of things for the fabrication of filth.
>
> (McGuire 1974: 207)

Freud calms his young friend and designated successor: 'To be slandered and scorched by the love with which we operate – such are the perils of our trade, which we are certainly not going to abandon on their account.' And he quotes Mephisto to support his statement: 'And another thing: "In league with the Devil and yet you fear fire?"' (McGuire 1974: 210f). Jung is relieved and thanks Freud for his 'kind and liberating words'.

Then at the end of May Jung gives notice that he is moving with his family from Zürich to Küsnacht. Also at the end of May Spielrein writes her first letter to Freud: 'I would be most grateful to you if you would grant me a brief audience!' (30 May 1909, Carotenuto 1982: 91). By now Freud is so irritated that he sends Jung a telegram and a letter asking him to telegraph an explanation: 'Weird! What is she? A busybody, a chatterbox, or a paranoiac?' (McGuire 1974: 226).

Gradually Jung reveals the truth: 'Spielrein is the person I wrote you about. [. . .] She was, so to speak, my psychoanalytic test case, for which reason I remembered her with special gratitude and affection. [. . .] She was, of course, systematically planning my seduction, which I considered inopportune. Now she is seeking revenge' (McGuire 1974: 228). Freud now also learns that Spielrein is a Jewess; and in order to explain his involvement with her, Jung refers to a philosemitic complex.

At this time Freud was convinced that only a personal successor could save his life's work, psychoanalysis, from downfall. '[. . .] if I am Moses, then you are Joshua and will take possession of the promised land of psychiatry, which I shall only be able to glimpse from afar' (McGuire 1974: 196f). The choice of Jung as crown prince and heir met with opposition among Freud's followers in Vienna and Berlin. Freud writes to Karl Abraham in Berlin: 'Please be tolerant [. . .] I nearly said that it was only by his appearance on the scene that psychoanalysis escaped the danger of becoming a Jewish national affair' (Freud/Abraham Letters 3 May 1908: 34).

And now a shabby game unfolds in which, out of calculating power politics, and in an endeavour to avoid any public scandal around psychoanalysis, Freud and Jung together draw up a design to checkmate the queen. First she is led up the garden path, pathologised, appeased. On 18 June Freud reports: '[. . .] and [I] suggested a more dignified [S.R.] procedure, something endopsychic, as it were' (McGuire 1974: 235).

In Zürich Spielrein and Jung finally manage to talk; the latter realises that he has suspected Spielrein unjustly. Following this discussion Spielrein writes to Freud:

> Ah, but you are a sly one, too, Professor Freud: *audiatur et altera pars* ('listen to the other side too'). The first logical conclusion was that you should have agreed to see me without putting up the slightest resistance. But one likes to spare oneself unpleasant moments. Right? Even the great 'Freud' cannot always ignore his [i.e. Jung's – S.R.] weaknesses. Well, the necessary corrections and explanations of his and my behaviour will be provided for you by Dr. Jung.
>
> (20 June 1909 S.S. to Freud, Carotenuto 1982: 104)

Jung hastens to follow up this pronouncement: 'I have good news to report of my Spielrein affair. I took too black a view of things. [. . .] Out of delusions in respect to the relationship [S.R.], understandable enough in the circumstances, I attributed the rumour to her [. . .]' (McGuire 1974: 236).

Freud apologises to Spielrein whom he has meanwhile begun to value. When he later gets to know the 'little girl' personally – as she is subsequently called in the correspondence between the two men – he writes to Jung: 'I must say she is rather nice and I am beginning to understand' (McGuire 1974: 469).

Further stages

In the winter term of 1910/11 Spielrein completes her medical studies. Her paper 'On the psychological content of a case of schizophrenia (dementia praecox)' is the first psychoanalytically orientated dissertation by a woman. It testifies to Spielrein's linguistic sensibility and her talent for grasping and deciphering unconscious processes. Freud and Jung are equally impressed. The text is published in 1911 in the *Yearbook for Psychoanalytic and Psychopathological Research*, and moreover as the leading paper.

In the spring Spielrein leaves Zürich. She spends the summer term in Munich: among other things she continues her musical education there and even considers changing her career to music. From Munich she goes to Vienna. At the extraordinary general meeting of the Vienna Psychoanalytic Society (WPV) on 11 October 1911 she is elected to membership: and indeed as the second *woman doctor*, as Freud expressed it. A year later we read in her diary:

> Vienna! Almost a whole year has passed, and what a difficult period! A reader would ask: 'How did it end?' There is no ending, many things happened, and still no conclusion. Away from Zürich and to Montreux on vacation (Chailly sur Clarens), from there – to Munich for art history, and here, where in complete solitude I finished my paper, 'Destruction as the Cause of Creation.' [. . .] Now I have actually become a member of the Psychoanalytic Society, on the strength of my dissertation. Prof. Freud, of whom I have become very fond, thinks very highly of me [. . .] I have two woman patients whom I am treating free of charge. Both are doing well; [. . .] During my vacation I was in Rostov for two weeks. [. . .] There I gave a lecture on psychoanalysis.
>
> (Diary 7 January 1912, in Carotenuto 1982: 40f)

By April 1912 Sabina Spielrein is mentioned in the minutes of the Wednesday meetings of the WPV. She takes an active part in the discussions, and gives several lectures; in addition she publishes in various psychoanalytic journals. Her first contribution on the analysis of children appears in the *Zentralblatt für Psychoanalyse*. Freud comes to value her and even sends her patients, but she cannot make a living in Vienna.

In the minutes of the WPV for 9 October 1912 we read: 'Dr S. Spielrein-Scheftel, Charlottenberg, Hardenbergstrasse 15'. She is now living in Berlin. At some point in the year 1912 Sabina Spielrein has married the Russian Jewish doctor Pavel Naumovitsch Scheftel. Presumably it was a traditional arranged marriage which took place in Rostov. In December 1913 Sabina is delivered of a daughter: she is named Irma Renata.

In Zürich in the winter of 1911/1912 a fierce public controversy blows up around psychoanalysis. In the *Neuer Zürcher Zeitung* alone twenty polemical articles appear in the course of January signed by Jung, Forel and Fritz Marti, among others. Dangerous psychoanalytic experimentation, eroto-mania, abuse, sectarianism, pseudo-science, smut and sleaze: these are some of the things for which psychoanalysis is blamed by its opponents. The fact that Jung, as the President of the International Psychoanalytic Association, energetically repudiates the 'offensive and extremely discrediting accusations' (NZZ 27 January 1912) is of no avail. 'Psychoanalysis even appears in the carnival newspapers,' he writes to Freud. 'Excuse this brevity, but I am in a state of war' (McGuire 1974: 486). But the relationship between the two men is heading for disaster too.

A few months later, in March, Freud reports to Abraham on his last visit to

Zürich. 'I have greatly retreated from him, and have no more friendly thoughts for him. His bad theories do not compensate me for his disagreeable character' (Freud–Abraham 27 March 1913: 137). A year later Freud is saying: 'So we are at last rid of them, the brutal, sanctimonious Jung and his disciples!' (Freud–Abraham 26 July 1914: 187) And Freud solves his succession problem by founding a Secret Committee to monitor correct theory.

For his part Jung gives up his academic career and enters on his Nekyia, or night sea journey – a 'creative illness' as Ellenberger (p. 953) calls it – which will lead him to the formulation of his basic psychological concepts.

In this archaic-sounding conflict between Freud and Jung, Sabina Spielrein holds a unique position. She does not allow herself to be dictated to; she preserves a relationship with Freud *and* with Jung; she even tries to reconcile the two of them. She preserves her own elbow-room and does not collude in fostering a sharp split between black and white, good and evil.

Shortly after the beginning of World War I we find her again in Zürich – and indeed without her husband. In spring 1915 she goes to western Switzerland. She looks in vain for a post in hospitals in Lausanne and Leysin: 'where am I to find patients? Would you recommend me if I came to Zürich?' she asks of Jung (19 January 1918, Carotenuto 1982: 82).

The tone of Jung's letters to Spielrein is variable. Sometimes his antisemitism – coloured by his clerical background and by his tragic break with Freud – gets in the way: 'There is a part of the Jewish soul which you are not yet living, because you still have your eye too much on the outside. That is – "unfortunately" – the curse of the Jew: [. . .] he is the murderer of his own prophets, even of his Messiah' (Chapter 3: 55). Then once more he has something important to say to her about her inner life and about his own experience:

> The love of S. for J. made the latter aware of something he had previously only vaguely suspected, namely of a power in the unconscious which shapes one's destiny, a power which later led him to things of the greatest importance. The relationship had to be 'sublimated', because otherwise it would have led to delusion and madness [. . .] Sometimes we must be unworthy to live at all.
>
> (ibid: 57)

At the sixth International Psychoanalytic Congress in 1920 at The Hague, Sabina Spielrein speaks on the theme of 'The origin and development of children's speech'. She develops an exciting theory about the significance of the mother's breast and of sucking for the development of the child. This lecture anticipates theoretically Melanie Klein's much later distinction between the 'good' breast and the 'bad' breast. In the obligatory group photograph of the participants at the Congress we see Sabina in the second row, on the far right, with a stylish short hairstyle.

In The Hague she gives notice that she is moving to Geneva. At the Jean-Jacques Rousseau Institute in Geneva she gives lectures on psychoanalysis and education; she does some clinical work; she conducts analyses and supervision; among other things she is the analyst of the well-known developmental psychologist Jean Piaget. She gives lectures; publishes several articles in professional journals; she writes an in-depth theatre criticism for the *Journal de Genève* and tries her hand at a short story. But her financial worries persist. And she does not get on to such friendly terms with her colleagues in Geneva. Spielrein does not agree with them about what passes for psychoanalysis there.

In 1923 Sabina Spielrein puts into action a plan which she has had in mind for some time: she goes to Russia for a few months to visit relatives and colleagues. After this journey she does not return to Switzerland. Initially she lives in Moscow where, together with Ivan Ermakov and Moshe Wulff she plans a training programme for future analysts at the Moscow psychoanalytic institute and works there as a training analyst and lecturer. Spielrein's 'Seminar on child analysis' is the course which, with thirty participants, is by far the best attended.

Recently discovered papers related to staffing for the Soviet People's Commissariat for national education, 'Narkompros', indicate that Sabina Spielrein held three posts from September 1923: as scientific contributor at the state psychoanalytic institute, as pedagogic medical consultant to the Third International (a kind of children's village), and as director of the child psychology department at the First Moscow University. Then with the fall of Trotsky the dark time of persecution set in which affected psychoanalysis too. About 1924 Sabina moves back to her home town of Rostov where she lives with her husband again and in 1926 her second daughter Eva is born.

Up to 1933 the name of Dr S.N. Spielrein appears on the membership list of the Russian psychoanalytic society. In the same year psychoanalysis is forbidden in Russia.

Also in 1933, on 10 May on an order from Joseph Goebbels, ritual book-burnings were carried out in several German university towns, including Berlin. To the cheering of the crowds, the first of over twenty thousand books which were burned that day were cast into the flames at 11.20. Goebbels' incineration order applied to Freud's works: 'Against the soul-destroying over-valuation of instinctual life, and for the nobility of the human soul! I consign the writings of Sigmund Freud to the flames' (Bergschicker 1982: 100). 'What progress we are making!' remarks Freud. 'In the Middle Ages they would have burned me, nowadays they are satisfied with burning my books!' (Jones 1961: 218).

In 1933 too, after the resignation of the German psychiatrist Ernst Kretschmer, C.G. Jung takes over the chairmanship of the government-approved General Medical Society for Psychotherapy which he held until the summer of 1940. In his foreword in December 1933 to the *Zentralblatt für*

Psychotherapie he explains his programme: 'The differences which actually do exist between Germanic and Jewish psychology, which have long been known to every intelligent person are no longer to be glossed over and this can only be beneficial to science' (Jung 1933, *CW* Vol.10, para. 1014). We can only be astonished at the depth of Jung's political naiveté in publishing such a text at that time. Yet we cannot doubt his subjective honesty when he protests in 1934: 'My relation to Germany [. . .] is due to idiotic altruism and not at all to political sentiment' (26 March 1934, Jung to Dr B. Cohen, Letters, Vol.1).

Forgetting

In comparison with other sciences and professions, psychoanalysis is very open to the participation of women. This was true particularly in the early years when the path from the role of analysand to the profession of psycho-analyst was not very long and not even unusual. In the written history of psychoanalysis we look in vain for Sabina Spielrein. In Ernest Jones's stand-ard work *Sigmund Freud* (1953) she does not appear; she is mentioned once briefly in Peter Gay's magnum opus *Freud* (1987) in connection with Freud's concept of the death instinct. Nancy Chodorow (1987), who at least addresses the 'Contribution of women to the Psychoanalytic Movement and to Psychoanalytic Theory', completely forgets her.

Just considering the range of Spielrein's publications – there are more than thirty of them, and they are in some cases very impressive – that is astonish-ing. In addition she is the very first woman to have written a doctoral thesis on a psychoanalytic theme, and furthermore hers is the first thesis to be given the prominence of being published in the *Jahrbuch*. Spielrein's pioneering achievements in her special field of child analysis have remained unnoticed until today. In the official view of psychoanalysis, Freud's daughter Anna features still, as she always did, as the founder of child analysis; Melanie Klein might also be mentioned in this respect. In fact in 1912 Sabina Spielrein and another 'forgotten' pioneer, Hermine Hug-Hellmuth (1871–1924), pub-lished the first contributions on child analysis in psychoanalytic history. Ten years later Anna Freud's first paper appeared; by this time twenty-five papers had been published by Spielrein, ten of them on child-analytic themes. We have to ask ourselves: what forces are at work here to cut off psychoanalysis from remembering and recording historically the myths of its origins?

Repression

The psychoanalytic concept of repression rests on the axiom that an earlier event A undergoes a re-working as a result of a later event B. Event A is thus endowed with new meaning and now develops a pathogenic effect. For this process the concept of *Nachträglichkeit*, or the recategorisation of experience, was coined. The question of repression can also be applied to the history of psychoanalysis itself. We could say: first Sabina Spielrein was forgotten. There were reasons enough for that. Her person, her name, undoubtedly recalled the break between Freud and Jung in 1913 which was so traumatic for the psychoanalytic movement. Spielrein was moreover an independent person and someone with a will of her own who would not allow herself to be slotted into the interests of the psychoanalytic movement as a mere apparatchik. In the patriarchal structures of psychoanalysis she caused offence again and again; Ernest Jones, the one time President of the International Psychoanalytic Association, could not stand her.

The reappearance of Spielrein's diaries and correspondence, and the publication of her scientific works in the 1980s, did not act as a memory trigger for psychoanalysis. People preferred to be spared the labour of remembering. Rather Spielrein was saddled retrospectively with a diagnosis indicating a severe psychic disturbance, a psychotic break with reality. Thus Aldo Carotenuto writes of a 'frankly psychotic episode', Bruno Bettelheim of a 'schizophrenic disturbance' and of a 'severe hysteria with schizoid characteristics'; Max Day calls her 'borderline'. Thus the support is in favour of Jung who lectured on the 'Spielrein Case' in a distorted and one-sided way at the International Congress for Psychiatry and Neurology in 1907 in Amsterdam. For Jung the enterprise ended in a fiasco; for Spielrein it still has consequences today.

Thus we are faced with the strange finding that, of all disciplines, psychoanalysis, which is founded on a belief in the healing power of memory, stubbornly resists its own history. And the handing down of a false diagnosis – which Sabina Spielrein was given retrospectively – ensures that nothing changes.

Epilogue: Flowers for joy and sorrow

Spielrein's brothers developed into successful scientists. All three were arrested under Stalin's reign of terror and lost their lives in the Gulag. Sabina too met a tragic end. On 22 June 1941, the day of the invasion of Russia by the German armed forces, Sabina Spielrein's daughter Renata, who had meanwhile been studying music in Moscow, returned to Rostov. As a strategically important bridgehead, the city suffered occupation by the German armed forces on two occasions during World War II. When Hitler's troops occupied Rostov for the second time on 27 July 1942, ten thousand civilians were slaughtered immediately. Sabina Spielrein was seen by neighbours for the last time in the summer of 1942. Supported by her two daughters Eva and Renata she was herded through the streets with a group of Jews to the outskirts of the city. There, according to information from Russia (Ovcharenko 1995, 1999), Jews and other victims were shot at the edge of a deep ravine.

Acknowledgement

In the above text several documents are referred to or quoted from, which concern C.G. Jung's employment at the Burghölzli Psychiatric Clinic (1900–1902, 1903–1909) and his teaching appointment at the medical faculty of the University of Zürich (1905–1914). The documents in question are housed in the State Archive of the Canton of Zürich (StAZ) under the signatures S 322.2, U 106f 2.76, and UU 2.63.

References

Bergschicker, H. (1982) *Deutsche Chronik 1933–1945. Ein Zeitbild der faschistischen Diktatur*. Berlin: Verlag der Nation.

Bleuler, E. (1910) Die Psychoanalyse Freuds. Verteidigung und kritische Anmerkungen, in: *Jahrbuch für Psychoanalytische und Psychopathologische Forschungen*, Bd. 2, H.2/2, pp 623–730. Leipzig/Wien: Franz Deuticke.

Carotenuto, A. (1982) *A Secret Symmetry. Sabina Spielrein between Jung and Freud*. Foreword by William McGuire. New York: Random House, Pantheon Books.

—— (ed.) (1986) *Tagebuch einer heimlichen Symmetrie. Sabina Spielrein zwischen Jung und Freud*. Vorwort von Johannes Cremerius. Freiburg i. Br: Kore.

Chodorow, N. (1987) 'Der Beitrag der Frauen zur psychoanalytischen Bewegung und Theorie', in *Psyche*, 41. Jahrgang, Heft 9, September: 800–31.

Ellenberger, H.F. (1970) *The Discovery of the Unconscious*. London: Allen Lane/The Penguin Press.

Freud, S. (1912) 'The Dynamics of Transference'. *SE* 22

—— (1914) 'On the history of the psychoanalytic movement'. *SE* 14.

Freud Sigmund–Abraham Karl. Letters 1907–1926. Frankfurt/Main: S. Fischer.

Gay, P. (1989) *Freud. Eine Biographie für unsere Zeit*. Frankfurt/Main.

Jones, E. (1961) *The Life and Work of Sigmund Freud*. New York: Basic Books.

Jung, C.G. (1902) 'On the psychology and pathology of so-called occult phenomena'. *CW* 1.

—— Briefe 1 1906–1945. Olten/Freiburg i.Br.: Walter.

—— (1906) *Experimental Researches. CW* 2.

—— (1908) *Freud and Psychoanalysis. CW* 4.

—— (1933) *Editorial. CW* 10.

—— (2001) 'The Letters of C.G. Jung to Sabina Spielrein (1908–1919)'. *Journal of Analytical Psychology*, 46, 1: 173–99, and this volume, Chapter 3.

—— (1961) *Memories, Dreams, Reflections*. Recorded and edited by Aniela Jaffé. London: Fontana, 1973.

McGuire, W. (ed.) (1974) *The Freud/Jung Letters*. London: Hogarth/Routledge & Kegan Paul.

Minder, B. (2001) 'Sabina Spielrein: Jung's patient at the Burghölzli'. *Journal of Analytical Psychology*, 46: 1, and this volume, Chapter 6.

Neue Zürcher Zeitung, Jg. 128, Nr. 348, 16.12.1907, *Erstes Abendblatt*: 2.

—— Jg. 133, Nr. 27 (119), 27.1.1912, *Erstes Morgenblatt:* 1.

Neumann, D. (1987) *Studentinnen aus dem Russischen Reich in der Schweiz (1867–1914)*. Zürich: Hans Rohr.

Ovcharenko, V. (1995) 'Le destin de Sabina Spielrein'. *L'Evolution Psychiatrique*, 60, 1: 115–22.

—— (1999) 'Love, Psychoanalysis and destruction'. *Journal of Analytical Psychology*, 44, 3: 355–73.

Protokolle der Wiener Psychoanalytischen Vereinigung, Bd. 3 1910–1911 & Bd. 4 1912–1918, eds. von Hermann Nunberg & Ernst Federn. Frankfurt/Main: S. Fischer.

Spielrein, S. (1911) 'Über den psychologischen Inhalt eines Falles von Schizophrenia (Dementia Praecox)', in: *Jahrbuch für psychoanalytische und psychopathologische Forschungen*, eds. Von E. Bleuler & S. Freud, Bd. 3, 1/2, pp.465–503. Leipzig/Wien: Franz Deuticke.

—— (1912) 'Destruction as the cause of coming into being'. *Journal of Analytical Psychology*, 39, 2: 155–86.

—— (1906–1907?) 'Unedited extracts from a diary', transl. into French by Jeanne Moll. *Le Bloc-Notes de la Psychanalyse*, *3*: 147–171.

—— (1986) *Ausgewählte Schriften*, Berlin: Brinkman & Bose.

—— (1987) *Sämtliche Schriften*, Freiburg i. Br: Kore.

Wackenhut I. & Willke. A. (1994) *Sabina Spielrein. Missbrauchüberlebende und Psychoanalytikerin. Eine Studie ihres Lebens und Werkes unter besonderer Berücksichtigkeit ihrer Tagebücher und ihres Briefwechsels.* (Sabina Spielrein. Survivor of abuse and psychoanalyst. A study of her life and work with particular reference to her diaries and letters.) Inaugural-Dissertation aus der Abteilung Geschichte der Medizin der Medizinischen Hochschule Hannover.

Weizmann, C. (1953) *Memoiren. Das Werden des Staates Israel.* Zürich: Phaidon.

Chapter 12

Kindred spirits

Nicolle Kress-Rosen

(Translated from the French by Barbara Wharton)

Documents discovered in 1977 in a cellar in the former Institute of Psychology in Geneva which, thanks to the enthusiasm of two Italian professors, Carlo Trombetta and Aldo Carotenuto, have allowed us to rescue the figure of Sabina Spielrein from oblivion, contain enough to satisfy even the most avid of puzzle enthusiasts. This collection of pieces – fragments of letters, scraps from an intimate diary – presents us in fact with a quite particular difficulty, since they are incomplete and there is no pattern to follow for reassembling them; we can imagine the pleasure of those who uncovered the image that was hiding there, even if it meant filling the gaps with hypotheses and constructions of various sorts. Those who discovered Sabina also invented her, and ever since we have continued to do just that, discovering her and inventing her at the same time.

The task was all the more exciting because the picture that was being reconstituted revealed the imposing figures of Freud and Jung at a particularly critical moment in their relationship and in the history of the psychoanalytic movement. In addition there was a spicy scandal based on a love story, and this played a significant part in the commotion caused by the publication of these documents. It was like a novel in which all the characters were represented: the young girl who is seduced and abandoned, the wicked seducer, even the confidant in the wings treacherously intent on pulling strings. It is a classic threesome; Faust comes to mind, Gounod's bourgeois version rather than Goethe's, although the only merit in this comparison is that both Freud and Jung referred to it. As for knowing which one was Mephisto, the question remains open . . .

However interesting the literature inspired by these documents, it is important that the reader discovering this story today approach it by means of the documents themselves, and if possible in the original language. Sabina's own writings, especially her first letters and her diary, will perhaps evoke the same reaction as they did in Freud when he read one of the young woman's letters at the end of June 1909. He had just received 'an amazingly awkward answer – is she a foreigner by any chance? – or very inhibited, hard to read and hard to understand' (McGuire 1974, 30.6.1909: 238). And Sabina's writings often seem like that – hard to read and hard to understand – to the extent that, with the heightened intensity of emotion and the absence of logic in some of her statements, we find ourselves wondering with Freud, 'What is she? A busybody, a chatterbox, or a paranoiac?' (McGuire 1974, 3.6.1909: 226). Reading the original documents has the advantage of revealing, better than the reconstructions of commentators, the passionate nature of Sabina's situation and the dislocation between the logic of her passion and the much more rational logic with which she is met. For this reason an impression of sadness emanates from these texts, a loneliness which makes one wonder whether she really did succeed in detaching herself from Jung, in spite of all her efforts to integrate herself into the life of the world.

In relation to this we have only to compare what she wrote in 1909 with the correspondence Freud and Jung exchanged about her. On the one hand we see the distress, the loneliness and the powerlessness of a woman who had devoted herself to an impossible love, a dream of merging in shared passion and glory, and who could claim only one thing from it all: the acknowledgement that Jung had loved her. On the other hand, the two men are completely immersed in and intensely preoccupied with their mutual relationship: they reason with each other, the one about his responsibility in this transference irregularity – responsibility, but not guilt – and the other, from a knowledge based on long experience, about how instructive routine incidents, 'little laboratory explosions' (McGuire 1974, 18.6.1909: 235), can be to the young analyst on what he will later call 'transference love'. Under pressure above all to get this problem out of the way for both of them, and without gauging its emotional significance for the woman who is calling him to witness, Freud thinks he can resolve it in the usual way: a bit more analysis and everything will be restored to order. It only remains for Sabina to try alone to mourn her love and the divine child, Siegfried, who for her was to be its fruition. As early as 1911 her diary documents her loneliness and bears witness to this psychic labour and to its ineffectiveness.

Despite her visible efforts to detach herself from her dream, despite her marriage the announcement of which in 1912 is intriguing, despite the birth of her child in 1913, a daughter named Renata, despite her departure from Zürich and her constantly renewed attempts to establish her work and her research somewhere else, we see the passionate note appearing once again in 1917 in long letters to Jung comparing her ideas with his and with those of Freud. Of course it is no longer now a question of claiming his love, but Siegfried is still present and his significance is plain. Her basic question is whether the fact of having renounced the possibility of bringing Siegfried into the world in an actual way, and of having tried to sublimate him, has allowed her to realise her vocation. While the idea of sacrifice is an essential issue in the Jungian conception of analysis, it also reveals the narcissistic basis from which passion develops. Thus we see the noise and fury of 1909 flaring up again in these chaotic pages in which Sabina concludes: 'I can say no more than that, after long amazement, which completely paralyzed me, I awakened as from a dream with the words "So he is alive after all, her Siegfried!"' (Carotenuto 1982: 88).

In the year 1910–11, as her diary shows elsewhere, she is working on her medical thesis, a new piece to fit into the puzzle. The fact is that during this time Sabina is a keen student, assiduously preparing her examinations, in order to meet the wishes of a much loved grandfather, himself descended from a line of great prophetic rabbis of whom she had to prove herself worthy by fulfilling an exceptional destiny. Her dreams of love thus mingle with dreams of a career and of fame, and Jung constantly reappears as friend, master and mentor. Certainly her director's influence appears on every page of her thesis. Although she begins by citing Freud, it can easily be seen that it is Jung who inspires her. Like him, who at the beginning of his career as a psychiatrist became passionately interested in listening to psychotic patients at the Burghölzli, she finds it quite natural to be attentive to her patient's delirious utterances and moreover to understand and interpret them. The empathy she displays with regard to her patient may well be based on their common love for the same man, 'Dr J.', and on the fact that she herself had seen him seven years earlier as a patient in the same clinic. This identification is doubtless the origin of her borrowing one of this patient's neologisms, which we find in her diary and in her letters, not as a quotation, but integrated into her own vocabulary. For her as for the patient, 'poetry' will indeed long signify Jung's love.

But it is also clear that she does no violence to herself in interpreting this delirium; she does so in an intuitive way without, she says, being restricted by 'existing dogmas', (Spielrein 1911: 9) and she arrives at the same conclusions as her masters according to whom the delirious utterances of psychotic patients 'obey the same rules as a dream, for example, which is a meaningful processing of contents' (Spielrein 1911: 65). But the fact that she refers to Freud and Jung on this subject is not to be taken lightly. Certainly it is still possible in 1911 to cite them both in the same text, but it is already clear that they no longer hold the same position. This is the year in which Freud publishes the analysis of Schreber's *Memoirs of my Nervous Illness* (Freud 1911) and it can be seen that it turns entirely on the Oedipal theory and the central place occupied by the father, whereas Jung, who was writing *Wandlungen und Symbole der Libido* during this period, will put forward his own conception of things in which the father is deprived of his dominant position and the Oedipus complex hardly plays a greater role in the psychic structure than any other myth. In Sabina's paper we find ourselves on Jung's side of the argument: her interpretations have a character of their own, being of a completely sexual order, but without the structure of the Oedipus complex which Freudian theory gives to sexuality.

Thus quite naturally she ends her presentation on the theme of the collective unconscious. It does not yet bear that name, but it expresses the idea that although '[i]t appears that the pleasurable feeling belongs to the new image content that we are presently enjoying[,] yet, in reality, our pleasures belong to past experiences' (Spielrein 1911: 66) and not only the past of the individual himself, but the past of the race. This explains the connection between the symbolism present in delirium and that embedded in superstitions and mythologies. It is on account of that that Jung, after a few criticisms, compliments her on 12 September 1910: 'The wine symbolism is thoroughly historical/ mythical. On that point I must decidedly congratulate you. Laokoon is marvellous. You know the Laokoon monument, don't you? Deeply symbolic' (Jung 1908–1919).

One might be tempted to attribute the 'Jungian' nature of this thesis to the exclusive influence of the man who for Sabina had been her only intellectual master up to that time. More subtly one can also see in it the trace of what makes her call Jung and herself 'kindred spirits'. We know that by that she meant everything which according to her made them similar, sensitive to the same things, sometimes thinking the same thoughts at the same moment; it was a kind of immediate communication which, if we are to believe her, never ceased to fill Jung with wonder. Thus they also both liked the works of Wagner, enjoying the same operas and sharing the same sensibility towards the heroic legends of Germanic mythology. This attunement went as far as telepathy: 'I was able to read Dr Jung's thoughts both when he was nearby and "à distance", and he could do the same with me' (Carotenuto 1982: 109). All that served as proof to her not only of an identity of interests, but of their fundamental identity as persons. There was no boundary between them, no difference, they spoke the same language and it will be no surprise that it was the language of passion. 'He cannot deny that he has assured me many times over that no one could understand him the way I could', she can write to Freud, to prove to him that whatever Jung's present conduct, he has loved her (Carotenuto 1982: 106).

Are we not just seeing in these claims to identity the illusion of fusion common to every passionate love? Certainly, to act as one is the most immediate metaphor of love, but in this particular case the formula rests on a truth which, without recognising all the implications, Sabina brought to a realisation. We know that Aldo Carotenuto sees the origin of Jung's countertransferential blunder in the interest that he first felt for this young woman patient at the Burghölzli whom he labelled psychotic; and because she 'must have expressed for him a typical image of the anima, attracting and repelling, wondrous and diabolical, exciting and depressing' (Carotenuto 1982: 161), and it is this 'secret symmetry', a common psychotic core, which provoked the encounter. Even if we pass over the romance that he reconstructs from the tiniest details from that point on, we can retain a portion of the truth he perceived, but we should be aware of different nuances in it.

Starting simply from the known facts, we can be sure that their meeting was real enough, in the sense that their innermost preoccupations echoed one another. Whatever animated Sabina most profoundly found a response in

Jung because for him, contrary to what we observe in Freud, passion had a value to which he himself strongly adhered. First there was everything that related to occultism with which he had been in contact since his childhood through the intermediary of his mother's family which was frequently visited by spirits. Moreover he was attracted to psychiatry by studying parapsychological phenomena which seemed to him to form an integral part of psychology. Jung dedicated his medical thesis in 1902 to 'The psychology and pathology of occult phenomena,' phenomena in which he never ceased to be interested. Sabina also had a link with the occult in her family, even though culturally it was different. She came from a very religious Jewish family: 'my great grandfather and my grandfather were both rabbis, and therefore – God's elect', she wrote (Carotenuto 1982: 21), but they were rabbis endowed with the gift of prophecy, in the Hassidic tradition, that is the mystical tradition in Judaism. And despite her father's teasing, for he had distanced himself from all religious practice, she herself was very religious up to the age of 13. Then, she says, 'Relinquishing God proved extremely difficult for me. What resulted was a void' (Carotenuto 1982: 23).

She was to find in Jung something to fill this void. Indeed from his earliest years the latter had never ceased to wonder about God, about faith, about revelation, and about evil. His spiritual preoccupations were not, as one might have thought, inspired by the protestant, clerical environment in which he lived. On the contrary, from a very young age he was strongly opposed to the teaching of his father and of his uncles who were also pastors; he took a gnostic view of religion which he continued to hold; this had developed as a consequence of an experience akin to a mystical encounter at the age of 11. The interest for us of this biographical detail consists essentially in the fact that it throws light on the concept of the unconscious that Jung would develop, a concept which would have nothing in common with the Freudian unconscious. We can get an idea of it from understanding what happened in the period following his break with Freud, when, in profound disarray, he decided 'consciously' to abandon himself to all the manifestations of his unconscious. That meant accepting without resistance everything that came to him, dreams, visions, impulses, with the same attitude he had adopted at the age of 11 in the face of the fantasy which had approached him unbidden and which at first he had tried to suppress. Everything that will emerge from the unconscious will have the same status as that thought, which came to him from God. And it is an idea of this kind that he ends up with, for he gradually reaches the certainty 'that there are things in the psyche which I do not produce, but which produce themselves and have their own life' (Jung 1961: 207). This 'something' 'which can say things that I do not know and do not intend, things which may even be directed against me' (Jung 1961: 208) is indeed the unconscious, but it is not the unconscious as Freud defined it. It is an unconscious which one can meet as one meets God, that is a revelation, an experience in which the Other manifests itself in one form or another. Whoever the imaginary characters are who proceed from the unconscious, or the dead who come from the 'land of the dead', another name for the same place, they are perceived not as the imaginary products of the individual's fantasy but as real beings whom the individual encounters. And this encounter occurs without mediation, in the same way that God had manifested himself to him.

We can imagine the attraction that such a concept could have for Sabina, the more so because she had experienced her encounter with Jung in the same fusional and mystical way. She will say repeatedly that he was her god, and the child Siegfried, who will remain a prevalent theme in her writings up to 1918, was to be the incarnation of this encounter between a woman and a god, hence the name he was given. The character of Siegfried, the sun hero, next to the gods in that he knows no fear, who comes victorious through the worst ordeals, to rediscover the treasure of the Nibelung and to rescue Brunhilde, was part of Jung's mythical world. At the same time he was to illustrate what Jung will later conceptualise as the heroic disposition which lies dormant in all of us and which it is the aim of analysis to uncover and bring to fruition. One last element did not escape the commentators on these documents. In the epic of the Nibelung, Siegfried is the son of King Sigmund. At the time when Jung was Freud's son and heir, this detail was certainly not unimportant in the transferential knot which bound these three people together.

But, as we have seen, for Sabina Siegfried remained closely linked to the question of her vocation and of the meaning he was to have for the direction of her life. This became even clearer when it proved impossible for Siegfried to be realised as an actual child and she then had to find in him a symbolic meaning. There too we see Jung's signature – what indicated for him the end of an analysis. Indeed here we reach an essential point: we can see in Sabina's insistence on the question of her vocation, with which she persists well beyond the end of her analysis, an echo of what Jung will later develop as his theory of transference and which must have been already present in him when they first met. Contrary to Freud, whose position on this matter he will moreover criticise, Jung will consider it insufficient to trace transference love back to its personal roots in the history of the subject in order to find a satisfactory resolution. According to Jung, the Freudian interpretation of transference, in the sense of the paternal transference, is merely a misunderstanding, for the unconscious only appears to lean towards a human person while in fact it is seeking a god. The true meaning of this love is defined thus:

> Could the longing for a god be a *passion* welling up from our darkest instinctual nature, a passion unswayed by any outside influences, deeper and stronger perhaps than the love for a human person? Or was it perhaps the highest and truest meaning of that inappropriate love we call transference, a little bit of real *Gottesminne*, that has been lost to consciousness ever since the fifteenth century?
>
> (Jung 1928, para. 214).

When this hypothesis was put to his women patients, even those who were agnostic, it had the effect of resolving situations which until then seemed insoluble. He can therefore formulate what he considers to be the final state reached in analysis:

> But as the influence of the collective unconscious increases, so the conscious mind loses its power of leadership. Imperceptibly it becomes the led, while an unconscious and impersonal process gradually takes control. Thus, without noticing it, the conscious personality is pushed about like a figure on a chess-board by an invisible player. It is this player who decides the game of fate, not the conscious mind and its plans.
>
> (Jung 1928, para. 251).

Passion for Jung then is not a dangerous drive which he must master at all costs by means of analysis; on the contrary it is a profound movement of the spirit to which analysis must give its fullest scope, with the aim of bringing its true object to recognition. Thus an analysis really reaches its conclusion when the patient recognises what links him to the universality of the archetypes which are active in the collective part of his unconscious. In 1946, in *The Psychology of the Transference*, he will go as far as establishing a relationship between the different stages of transference and the course of analysis, and those that alchemy, as a mystical philosophy, sets out for reaching the goal of the work, a new birth. Analysis is conceived here, even more clearly than in Jung's previous works, as a spiritual journey in which the individual will have to rediscover the deepest roots of his being. In this odyssey, which at times takes on the qualities of a descent into hell, and which evokes in many respects his own experience of his 'confrontation with the unconscious' between 1913 and 1916, transference in its proper sense, that is the loving transference, occupies a necessary place, but simply as a stage on the way towards wholeness. For Jung the supreme end of analysis is therefore to allow the individual to realise his destiny or his 'vocation', and what appears as 'transference love' must find its realisation and its achievement in a passionate endeavour.

We can see now where the encounter between Sabina and Jung really took place: in a common conception of the purpose of existence which must, through analysis, lead each person to recognise and realise his vocation, whatever it may be. She herself is an example of this, in her unceasing search for 'Siegfried', which found its ultimate realisation in 1923 in her return as a missionary for psychoanalysis to Russia, which since her departure had become the Soviet Union. But like any vocation and any passion it could be realised only at the cost of sacrifice. The removal of Sabina's name from all papers, and her disappearance from the stage where the careers and reputations of those first analysts were played out, were no doubt the price she paid to fulfil her destiny which history came to mark finally with the seal of tragedy.

Not only was her name forgotten but also the works to which it was attached. The first reason for this lay precisely in her 'kinship' with Jung. For, if they thought the same thoughts, how could they avoid both of them being confronted with the problem of plagiarism? This issue appears first in August 1911 in relation to 'Destruction as the cause of coming into being', which Sabina wrote immediately after her thesis. She sent the manuscript to Jung who replied that, although he had not yet had time to read all of it, he is 'surprised at the abundance of excellent thoughts which anticipate various ideas of my own. But it is good,' he adds, 'that others see things the same way as I do' (Jung 1908–1919, 8.8.11). He goes on to explain to her why her paper is not best suited for the *Jahrbuch*, and that it would be better to publish it separately, or alternatively among Freud's *Papers*. He will again postpone his reading of her paper, under various pretexts, till 13 November when he tells her that he is citing her ideas several times in the second part of the *Wandlungen* and he hopes to do the same with her new paper. 'Thus we are in harmony' (Jung 1908–1919, 13.11.11).

We know what a cool reception Sabina received when she read her paper at the Vienna Psychoanalytic Society on 29 November. She was clearly being used to target Jung, at a time when relations between Vienna and Zürich were becoming increasingly strained, notably over the publication of the *Wandlungen*.

Freud's brief comment the next day is evocative enough of the climate; he points to the 'similarity' of this work with Jung's: 'Fräulein Spielrein read a chapter from her [ihrer] paper yesterday (I almost wrote the "ihrer" with a capital "I" [which would have meant "your", trans]), and it was followed by an illuminating discussion. I have hit on a few objections to your [Ihrer] (this time I mean it) method of dealing with mythology, and I brought them up in the discussion with the little girl' (McGuire 1974, 30.11.1911: 469). Jung consoles Sabina by assuring her that her paper will be published in the *Jahrbuch*, if Freud agrees, and congratulates her warmly on her success, which neverthe-less was not outstanding. But its publication will continue to create problems for several months to come, Freud and Jung apparently passing the responsi-bility back and forth between them. Sabina's insistence will overcome these resistances, but the question of whom her ideas belong to remains in sus-pense. On 18 March 1912 Jung writes to her:

> As I read your paper I found uncanny parallels with my own new work appearing in it which I did not at all suspect, for until then I had always read your title incorrectly: "distinction" instead of "destruction", and was puzzled by it. Now I find considerable parallels which show the results one gets if one goes on thinking logically and independently
>
> (Jung 1908–1919).

We too can be surprised at this misreading of a manuscript that he had had in his hands so long, and at the reasoning that the parallels he discovers between their ideas would stem from their mutual independence. But his words upset Sabina, since he is obliged to explain himself in his next letter:

> You are upsetting yourself unnecessarily again. When I said there were "uncanny" similarities, you again took that much too literally. I was intending it much more as a compliment to you. Your study is extraordinarily intelligent and contains splendid ideas whose priority I am happy to acknowledge as yours. . . . I express myself so differently from you in my work that no one could imagine that you had borrowed from me in any way. . . . Perhaps I borrowed from you too; certainly I have unwittingly absorbed a part of your soul, as you doubtless have of mine.
>
> (Jung 1908–1919, 25.3.12)

This exchange is all the more interesting in that it resonates with the problem which Freud and Jung face during this same period. Since the summer of 1911 Freud had begun work on the origin of religion – it will be *Totem and Taboo* – that is, the theme on which he knows Jung has been working for more than a year, but from which he has carefully distanced himself. When he read the first part of the *Wandlungen*, he wrote to Jung on 1 September: 'I can see from a first reading of your article in the *Jahrbuch* . . . that my conclusions are known to you, I find, much to my relief, that there is no need for secrecy. So you too are aware that the Oedipus complex is at the root of religious feeling. Bravo!' (McGuire 1974, 1.9.1911: 441). By speaking of 'his' conclusions he enjoins Jung clearly to acknowledge the anteriority of the Freudian discovery of the Oedipus complex and hence the debt Jung owes him. So at a time when Jung was trying with all his might to put forward his own ideas and to extract himself from the position of son which Freud had imposed on him from their first meeting, this reflection could not have come at a worse moment. The effect was an increasingly rapid deterioration in their relationship, and the necessity with which Jung found himself faced, to have to spell out his difference more clearly by abandoning in the second part of the *Wandlungen* the precise theoretical point of which Freud had claimed paternity: the Oedipus complex.

We can understand that at such a time when there was a major issue between them they had not been able to hear what Sabina was saying. It had escaped no one that in 1911 Freud had shown no interest in the theme of destruction as the cause of coming into being, which nevertheless contained certain characteristics anticipating the death instinct which he himself was to develop many years later. But we can wonder about the fact that, although Jung often cited Sabina in the *Wandlungen*, her name was erased from all his writings. Certainly in what happened from now on between the two men there was no longer any room for her, but why was she not able to find her own path and imprint her name on it? Why, for example, could she not make up her mind which side to take, when Freud challenged her to do so in 1914? This alienated her from them both and doubtless prevented her really integrating herself into one group or the other. Her membership of the Viennese society was in effect constantly contradicted by the interest she continued to show in Jung's work, which during this period of hate was inconceivable to the Freudians. Why did she continue to wander from one city to another until 1923, without succeeding in finding a place for herself or getting her original ideas heard? The break between Freud and Jung, which left each of them as bruised as the other, did not stop them, each in his own way, from obtaining recognition for the originality of his ambition and of his thought. We can even imagine that, without her, and with such a collaborator as Freud, Jung might not have succeeded. Why could Sabina not do as much?

The fact is that her passion swept her along elsewhere, an 'elsewhere' whose shimmer she had glimpsed with Jung and which had left her dazzled. The dream of Siegfried, of an ego ideal whose fullness she was to be able to recover through the love of the one she called her god, guided her erratically along a path which she saw as sublimation, but which for a long time was a path to her own destruction. Jung's slip in reading the title of her 1911 essay was doubtless no accident. To be singled out among women by a god to bring a hero into the world was indeed a narcissistic dream which underpinned her passion and it was precisely the pursuit of that 'distinction' which led her to her downfall. By dint of seeking the best means of realising her 'vocation', she sacrificed everything that constitutes ordinary ambition, success, a position, a name, even to the point of effacing herself completely, after the fashion of the mystics for whom the things of this world are as nothing beside the love of God, who alone can fulfil their expectation.

The interest in Sabina's story which has developed since the discovery of the Geneva documents can no doubt repair what, according to the usual criteria, we might otherwise see merely as the failure of a life and of a career. By rescuing from unjust oblivion a figure connected with the beginnings of the history of psychoanalysis we are responding in effect to one of her dearest wishes, making her into a romantic or tragic heroine. But if we look at things from the point of view of her passion, what we see as failure is perhaps the highest realisation of her 'vocation'. In the darkness and suffering she endured, perhaps she was closer to her truth than she would have been in the light we are projecting on to her life today. And from this point of view, which it is tempting to equate with some kind of madness because it escapes common logic, we can only respect the mystery. Once the limits of this are defined, to repeat Jung's quotation in his last letter to Freud leading to their break, 'the rest is silence' (McGuire 1974, 6.1.1913: 540).

References

Carotenuto, A. (1982) *A Secret Symmetry: Sabina Spielrein between Jung and Freud*. New York: Random House.

Freud, S. (1911) 'Psycho-analytic notes on an autobiographical account of a case of paranoia (dementia paranoides)'. *SE* 12.

Jung, C.G. (1908–1919) 'The Letters of C.G. Jung to Sabina Spielrein'. *Journal of Analytical Psychology*, *46*, 1, and this volume, Chapter 3.

—— (1928) *The Relations between the Ego and the Unconscious. CW* 7.

—— (1961) *Memories, Dreams, Reflections*. London: Collins/Fontana 1967.

McGuire, W. (1974) (ed.) *The Freud/Jung Letters*. London: Hogarth/Routledge & Kegan Paul.

Spielrein, S. (1911) '*On the psychological content of a case of schizophrenia (dementia praecox)*'. (Translated by Kenneth J. McCormick 1992, unpublished).

Chapter 13

Three psychoanalytic studies

Sabina Spielrein

(Translated from the Russian by C. J. Wharton)

1. The unconscious phantasies in *Kuprin's Duel*

As an interesting piece of information about how close Freud's theories are to modern thinking, I should like to take the following quotation from *Kuprin's Duel*. It should be noted that this particular story by a well-known Russian writer was written some twenty years ago, that is, long before the name of Freud was known in his native land.

> While driving at about five o'clock in the afternoon to the house where the Nikolayevs were living, Romashchov noted with surprise that his cheerful conviction of the morning that the day would be a success had given way to some strange and inexplicable disquiet. He felt that this had not suddenly happened, right there and then, but much earlier; evidently he had at some stage or other started to become afraid without noticing it. What could it be all about? There had been such occasions previously, from very early childhood, and he knew that in order to relax he would need to identify the original cause of his vague fear. Once, having spent the whole day worrying, he remembered only towards the evening that in the middle of the day, while crossing the railway line to the station, he had been deafened by the whistle of a steam-engine, that this had startled him, and that, without being aware of it, he had become bad-tempered; but he recalled that he had relaxed immediately, and even become cheerful.

The analysis is not a full one: we are given no explanation of why the trauma (the whistle of a steam-engine) was suppressed from consciousness, for it was not without meaning in his mind, otherwise it would not have produced so long-lasting a sign of his 'upset'. If it did have a meaning in his mind, then there must have been some reason for forgetting about it; yet at the same time he had experienced a hint of some negative emotion, which must not enter his consciousness, so a whole series of associations were suppressed. Romash-chov's negative feelings do not fit the description of the experience; he should have been happy that the fear was unfounded and that there was nothing more threatening his life.

Despite there not being a full analysis, the symptom disappeared. We know from experience that cases like this do occur. The individual can 'suppress' a part of his experience without any harm. If linked to a further experience of the same kind, the later one becomes assimilated into the earlier one. Pathogenic influences build up and cause the symptoms to occur.

So Romashchov – owing probably to some momentary 'similarity' – consciously or unconsciously made a link between the whistle and another experience, having been touched by feelings which tormented him. The experience (that of the whistle), being of the same nature as the other experience, thus became traumatic and was also suppressed. Now what had been suppressed was so strong that it became pathogenic, so that in this case it put him in a bad humour for no apparent reason. As a result of clarifying the reason which had brought the feeling about at the outset, some relief was achieved: what had been suppressed was reduced to its former bearable level. However, the reason for the disquiet was not established and could possibly continue to convert each new similar experience into a pathogenic one. Romashchov provides us with evidence for this: he talks of the bad moods which frequently occur, caused by forgotten (suppressed) events. And now without any conscious reason a change in his state of mind will suddenly come about, and once more he is forced to think about a traumatic experience in childhood which for so long has remained in his memory.

Acknowledgements

This paper first appeared in *Imago*, 1913, no. 2. It was also published in Russian in the journal *Archetype*, 1995, 1, and in English in the *Journal of Analytical Psychology* in Vol. 46, 1, 2001.

2. Animal symbolism and a boy's phobia

Little Misha was physically a healthy, cheerful child, quite happily spoilt by his mother. She usually called him 'Moonya', or even more lovingly 'Moonitchka'. It is a Russian abbreviation from 'Mamoonya', a pet name for 'Mama'. The name of one's first love-object – 'Mama' or 'Mamotchka' – is often used in Russian as an endearment, not just for females but also for males.[1] Educated women use this form of endearment only with children and then it has another psychological basis. For example, a mother will say to her small child, 'Come here, Mamotchka, do this for me'. She feels herself to be so much a part of her child that she makes no great distinction between herself and him. This process is particularly evident when the mother has loving dreams: here the child is regularly the mother's 'wished-for personality', i.e. the symbolic representation of herself with her own physical and spiritual pains, desires and fears.

Misha's mother too identifies with her small son, and at the same time the boy, owing partly to similar feelings, always uses male terms of endearment to his mother. It is impossible not to recognize in this aspects of irony: 'You too have to be manly'. For a long time Misha chiefly called his mother either 'the grey hare' or the 'devil-lad'. Both are characters from the world of Russian stories. 'The grey hare' is a small timid animal which suffers much from the unfairness of those who are stronger, and so is in need of protection. 'Amongst mothers you are the grey one', Misha often said to his mummy. Nannies as a rule called their wards 'short hare',[2] which means 'young hare'. Misha too had a country nanny like that, his previous wet nurse. Now he calls his mother by her former names. 'The devil-lad' in contrast to the grey hare has a fully independent and sly personality, which ought long ago to have been punished, if only it could have been caught and driven off. Misha finally united these two contrasting characters of his mother in a new endearment for her, namely 'the old rogue'.

It was as if by this new name he wanted to say, 'You are a small frightened creature, you know, and yet so crafty that I am frightened of you; you may be a man, so you are sharp, just look at that man – yet you are at the same time a little grey hare'.[3] 'Oh, how crafty he is, this grey one!' the boy would sometimes call out, pointing to his mother with admiration. One of his favourite occupations was to deceive his mother. When she caught him out in this, he would laughingly admit, 'It's only you, you know, that I'm deceiving, you're the only one that's cunning, you're the grey hare. I get a lot of pleasure from deceiving you'. For a long time the boy could not bear to have anyone around his mother except his father, towards whom he behaved lovingly, whilst towards others, especially other strange men, he was extremely jealous. It took a long time for him to forgive his mother when, in some discussion – for example where to go for a walk – she would consider changing her mind. Once when it happened he went wild and wanted to pinch and bite his mother. When he had quietened down he came up tearfully to beg her forgiveness, saying that he himself didn't know why he was trying to torment his beloved mother; he was terribly sorry because he knew he was behaving very badly but he couldn't stop himself.

Misha was a very nervous child, and the longer it went on, the more his nervousness increased. For example, at the age of ten he developed a phobia about monkeys. His terror was so great that he could not bear to stay alone in a room. He could not even bring himself to go to the toilet, unless his mother waited by the door for him. He felt as if a monkey was going to spring out at him. By chance I remembered that the boy had earlier liked to call his mother 'you bad marmoset',[4] something he had now completely forgotten. In order to bring it back to his mind I asked his mother whether somewhere he had seen that type of monkey. Yes, he remembered having seen one at the zoo. It had been a marmoset. I asked whether it reminded him of someone. Yes – he remembered that his mother had once been very angry with him; he had thought that she wanted to spring out upon him. From that time on he called her 'you bad marmoset'.

In Russian there is a children's story about a boy who, despite his mother telling him not to, had teased a marmoset in a cage and got punished by the enraged animal. Misha's phobia about monkeys had developed in a similar way; clearly he wanted to do something that would greatly upset his mother. The mother was threatening him and the child got some satisfaction for himself out of this threat by identifying in an amusing endearment the mother he loved with the marmoset who punished. In time the relation between animal and mother had been pushed back into his subconscious. Misha must have remembered from far back in his mind the association between the marmoset and his mother. 'Marmoset' became the symbol of punishment for a careless major misdemeanour and consequently induced the former state of dreadful fear. What the misdemeanour had been, I unfortunately could not know, as I was rarely able to see the boy. The child's father told me that his parents had also been symbolised in the form of dogs. Misha had this dream: he saw a kitten being chased by some dogs and was extremely sorry for the small animal. The father had no difficulty in linking the dream with reality: the previous day Misha had on frequent occasions been reprimanded by his parents and threatened with punishment. Now, in his dream, his parents had become the dogs which were pursuing him, a poor little kitten. In his *Interpretation of Dreams* Freud had analysed a boy's phobia about a wolf.

My short paper does not of course present a full and complete analysis. The story of little Misha only shows how animals can both give pleasure and evoke terror in a child: this corresponds with Freud's claim that they can represent to a boy his own parents, especially his mother. In parallel with this I was reminded of an amusing story which I heard by chance from a doctor acquaintance. Two children, a boy and a girl, were happily playing mothers and fathers. The father was represented by a rabbit and the mother by a goat. The animals were even given the parents' names – Leo and Mary. The children were severely reprimanded for their 'naughtiness'. The parents' aim was achieved, namely the children no longer called their parents 'Leo' and 'Mary' but 'Treasure', which is how the father and mother often addressed each other. The children related the reprimand only to the names, since it had not yet entered their young heads that a father and mother have higher status in the animal hierarchy than a rabbit and a goat.

Notes

1 In contrast the well-known Russian expression 'Batyushka' (old chap) is applied only to men.
2 The analyst should remember that a hare has a short tail. Hence, probably, 'short hare'. Whether this is a generally accepted association, I do not know.
3 Misha sometimes gives his mother another name, which includes the word 'short'. This name is not a very nice one, though neither mother nor child notice that.
4 Marmoset in Russian is a type of female monkey.

Acknowledgements

This paper first appeared in the *Internationale Zeitschrift für ärztliche Psychoanalyse*, 1914, no. 2. It was also published in Russian in the journal *Archetype*, 1995, 1, and in English in the *Journal of Analytical Psychology* in Vol. 46, 1, 2001.

3. The mother-in law

The problem of the mother-in-law is one of the most grievous and at the same time one of the most interesting of psychological problems. In his article 'The fear of incest among primitives and neurotics',[1] Freud points out that primitives have a resistance towards their mother-in-law, and take a series of precautions against her. Freud deduces part of this resistance from the fact that the mother-in-law, as the older woman, is a reminder to her daughter's husband of the rapid ageing of his young wife. However, the mother-in-law is certainly not always an ugly old woman, as popular belief usually has it. Especially today she is frequently the modern woman in full flower that many men find desirable. She is seen not as a mother but as their daughter's older sister. Some mothers-in-law are so full of vitality and power that they want to rule over the young married couple, as if these were their own children; they interfere in everything, require obedience and by doing so create difficulties for their sons-in-law, although these are a minority of cases.

First, why is so much heard about bad mothers-in-law and so little about fathers-in-law? To answer that question we need first of all to start with an understanding of female psychology; a woman has considerably less ability in real life to fulfil her own personal desires. To compensate for this she has a much greater ability to 'identify' with others and so to experience her life through them. One only has to think, for example, of how old maids, who have themselves been denied the happiness of love, will assist in other people's weddings. I find in the very widespread exercise of this gift of identification the reason why women, while in no way yielding advantage to men in their level of development and power of imagination, have nevertheless not created any works of art of equal importance. In order to create a work of art, one must to some extent objectivize either one's own experience or that of another so that it can be assimilated in an impersonal way, as the world outside, and only then can one talk about a form of representation which expresses the essence of a work of art. This objectivization brings some relief to the artist. Women's ability to do this is much less, for as a rule it is outweighed by a counter-mechanism; a woman conjectures about others' experiences in ways which correspond with her desires or fears and makes them her own, she frees herself from her feelings, mentally goes through these experiences for herself anew, and transforms them along the lines of her own desires.[2] It is in this ability to live through another person that a woman's great distinctive social significance is to be found, and I do not know how far it is either possible or desirable to wish to embody in women the masculine aspects of feeling of the 'highest' sort of quality. In any case I believe that it would scarcely succeed in full; the woman's biological roles, as mother and as governess of the human race, are roles which make such great use of the gift of sympathetic feeling that fundamentally the woman can rearrange only a comparatively small part of her feelings in her objectivization. There will of course be creative female artists around, as there always have been, but it seems to me that they will always lag behind the greatest of the male artists. Of course, when discussing such important questions one always needs to be careful and prepared to be mistaken.

In the first instance a mother lives in the life of her own children and would like to direct them in the way that she, benefiting from her experience, would like to lead her own life.

Her daughter, being female, is closest to her mother, and hence there is an intimacy but also a continual competition between mother and daughter over relationships. The good mother always loves to be loved by her child, even more so when the child who loves her is male. In this way she relives her own youth and would like to appear pleasant and attractive to her son-in-law: both of them buy new clothes, they surgically remove a few minor flaws to their beauty, blotches to which they never used to pay attention, and so on. To excuse this coquetry, the mother persuades herself that she is doing it for her daughter's good; the husband will love his wife still more if her mother's ugly example does not frighten him away, and we analysts might also add that some small part of this love, which of course has its uses for the daughter, is subconsciously often tied up with being a beautiful mother-in-law. All the same, these high-sounding reasons are not the only ones, for if she is quite honest with herself, the mother-in-law has to admit to being ashamed of being considered ugly by the son-in-law, as if it were she who were being subjected to critical examination as his love object.[3] The loving mother does not allow to enter her consciousness the thought that her daughter's freshness and youthfulness are to be envied, but she does feel young and fresh herself when she sees those qualities in her daughter. The mother-in-law is often quite sensitive and easily hurt; she would not be like that, were she thinking only of her child's good. Nevertheless she also tries to get her new 'child' to love and appreciate her as if she were his real 'mother'. Because she continually identifies with her daughter, she projects her own feelings of dissatisfaction on to her daughter; it occurs to her that her daughter is not loving enough, that she must prepare for everything and protect her not only with advice but with her actions. And this emotional set-up gives rein to every possible combination of action which of an instant turns the most desirable and dearest of mothers into the most dangerous of mothers-in-law.

Contemporary society pays attention almost exclusively to the husband's mother-in-law, although young wives too, especially those among the less well-off, certainly have difficulties with their mothers-in-law. On average the wife's mother is much happier than the husband's mother about the wedding. The reason is to be found not only in a woman's lack of social independence, but also in the fact that one loses a son, while the other, who is living through her daughter, gains a son. We know that a mother's relationship to her son differs from that with her daughter; it contains more of the erotic and less of the intimate. Especially where families are fatherless, a son will be seen by his mother as the man of the house, to whom she can come for advice and protection. In the subconscious world of fantasy he is the boyfriend. That is why she is not easily able to identify with his love for another woman. Her daughter-in-law continues to be a rival until such time as her love as a mother freely enables her to accept without envy her son's good fortune in loving another.

That marriage where a man and a woman are totally free of their parents' families, so that the two could belong completely to each other, would be the ideal one. Only an analyst lacking in experience could look for this: if a man and woman's love were completely separate from their love of their parents, then their love of the parents would not disturb the harmony of their marriage, as is actually almost always the case. There are quite a number of neurotic men and women who are unable to love anyone, because they are too closely attached to their own family. There are people who are able to love the object of their affections so long as that object does not develop a closer relationship with their family; when that happens, the object immediately loses its attraction.

The natural impulse of a lover is to love the relatives of his beloved, so that they may belong to him too, but there is a counter-impulse which affects surface consciousness in a way which we understand but little: our leanings towards our own family which we love, and which remain fundamentally heartfelt. Along with this is also the feeling of having betrayed one's father, or one's mother in the case of a son, by giving the love and attention which are hers by right to another's mother who in the child's mind will after all never measure up to the real mother. A partly conscious but basically unconscious comparison will reduce still further the standing of his or her mother-in-law. Deep down the real mother will always remain young and attractive. Hence every other woman not conforming with one's image of mother will be old and unattractive by comparison. This is the attitude to the mother-in-law on either side who has unfairly taken for herself the happiness which rightly belongs to the mother. Sensitivities can be so heightened, pathologically speaking, that the son, himself a future husband, who is much more strongly attached to his mother, develops an antagonism, indeed hatred, towards his mother-in-law, finding in her every word some slighting reference to his family or criticism of his mother. This is even more likely if he is similarly critical of her, and he justifies himself by blaming his behaviour on his mother-in-law.

In this situation any loving treatment of the wife's parents is useless, for love demands that love be returned, something which he cannot achieve. Only a well-analysed knowledge of the processes of one's own mind can help. This will tell us that from the very beginning every small child sees his parents as the sole godlike authority; there then follows a phase of breaking free from parental power, beginning with intense opposition to and criticism of everything his parents do. Later these two extremes will even out, and the boy or girl will learn to love others without blaming themselves for betraying their own family, so that they can also hold on to the love and gratitude due to their own parents. It is where, because of an excessive fixation, such a development fails to occur smoothly, that the prerequisites for neurosis are to be found. In such cases analysis will help by creating out of an anti-social being, who acknowledges only himself and what is his, a social being who can also love and appreciate other people. True, despite every conscious effort, some people cannot escape a feeling inside them that they themselves and their own parents are the most important people in the world. This feeling can give them peace: it is not so much a matter of coping with this feeling inside themselves as of not showing it and, if it becomes difficult to retain a sense of balance, then it is better to let the contrary feelings take over, in other words to treat others rather more kindly than one's own relatives.

Notes

1   *Imago* [trans. The image] 1st year edition, issue no. 1.
2   In her unconscious, a woman is able to objectivize much more, and hence, generally speaking, totally uncreative women can sometimes in their dreams or in dreamlike states see themselves as poetesses.
3   An experience similar to that in the saying of Rabbi Jeshua ben Levi: 'Where the first son-in-law is concerned, look after your wife.' Quoted from 'Sexual problems', November 1913: 783.

Acknowledgements

This paper first appeared in *Imago*, 1913, no. 2. It was also published in Russian in the journal *Archetype*, 1995, 1, and in English in the *Journal of Analytical Psychology* in Vol. 46, 1, 2001.

Chapter 14

Sabina Spielrein, Jean Piaget – going their own ways

Fernando Vidal

(Translated by Pramila Bennett in collaboration with Fernando Vidal)

There is hardly any documentation on the relationship between Jean Piaget (1896–1980) and Sabina Spielrein (1885–1942), who was his psychoanalyst in Geneva in the early 1920s. There are some indications of their mutual sympathy, as well as traces of a shared project. Spielrein and Piaget had common intellectual roots in the Zürich psychiatric and psychoanalytic school. Moreover, Spielrein had started to study child psychology before meeting Piaget. Yet the collaboration between them, which was to deal with the theory of symbolism, never came into being. This may be explained by the divergence in intellectual focuses: psychoanalysis for Spielrein and epistemology for Piaget. But it is perhaps their contrasting attitudes to symbolism that best account for the failure of the project. Piaget mistrusted symbolic thought for intellectual and personal reasons that can be traced to his adolescence, and considered it as a lower stage in the growth of intelligence. On the contrary, as is apparent in both the form and content of her writings, Spielrein emphasized and valued the unconscious roots of symbolism, in which she saw the 'sap' of all thinking.

Jean Piaget was analysed by Sabina Spielrein. Each has mentioned the other in their writings and there are traces of their intellectual understanding. Some chronological parallels have been established (Volkmann-Raue 1993), and Spielrein's works have been collected (Spielrein 1986, 1987). But nothing so far allows us to guess what their true relationship was, nor to go beyond what can be gleaned from a few memories and scientific publications. It would very interesting, were it possible, to reconstitute the meeting of these two exceptional persons in a city which was a centre of psychoanalysis, and which played a crucial role in introducing Freudian thought into France.

The production on Wednesday 11 January 1922, at the Theatre Pitoëff in Geneva, of a modern tragedy by Henri-René Lenormand entitled 'The Dream Eater' (Lenormand 1922), was indicative of the place psychoanalysis occupied in the city's cultural life at the beginning of the 1920s (on Lenormand, see Blanchart 1951; on the play, Cifali 1982: 118–27). The dream eater is the psychoanalyst Luc de Bronte, a 'Don Juan in the guise of a healer' (Lenormand 1943: 66). After revealing to his patient Jeannine the oedipal source of her refusal to love, he becomes her lover. However, the young woman is obsessed by remorse. While she is gradually becoming conscious of the origin of her anguish, an ex-patient and mistress of Luc reveals it to her abruptly, and at the same time provides her with a weapon. Jeannine commits suicide.

The public received 'The Dream Eater' with a kind of frenzy (Piachaud 1922). The actors were acclaimed, as was Georges Pitoëff's abstract and suggestive *mise-en-scène*, including a set of coloured ribbons against a black velvet background (Lenormand 1943: 67). A highly regarded lecturer, the psychologist Edouard Claparède, was called upon to introduce the play. This progressive and cultured aristocrat was aware of speaking to the initiated: no other city, he said, was more appropriate than Geneva to host the 'The Dream Eater'; even Paris was hardly acquainted with psychoanalysis, whereas the Genevan public 'knew all about it'. Claparède took pains to dissociate himself from Luc, a 'rather unsavoury character' (Claparède 1922: 138). Some days later, in the *Journal de Genève*, Sabina Spielrein concluded that the attitude of the character was antithetical to the 'sensitive method' of Sigmund Freud, and that he was not a 'true psychoanalyst' (Spielrein 1922).

Lenormand claimed his play was based on personal experience. He also recognized that the initial sketches of the subject 'bristled with darts aimed at psychoanalysts' (Lenormand 1949: 279), and that the final version contained 'a bitter criticism of Freudian theories' (cited in Küppers 1938: 19). While several critics saw a direct influence of Freud in his plays (Cazamian 1924: 450, n. 2; Küppers 1938, ch. 2), and while indeed 'The Dream Eater' made a psychoanalytic breakthrough in Paris when it was produced there in February 1922, the playwright always denied having intended to write a Freudian play. The characters of 'The Dream Eater', he said, were those of a tragedy in the course of which Freudianism was revealed to him by the 'observation of persons profoundly steeped in Freudian ideas and methods' (cited in Küppers 1938: 18). He was of course interested in psychoanalysis; at the invitation of Claparède, he even attended a gathering of the Psychoanalytic Group of Geneva, which met informally in Claparède's psychology laboratory (Cifali 1982: 127). He nonetheless saw psychoanalysis as a 'poetical intuition' and as 'an artistic interpretation of the soul' (Lenormand 1949: 270–1).

Lenormand, who had an international reputation and was one of the best known French avant-garde playwrights between the two world wars, has been forgotten. The mixture of symbolism and truculence of 'The Dream Eater' makes it too didactic and not to the taste of today's audience. The play, however, appealed to the public. Spielrein and Claparède discredited its hero, but their interest confirmed its success. As remarked by the Genevan critic René-Louis Piachaud, who found the play irritating, decadent and pernicious, 'the psychoanalysts admire Mr Lenormand for the love of psychoanalysis' (Piachaud 1922a). These 'psychoanalysts' included at least Sabina

Spielrein and Edouard Claparède, who both attended the premiere in Geneva.

Claparède had founded the Jean-Jacques Rousseau Institute in 1912 with the aim of combining the training of teachers with experimental pedagogy and research in child development; psychoanalysis was one of his many interests. At the time, he was also president of the Psychoanalytic Group of Geneva and wrote the entry 'Psycho-analysis' for what was to become André Lalande's reputed *Vocabulaire technique et critique de la philosophie* (Technical and Critical Vocabulary of Philosophy). With his introduction to the first translation into French of a text by Freud (the *Five Lectures on Psychoanalysis*), he had performed a pioneering task; and although he reproached the psychoanalysts with frequent tendencies to sectarianism and dogmatism, he attached great value to their theory (Claparède 1920).

In 1920 Spielrein, a 'shy and tenacious Russian', came to the Jean-Jacques Rousseau Institute (Bovet 1932: 101; cf. Kerr 1993: 492–7, a superficial and inaccurate treatment). She claimed to be Claparède's assistant (see Cifali 1982: 125, n.) and gave a seminar, the only trace of which is in an article where she describes an experiment carried out with 14 of her students at the Institute in the winter semester of 1922–23 (Spielrein 1923). An advertisement which appeared in the *Journal de Genève* in February 1922 gave notice that Mme Spielrein, 'former assistant of Professor Freud' (which was incorrect), would be available every Tuesday evening at the Institute for 'free consultation with people desirous of information on educational and scientific psychoanalysis' (cited in Cifali 1988/2001: 253/129). She returned to Russia in 1923. During her stay at the Institute, she analysed several colleagues. But only Piaget, in Geneva since 1921, spoke about his experience.

Piaget recalls that he had 'his didactic analysis' every morning 'at eight o'clock for eight months' – he wanted to be analysed 'as a learning experience', and was 'glad to be a guinea-pig' (Bringuier 1977, p. 182). Why did the experience come to an end? Piaget gave two explanations: the first was that the analysis lasted long enough to satisfy the analyst (Piaget 1977). The other suggests almost the opposite: having discovered that he was 'impervious to the theory' and that she would never convince him, Spielrein decided that it was not worth continuing. Piaget, however, was 'deeply interested' in the process and found it 'marvellous' to discover his complexes: 'it was she who brought it to an end' (Bringuier 1977: 182–3). This is very different from the tendentious claim that he 'reneged his analyst' (Roudinesco 1982: 363).

It would be justifiable to perceive a note of regret in Piaget's comment. At the beginning of the 1920s, though ambivalent about it, Piaget was strongly attracted to psychoanalysis. In 1916, at a gathering of the Swiss Christian Students Association (Vidal 1987), he had heard Théodore Flournoy talk about psychoanalysis and religion and compare the Viennese and Zürich schools. In his 1918 autobiographical novel *Recherche* (Research), psychoanalysis, as understood by Flournoy and the Zürich analysts, gave him some of the conceptual tools necessary for a self-analysis by means of which he tried to understand and change himself. He used the idea of complexes and branded his earlier mystical and metaphysical tendencies as instances of autistic thought (Vidal 1994, chap. 14).

At the end of 1918, having finished his studies in natural sciences, Piaget left his native Neuchâtel and went to Zürich, at the time the Protestant capital of psychoanalysis. Later, during a stay in Paris from 1919 to 1921, he lectured to an audience of educators on the 'currents of pedagogical psychoanalysis'. Like the ideas of 'autism' and 'complex', the subject was at the time a Swiss speciality. The published version of this lecture, 'Psychoanalysis and its relationship with child psychology' (Piaget 1920), was Piaget's first article in psychology. In a review of this article, the Zürich psychoanalyst and Protestant pastor Oskar Pfister wrote that Piaget 'had energetically initiated himself into the theory and practice of psychoanalysis'; he went on to 'emphasize the value of his detailed personal research' and praised the 'young scholar from whom the psychoanalytic movement is entitled to expect important contributions' (Pfister 1920).

Piaget became a member of the Swiss Society for Psychoanalysis in 1920. The first psychology congress he ever attended was the International Congress of Psychoanalysis (Berlin, 1922). He participated in it with Spielrein. Moreover, he was to act as a messenger to Freud. 'I hope', wrote Freud to the Genevan psychoanalyst Raymond de Saussure in July 1922, 'that your friend J[ean] P[iaget] will explain to us all here in Berlin the numerous advantages of your project concerning the Geneva congress' (Freud 1922). A reviewer of the 1922 conference of the Swiss Christian Students Association, where Piaget spoke about psychology and religious values, called him a 'master of psychoanalysis' (Abauzit 1922). Spielrein too described him as a 'psychoanalyst' (Spielrein 1923a: 318). Such descriptions ring true. Apart from the 'young autistic person' that Piaget claimed to have analysed with some success (Piaget 1977), he analysed a student of the Rousseau Institute for two months in 1924 as an experiment; and it is for reasons that cannot be explained by simple scientific curiosity that (according to the recollection of his sister Marthe) he attempted to psychoanalyse his own mother (Vidal 1986).

In the early 1920s, at the time Sabina Spielrein was in Geneva, psychoanalysis was a central element in Piaget's intellectual world. The young psychologist was studying the thought processes of children. To him childhood thought was characterized by 'egocentrism', that is, by the inability to perceive and adopt someone else's point of view and a tendency to regard all reality as resulting from one's own activity. According to Piaget, spontaneous thought in the child, being syncretic, animistic and magical, resembled 'primitive' thought, and especially the 'autistic' thought described by Eugen Bleuler (e.g. Piaget 1924: 17–18). Bleuler, a distinguished psychiatrist who directed the Burghölzli clinic in Zürich, elaborated on the concept in many articles and writings. Among these are his 1911 treatise on schizophrenia (Bleuler 1911) and his 1916 *Textbook of Psychiatry* (Bleuler 1916). In order to avoid mis-understandings such as the conflation of autism with schizophrenia, he pro-posed (unsuccessfully) to replace the term 'autistic thought' by '*dereistisches Denken*', a neologism formed from the Latin 'reor', to think (Bleuler 1923: 34). For Piaget, who declared himself to be a pupil of Bleuler (Piaget 1951: 46), dream, dementia and mystical imagination are 'pre-logical' aspects of intelligence that show a loss of contact with reality, as well as a lack of conscious 'direction' in the temporal and logical organization of judgement. It is gradually through contact with others and the 'grasp of consciousness' (a key concept of Claparède's psychology) that childhood thought adapts itself to reality; its development therefore depends on its gradual socialization.

In broad terms, such a description of the development of thought was felt to be consistent with the basic principles of psychoanalysis. Piaget himself emphasized that. Spielrein reported that, in his seminar on 'autistic thought' (winter of 1921–2), he said that we are indebted to Freudian psychoanalysis for the knowledge we have of the primitive mechanisms of childhood thought (Spielrein 1922a: 264). In 1923, in his first book on child psychology, Piaget drew the reader's attention to what he had 'borrowed from psychoanalysis', which to him seemed 'to throw new light on the psychology of primitive thought' (Piaget 1923: 4).

It is not surprising then that Spielrein and Piaget found common areas of understanding and intellectual companionship. By the mid-1920s, Piaget had become an authoritative figure. At the Institute, Spielrein attended his course on autism. She quoted his work (Spielrein 1922a; 1922b: 262, n. 26; 1923b: 318–19); in her last known article (Spielrein 1931: 383, n. 13), published in 1931, she refers to Piaget's first four books and to his 1921 article on verbal comparison in the child (Piaget 1921). Initially, however, their relationship seems to have been rather symmetrical. Ten years older than Piaget, Spielrein had assimilated the research and ideas of the Zürich school at a time when her future colleague at the Rousseau Institute was still studying natural his-tory and had had contact with neither philosophy nor psychology. Many of the articles she published after her medical thesis on a case of schizophrenia (1911) are about children – sometimes her own daughter Renata, born in 1913. Some are only brief observations; others have a more clinical or more theoretical orientation. Yet they all reveal Spielrein's conceptual openness, as well as her conviction that the study of child psychology is important for the future of psychoanalysis (Spielrein 1912: 144) and that the psychoanalytic approach should be combined with other methods (Spielrein 1923: 271).

Considering the stature acquired by Piaget since the 1920s, it is tempting to attribute to him the intellectual initiative. Aldo Carotenuto, for example, commenting on Spielrein's work 'Time in the Subliminal Life of the Mind', suggests that it is probably along the lines of Piaget that she studied the development of the concepts of time, space and causality (Carotenuto 1982: 194). It seems more accurate, however, to speak of reciprocity and exchange.

First, in 1923 Spielrein rightly remarked that it had long been known that the concepts of time, space and causality are not Kantian a priori categories, but concepts acquired with individual development (Spielrein 1923a: 319). The idea was basic for Piaget's psychology and epistemology, but Spielrein's remark did not derive from him. Secondly, some of her observations on the concept of time relate to her daughter Renata aged two, and therefore go as far back as 1915. Thirdly, her hypothesis on the existence of languages that do not make time distinctions (and are thus analogous to the 'language of dream'), as well as her incursion into the field of linguistics with the help of the Genevan professor Charles Bally, show a sensitivity to linguistic phenomena that is qualitatively different from Piaget's. Fourthly, Spielrein interprets the results of her studies of an aphasic patient's drawings as illustrating a lack of direction in thought. This lack is for her consistent with pre-conscious thought and with children's thinking; from the point of view of the notion of time, it manifests a deterioration in the representation of temporal direction. Spielrein also uses the same case to illustrate the general difficulty the patient has in 'keeping to a fixed direction in his thinking' (Spielrein 1923b: 318). Some of her psychological vocabulary coincides with Piaget's, but she approaches the problem of time in her own manner.

The way Spielrein and Piaget each address the study of childhood thought is revealing. Both consider it as essentially 'symbolic' and base their theories on its similarities with pre-conscious thought (Spielrein) or with autistic thought (Piaget). For Piaget, nevertheless, who in the early 1920s was still constructing his own viewpoint, the data and vocabulary of psychoanalysis held mainly a heuristic value. Spielrein's theoretical discourse, on the contrary, belonged to a conceptual space that, while not being strictly Freudian, was specifically psychoanalytic. In 1929, for example, she considered it simplistic that a phenomenon such as regression could be explained only from the point of view of the 'construction of reality', whose development was being studied by Piaget. Rather, the interaction between instincts and other aspects of the personality (the 'construction of reality' among them) was for her the determining factor. Those aspects, she explained, are under the direct or indirect influence of 'bio-, physio- and socio-genetic factors. The principal object of the psychoanalyst's research is the influence of the sociogenetic factors' (Spielrein 1929: 340; cf. Spielrein 1929a: 210).

By 1917, Spielrein had adopted the notion of 'subconscious', and reserved 'unconscious' to name the area of the subconscious which is blocked by censorship. She concentrated on the subconscious, whose symbolic language she called 'subliminal'. Subliminal language served to express problems, preoccupations and complexes suppressed by 'directed thinking'. In her letters to Jung of 15 and 20 December 1917 (Carotenuto 1986: 149–61), she distinguished '*Unterdrückung*' (suppression) from '*Verdrängung*' (Freud's notion of repression): the former, she explained, operates from the conscious to the subconscious, the latter from the subconscious to the unconscious. Later on

(Spielrein 1923a), she subsumed the pre-conscious and the subconscious under the expression 'subliminal psychic life'; and she studied its 'thought functions' through observations of the subliminal language of images, childhood language, linguistics and language disturbances. As Spielrein herself recognized, such an approach was Jungian in inspiration.

On the subject of her work 'Destruction as the cause of coming into being' (1912), Spielrein declared to Jung that she had always wished to replace the word 'unconscious' with 'subconscious', even before realizing that by 'unconscious' she meant something fundamentally different from Freud's concept. 'As your pupil', she went on, 'I was used to conceiving of the "unconscious" in your sense of the "non-conscious", and only later did I realize that you and Freud meant entirely different things by the expression' (Letter of 15 December 1917, Carotenuto 1982: 61).

Moreover, it is from Jung that Spielrein borrowed the concept of 'directed thinking'. In his 1912 *Transformations and Symbols of the Libido* (1912, chap. 2), Jung distinguished between two kinds of thinking. 'Reality thinking' or 'directed thinking' is logical, verbal, conscious and adapted to reality; it is governed by a 'superior representational capacity' that gives rise to a 'sense of direction'. 'Non-directed' thinking, in contrast, is neither determined nor conscious; it is subjective, symbolic and imaginative, fed by affects emanating from the self and made up of a succession of images and feelings. Whether it takes a pathological, especially a schizophrenic form, or whether it manifests itself as dream, fantasy, myth or artistic creation, it always betrays a 'childish state of mind', rooted both in the person's individual history and in the 'past of humanity'. This, according to Jung, demonstrated the link between myth and the unconscious, as well as a 'historical stratification' of the mind. Here Jung follows Freud's ideas on the reality and pleasure principles, but without adopting the Freudian terminology.

While by no means Jungian, Piaget, like Spielrein, uses the concept of directed thinking and develops a concept of psychoanalysis which is closer to Zürich than to Vienna. In his 1920 Paris lecture on psychoanalysis and pedagogy, he clearly came down in favour of the 'Zürich school', and characterized 'the original fault of psychoanalytic theories' as their 'excessively rigid distinction between consciousness and the unconscious' (Piaget 1920: 52). Later on, he pointed to Jung's effort 'to show the generality of symbols and the existence of "symbolic thinking" as a sort of primary language' common to all, and directly conveying 'affective tendencies, without any necessity for disguise or suppression' (Piaget 1945: 170–1). In sum, Spielrein and Piaget are brought closer together through their common Zürich affiliation, especially where the notions of the unconscious and symbolism are concerned.

Spielrein's article 'The genesis of the childhood words Papa and Mama', takes as its starting point a report presented in September 1920 at the International Psychoanalytic Congress at The Hague; this was before she met

Piaget and before he began to publish his research on the language and reasoning of the child. But her text did not appear until 1922. In the meantime, Spielrein attended Piaget's course on autistic thought where, she reported, he spoke of the child's different attitudes towards reality. Spielrein commented that his description of the evolution of child thought from the absolute to the relative corresponded to psychoanalytic experience (Spielrein 1922b: 253; see also Chapter 15: 299). Thus, Piaget's work supported Spielrein's hypotheses and observations.

In the first place, for Spielrein, the question is not whether the child himself creates his own language or receives it simply from adults, but rather whether he is a 'social being endowed with the need to communicate' (Chapter 15: 291). This is the same 'functional problem' that Piaget confronts in *Language and Thought of the Child*: 'What needs does the child seek to satisfy when he speaks?' (Piaget 1923: 9 & 7). In both cases, the use of the words 'need' and 'function' reflect Claparède's vocabulary (e.g., in Claparède 1920a, chap. 3).

In the second place, like many other observations, those of Spielrein on the genesis of the words 'papa' and 'mama' seem to Piaget to show that expressions to which adults give conceptual meaning have for the young child an affective and almost magical sense which needs to be studied as such. This is what Piaget tries to do, 'by removing himself a long way from the commonly held idea that a child uses language to communicate thought' (Piaget 1923: 10–11). Spielrein is of the same opinion: 'I use "language" here in the usual sense of a means of communication. We will see that in its origins language was not that' (Chapter 15: 304).

Finally, for Spielrein language development corresponds with that of Freud's reality principle. In the 'autistic' stage a word does not signify an action: it is the action itself. In the 'magical' stage, the word replaces the action and is used to conjure up reality. In the 'social' stage, words are used to communicate. Piaget made similar connections between the transformations of childhood thinking and the reality principle. During the 1920s, he emphasized the development of thought as a socialization process; his concept of the different stages accorded with Spielrein's, and both incorporated views then current in psychology, ethnology and philosophy.

In short, Spielrein and Piaget agree on the functional approach, the interpretation of childhood language and the stages of development. These three fundamental points of their psychology must be added to their common intellectual roots in the psychiatric and psychoanalytic school of Zürich, and to the interest they shared in childhood and in the development of the basic concepts of thought.

The last area of the common ground between Spielrein and Piaget which I will refer to here, and undoubtedly the one in which they progressed together furthest, is the theory of symbolic thought.

In his lecture in Berlin in September 1922, Piaget talked about ideas he had in common with Spielrein and announced the forthcoming publication (which never saw the light of day) of his colleague's 'very suggestive' theory of symbolism. He declared: 'We hope to develop these hypotheses together' (Piaget 1923a: 286). And in his book on the child's representation of the world (Piaget 1926: 128 & 318), he cited some of Spielrein's observations on children's beliefs about the origins of babies (Spielrein 1912: 40).

In 1923, Spielrein recounted how, when she was studying the pre-conscious thought of the child, she met in Geneva 'a researcher of great standing' who was also exploring childhood thought. 'Since then', she added, 'though separately [*wenn auch jeder für sich*], we have been essentially working in the same area' (Spielrein 1923a: 318). Why 'separately'? What became of their collaboration? Why did Spielrein not publish her theory? There is nothing that allows us to answer this with any degree of certainty nor even to venture a probable hypothesis. It is however possible to establish a number of textual symmetries.

In her 1917–18 letters to Jung, Spielrein explained that symbols 'are reversible'; the subconscious symbolizes consciousness and vice versa. For example, when we are consciously trying to solve a hard problem whose unconscious 'parallel image' is submergence in a dark sea, we tend to think of the subconscious image as symbolic. However, if we take the subconscious 'as "reality", then all our conscious thought merely constitutes a barely successful attempt at portraying this reality in some symbolic form' (Carotenuto 1982: 67). From the point of view of the unconscious, the subconscious image symbolizes a repressed desire; from the point of view of the non-repressed subconscious, the same symbol represents both the problem which one is consciously thinking of, and the subconscious thoughts that are inherent in it. From the point of view of bodily sensations, the symbol and the difficulty experienced during conscious work express an organic state. Conscious thoughts would then be merely 'symbolic offshoots of the original symbol' (ibid: 67). Spielrein here suggests a hierarchical process of symbolization and a composite origin of symbols: organic, unconscious, subconscious.

The idea of a composite origin of symbols runs through the later work of Spielrein on symbolic development. 'Motor-verbal images [she wrote] are but a group of kinaesthetic images which are . . . at the origin and base of our thought'. While conscious thinking is mainly verbal, the subconscious thought that (according to Spielrein) always accompanies it maintains its primitive character in that it remains primarily kinaesthetico-visual. As Spielrein explained, 'subconscious thought expresses in images what conscious thought would have expressed in words. . . . Kinaesthetico-visual images nourish our conscious thought' (Spielrein 1923b: 320 & 321). As examples, she cited hypnagogic states and the phenomenon of coloured hearing. Now, her work on genesis of the child's words 'papa' and 'mama' shows that her theory has wider implications. According to Spielrein, the formation of the syllables that make the word 'mama' (her main theme) is initially linked to a satisfying action, that of breastfeeding. By reproducing suckling, the word serves to prolong the event and procure a substitute satisfaction of the desire; only later does it become a means of communication (Chapter 15: this volume).

This is the theory that Spielrein and Piaget hoped to work on together. Both were interested in the affective functions of the symbol, but equally, perhaps even more so, in the acquisition of cognitive and semiotic functions. Melanie Klein, in contrast, interpreted Spielrein's observation of the role of suckling in the origin of the words 'papa' and 'mama' as evidence for the importance of libidinal investment in language development. In speech, Klein explained, there are sublimated perverse fixations, specifically oral ones in the case studied by Spielrein (Klein 1926). In spite of the differences which separate both Piaget and Spielrein from an approach (such as Klein's) focused on the Oedipus complex, a comparison of the articles they published one after the other in 1923 in the Genevan journal *Archives de Psychologie* reveals not only considerable theoretical agreement, but also serious divergences of aim and attitude.

In 'Some analogies between the thought of the child, that of the aphasic and subconscious thought', Spielrein began by distinguishing – thereby following Jung, but without naming him – between 'directed' thinking and 'non-directed' or spontaneous thinking (Spielrein 1923b: 305). According to her, the responsibility of the psychoanalyst is to be concerned with the laws of the second type of thought, to study them in free association, dreams, mental illness and the child's psychology (Spielrein 1923b: 306).

Spielrein first discussed the thinking of a child aged two and a half. At that age, the child behaves in the same way we do when we dream and distort reality accordingly (Spielrein 1923b: 307). To study this phenomenon, she skilfully combined the 'clinical method' whereby Piaget aimed to reach beyond observation while avoiding the drawbacks of testing (Piaget 1926, Introduction), with the association studies of Jung and his colleagues (published together as the 1906 *Diagnostiche Assoziationsstudien*). She recorded the spontaneous language of a child and discovered, in a total of 73 successive phrases, four 'groups of ideas' with which the phrases are associated. She concluded that associations are based on two mechanisms. The first is 'perseveration'. For example, when a child has to give up an object he desires, he does not go as far as abandoning the 'group of ideas that surround it' and this group 'continues to live inside him while assimilating the new object' (Spielrein 1923b: 306). The second mechanism is 'convergence': two groups of ideas can be condensed into one phrase, but dissociated in the phrases which precede or follow it. The child's thought is not 'directed' because when he comes across a new idea, the old one persists and produces the phenomenon of 'convergence' by grafting itself on to the new one.

Subsequently Spielrein examined the similarities between the mechanism of childhood thinking and the thinking of an aphasic who had been introduced to her by Claparède. The patient could point to the object whose name he was given, but was incapable of naming the object which he was shown.

The name he produced was determined by the preceding word: if he said 'chambre' just before being asked to name a table (French 'table'), he uttered 'timbre'. As in the word associations of the young child, there are here perseveration and convergence. The same mechanisms explain why when a patient is asked to draw a square, he produces a mixture of two rectangles, or when a child is asked to copy a diamond-shape, he draws a rectangle with a pointed corner (this last observation was made by Piaget). In all cases (children's drawings and word associations, an aphasic's verbal and graphic errors), Spielrein interpreted the observed phenomena as the incapacity of the subject 'to maintain a fixed direction in his thinking' (Spielrein 1923b: 318).

For Spielrein, language, whether verbal, graphic, musical or in the form of a gesture, is always an expression of thought; 'we infer the mechanism of thought from the type of language in which it is expressed' (Spielrein 1923b: 315). Intelligence and language are therefore interconnected. The child acquires language when he begins to emerge from the autistic stage and it is thanks to the spoken and 'socialized' word that thought 'becomes logical, adapted to the demands of reality' (Spielrein 1923b: 319). Pathological phenomena such as aphasia constitute a return to the type of thought dominated by the pleasure principle; in morbid states, directed thinking reverts 'in some measure to the primitive thinking of the child'; from the point of view of its mechanisms, it is then more like subconscious, 'organic', 'hallucinatory' and 'kinaesthetic-visual thinking' (Spielrein 1923b: 320).

In his paper 'Symbolic thought and the thought of the child' presented at the 1922 Psychoanalytic Congress, Piaget intended, like Spielrein, to elaborate these analogies. Psychoanalysis, he said, has the merit of showing that different mental phenomena (dream, imagination, dementia) originate from a single type of thinking: symbolic or autistic. However, as in the Paris lecture of 1920, Piaget emphasized the continuity of autistic and logical thought. According to him, the Freudian approach opposes one to the other, while in fact autistic thought constitutes 'a beginning, one of the primitive forms of logical thinking' (Piaget 1923a: 275).

Treating symbolic thought as a function, not as 'an entity which is dormant in the unconscious', Piaget reckoned that the child is not an 'antilogical' being (Piaget 1923a: 301 & 274). Children's thought is 'pre-logical' rather than 'paralogical', and is 'intermediate' between symbolism and logic, 'between complete autism with its incommunicable fantasies, and the social nature of adult intelligence' (Piaget 1923a: 275 & 284). Piaget called this intermediate form 'egocentrism', and studied its similarities to symbolic thought.

Like Spielrein, Piaget emphasized the lack of directedness and the relative unconsciousness in a child's thinking. Also like Spielrein, he explained the autism of the dream and of symbolic thought, as well as the 'egocentrism' of the child, by the lack of differentiation between the self and the non-self, between the world of subjective representations and the world of external representations. In dreams, for example, the limits of the subjective are blurred; in the same way, the child is not aware that his thoughts or his dreams are subjective phenomena. This is in line with Spielrein's theory of symbolism, according to which, Piaget explained, 'organic symbols consist of objectivized kinaesthetic impressions, which have been objectivized precisely because there is no sense of self [*sentiment du moi*]' (Piaget 1923a: 286, n.).

For Piaget, the analogies between symbolic and egocentric thought resulted from their kinship to play and the predominance of the pleasure principle (Piaget 1923a: 303). At the same time, Piaget highlighted his loyalty 'to the numerous psychoanalysts who have a sense of the problems and show caution in research' (ibid: 301–2), and explained that symbolic and childhood thinking can be interpreted in terms of their 'weak tension', the 'narrowness of the field of attention' and the 'loosening [*relâchement*] of consciousness' – all concepts from the psychology of Pierre Janet.

If, as Spielrein pointed out, she and Piaget were working 'essentially in the same field', they did so for different reasons. Piaget reported that he became interested in symbolic thought through research that was not organized to find traces of this type of thought in the child; it was while studying children's language, judgment and reasoning that he was struck by similarities between the mechanisms at work in dreams and in the thought of the child (ibid: 276–7). In his epistemological framework, symbolic and especially egocentric thought were primitive forms destined to be overtaken and replaced by socialized, logical and objective thinking.

Autistic or symbolic thought, as a model of the child's egocentrism, fascinated the young Piaget; but it probably held a fascination for him also because he had seen it as a danger to be neutralized. In his article on symbolic thought, he defined as autistic 'most of the mystical and metaphysical ideas of adolescence', and recognized, 'especially in mystical thought', the absence of a sense of self and the projection of the self onto the world (Piaget 1923a: 283 & 286). The idea was not a new one – Bleuler (1923, chap. 1) had already subsumed belief, mythology, poetry and philosophy in autistic thought. But this had for Piaget a personal meaning. As already mentioned, in the autobiographical part of his 1918 book *Recherche*, he had presented himself as having experienced autistic thought through metaphysics and mysticism (in Vidal 1994, chap. 14).

For Spielrein, on the contrary, subconscious thought, the source of symbolism, remained 'our principal mode of thinking'. Left to itself, it loses its characteristic of 'creative thinking'; only in collaboration with conscious thought can it result in creative work (Spielrein 1923b: 322). The difference between the two researchers is clearly of an intellectual nature, as Piaget never put himself entirely in the camp of psychoanalysis and pursued an epistemological goal. But it is also affective: Piaget's distrust of subjectivity and the unconscious was in opposition to Spielrein's willingness to allow them to exist side by side in a discourse combining conceptual acumen and originality with a powerful poetic sensitivity and a wish to understand the roots of suffering.

Jean Piaget tried to restrict himself to what he saw as objective thought, and to understand its progress, for him characterized by an increasing capacity to assimilate reality without generating contradiction. Mysticism had become forbidden to him since he could not approach it without, in his view, risking a dismemberment of his personality. Like his epistemology and his psychology, his religion rested on the assumption of the immanence of the impersonal norms of reason (Vidal 1998). 'Autistic thought' (here including poetry, mysticism and metaphysics) could not open legitimate paths to knowledge. Sabina Spielrein, on the other hand, was not afraid, in her personal writings as in her publications, to give meaning and value to intuition, or follow the meanderings of a thought which drew on subliminal life for its 'nourishment'. It is thus not surprising that she was accused of being a sort of mystic, as did Paul Federn in his comments of 'Destruction as the cause of coming into being' (Federn 1913: 92–3). Indeed, by fusing discourse with desire in brilliant flashes of writing, Spielrein could evoke Nadja – 'one of those spirits of the air which certain magical practices allow us to attract temporarily, but which cannot be subdued' (Breton 1928: 130).

Acknowledgement

This article is a revised version of 'Sabina Spielrein, Jean Piaget: chacun pour soi' published in *L'Evolution Psychiatrique*, *60*, 1, 1995, 1–17.

References

Abauzit, F. (1922) 'Du premier Sainte-Croix au dernier Sainte-Croix. Impressions d'un témoin'. *La semaine littéraire* (Genève), 4 November, 548–50.

Blanchart, P. (1951) 'Notes et documents sur H.-R. Lenormand (3 mai 1882–16 février 1951)'. *Revue d'histoire du théâtre*, *3*, 167–76.

Bleuler, E. (1911) *Dementia Praecox; or, The Group of Schizophrenias*, trans. J. Zinkin. New York, International Universities Press, 1950.

—— (1916) *Textbook of Psychiatry*, trans. A.A. Brill. New York: Macmillan, 1924.

—— (1923) *Lehrbuch der Psychiatrie*. Berlin: Julius Springer, 4th ed.

Bovet, P. (1932) *Vingt ans de vie. L'Institut J.-J. Rousseau de 1912 à 1932*, Neuchâtel: Delachaux & Niestlé.

Breton, A. (1928) *Nadja*. Paris: Gallimard, 1987.

Bringuier, J.-C. (1977) *Conversations libres avec Jean Piaget* (Conversations with Jean Piaget). Paris: Laffont.

Carotenuto, A. (1982). *A Secret Symmetry: Sabina Spielrein between Jung and Freud*, trans. A. Pomerans, J. Shepley, K. Winston. New York: Pantheon Books.

—— (1986) *Tagebuch einer heimlichen Symmetrie. Sabina Spielrein zwischen Jung und Freud*. Freiburg i. Br: Kore.

Cazamian, L. (1924) 'La psychanalyse et la critique littéraire'. *Revue de littérature comparée*, *4*, 448–75.

Cifali, M. (1982) 'Entre Genève et Paris: Vienne'. *Le Bloc-notes de la psychanalyse*, *2*, 91–127.

—— (1988/2001) 'Une femme dans la psychanalyse. Sabina Spielrein, un autre portrait'. *Le Bloc-notes de la psychanalyse*, *8*, 1988, 253–65; *Journal of Analytical Psychology*, 2001, *46*, 1, 129–138.

Claparède, E. (1920) 'Freud et la psychanalyse'. *Revue de Genève*, December, 846–64.

—— (1920a) *Psychologie de l'enfant et pédagogie expérimentale*. Geneva: Kundig, 1920, 8th edn.

—— (1922) 'Le mangeur de rêves', manuscript notes for the lecture presenting Lenormand's piece (21). *Le Bloc-notes de la psychanalyse*, *2*, 1982, 133–8.

Federn, P. (1913) 'Sabina Spielrein, Die Destruktion als Ursache des Werdens'. *Internationale Zeitschrift für ärtzliche Psychoanalyse*, *1*, 89–93.

Freud, S. (1922) Letter of S. Freud to Raymond de Saussure, 3 July 1922, trans. J. Moll. *Le Bloc-notes de la psychanalyse*, *6*, 1986, 191–2.

Jung, C.G. (1912) *Wandlungen und Symbole der Libido. Beiträge zur Entwicklungsgeschichte des Denkens* ('Metamorphosis and symbols of libido', *CW* 17). Leipzig: F. Deuticke.

Kerr, J. (1993) *A Most Dangerous Method. The Story of Jung, Freud, and Sabina Spielrein*. New York: Knopf.

Klein, M. (1926) 'Infant analysis'. *International Journal of Psychoanalysis*, *7*, 31–63.

Küppers, J. (1938) *Henri René Lenormand und seine Dramen*. Würzburg: Richard Mayr.

Lenormand, H.-R. (1922) 'Le Mangeur de rêves', in *Théâtre complet*, vol. 2, Paris: G. Crès, 1922/Albin Michel, 1942.

—— (1943) *Les Pitoëff. Souvenirs*. Paris: Odette Lieutier.

—— (1949) *Les confessions d'un auteur dramatique*. Paris: Albin Michel, vol. 1.

Pfister, O. (1920) 'J. Piaget: La psychanalyse et la pédagogie' [1920], trad. J. Moll. *Le Bloc-notes de la psychanalyse*, *1*, 1981, 89–92 [German original in *Imago*, *6*, 294–5].

P[iachaud], R.-L. (1922) '"Le mangeur de rêves" au Théâtre Pitoëff'. *Journal de Genève*, 12 January, 6.

—— (1922a) '"Le mangeur de rêves" au Théâtre Pitoëff'. *Journal de Genève*, 18 January, 5.

Piaget, J. (1920) 'La psychanalyse dans ses rapports avec la psychologie de l'enfant'. *Bulletin de la Société Alfred Binet*, 18–34 & 41–58.

—— (1921) 'Une forme verbale de la comparaison chez l'enfant. Un cas de transition entre le jugement prédicatif et le jugement de relation'. *Archives de psychologie*, *18*, 141–72.

—— (1923) *Le langage et la pensée chez l'enfant* (*The Language and Thought of the Child*). Neuchâtel: Delachaux & Niestlé.

—— (1923a) 'La pensée symbolique et la pensée de l'enfant'. *Archives de psychologie*, *18*, 275–304.

—— (1924) *Le jugement et le raisonnement chez l'enfant* (*Judgement and Reasoning in the Child*). Neuchâtel: Delachaux & Niestlé.

—— (1926) *La représentation du monde chez l'enfant* (*The Child's Conception of the World*). Paris: Presses Universitaires de France, 1972.

—— (1945) 'Hommage à C.G. Jung'. *Revue suisse de psychologie*, *4*, 169–71.

—— (1951) 'Pensée égocentrique et pensée sociocentrique'. *Cahiers internationaux de sociologie*, *10*, 34–49.

——— (1977) 'Réponse de Jean Piaget au Dr. Olivier Flournoy'. *Journal de Genève* (Samedi littéraire), 5 February, p. v.

Roudinesco, E. (1982) *La bataille de cent ans. Histoire de la psychanalyse en France*, vol. 1. Paris: Ramsay.

Spielrein, S. (1911) 'Über den psychologischen Inhalt eines Falles von Schizophrenia (Dementia Praecox)', in: *Jahrbuch für psychoanalytische und psychopathologische Forschungen*, hrsg. von E. Bleuler und S. Freud, Bd.3, 1/2, pp.465–503. Leipzig/ Wien: Franz Deuticke.

——— (1912) 'Beiträge zur Kenntnis der Kindlichen Seele', in Spielrein 1987.

——— (1920) 'Renatchens Menschenentstehungstheorie', in Spielrein 1987.

——— (1922) 'Qui est l'auteur du crime?' *Journal de Genève*, 15 January, p. 2. Also in Spielrein 1987 and in *Le Bloc-notes de la psychanalyse*, 2, 1982, 141–6.

——— (1922a) 'Schweiz', in Spielrein 1987.

——— (1922b) 'Die Entstehung der Kindlichen Worte Papa und Mama', in Spielrein 1987.

——— (1923) 'Die drei Fragen', in Spielrein 1987.

——— (1923a) 'Die Zeit im unterschwelligen Seelenleben', in Spielrein 1987.

——— (1923b) 'Quelques analogies entre la pensée de l'enfant, celle de l'aphasique et la pensée subconsciente'. *Archives de psychologie*, *18*, 305–22. Also in Spielrein 1987.

——— (1929) 'Zum Vortrag von Dr. Skal'kovskij', trans. in Spielrein 1987.

——— (1929a) 'Referat zur Psychoanalyse', trans. of the same Russian original as Spielrein 1929, in *Ausgewählte Schriften*. Berlin: Brinkmann & Bose, 1986.

——— (1931) 'Kinderzeichnungen bei offenen und geschlossenen Augen', in Spielrein 1987.

——— (1986) *Comprensione della schizofrenia e altri scritti*. Naples: Liguori.

——— (1987) *Sämtliche Schriften*. Freiburg i. Br: Kore.

Vidal, F. (1986) 'Piaget et la psychanalyse: premières rencontres'. *Le Bloc-notes de la psychanalyse*, *6*, 171–89.

——— (1987) 'Jean Piaget and the Liberal Protestant Tradition', in M.G. Ash & W.R. Woodward, eds., *Psychology in Twentieth-Century Thought and Society*. New York: Cambridge University Press.

——— (1994) *Piaget Before Piaget*, Cambridge, MA: Harvard University Press.

——— (1998) 'Immanence, affectivité et démocratie dans "Le jugement moral chez l'enfant"'. *Bulletin de psychologie*, *51*, 585–97.

Volkmann-Raue, S. (1993) 'Psychologie-historischer Kommentar zu Jean Piaget, Sigmund Freud und Sabina Spielrein', in S. Volkmann-Raue, ed., *Jean Piaget. Drei frühe Schriften zur Psychoanalyse*. Freiburg i. Br: Kore.

Chapter 15

Part I Comment on Spielrein's paper 'The origin of the child's words Papa and Mama'

Barbara Wharton

This paper, published in 1922, is striking in that it expresses ideas and a quality of attitude and insight far in advance of its time. Not only does Spielrein perceive the importance of the infant's relationship to the breast for its psychic development, anticipating the work of Melanie Klein whose paper 'Weaning', on the theme of the 'good' and 'bad' breast, appeared in 1936, but Spielrein also records her observations on her daughter as an infant and young child (collating numerous similar observations from other writers) with a precision and sensitivity which seem to point forward to the work of Winnicott and Fordham, among others. Spielrein's focus here is intentionally restricted to the emergence of language, specifically of the two words, 'mama' and 'papa'. When however she writes of mothers who 'adapt themselves instinctively to the kinds of language that the child is ready to produce' one cannot help thinking in a wider context of Winnicott's description of the spatula game (in 'The Observation of Infants in a Set Situation', 1941) and of the profound significance of his perception of 'the infant's spontaneous gesture' for the development of the personality and the ability to relate to others (cf. 'Ego Distortion in Terms of True and False Self', 1960).

Spielrein describes how adults 'play' with babies verbally, 'feeling into' the baby's mind from the 'depths of their own mind' and their own earlier experience. She poses the question of whether the child makes his language, or whether he simply inherits it; putting this another way, is he 'by natural inclination a social being who has a need to communicate' which would lead him both to 'seek [language] and to invent it'? Here there is an uncanny foreshadowing of Winnicott's concept of transitional objects and the question 'Did you conceive of this or was it presented to you from without?' ('Transitional Objects and Transitional Phenomena', 1951). Spielrein is convinced, like Fairbairn later, of the essential sociability of the infant, of his need to communicate and to relate. She sees that the development of language lies in a transitional area, the area of play: the baby playing at the breast, playing with letting it go and latching on to it again, creating an emotionally charged fantasy of it through sensorimotor experience when it is no longer available, and through these experiences making momentous discoveries about presence, absence, and its own being.

Spielrein is grappling here with issues which preoccupied psychoanalytical thinkers throughout the century and to the present day, issues relating to the nature and development of the self, individuality, separateness, and the function and meaning of loss. She is working in the same area as Fordham later when he insisted on the infant's own distinct and active personality, and when he formulated his theory of deintegration and reintegration to describe the development of the ego and the personality from the primary self (cf. Fordham, *The Life of Childhood*, 1944, later published as *Children as Individuals*, 1969, and also *Explorations into the Self*, 1985). Spielrein traces back the infant's growing awareness of itself and the external world to the resistance it experiences in relation to the mother's body. In Fordham's theory the processes of deintegration too depend on the infant's self meeting a certain optimum resistance in its interactions with the outside world.

Spielrein's paper conveys an impression of a richly creative and profoundly sensitive and insightful mind. It is a great loss that her work and thinking in the area of early developmental processes were not further elaborated and more widely known and appreciated at the time. She has indeed been sadly neglected.

References

Fordham, M. (1944) *The Life of Childhood. A Contribution to Analytical Psychology.* London: Kegan Paul, Trench, Trubner.
—— (1969) *Children as Individuals.* London: Hodder and Stoughton.
—— (1985) *Explorations into the Self.* London: Academic Press/Society of Analytical Psychology.
Klein, M. (1936) 'Weaning'. In *Love, Guilt and Reparation and Other Works 1921–1945*. London: The Hogarth Press & The Institute of Psycho-Analysis, 1975.
Winnicott, D. W. (1941) 'The observation of infants in a set situation'. In *Through Paediatrics to Psycho-Analysis*. London: The Hogarth Press & The Institute of Psycho-Analysis, 1987.
—— (1951) 'Transitional objects and transitional phenomena'. In *Playing and Reality*. London: Tavistock Publications.
—— (1960) 'Ego distortion in terms of true and false self'. In *The Maturational Processes and the Facilitating Environment*. London: The Hogarth Press & The Institute of Psycho-Analysis, 1965.

Chapter 15

Part II The origin of the child's words Papa and Mama. Some observations on the different stages in language development

Sabina Spielrein

(Translated from the German by Barbara Wharton)

1. The different forms of language

When we adults speak of languages we think of verbal content and overlook the role played, even in written texts, by contributions from the field of rhythmic/melodic language, such as exclamation marks, question marks, and so on. These melodic means of expression become even more important in spoken language; here a third factor is added, imitation and gesture, means of expression which we could call visual language, and which indeed play such an outstanding part in dreams as a distinctive picture language. Accordingly we must differentiate from verbal language other types of language such as that of melody, visual (picture-) language, the language of touch, and so on. As a conscious means of communication the sound-based languages (melody, and above all words) play a vastly predominant role and thus they deserve above all others to be called 'social languages'. Lazarus says with justification that people became social beings first through language, by which he meant verbal language: 'the world now consists no longer of a Not-I and an I, that is my I, but of Not-I and very many I's, as many in fact as speak, as understand one another and can find a witness to their common, shared consciousness', and further: 'if we remember that language exists only in society, a human being can realise himself as a Self and an I only by being alongside other Selves and other I's.'

One has only to compare the usually shy, wary, spiteful nature of deaf-mutes with the character of blind people to value the high social significance of verbal language in comparison with other languages.

Since it was the one best suited for social purposes, verbal language soon pushed all others into the background, and they thus sank to the position of auxiliary languages, unconscious languages, or alternatively were transformed into artistic languages. Genetically however verbal language is far from being the first, either among human beings, or in the animal world. The language of melody, music, in its most primitive form of rhythm and tone, precedes verbal language by a long way: long before the first signs of verbal language appear, crying is a reliable means of communication between the infant and its caretaker. Attentive mothers and nurses know very well that their little charge cries in quite different, specific ways, according to whether he is wet, hungry, in pain, or whether he simply wants the caretaker to be there. The infant expresses his state and his desire – intentionally or not – first through the different rhythms, pitch, tone and intensity of his cry, in other words in a primitive, melodic language. It is also tone that he first understands and only much later words. – To animals too the melodic element of our language is usually what is accessible.

After these reflections the widespread popularity of music becomes understandable, and incidentally that goes for the popularity not of music as a work of art, which is not so easy to understand, but of music as language. The products of the plastic arts were originally representations which served magical purposes.[1] As language, except as an autistic one, that is a language which exists only for its own sake, or a 'magical'[2] language, plastic expression is much more clumsy and thus much less reliable. The products of the plastic arts can be enjoyed on their own in silence. Music on the other hand, in its most primitive form of song, even if it began as a means of self-enjoyment, soon became a method of communication *par excellence*, a call for attention, a prayer, a complaint directed to God or to fellow human beings demanding their involvement. With the development of verbal language the two related acoustic languages emerge consciously and in combined form in prayer, in folksongs, and later in works of art (choral music, opera, among others). But the combination of word and melody in folk-music also shows that there are two independent languages, each with its own character, and each partly excluding the other: in most cases either the melody or the text becomes obliterated. The melody is the general, the verbal language the more concrete, adapted to the environment. In all prayers the melody fits the text and in the oldest prayers is reduced almost to pure rhythm. In folksongs the often simple and crude text is particularly striking alongside the stronger accent and greater differentiation of the melody. Just as there are great poets who have remained musically primitive and cannot even sing a tune, so on the other hand there are composers of music who are incapable of writing a verse to fit a tune. Probably there is evidence here of racially based differences.

With my daughter I paid a great deal of attention to when and in what form she produced her first musical communications. In spite of that I did not succeed in noting the first one. Soon, however, several followed which were in essence analogous: they were all attempts to make a tune from speech. In the sense of musical feeling it was not yet a real melody, much more a rhythmic drawing out of syllables, comparable to so-called 'verses without rhyme', a melody such as children 'without hearing' sing. The text of such a song runs:

Von der Kiiissen Nadel pickt
Von der Naaadel picke di.[3]

The needle from the cuuushion pricks.
You prick yourself on the neeeeeedle.

We often amused ourselves singing all kinds of folksongs with our little daughter 'just as they came to mind'. In the course of this it occurred to me that I associated the next song to the previous one according to the similarity of its verbal content, while the child, then between two-and-a-half and three years old, associated according to the similarity of the melodic shape. This could not have come from ignorance on the child's part, since in every case she knew the content of the texts and to a large extent knew the words by heart. When she was older, my daughter began to associate according to the similarity of verbal content. In normal adults, in an overwhelming majority of cases, association according to verbal content seems to predominate.

2. Papa and Mama

In what follows we shall be concerned only with verbal language and particularly with the words 'Papa' and 'Mama' which according to common belief are the child's first words.

Who invented verbal language? Was it the adult or the child? Is the child capable of spontaneous creativity in language, or does it simply acquire the language handed down by adults which it adapts to its needs? This much debated question remains unsolved to this day. Here psychoanalytic experience can be helpful.

Language is essentially created out of the unconscious (more correctly, the subconscious) and the unconscious always leads us back, as Freud and his pupils showed, to infantile experience and thought processes.

We must always keep in mind that the ancestor sleeps within the child, and the child within the ancestor. If the adult really invented language, he created it in its earliest origins out of the childlike stage of his psyche. Does the child himself make his language, or is it simply handed down from adults? In my opinion this question should be formulated differently, thus: is the child by natural inclination a social being who has a need to communicate? If it has inherited a need to communicate, and if it belongs among people who speak, then it has inherited a need for language which leads it both to seek it and to invent it.[4] Of course the adults come to the aid of the young mind in its struggle; through their own talking and mimicry in the child's presence, they encourage it to develop the speech mechanisms for which it is prepared by heredity; mothers and nurses adapt themselves instinctively to the kinds of language that the child is ready to produce: they feel into the young psyche, finding material in the depths of their own mind, in their own earlier stages of development, and allowing this to speak to the child in an unconscious way. An example might explain how child and caretaker collaborate in the formation of language: Stern reports that at eight months his daughter spontaneously produced the labial sound 'p'. The adults encouraged her and said the word 'Papa' to the child. The child repeated what she had first said, just the labial sound 'p'; after a pause of five to ten minutes the child said spontaneously 'Pa-pa-pa', though of course without understanding the meaning of what she had said. The child learned to say the word 'Papa' so quickly because she modelled it on the spontaneous sound 'p'; however she did not yet repeat 'Papa', but 'Papapa', because to restrict it to two syllables was not yet appropriate to her phase of development; thus for the time being she used the word 'Papa' just as a number of 'babble' syllables without any actual verbal meaning.

It is remarkable that according to general opinion it is always the same words, Papa and Mama, which are seen as the child's first words. The labial sound 'p' is replaced in different languages by the genetically related labial-dental sounds. Thus in Russian we have 'Papa', in French and German 'Papa', in English 'Papa', in other Slav languages 'tàte', 'tiatia', in Greek 'baba',[5] and so on.

The word Mama remains more or less the same in all languages. Russian 'Mama', French 'Maman', German 'Mama', Ukraine 'Maty', but also 'màmo', Greek 'Mama' and so on. The labial sound 'm' does not seem to change except that there are languages in which the order of the sounds is reversed, that is where instead of 'Mama' we would have 'amam'.[6]

Are Papa and Mama really the first words for all children? This question is very hard to answer because as well as the observational material being sparse in itself, there is in addition the difficulty of distinguishing between the word and meaningless babble. This difficulty of differentiation is already evident in a baby's crying. The crying may originally be a reflex phenomenon but it does not remain so for ever. Yet we cannot fix with certainty the point at which it is no longer a reflex phenomenon, when the baby uses its cry for the first time consciously or unconsciously with a particular intention. Fathers and mothers are inevitably inclined to make different claims regarding this moment; a mother generally is not satisfied with the idea of a reflex phenomenon. As with crying, so it is with the voluntary factor in the first words; we call the babble a 'word' as soon as it contains a meaning we understand or should understand, because it is produced with a particular intention.

A mother wrote to me about her baby: 'The first word which Lili definitely knows the meaning of is "a-a",[7] but she doesn't say it; other words, which she does say, she does not understand,' that is, she does not understand them in our sense. The mother did not record the first word that Lili spontaneously said and understood at the same time.

Stern reports that *Dida* (clock) was his daughter's first word. This word arose from its being repeated in her presence by adults, at the same time as the child's attention was deliberately drawn to the actual clock. Another writer reports on *Lululu* which appeared spontaneously after the child heard the sound of water. Why these impressions in particular, among the many that reach the child, should have taken priority and should have provided an occasion for the formation of the first word, we cannot say: the observational material is grossly insufficient. Might Papa and Mama be these children's first words too, but overlooked, even though they do not appear as such in either form or meaning? What are the grounds for the widespread public belief which gives them this priority? Why is it also that the child reproduces words inaccurately, in a corrupted form? We will turn our attention first to this question. There are many theories about this of which I will briefly select a few: The so-called '*Loi du moindre effort*'[8] is, according to Ament, to be traced back to Maupertuis. Buffon applies this rule to articulation and says that of the vowels A, and of the consonants P, B, M are the easiest to pronounce. Thus the child's first words would consist of these sounds (Baba, Mama, Papa). Schultze says that the child moves from the sounds linked to the least physiological effort to the more difficult ones; he formulates the following law of sound-shift, sound corruption or sound-conversion in children's speech: 'The child replaces the sound it cannot yet pronounce (vowel or consonant), with the one most closely related to the difficult one, and one which can be spoken with the least physical effort, and if it cannot achieve this either, it simply leaves it out.'

Gutzmann, Franke and Toischer too speak of the different levels of physical effort, suggesting that the easier levels are preferred. Like Kussmaul, Gutzmann differentiates periods of language development and says that in the second period the child produces sounds which already resemble the mother-tongue. 'It is natural,' he says, 'that these first speech sounds lie in the first and second articulation system: lips and the tip of the tongue are the parts which are prepared for articulation by sucking. For that reason the names for father and mother are similar in almost all languages, and very often the same.'

Thus for Gutzmann it is the act of suckling which paves the way for our first words, Papa, Mama, Baba, etc. Gutzmann's fallacy lies in his assumption of the principle of a sequence according to least physical effort. Well-founded objections have been raised to this principle. Preyer, Sully, Rzesnitzek among others do not recognise it as a regular pattern. Rzesnitzek speaks of a playful involvement with the tools of speech. Finally Ament provides evidence that in babble monologues the most difficult sounds K, G, R etc. are used long before the child speaks his first word of language.

Irene D for example at the age of 288 days babbled *rrr* (rolled), *errau* (nasal), *abrrr* and such like; Gertrud Z, at 190 days, babbled *abrrr, abruh*; Elisabeth M at around 390 days *rollewollegogu* etc. So Ament replaces the old theory of sequence according to least physical effort with his theory of sequence according to physical preference. Although the child is already able to say the most difficult sounds, it prefers to substitute them with labial or dental sounds respectively; it prefers these sounds because in suckling it has particularly cultivated them in the course of its development. Accordingly Ament's theory is also essentially a physiological one. Quite definitely physical preference in Ament's sense plays a big role in the choice of sounds in the child's first words. Unfortunately it is not possible for me here to expand in more detail on the interesting work of Ronjat.[9] Ronjat actually formulates laws according to which the child rearranges the common words of the language, for example in his chapter called Assimilation:

at 15 months I was able to identify in French, and to have identified in German, a series of words which permit the following formulas to be established:

An occlusive or nasal explosive[10] in a tonic syllable[11] assimilates an implosive consonant in a tonic syllable or a consonant in any position in an atonic syllable. In a post-tonic syllable Louis is not able to produce any implosive other than a non-rolled 'r', which is a kind of vocal resonance prolonging a post-tonic (s); this very faint sound, which is by nature hardly a consonant, remains as it is.

In a pretonic syllable I have no example of an implosive consonant other than Armband (ambam)[12] where m rm[13] already belongs to the same category as the explosive b in the tonic syllable.

The inducted phoneme takes the point of articulation from the inductive phoneme, but retains its own mode of articulation.

Thus a labial nasal[14] inducted by a dental occlusive[15] becomes a dental nasal,[16] m x d = n, an example in French being dame > (dam > dan), a voiced dental occlusive (= d) inducted by an unvoiced labial occlusive (= p) becomes a voiced labial occlusive (= b), d x p = b, an example from German being Puder > (puds > pubs) and so on.

These examples show that a strict regular pattern emerges in the way children rearrange words, and that this can indeed be explained by physiological preference. When the child says 'dan' instead of 'dam', it makes the task easier for itself by forming a dental sound out of the following consonant, a sound which lies in the same articulation system. It is quite certain that labial and dental sounds are preferred in the child's first words because these particular sounds were produced in the child's development in the act of suckling. In all honesty however these theories leave essential points unexplained: how does it happen that in children of all races the same comparable terms for father and mother are found (papa and mama)? How is it that these are the child's first words, or perhaps more correctly that they are held to be such? How is it in any case that a sound produced by a child contains verbal meaning? The first two questions have not been answered; we actually know a lot of theories for the origin of words of which it seems to me the reflex theory and the onomatopoeic theory deserve the most consideration. Both these theories agree that human beings use sounds they have learnt by hearing them naturally and fitting them to a particular meaning (verbal meaning).

According to all earlier theories language knows no other stage than this: that a sound having arisen naturally, either as a reflex or from being meaninglessly repeated, becomes a word as soon as it is used with the intention of conveying meaning.

Now I would like to place my ideas about psychological preference alongside these theories. I will anticipate straight away that I would distinguish three stages in the development of language: first the autistic stage, in which language exists for its own sake; second is the magical stage, in which a word contains an extra significance which conjures up reality; the third is the present stage of a social language intended for our fellow human beings.

These three stages would correspond with the well-known sequence in the development of Freud's reality principle; in Freud the autistic and magical stages merge into one and the same stage in which the wish is more powerful than reality, phantasy more important than fact, and in which the omnipotence of thought reigns supreme. Let us follow Freud for a step in his reflections on 'Animism, Magic and the Omnipotence of Thought':[17]

It must not be assumed,' writes Freud, 'that mankind came to create its first world system through a purely speculative thirst for knowledge. . . . We are therefore not astonished to learn that something else went hand in hand with the animistic system, namely the elaboration of directions for making oneself master of men, animals and things, as well as of their spirits. S. Reinach wants to call these directions, which are known under the names of "sorcery and magic", the strategy of animism. With Mauss and Hubert, I should prefer to compare them to a technique

(*Totem and Taboo*: 110–111)

The principle of magic rests on the 'similarity between the performed action and the expected happening. Frazer therefore calls this kind of magic "imitative or homoeopathic". If I want it to rain, I have to produce something that looks like rain or recalls rain.'[18] (ibid: 114).

'The motives which impel one to exercise magic are easily recognised; they are the wishes of men. We need only assume that primitive man had great confidence in the power of his wishes' (ibid: 117–118) For the child, as for primitive man in his magical acts, wishing is the same as experience.

In the case of the child which finds itself under analogous psychic conditions, without being as yet capable of motor activity, we have elsewhere advocated the assumption that it at first really satisfies its wishes by means of hallucinations, in that it creates the satisfying situation through centrifugal excitements of its sensory organs' (ibid: 118). (Cf. Freud:

'Formulierungen über die zwei Prinzipien des psychischen Geschehens'.
Jahrbuch, Vol. 3, 1912: 2.)[19]

The person who believes in magic is like a child for whom 'objects as such
are over-shadowed by the ideas representing them; what takes place in the latter
must also happen to the former, and the relations which exist between ideas are
also postulated as to things' (*Totem and Taboo* 119).[20] We often meet this kind
of magical belief in mental illness, in so-called 'schizophrenia' (Bleuler). One
of my patients for example was upset about the various bad ideas that people
had about her. I said that she did not need to get upset about them because
they were only ideas, to which she replied: 'The idea could become a fact in
order to demonstrate its existence.'[21] It is enough to think something for it to
happen; this thought, however, is always an expression of a wish or a fear.

When the baby produces its first babble-sounds it does so because for
various physiological reasons to do with breathing, muscular tension and so
on babbling gives it pleasure. In Stern for example we read:

From the seventh week the baby sometimes produced sounds of contentment after a satisfying feed, something like "krä-krä"; at two months
the sound of pleasure was more like "erre-erre". In the eleven week-old
baby it was noted that the babbling becomes more sustained and is
always a sign of deep contentment.

According to Stern the development progresses 'from the affective/will-based
position to the objective/intellectual.'

Let us now turn to the first words 'papa' and 'mama'. It is very important
to pay attention to how the baby pronounces these words. He does not at first
say 'mama' and 'papa' but 'mö-mö-mö', 'pö-pö-pö': the vowel sound is thus
roughly an *ö* and the number of syllables to begin with is unrestricted. If we
carefully watch the baby's mouth as it says 'mö-mö-mö' and then try to
imitate its movements ourselves, we see how closely these movements are
related to those of suckling. The act of suckling is present in the 'mö-mö-mö'
sounds. When the baby is returned to its cot after a feed the nervous impulse
needed for sucking is not immediately brought to a standstill; thus the movements are continued and consequently the word 'mö-mö-mö' is produced.
The movements which produce 'mö-mö-mö' must be extremely pleasurable
for the baby, partly for physiological reasons, because they are modelled on
the act of suckling and are therefore easily produced, but even more for
psychological reasons: by reproducing the act of suckling in its movements, it
must somehow relive the sensations it has enjoyed in the act which has just
taken place. I do not want to go as far as James in stating: 'We do not weep
because we are sad; we are sad because we weep.' But it must be the case that
at the earliest age the connection between certain movements and the sensations accompanying them is already laid down. It is therefore not a daring

conclusion to assume that when the baby first utters 'mö-mö-mö', sounds which are linked to certain movements in suckling, it also experiences the pleasurable sensations of suckling.

We do not need to imagine that there are clear images in the baby's mind: they need not be either the image of the mother or of suckling itself, they could be quite vague sensations of warmth, of softness (in contact with the mother's body), of liquid, of fullness, etc. The baby will naturally always want to repeat these sensations; so it will instinctively bring its mouth into a position which produces the sounds we have been discussing. The connection between the 'mö-mö' sounds and the corresponding sensations becomes increasingly close, it becomes constant; the baby will seek to produce these sounds in order to invoke in itself a certain group of sensations which are both desired and familiar. Because certain sounds are now linked to quite specific psychic contents, to sensations, perhaps even ideas, we can already talk about words which indicate these contents, or indeed represent them.

These first words are still autistic, that is they exist only for their own sake. This first autistic stage is distinguished from the later 'magical' stage to the extent that magic assumes an external world which can be influenced, whereas in this first autistic stage we do not yet need to assume an external world separate from the child. The emergence of the word 'mö-mö' already in the autistic stage however throws light on the origin of magic, namely the belief in the omnipotence of words and especially of a name.

As everybody knows, in magic the name stands for the person. And in this respect the image is equivalent to the name: if for example someone wants to invoke the death of an enemy he takes a candle the same size as the enemy and lets it burn down completely; the same result can be obtained by speaking the enemy's name with evil intent.[22]

Just as we may not approach a sacred animal or a king, and just as we ourselves must avoid objects, especially food, which are used by that person, because otherwise we would die on the spot, so we may not speak his name.

The same goes for the names of spirits, of the dead, and so on. Freud explains this equivalence of name and person, of word and deed, in the same way as we have shown above how the idea, the thought becomes more important than the reality, as it does with the baby; every wish was originally satisfied through hallucination, and only in retrospect did the child have to learn that there is a reality which makes many things impossible for him and which must first be mastered.

The emergence of the child's first words shows that we do not need to assume that its origin lies in an intentionally induced hallucinatory wish-fulfilment. When the baby cries 'mö-mö' it does so at first not because this word reminds it of an action, suckling, which is linked to pleasurable sensations: originally the word did not mean an action,[23] it was the action itself. It is to this fact that the belief in magic returns: the word can replace an action because the first word was originally an action. The word 'mö-mö' in the sense of a separate object becomes differentiated only in retrospect from a certain ill-defined cluster of sensations which is constellated in the act of suckling.

Speaking a word or thinking it gives rise to the same sensations as the action itself, such as the movements of the mouth in suckling, because since it is a direct result of these movements this word copies them exactly. When in time and with further psychic development the idea of an object, the mother, becomes differentiated from the ill-defined cluster of sensations, the original connection between action = word and the now differentiated object 'Ma-ma' (later mother), persists. By speaking the name it would be possible actually to evoke a certain group of sensations which will later be represented by a person. If this name is altered or damaged in any way, the psychic content connected with it (in this case = the person) is also damaged. Thus it happens that in magic the name of a person represents the person himself and whatever happens to the person's name will happen to the person himself.

The separating of the word (name) from the event is a secondary process; originally it was one and the same. In magic it becomes reunified in that the name stands for a person, an event, and the word for an action.

In the first stage of development, when the child does not yet know a world separate from himself, and a world to be conquered, the word is meant for self-enjoyment. It evokes certain clusters of sensations which it ends up by representing.[24] The baby must have become aware retrospectively that between the 'apparent gratification' which it had on speaking the first words, and the actual gratification in suckling there is an essential difference. It must have owed its first experience in this respect to the feeling of hunger, which was not always amenable to being removed in an 'apparent' way. Here lies one of the factors which must have made the child aware of the opposition between the wish and the resistance (obstacle); here lies the core of the beginning of the centring of the I in respect of a something, which will later become the external world. The second factor lies in the act of suckling itself. Compayre says: 'It is perhaps in pressing the mother's breast inside its mouth that the infant acquires the first confused notion of exteriority.' It is the resistance on the part of the mother's body, the resistance which meets our every movement, that actually allows us to experience a movement. This external world which offers resistance is however at the same time endowed with the most pleasurable sensations. Now the adults again come instinctively to the young child's aid. In accordance with the experiences coming to them from the dim reaches of their own childhood they relate the 'mö-mö' sounds to the feeding mother; these sounds are repeated lovingly and at the same time the mother's breast with its desired nourishment reaches the baby's eager mouth. In this way the 'idea' is formed in the infant's mind that we can 'conjure up' actual reality through an 'apparent' action, such as we have with the words 'pö-pö' and 'mö-mö'.[25] It is enough to utter the word 'mö-mö' to produce the corresponding cluster of sensations which is now recognised as external and not always present, the cluster of 'mö-mö' sensations. Thus we are in the second stage of word development, the 'magical stage'.

The child's first words however have a quite different general meaning from ours. Paolo Lombroso for example reports on a little girl who shouted 'Pello' (= hat = cappello) for all the possible things she wanted. My little Renate too gives us a nice example of this from the relatively advanced age of one and a half years. At that time I wrote: 'It gives her great pleasure to open and shut windows, doors and all possible objects. As she did it I would say "open – shut". Now she often shouts "open" when it is not appropriate, simply when she wants something. I cannot guarantee it, but I think it simply means for her the name of a thing, an object, in the vocative.' This was written seven years ago; now I would correct it in so far as 'open!' was not summoning a thing but was rather a call or a wish for the pleasant sensation which the child had assimilated in shouting 'open' to the earlier sensation of pleasure she had in opening and shutting doors. It is as if it were saying: 'let this nice thing happen now.' At a year and a half the child has already come to terms with the relationship between subject and object but – let us not deceive ourselves! – not for a long time with the clarity with which we adults think of it! Even at four and a half years Renate was asking me: 'When I close my eyes I can't see; why is it that, when I close my eyes it is not Louise (the maid) who can't see?' The child would not have put this question if the demarcation of her own ego from the external world had been familiar enough to her, if she had been able to see herself from the outside, from the point of view of the external world (i.e. from Louise's point of view).

The word 'open' of course is not a direct derivative of an action like the word 'mö-mö', but the original experience word = action, which 'wishes into existence' the desired object, cannot be destroyed so soon. That takes longer. For a child every thought, every wish and every fear is at first an external fact. Piaget spoke in one of his lectures about the child's different attitudes to reality;[26] according to him the child progresses from the absolute to the relative, as indeed corresponds with psychoanalytic experience. Doubt develops much later: when the child asks a question, it is not to clarify the real facts for itself but to get an answer it wants. Here again my daughter provides good examples. At first she knows no past, only the present. If I say: 'Renate was a good girl, she ate her food up nicely,' she immediately wants food, even when she is not hungry at all. What is said must happen immediately. The child's first sentences are affective-affirmative (or interjectional); that corresponds with Stern's observations of his daughter. He writes thus of a one and a half year old child:

Affective sentence formations still predominate; the short interjectional sentences of the earlier time have become distinctly volitional (expressions of desire) and they appear in many forms. At the same time questions are appearing; they consist no longer merely of "what questions" but also of "where questions" and "making sure" questions. Sometimes she answers these questions herself.

With the 'What's that?' question the child wants to know the name of the thing which for him stands for the thing itself. In contrast to that, the 'where' question indicates a great advance; here the active stage begins: the thing is not always available; you have to make it your own, you have to know how to find it. Here too the search is at first just an 'apparent' search, because the idea is superior to the reality. At the age of two years three and a half months Renate asks questions as if to get the answers she wants. We have often played 'hiding' games with her, in which there is a 'where?' and then a 'there!' Now it is 'Where? – there!' with everything. For example: 'Where's the pussy-cat? – There's the pussy-cat!' She answers 'there' without worrying whether this corresponds to reality or not. To a child the world is not as it is but as it should be (Spitteler: 'My earliest childhood experiences'.) She did indeed learn the interrogative sentence structure from me, but these questions held for her an affirmative character, so that I noted: 'She often uses sentences in the interrogative, and in situations where they are not appropriate, for example when she wants a biscuit she says: "Do you want a biscuit?" or "Do you want something to eat?" etc.'

Some days later I wrote: 'Go on, knock: do you hear all the noise? Shall Mama take you? (instead of "Mama will take you" = "take me, Mama.") Do you want the book closed? – the book is closed (here is the separation between the question and the immediately completed desired action "book closed"). Or put it on the table? (she puts the object on the table). Or have that? (bread) Or not have it? Not? (= I want the bread; no, I don't want it.)' Renate at two years eight months: 'Or we can drive both cars now. If we take both cars with us.' Even this new sentence form beginning with 'if' is not yet a conditional: it is not followed by a further sentence which supports the 'if'. The child means: 'Now I want to drive both cars' or simply 'Now both cars are going' (the cars she is playing with); it is possible that the 'if' here means 'so' or something similar, but it has no sense of a condition. The interrogative, and finally the conditional sentences, which the child has picked up from hearing me, contain for her a meaning appropriate to her psychic development. In Anatole France there is a beautiful passage:

> Now that I could write a little, I thought that nothing would stop me writing a book. Under the supervision of my dear mama I undertook a short theological and moral treatise. I started it like this: "What is God" . . . and straight away took it to my mother to ask her whether that was all right. My mother replied that it was all right, but that there should be a question mark at the end of the sentence. I asked what a question mark was.
>
> It's a sign, said my mother, that means it's a question, that you're asking

something. You put it at the end of every question. You have to put a question mark because you're asking: "What is God".

My reply was superb: I'm not asking. I know. – Oh yes, you are asking, my child. I repeated twenty times that I was not asking because I knew, and I absolutely refused to put the question mark which seemed to me like a sign of ignorance. My mother reproached me severely for being so obstinate and told me I was just being stupid. My pride was hurt and I replied with some impertinence for which I was punished. I've changed a lot since then; I no longer refuse to put question marks in all the usual places.

I would even be tempted to put very big question marks after everything I write, everything I say and everything I think. My poor mother, if she were alive, would tell me that perhaps now I am putting too many.

Only when reality is recognised alongside phantasy, when fellow human beings are perceived alongside oneself, and when words contain not an enforcing meaning but an optional one, does that emerge which we adults generally understand as language. This is the third stage, the stage of a social language intended for fellow human beings.

I should now like briefly to summarise what I have been saying:

The child's first words, which in the overwhelming majority of cases consist of labial and dental sounds, owe their origin to the act of suckling. The process of suckling, continued when the baby is separated from the mother's body, easily gives rise to the sounds 'mö-mö'. Originally the word was an action. As a result of the child's repeating this action countless times, that is the word 'mö-mö', a close connection must have formed between this word (the movement of the mouth that produced it) and a quite specific and constant cluster of sensations which the child experiences every time it suckles. By uttering a certain group of sounds the child could finally call up this specific cluster of sensations as often as it wished.

The sensations are elements of the later perceptions and finally ideas (perhaps we already have perceptions and ideas at this stage). The connection from the sound to a specific cluster of intellectual and affective elements,[27] which has now become constant, allows us to say that this group of sounds has become a 'word'. Here it is naturally a question of terminology.[28] Whether we want to speak of a 'word' already or whether we prefer another term, in any case these first words, originating in the act of suckling, go through the stage where they are reproduced for the sole purpose of pleasure, and where uttering them gives direct pleasure because in the process movements come into play which evoke the sensations of suckling. This stage, in which an external world is differentiated, in which language exists for its own sake, is the autistic stage. Once the child has discovered from experience the difference between true satisfaction through suckling and 'apparent' satisfaction through speaking the first words, and has a vague idea of an external world to be mastered, it has reached the second 'magical' stage, the stage in which what is desired can be conjured up by reproducing it in an action = word.

In this second stage we are still dealing with an overvaluation of the wish, of the subjective, of the psychic in contrast to reality, and with the belief in the 'omnipotence of thought'. The child learns only slowly to draw a sufficiently clear line between itself and the external world to enable it to see itself from the point of view of its fellow human beings. Many, if not all of us, never learn it completely. We learn to restrict our desires and to attach optional meaning to words. With the awareness of our own inadequacy and dependency on the external world, the need arises ever more insistently to retain the support of our fellows, to communicate, to feel understood, and finally to understand. Thus language enters the third 'social' stage.

Until now we have been concerned only with the emergence of the word 'mö-mö'. As the word 'mö-mö' undergoes a shift in meaning to mean finally the person who is closest to the child, the mother, the word 'pö-pö' undergoes a similar process. The word 'pö-pö' shows its descent from the act of suckling in many ways. In Russian nursery language for example bread is called 'Papa'. The Christian faith in which the body of Jesus is eaten in the form of bread, shows that we are dealing not just with a rational connection, Papa = bread, because the father is the bread-giver, but with a much older, closer link. The humorous statement 'Man ist, was man isst' ('You are what you eat') is taken seriously by primitive peoples; they assume the qualities of a sacred animal they have eaten. The closest community is symbolised through the act of eating. This belief seems natural to us when we think that once in our life we really did feed from a human being, one human being who gave us life and with whom we were formed from time immemorial. For that reason identification is symbolised through the act of eating.

The Russian word 'niania' is generally well known. In nursery language in the Don region I often heard the expression 'niamniam' for eating. It has obviously developed onomatopoeically; the word 'niania' derived from the act of eating was then applied to the care-taking person who provided the food.[29]

It is very interesting to see in which circumstances the baby babbles 'mö-mö' and in which 'pö-pö'. There seems to be a quite characteristic difference. I wrote in my diary: 'Tomorrow Renate is ten months old; she is still very helpless: she has no teeth, cannot sit up on her own, does not understand what "Papa" and "Mama" mean although she quite often babbles these words during the day. I don't know whether I have noted this already: when Renate is content she says "Papa", when she is unhappy or wants something it is "Mama".'[30] Stern, writing about his daughter, also reports that Papa is a sign of contentment and Mama a sign of sadness, and I think Sully does so too. Since then a few mothers have given me similar information. Dr

Hug-Hellmuth who heard my congress paper said I had taken the words right out of her mouth on this subject. Since for the time being no contrary evidence has been put forward, we could possibly be talking about a widespread fact. How could this strange phenomenon be explained? When I wrote my observations I did not yet know of similar findings by Stern and others, so the possibility of the idea being suggested to me by them is ruled out: there is comprehensive evidence that the infant does not yet understand the words Papa and Mama. Thus 'Mama' as a sign of sadness cannot stem from an idea in the child which first leads it to seek protection with the mother. The bottom of it seems to me this: the different sounds in question do not stem from the same mouth positions; they arise in different phases of suckling. The word 'mö-mö' reproduces suckling in its truest sense. 'Pö-pö', 'bö-bö' etc correspond more with the time when the satisfied infant is playing with the breast, now letting go of it, now latching on to it again. If the baby is not too hungry and is thus in a good mood, it enjoys repeating the movements that produce 'pö-pö', 'bö-bö' and similar sounds. But when the feeling of hunger becomes more imperious the sucking movements become more energetic and the mouth takes on the specific shape for suckling, for grasping the nipple firmly. This shape produces the 'mö' sound. If the hunger becomes altogether too severe then every 'sensible' sound stops and gives way to a reflex process, crying. Among certain mammals the noises arising from labial sounds remain their only language for their whole life. With others it is not the case. Why should that be so?

What is decisive in these cases for the formation of the sound? I do not want to go into this complicated question. It was not my task to consider all the possible sources from which the various forms of language could come into existence. Also I am not claiming that it is suckling alone which gives rise to children's speech. What we see is that in an overwhelming majority of cases the child's first words consist of labial and dental sounds. They thus suggest a close connection to suckling.

My task was to trace the emergence and development of the words Papa and Mama. This investigation throws light on a whole range of psychological issues, above all the problem of the different stages in the development of language (the autistic, the magical, and the social.)

The word 'Mama' (in baby pronunciation 'mö-mö-mö') reproduces the act of suckling. The word Papa (= 'pö-pö') stems from the phase when the satisfied infant is playing with the breast. Both words owe their origins to suckling. Like no other, the act of suckling is fundamental to the most important experiences of the child's life: here it gets to know the bliss of having its hunger stilled, but it learns too that this bliss has an end and has to be won all over again. The infant experiences for the first time the fact that there is a world outside itself; its contact with the mother's body plays a part in this by offering some resistance to the movements of the infant's mouth.[31] And finally the infant learns that there is a refuge in this external world which is desirable not only because there its hunger is satisfied, but because it is warm and soft and protected from all dangers. If we have once in our lives felt 'Let this moment last for ever, it is so beautiful' it was surely at this time. Here the child learns for the first time to love, in the widest sense of the word, that is to experience contact with another person, independently of feeding, as the highest bliss.

For all these reasons it is understandable that a quite special significance attaches to the words that are generated by the suckling movement. If then Papa and Mama are not the child's first words, as is very possible, they will nevertheless always be regarded as such in popular culture.

Notes

1 See Freud: *Totem and Taboo*.
2 We are on the point of saying that language originally exists for its own sake and develops only later into a social language intended for one's fellow beings.
3 *Die Nadel vom Kissen pickt (sticht). An der Nadel 'pickst' du dich.*
4 Here I mean 'language' in the normal sense of the word, that is language as a means of communication. As we shall see shortly, language, in its origins, is not that.
5 In all words which appear rather more complicated, as for example '*batjka*' and so on, we always have to remember that this is not the first form that the child uses.
6 I shall consider the phonetic side elsewhere.
7 To indicate a bodily function.
8 'Law of least effort'.
9 'The development of language observed in a bilingual child': Jules Ronjat, Paris 1913.
10 'Explosive' means that the sound at the beginning of the syllable is dominant, implosive that the sound or sounds following the vowel sound of the syllable is dominant.
11 On which the accent falls.
12 That is: instead of '*Armband*' Louis says *ambam*. For more clarification on the expressions I am using following Ronjat, I refer the reader to the original.
13 That is, where 'm' replaces 'rm'.
14 = m
15 = d
16 = n
17 Freud: *Totem and Taboo* 1913.
18 Salve from a weapon that has inflicted a wound can heal the wound. With this so-called 'contagious magic' there is no question of a connection in space, contiguity, or at least imagined contiguity. But since similarity and contiguity are the two essential principles of association processes, the supremacy of thought association turns out to be an explanation for all the stupidity of magical formulations.
19 The text continues: *The adult primitive man knows another way. A motor impulse, the will, clings to his wish and this will, which later will change the face of the earth in the service of wish fulfilment, is now used to represent the gratification so that one may experience it, as it were, through motor hallucination. Such a representation of the gratified wish is altogether comparable to the play of children, where it replaces the purely sensory technique of gratification.*
20 Spitteler: *Meine frühesten Kindheitserlebnisse.* (My earliest childhood experiences).

21 Spielrein: *Über den psychologischen Inhalt eines Falles von Schizophrenie*. (On the psychological content of a case of schizophrenia). *Jahrbuch für psychoanalytische und psychopathologische Forschungen* BD.III 1911. *Yearbook of Psychoanalytic and Psychopathological Research*. Vol. 3, 1911.

22 I am extracting the following passage from a case study which Dr Papadaki (Director of a psychiatric clinic in Geneva) very kindly put at my disposal. Appearance of certain manias through anxiety: if while working for example at embroidery the idea of death crossed her mind she was filled with scruples lest that should bring ill fortune to the person whose name might have crossed her mind at the same time, and she would undo a few stitches in order to stitch them again with a less disagreeable idea. If she decided that was absurd and continued she was seized with a fear of hot flushes, of a terrible malaise, which made her very unhappy.

23 It signified the group of sensations, not the action.

24 It stands for them.

25 Cf. Sperber: *Der sexuelle Ursprung der Sprache* (The sexual origin of language).

26 'Autistic thought'. Winter term 1921/1922. Geneva psychological laboratory.

27 That is: with sensations with their own accompanying feeling reaction. The idea emerges from the sensation through the abstraction of the essential element. I do not want to give a precise definition of an 'idea' here. I will speak of how this process comes about in my work on symbol formation which will follow shortly.

28 I am not insisting on the term 'word' in this study. Here we could even speak for example of 'embryo words'. The terminological questions do not in any way change the facts.

29 In the Don region I also heard '*ham-ham*' (with an aspirated 'h') used by children for food.

30 The pronunciation is always '*pö-pö*', '*mö-mö*'. Even at one year of age the child said '*pö-pö*' instead of Papa.

31 Of course I am not claiming that it is the act of suckling alone from which the child gains knowledge of the external world. I would like to stress again particularly that I am speaking only of the child's words Papa and Mama. The term which adults use for father and mother could be derived from various sources and various realms of thought; they could possibly no longer contain the elements which represent their connection with suckling.

Index